EMBEDDED COURTS

Embedded Courts are laden with tension. Chinese courts are organized as a singular and unified bureaucracy and yet grassroots courts in urban and rural regions differ greatly in the way they use the law and are as diverse as the populations they serve. Based on extensive fieldwork and in-depth interviews, this book offers a penetrating discussion of the operation of Chinese courts. It explains how Chinese judges rule and how the law is not the only script they follow – political, administrative, social and economic factors all influence verdicts. This landmark work will revise our understanding of the role of law in China – one that cannot be easily understood through the standard lens of judicial independence and separation of powers. Ng and He make clear the struggle facing frontline judges as they bridge the gap between a rules-based application of law and an instrumentalist view that prioritizes stability maintenance.

Kwai Hang Ng is Associate Professor of Sociology at the University of California, San Diego. He has written a series of articles (with Xin He) on different aspects of the Chinese grassroots courts, addressing topics including courtroom discourse, mediation, criminal reconciliation, domestic violence, and divorce petitions.

Xin He is Professor and Director of Centre for Chinese and Comparative Law at the School of Law, City University of Hong Kong. He has published more than forty articles in the fields of law and society, comparative law, and the Chinese legal system.

Embedded Courts

JUDICIAL DECISION-MAKING IN CHINA

KWAI HANG NG
University of California, San Diego

XIN HE
City University of Hong Kong

CAMBRIDGE
UNIVERSITY PRESS

CAMBRIDGE
UNIVERSITY PRESS

University Printing House, Cambridge CB2 8BS, United Kingdom

One Liberty Plaza, 20th Floor, New York, NY 10006, USA

477 Williamstown Road, Port Melbourne, VIC 3207, Australia

314-321, 3rd Floor, Plot 3, Splendor Forum, Jasola District Centre, New Delhi - 110025, India

79 Anson Road, #06-04/06, Singapore 079906

Cambridge University Press is part of the University of Cambridge.

It furthers the University's mission by disseminating knowledge in the pursuit of education, learning and research at the highest international levels of excellence.

www.cambridge.org
Information on this title: www.cambridge.org/9781108430364

First published 2017
First paperback edition 2018

A catalogue record for this publication is available from the British Library

Library of Congress Cataloging in Publication data
NAMES: Ng, Kwai Hang, author. | He, Xin (Professor of law), author.
TITLE: Embedded courts : judicial decision-making in China / Kwai Hang Ng, Xin He.
DESCRIPTION: Cambridge [UK] ; New York : Cambridge University Press, 2017. | Includes bibliographical references and index.
IDENTIFIERS: LCCN 2017030488 | ISBN 9781108420495 (hardback)
SUBJECTS: LCSH: Judicial process – China. | Courts – China. | Justice, Administration of – China.
CLASSIFICATION: LCC KNQ1679 .N45 2017 | DDC 347.51/05–dc23
LC record available at https://lccn.loc.gov/2017030488

ISBN 978-1-108-42049-5 Hardback
ISBN 978-1-108-43036-4 Paperback

Contents

Preface and Acknowledgments

Embedded Courts represents the fruits of our academic collaboration in the past decade. We came from different but related disciplinary and intellectual backgrounds. Underlying our collaboration is a shared belief that to gain a meaningful understanding of the Chinese legal system, one must study how the courts operate in action. It may help if, from the very beginning, we give up on the ambition to cover everything that can be said about the Chinese courts. There are many books that offer systematic overviews of the Chinese judicial system. This book is shot through with an issue that in our view is most central to understanding the Chinese courts: namely, the intimate, delicate and complex relationships between the courts, the party-state, and the society. The genesis of this book is also owed to a set of puzzles we have grappled with over the years as we have tried to make sense of the Chinese court as a unique bureaucracy within the party-state of China. This book is the result of our joint labors at thinking through the puzzling nature of the Chinese courts that we identify in Chapter 1 – a weak and highly malleable institution that is supposedly bestowed with the authority to carry out some of the most intrusive laws of an authoritarian party-state.

We would like to thank the judges who helped make indispensible arrangements to facilitate our fieldwork at various grassroots courts in China. We would also like to thank the judges and litigants who agreed to be interviewed for the book, without whom we would never have been able to do the research necessary for producing this book. Specifically, Ju Xiaoxiong generously opened the door of a basic level court for Xin He to start the research on Chinese courts. His vision, courage, insights, ideas and suggestions had significantly shaped many studies on which this book is based. Randy Peerenboom always encouraged Xin He to write a book on Chinese courts and he has offered invaluable advice on the book publishing process. Sida Liu also offered useful suggestions. The anonymous reviewers asked incisive questions and offered very practical recommendations.

There are colleagues and friends whose engagement with the arguments made in this book at various stages have pushed us to be attentive to issues that would otherwise have been overlooked. Their questions prodded us toward greater clarity. Some of them endured the tedium of reading rough early drafts. We would like to thank Bjorn Ahl, Lei Guang, Michelle Hsieh, Hou Meng, Elena Obukhova, Charles Qu, Gwo-Shyong Shieh, Jeffrey Sachs, Yang Su, Ting-hong Wong, Horng-luen Wang and Frank Upham. Xin He is grateful for the help offered by his assistants and doctoral students Jing Feng, Kege Li, Yaqing Wang, Huina Xiao, Yan Ye and Yixian Zhao.

Kwai Ng was supported by a Taiwan Fellowship that afforded him time and space to work on the chapter drafts and to rethink this work under the changed conditions triggered by the latest judicial reform. He would like to give the warmest thanks to the Institute of Sociology, Academia Sinica, for providing a quiet and genteel environment for writing. At UC San Diego, Ng received a Center for the Humanities Fellowship that provided some extra time for revising the manuscript. He would like to thank the Center's director Stefan Tanaka for his support. He would like to extend his thanks also to the fellows at the Center for giving a close read of an early draft of the first chapter. Sarah Schneewind, in particular, offered some great advice. Ng would also like to express thanks for the research help provided by Gary Lee.

We also shared and tested our evolving theory of the Chinese courts at a workshop held at City University of Hong Kong in the summer of 2016. We would like to thank Peter Chan, Baifeng Chen, Albert Chen, Yuqing Feng, Hualing Fu, Ling Li, Susan Finder and Susan Trevaskes for their critical engagements.

Research for the book was supported by the National Science Foundation (Grant No. 1252067). Xin He acknowledges the grant support from the Research Grants Council of Hong Kong (Projects: CityU 143612, 142013, 11403114, 11613315).

Much of the analysis in this book is based on new interviews and field works we conducted in the past few years. Given the synthetic nature of our project, it also draws on some of our previous studies. These reports have been substantially rewritten and updated to fit within the broader framework of embeddedness. A different version of Chapter 6 was published as an article entitled "'It Must Be Rock Strong!' *Guanxi's* Impact on Judicial Decision-Making in China" in *American Journal of Comparative Law* (2017). The discussion of the adjudication committee in Chapter 4 drew from a study by Xin He ("Black Hole of Responsibility: the Adjudication Committee's Role in a Chinese Court," *Law & Society Review* 46(4):681–712, 2012. Chapter 5 also drew from some of He's previous studies, including "Routinization of Divorce Law Practice in China: Institutional Constraints' Influence on Judicial Behavior," *International Journal of Law, Policy and the Family* 23(1):83–109, 2009, "Judicial Innovation and Local Politics: Judicialization of Administrative Governance in East China," *The China Journal* 69:20–42, 2013, "Maintaining Stability by Law: Protest-Supported Housing Demolition Litigation and Social Change in China," *Law & Social Inquiry* 39(4):849–873, 2014, and "'No Malicious Incidents': The Concern for Stability in China's Divorce Law Practice," *Social & Legal Studies* 2017. Chapter 7 reproduces a table (Table 7.4) that first appeared in "Court Finance and Court Responses to Judicial Reforms: A Tale of Two Chinese Courts," *Law & Policy* 31(4):463–486, 2009.

Our families have provided us with unwavering support for the work. Kwai Ng dedicates this book to his wife, Ngai Ling. Completion of this book would have been impossible without her quiet and steady support and company. He would also like to thank his sister Chui for hosting him during his visits to China and Hong Kong. Xin He's father, Xiuxin Tao, always encouraged him to publish a book. His wife Lixin Chen, over the years, consistently shared more family responsibilities, despite the heavy professional demand of her own work. She complained that Xin He had not published a book earlier than did their son Tim He, whose "History of 3B" has been put up on his school website. For this and other reasons, Xin He dedicates this book to her.

Chinese Courts as Embedded Institutions

SCENE ONE

In an economically backward hinterland of northern China, a woman in her forties arrived at the court building early in the morning. She was ranting to every member of the court staff. She requested that the court's president come out and see her. She said she filed her divorce petition five months ago but the judge responsible had been ignoring her. The judge stalked her petition, she complained. She wanted a different judge to handle her case. After making a scene for an hour, the court agreed to the woman's request and sent in a new judge.

A few days later, we talked to the new judge, a middle-aged "old-hand" at the court, who admitted that this was a tough assignment. She said:

> There is no way we'll approve her divorce petition. This woman is better off than her husband economically and socially. Her husband has just been laid off from a local state enterprise. He's hurt emotionally. And they have a son attending college now. We can't allow her to divorce the husband. It'd be too big of a blow to the man. All I can do is to keep talking to her, to calm her down. I'm in for many meetings with this woman.[1]

SCENE TWO

It was the second day of our fieldwork in a grassroots court located in a big city in southern China. We were sitting in on the second divorce trial of the morning in Civil Court Number 1. The presiding judge was an old hand who has worked in the courts for over a decade. The defendant (the plaintiff's wife) did not show up. The presiding judge asked the husband a few questions. The man, in his late fifties and wearing a grey suit, was accompanied by a lawyer. He said there was no love lost between him and his wife. This was his second time of filing for divorce. Not long ago he agreed to withdraw his first petition after the court indicated to him that his petition would not be approved. He told Judge Wang that he had left his family in

2008 and had been separated from his wife since then. The judge said very few words. In fact, she remained silent most of the time. She went through pages in the case file to double check if what the husband said conformed to the written records. Toward the end of this short trial (which lasted for about half an hour), the man said to the judge:

> [Plaintiff] In fact, I don't want to divorce. We once both dreamed of a wonderful future together. Throughout all these years of conflict, we've talked and tried to iron things out. Now, there is really *no road for me to walk* [emphasis added].
> [Judge] So do you want a divorce or not?
> [Plaintiff] I insist on a divorce.

The formulaic expression "no road to walk" (无路可走 *wu lu ke zou*) was used by the applicant to convey how reluctant and regretful he was to decide to divorce. He could not go on (no road ahead) even if he wanted to. He tried to avoid any remaining moral stigma against divorcees by suggesting that it was not his fault that the marriage had to end. The litigant in this case was greeted coldly by the judge: "So do you want a divorce or not?" She was probably thinking about if she could finish her third divorce trial in the morning. Realizing that the judge was not in the mood to moralize, the man responded: "I insist on a divorce."

HOMOGENEOUS COURTS?

Ever since the opening up of China's economy in the 1980s, both domestic and foreign attention to China's judiciary has increased in tandem with the country's growing international presence. This is so even though Westerners generally view its socialist legal development with skepticism. Major news outlets such as *The New York Times* and *The Economist* now commonly report the major trials of China, from the televised trial of former Chongqing party chief Bo Xilai to multi-billion-dollar civil trials targeting transnational Fortune 500 giants like Apple and Qualcomm.

The courts' veil seems to have been gradually lifted. Among the Western audience, there is now a vague sense of familiarity, as changes since the 1990s have produced apparent similarities between the Chinese courts and their Western counterparts. Gone are the makeshift courtrooms in old, rundown government buildings. In the big cities, courthouses are grandiose and modern; many feature a set of wide stairs leading up to the entrance, literally elevating courts to a higher level; some with added steel gates to protect the safety of judges, but also to create a sense of intimidation that mimics traditional Chinese courts, or yamen [衙门] (Jones 2013). Newer and younger judges are educated in law and trained in procedure, palpably different from the autocratic cadres of the Maoist era. They also look different. Right until the onset of the reform era in 1978, judges not only acted like military officers but dressed like them as well. It was not until 2001 that judges, when hearing cases, traded their old green military-style uniforms for Western-style pitch-black judicial robes, decorated with a red stripe down the front (People's Daily 2000). Nowadays, they also wield and bang their gavels authoritatively, just like judges in the United States.

The growing literature of the past two decades studied the Chinese courts from a wide array of perspectives. A good deal of the works continue to be dominated by overviews of the law on the books rather than on how law is practiced. This legalistic approach treats the courts as no different from courts in Western democracies. One problem with this approach is that it takes the law on the books too seriously. It sounds heretical for us – academics who study the legal system as our careers – to make this claim. While the law on the books seems predictable and clear, the law in practice is flickering when the court runs up against the limit of its power. No reputable scholar would dispute that the written law was often not strictly followed in China. This sort of gap is not exclusive to China, of course, but China's gap is remarkable. Without keeping this in mind, any grounded understanding of how law works in China would be impossible.

There are also some empirically oriented studies. Yet, these works share an approach that treats all Chinese courts as parts of a homogeneous system. It is a top-down, monistic approach that focuses on the major policies of the Supreme People's Court (SPC). This approach finds support in successive SPC presidents' adoption of shifting policies during their reigns. For example, the 1990s witnessed the emergence of adversarial trial, but then the pendulum swung to the other end as mediation was prioritized in the 2000s, and now we are in the decade that promotes the use of law in governance. The Xiao court, named after SPC President Xiao Yang (1998–2008), was the court of professionalism, privileging the import of Western jurisprudential ideas and practices. The Wang court, presided over by Wang Shengjun (2008–2013), was the court of traditionalism, privileging social harmony and stability over the legal rights of individuals. And now the Zhou court, since Zhou Qiang's appointment in 2013, while still evolving, seems to be a hybrid, but with more Xiao than Wang so far.

Such an approach is appealing in its simplicity and clarity, an appeal similar to the "great man" narratives in history books. The approach makes sense in some contexts. It offers an easy way to intuitively make sense of the maelstrom of forces that influence the courts. However, this simplicity comes at a cost. It adopts a methodological premise that takes for granted the Chinese courts as a coherent unity. The approach treats the many Chinese courts as a highly coordinated, homogeneous organ at the command of the party-state. China, however, has the largest establishment of judges in the world (Zhu 2011). The total number of judges in China, by a recent estimate, has reached 195,000. The number should not come as a surprise, given the size of China and its status as the most populous country of the world. What is surprising is that for a country not known for its strong rule of law, China features one of the highest numbers of judges per capita. According to one calculation, China has 18.8 judges per 100,000 people. In comparison, the corresponding figure in the United States is 5, in England, 1.8, in France, 8.1 and in Japan, 1.7.

Among developed countries, only Germany recorded a higher number: 22.2 judges per 100,000 people (Zhu 2007:196). The contrast is even bigger when compared to other developing countries of similar size. India, for example, has 1.4 judges per 100,000 people (Government of India 2008). Of course, not all judges judge, a problem that the latest judicial reform is attempting to rectify.[2] But the sheer size of the judicial establishment does show one thing: the court system of China is a huge, complex bureaucracy.

In an unintentional but consequential way, this methodological premise of treating the courts as a unity coincides with the political premise promoted by the Chinese central government. It portrays the court system as constituted by a powerful central court with tentacles running into different corners of the country. But it is important not to conflate the ideology promoted by the party-state with the reality on the ground. From the standpoint of the former, the reach of the central state is never challenged or questioned. This is, of course, an implausible picture. Not even the Supreme Court of the United States, arguably the most powerful central court of Western jurisdictions, commands this degree of control of the everyday operations of its district courts. This also flies in the face of a long tradition of research that sees China as decentralized and "cellular." Central policies promulgated downward certainly shape the institutional activities of local courts, but as has been shown by scholars, other sectors in China evince weak policy implementation, even fragmentation (Lieberthal 1992, 2004; Shirk 1993). It is unrealistic to assume that the vast court system is immune from diversity and fragmentation.[3] A top-down perspective inevitably offers little in terms of an analytical framework to account for the great variance across frontline courts situated in different locales of China. Implicitly, courts are seen to operate more or less in the same way, and that any differences, if existed, are secondary for formulating a clear-eyed understanding of the Chinese courts. This is most obvious in works that focus on analyses of the legal reforms and transitions (see Diamant, Lubman, and O'Brien 2005; Lubman 1999; Peerenboom 2002; Potter 2004; Zou 2006). It is also obvious among works that study specific sectors of the Chinese courts – for example, works that analyze how divorce cases have been handled in China (Alford and Shen 2003; Huang 2010; Woo 2003). In his otherwise-sophisticated treatment of the development of civil justice in China, Huang (2010) subscribes to a periodization analysis that sees the development of divorce law practices from a coercive reconciliation system to a formalized system of mediated settlement. While the work offers a nuanced and insightful treatment of the changing moral overtones of the Chinese civil justice system since 1949, it does not address the issue of synchronic heterogeneity within the Chinese courts, which is becoming more pronounced as the legal system evolves.

The overreached case of homogeneity also persists in works that study the Chinese court as a legal institution. For example, in his critical review of the question of judicial independence of China, Peerenboom (2010) adopts the similarity thesis and argues that Chinese courts are more similar to Western courts than many pundits have argued. Peerenboom (2010:75–77) further argues that the critique of the lack of judicial independence in China is often overstated and based on vague, shaky assumptions. For example, Chinese judges decide most of their routine cases, and increasingly so, on their own. There is evidently growing independence and authority of the court. The public has become more reliant on the courts for dispute settlement. National regulations have sought to strengthen the personal independence of judges by limiting the practice of penalizing judges for reversals on appeal. And appointments and promotions are now also more merit-based. The general trend has been toward increased emphasis on professional skills and a greater role for judges in the same level and higher courts in decision-making.

Peerenboom is right that the developing trends identified above are happening in *some* courts in China, and his points are important, since Western scholars often ignore these developments when it comes to Chinese courts. The question, however, is whether changes are happening uniformly across the country. Here, treating the Chinese court system as a homogeneous institution overlooks important internal variations. Beyond their surface homogeneity, courts in China differ greatly from each other.

The two examples in the opening pages show the contrasting behavior patterns of the litigants and the courts' responses. Both were divorce cases. And yet, they display, in a clear, albeit simplified manner, an internal complexity often ignored if one looks at the Chinese court system on paper, or from a top-down view. Regional differences of judicial practice within China are plainly remarkable (see e.g., He 2009b, Woo and Wang 2005, Saich 2015, Su 2000),[4] so much so that it is more misleading than useful to conceive of the Chinese courts as parts of a unified, homogeneous institution. The *social* organization of the Chinese courts is varied. On the surface, it adopts a unitary, four-tier system that resembles unitary court systems of some European countries, such as that of Italy or of France. However, the vast size of the country and the "cellular" nature of local governments mean that, horizontally, this simple structure is fragmented. Among the unitary (non-federal) judiciary systems in Europe (e.g., Italy, France, Spain) and in East Asia (Japan, South Korea, Taiwan), the Chinese system is institutionally the most fragmented and diverse (Chen 2008; Keith et al. 2014).

In theory, basic-level courts are the local extension of the state's unified judicial authority. The SPC is supposed to exercise control over subordinate courts, as it has the broad power to promulgate judicial interpretations and directives, and sometimes to hear appellate cases on questions of both fact and law. In practice, however, the SPC does not command unquestioned allegiance from its lower, grassroots courts. The extent of its actual control varies socio-spatially. Indeed, grassroots courts are often an arena for both symbiotic cooperation and power struggles between the central and local governments. True, the central government has greater (but not complete) control over the "software" of the system – the law. But on the "hardware" of the system – personnel and finance – its control is iffy at best. Regional differences are a result of the dynamic interplay between the central and the local and the adaptation of the latter (Zhou 2010; Nee and Mozingo 1983). Variations across the 3,500 different courts in China should not and cannot be overlooked. Consider the mosaic of snapshots of judges and their courts that we gathered:

- A judge in Shanghai works in her office until 11 PM in December. It is the umpteenth time she has worked overtime this month. She still needs to close a dozen more cases to make sure that her numbers this year beat those of last year.
- A young judge in Hulunbuir, Inner Mongolia, spends her December quietly. In fact, her court is closed most of the time during the harsh winter there. Sometimes she holds mobile court sessions in the neighborhoods of the litigants. It is too difficult for them to get to the courthouse.
- In a public hygiene campaign initiated by the local government, the president of a grassroots court in a poor inland province requires that all his judges stop working on cases for half a day to participate in the campaign, literally to help clean up the streets. Judges take off their robes, roll up their sleeves, pick up the brooms and sweep the streets and alleys.
- A grassroots court in Dongguan, Guangdong, thumbs its nose at the local government. The township government chided the court for being uncooperative. For two consecutive days, the government published a stern warning in a local semi-official newspaper, criticizing the court's decision to "unilaterally auction a piece of local land."
- A judge from the Pearl River Delta closed about 500 cases a year. He adjudicated over 80 percent of the cases he presided over. When asked if he would like to mediate more, he said: "Not really. I don't have much time for mediation but I'm OK. My court has ways to boost my mediation rate."
- An inexperienced judge from Yunnan closes the year with a tally of around 100 cases. By his own assessment, he works too slowly. He mediates over 80 percent of his cases, yet he still considers himself pedestrian. Some of his colleagues boast a near-perfect mediation rate of over 90 percent.

THE TWO HEMISPHERES: WORK-UNITS AND FIRMS

This book accounts for these variations. We argue that the variations of court behaviors are primarily the outcomes of the changing environment that the courts face. This changing environment of judging is shaped by four types of forces: administrative, political, social and economic. The interplay between external and internal developments creates courts with palpable differences. Beyond offering a train-window view of Chinese courts, we will offer an analytical account. We are interested in not just describing but also explaining the recurring variations. The challenge is to make sense of the pattern underneath the surface of chaos, the "patterned contingency" of the practices of the Chinese courts.

We argue that these variations can be analytically understood as the differences between two types of courts: "work-units" and "firms." We use the terms to signify two distinct bureaucratic types. The two differ in many aspects. Some differences are legal. They differ in how they interpret, and at times supplement, the laws passed by the central government, particularly in the civil and commercial areas of the law (deLisle 2014:243). They also differ in their sentencing practices (Trevaskes 2010). Most important, though, they differ in how much of the law is used. Some courts use more law; some use less.

At first sight, it is baffling that Chinese courts display different *propensity* to use the law. Some courts prefer to adjudicate; some, however, prefer to mediate. These variances are buried in official statistics that report the national averages.[5] Even within the same court, not all cases receive the same treatment. Some cases are quickly dispensed of, some are stalked; some cases are highly sought after, while some are avoided at all costs (see Clarke 2003). Sometimes, the courts embrace cases like sunflowers turning toward the sun. Other times, they retreat from cases like shy, shrinking violets.

Firms and work-units are characterized by their distinct clusters of institutional characteristics concerning organization, control, logistics, and communication – that is, the capacity to organize and control judges and other personnel and also to obtain material resources. They organize in ways that are practically preferable and feasible in some settings, but not in others. Their priorities in performance are also different. Firms prioritize on output. Work-units prioritize on outcome.[6]

The institutional distinction between the two types is in part a consequence of the deepening urban-rural divide that the Chinese society has experienced in the past few decades. It is no coincidence that courts that are most firm-like reside in big cities while courts resembling work-units are mostly located in the rural regions. In our view, the process of urbanization since the 1980s remains the most fateful force shaping the environment in which courts operate.[7] Indeed, China is at a critical point of urbanization. The picture of a small but concentrated urban China and a vast rural hinterland is outdated. In 2011, for the first time in its history, over half of its population lived in urban areas (Saich 2015:224). Other labels have been used to distinguish the external environment in which courts reside, including, for example, coastal vs. inland (central and western regions), developed vs. less developed. But there are "hybrid" distinctions locatable on the urban-rural continuum. The urban-rural divide bespeaks an internally differentiated court system that is now made of two hemispheres – firms and work-units.

As analytical concepts, the firm and the work-unit serve to make sense of the internal variances within the Chinese judicial system. They are ideal types in the Weberian sense. Any court in China today exhibits traits of both. In reality, the distinction across the courts in China is neither all-firm nor all-work-unit. The terms are used to denote "firm-ness" and "work-unit-ness" that specific courts display to a greater or lesser extent. They are tools to get at the structural patterns that are otherwise unavailable for inspection. We will explore the institutional character of the Chinese courts by illustrating how the two types behave differently from one another. In so doing, we will draw from our interviews and observations conducted in courts of both types, from the Supreme People's Court to rural dispatched tribunals.

Admittedly, the distinction between firms and work-units is just one way, albeit a powerful way, to make sense of the variations within the court system. Courts may be distinguished, for example, by the extent to which they accommodate to local legal customs. Erie (2015), for example, suggests a strong presence of legal pluralism among Chinese Muslim minorities (the Hui) in Northwest China, which in turn points to a harmonious relationship between state law and local practices. We make the conscious decision to leave aside the ethnic-cum-cultural distinction. Since most courts reside in areas dominated by Hans majority, sticking with the firm vs. work-unit dichotomy allows us to articulate most sharply the structural patterns that affect grassroots courts on the broadest scale.

THE WORK-UNIT COURT

Work-unit courts are organized and operated within the framework of the system of employment typical of the collectivist and socialist legacy: the *danwei*. We use the term "work-unit," or *danwei* (单位) in Chinese, with great caution. It is a term steeped in history, and much contested among scholars of China (Lü and Perry 1997; Whyte and Parish 1984; Walder 1986).[8] For our purpose, the term underlines an institutional form with four key attributes: vertical hierarchy, administrative nature of the decision-making process, an organization-oriented model of promotion that values political assets over legal assets, and the role of the court not merely as an employer, but as a nexus of valuable resources for its judges.

Work-units prioritize tight vertical control over efficiency. One of the original functions of the *danwei* was to allow the Chinese party-state to track the political loyalty of its citizens. Citizens who worked for a *danwei* were monitored by the *danwei* (Belcher and White 1979). For each individual, the *danwei* maintained a dossier that personified the individual in the state bureaucratic system (Yeh 1997). This controlling nature of the *danwei* continues in the work-unit court. A strong vertical administrative hierarchy makes up the humming heart of the work-unit court. It serves as a "patrolling" system of political supervision (Shirk 1993) and as a means through which the balancing of interests within the local party-state is factored into the decision-making process of the court. For court leaders, tight hierarchical control minimizes risks and uncertainties. At the top of the hierarchy is a highly oligarchic decision-making body made up of senior judges and officials of the local party-state. Through the control of the administrative hierarchy, the court becomes an integral part of the local coalition of governance. Hierarchical organization and associated controls lead to the limited capacities of frontline judges to cope with the complexity and uncertainty with which they are confronted. This limitedness is most visible when the court internally reviews cases that are considered potentially controversial. Explaining the root structure of hierarchical organizations, Reinhard Bendix refers to the epilogue of Leo Tolstoy's *War and Peace* to describe the hierarchical organization as a perfectly shaped cone: "As men unite for common action, the largest number of them take a direct share in the action, while a smaller number takes a less direct share. The commander-in-chief never takes part directly, but instead makes general arrangements for the combined action" (Bendix 1977:139). The Chinese work-unit court is more supervisory and controlling than the typical hierarchical organization that Bendix describes. Its operation requires that the most senior officials be *sometimes* "hands-on" in the decisions of individual cases. But this occasional "hands-on" nature means that internal controls are quite erratic and are not rule-based. Noncontroversial matters remain loosely controlled.

Since erratic control is a consequence of the *administrative* nature of the court's decision-making process, the system needs a mechanism to prevent it from going wild. As a result, the second feature of the work-unit court is the central role played by the vertical hierarchy as a replacement for the formal judicial process. Tight hierarchal control ensures that a judicial decision, when required, has adequate opportunities to allow for the input of political savvy and privileged information by the leaders of the court.

The decisions that Chinese courts make can be divided into three categories: (1) decisions too trivial to cover with legal rules; (2) decisions covered by legal rules; and (3) decisions too important to make without being reviewed by the vertical hierarchy.[9] Compared with firms, work-units make more decisions in categories (1) and (3). Decisions that fall within category (1) are family and neighborhood disputes that are too personal or just too trivial to be dealt with by law. It is best left to frontline judges to placate the parties involved and settle the conflicts. But work-unit courts also entertain a more expansive category (3). Work-unit courts tend to adopt a broad definition of "reviewable" cases – they would rather err on the side of caution. These criteria are developed locally and administratively by the court president and his group of senior judges. As such, whether a case is to be reviewed or not is more an act of political discernment than an application of legal rules. The boundary separating non-routine from routine cases is nebulous and ever evolving. Cases are reviewed not so much because they constitute *de novo* legal puzzles or because of procedural rigor (i.e., the legal sub-decisions leading to final decisions appear to contradict themselves), but because they constitute real-life conundrums that courts cannot resolve by following the law.

Some of these courts operate in the most uncertain and adverse environment for judging – a public with less knowledge and little trust of the law, a lack of quality frontline judges, an undeveloped economy that leads to an outsized proportion of disputes for litigants engaged in multiplex relationship (family disputes and divorce), and, in some multi-ethnic regions away from the coastal area, a community divided by languages and ethnic cultures. For these courts, a high percentage of daily cases – in some cases almost all cases of an entire category (e.g., criminal) – are fed into the administrative hierarchy for review. It is clear that decisions on controversial cases are not motivated solely, and often not even primarily, by legal consideration. Political consideration, be it the welfare of the local party and government, or the interest of a major state-owned enterprise, or the repercussions of a certain decision on the public, looms large (Peerenboom 2002:280–343; Fu 2003). In Chapter 4, we account for the setup of the administrative hierarchy that concentrates the power to decide in the hands of the president and his lieutenants.

This brings us to the third point – the valuing of social and interpersonal skills over legal expertise in personnel decisions. Once they are recruited into the court, judges are rewarded and promoted according to their "people skills" and political acumen rather than their legal expertise and judicial experience. Within the work-unit court, judges are, in an important sense, no different from bureaucrats working in other state bureaus. They face the same problem as other political actors face: an institutional environment that is highly fluid and rule-deficient. Judges, from court presidents down to new assistant judges, are aware of the precariousness of their careers. Their power could be taken away, their budgets reduced, their standing among peers undercut, and in the most severe situation, their careers ruined. To make things worse, the judiciary is traditionally a weak player. Its function, from the standpoint of the party-state, is preventive. It averts social unrest. It consumes rather than generates resources (Lieberthal 1992:17). It lacks financial clout. Traditionally, it was also the weakest of the three public security bureaus. Chinese bureaucrats talk about the bureaucracies of the police, the procuratorate, and the court as *gong* (公), *jian* (检), *fa* (法), with the court (*fa*) routinely coming last.

Senior judges of China exhibit a different disposition from the low-key, aloof personality one usually associates with Anglo-American and European judges (this is, of course, a stereotype, which is an exaggeration of some typical traits). As leaders of a weak bureaucracy, they devote their energy in cultivating and nurturing personal ties with equal- or higher-ranked officials, not just in the police and the procuratorate, but also among other local government and party officials. This is particularly true for leaders of work-unit courts (see, for example, Balme 2010; Xiong 2014a). In an interesting empirical study, Zuo Weimin (2014) found that among the 200 judges surveyed in Province S, an inland province in southwest China, less than one-fifth of them ranked the role of a legal expert as being important for their presidents. By comparison, over half of them considered it important for their court presidents to act as a manager (56.5 percent) and politician (53 percent)! Most judges we interviewed referred to their presidents as the "number one leader," or *yibashou* (一把手) in Chinese, rather than the most senior judge of the court.

Personal assets are, for Chinese bureaucrats, precious political capital. The personalized networks developed by senior judges can be viewed as a form of local knowledge. The ties and the special knowledge generalized from these ties are so localized that they become specific assets. For this reason, there have not been a lot of lateral movements among Chinese judges. Limited mobility is a known characteristic of the *danwei*. Judges' personal networks are too localized to be of use when uprooted. This "knowledge edge" that senior judges hold over their subordinates offers an institutional justification for court leaders to participate in the decision-making process of tough, difficult cases.

The fourth and the last feature of the work-unit court is that it binds its judges by a network of relationships encompassing work, home, neighborhood, and social life (Walder 1986). The presence of the vertical hierarchy, coupled with the intervention of senior judges, mean that frontline judges are much less free than their Western counterparts. But frontline judges in work-unit courts are generally willing to subject themselves to the scrutiny of senior judges in exchange for internal support, should their decisions go wrong. The control to which frontline judges are subjected is also made more palatable by the broader socioeconomic benefits that the work-unit court provides. As Andrew Walder (1986) points out, the *danwei* before the economic reform period of the 1980s functioned not only as the employer for the employee, but also as the conduit for the distribution of social services. Other scholars also point out that the *danwei* operates like a self-sufficient social community (Lü and Perry 1997). Certainly, things have changed after more than three decades of reform. The *total* nature of the *danwei* has been somewhat attenuated. More public goods are now available through the market mechanism. Yet, in some of the inland rural localities, frontline judges remain dependent on their work-unit courts for social and economic resources. They lean on the bureaucratic network of the court to provide services ranging from housing, health care, and schooling of young kids, to retirement benefits.

Work-unit courts still populate the judicial landscape of China. Many courts continue to follow a hierarchical decision-making process that vested a lot of the power in the senior judges at the top of the hierarchy. Of course, as with courts elsewhere, the majority of the cases they deal with are of a routine nature. Yet court leaders keep a tight rein on their subordinates, even when they are handling seemingly straightforward, routine cases. The court is able to survive in uncertain environments because power is centralized in the few senior judges who are most connected with the local network of governance. Yet, precisely because the decision-making process is monitored and regulated vertically, it is inefficient. As said, the work-unit court prioritizes outcome over output. It is more important to get the "safe" outcome for the cases than to process as many cases as possible. Bargaining among Chinese bureaucrats is infamously time-consuming. The game follows what political scientists call the method of "management-by-exception." Every agency representative must decide whether to sign on to a lower-level decision that does not entirely satisfy its preferences, or to hold out and force the intervention of the higher levels. Under this system, minorities have the power to delay action by refusing to compromise and referring it to a higher authority for resolution (Shirk 1993). This process of bargaining has a further tendency to sideline the use of law, as the dichotomous logic of law (legal/illegal) is not amenable to the give-and-take that bargaining requires.

Frontline judges have limited autonomy to make decisions on their own, as vertical supervision is strong. Furthermore, this embedded system is sometimes complicated by agents who employ their authority toward their own selfish ends. Senior judges have career and institutional interests that at times conflict with the role of the court as a government bureaucracy. Issues of corruption and old-fashioned patronage beset the efficacy of the mechanism (see Chapter 6). The transaction costs of supervising and coordinating, and sometimes haggling and rent-seeking, are high.

THE FIRM-TYPE COURT

In the sociological literature, the concept of the firm has been persistently shaped by the writings of Max Weber on bureaucracy. Our conception of the firm, however, differs from the classical Weberian conception of a bureaucratic enterprise. Instead, our adoption of the concept highlights the many attributes that newer, leaner, modern twenty-first century firms exhibit (DiMaggio 2001; Powell 1990; Sabel and Zeitlin 1996). Among these attributes are a flatter hierarchy that replaces vertical supervision with more lateral communication, the greater use of law in the decision-making process of the court, the growing importance of professional assets, and competition with the outside market for qualified personnel, especially among the younger segment of the legal workforce.

The first distinguishing feature of the firm-type court is its weakened hierarchy. Though the vertical hierarchy remains in place, the firm coordinates its actions through what can be described as a quasi-market mechanism; though the court monopolizes its services, it pays greater attention to "cost-and-revenue" calculations. The firm is adept at allocating its personnel to cater to case types that generate revenue. The responsiveness required to deal with a more complex litigation market pushes court leaders to opt for a more horizontal mode of governance, one that unsettles established ways in a vertical, hierarchical environment. To borrow a pair of metaphors used by political scientists Mathew McCubbins and Tom Schwartz (1984), if work-units with their vertical hierarchy adopt an interventionist "police patrol" approach, the firms opt for the in-the-background approach of the "fire alarm."[10]

There is also more "structural contingency" (versus the political contingency in the work-unit court), in the sense that organizational supervision varies substantially depending on the tasks at hand. The more routine the tasks, the greater the extent to which an organization can rely on a fine-grained division of labor based on skills and knowledge (DiMaggio 2001; Perrow 1967).

The second feature of the firm is a tendency to use *more* law. As mentioned, the scrutiny of vertical hierarchy is inefficient. The move to a more horizontal structure is motivated by the quest for higher efficiency. Economic liberalization since the 1980s have produced more lawsuits in the urban cities of China, in both the civil and the criminal areas. Most important, commercial cases with substantially bigger claims are now the fastest-growing category of cases in the most economically developed region. As we will see in Chapter 7, just like the economic activities that the law regulates and adjudicates, this economy-backed legal development is marked by sharp regional differences.

The firm faces a bigger caseload. It also operates in a relatively less volatile, less risky environment of judging. The combination of the two imparts a characteristic largely absent in the work-unit court: the firm values output. In the unique context of China, in order to increase output (i.e., to take up and close more cases), the court has to get ready to adjudicate more. It is less common (though it remains a possibility) in the firm environment for a court's hierarchy to micromanage the outcome of a particular case. The firm-type court is organized and managed toward adjudication. The complexity of the urban makeup, coupled with strong media scrutiny, means that adhering to the law has become, more often than not, a viably "safe" option for the courts. Of course, adjudication done by the firm is not entirely rule-based. The firm is also subject to influences from the external environment (see below). Yet the extent and intensity of these influences are more intermittent and varying.

The availability of more cases presents new options for court management. In a more predictable environment of judging, a high volume of adjudication produces benefits to the firm-type court that outweigh its exposure to adjudication-related uncertainties. As a "volume" court, the reward of dealing with more cases, besides achieving a higher standing among competing courts, is found in more revenue from court fees (calculated as a percentage of the monetary damages plaintiffs sought to recover) and other court-related charges, to the point where these courts do not require substantial subsidies from their local governments (Wang 2010). Quantitative change leads to qualitative change. This growing stream of income confers a new sense of financial independence for courts. It feeds back into the dynamics governing the interaction between the court and the local party-state. The reduced financial dependency on local government and party further makes for a less risky judicial environment. Hence, the demand to meet the *economic* criteria of efficiency is itself a *political* change that has broad consequences for the nature of the court and the quantity and quality of law it delivers.

The third feature is the enhanced role of legal knowledge and expertise. The emergence of a more diversified and complex judicial market prompts the firm to opt for a more refined division of judicial labor. In a typical big-city court in China today, its civil branch is subdivided into different divisions, or in Chinese, *tings* (庭). Besides the Civil Division Number 1 (民一庭 *minyiting*) that deals with traditional family and tort cases, there are newer divisions (2 to 4) that deal with commercial cases (contracts, companies, and securities), intellectual property disputes (copyright, trademark, and patent infringements), cases involving foreign companies, and maritime disputes.

Judges working in the firm have noticeably better credentials. For courts located in the major cities of China, a master's degree is a *de facto* prerequisite for an entry-level judicial position. In contrast, courts in the inland region struggle to find enough college-educated judges to fill their vacancies.

These young cohorts of urban judges resemble the knowledge-based professionals in Western societies. They tend to value their professional knowledge above everything else, as this is an area in which they can claim expertise, and thereby authority, often even over their superiors.

But firms have to compete with other sectors of the litigation market for the service of their frontline judges. The fluidity of employment is the fourth feature of the firm. Frontline judges working in the firm no longer think that they are "owned" by their *danwei*. The idea of a lifelong employment in the judiciary is quickly receding for the younger generation of judges. They do not see themselves as permanently attached to the court. Some view it as a stepping-stone to the commercial law firms in the big cities, a growing sector where people with government ties can earn a lucrative salary many times higher than the court is able to offer. Others are prepared to move on to other bureaucratic units after trying their hand at the judiciary. Chinese scholars in particular are concerned about the phenomenon of the rising attrition of younger judges. We explore this question further in Chapter 3.

INSTITUTIONAL ENVIRONMENT OF JUDGING

We have outlined, in an ideal-typical fashion, the features that distinguish the two types of courts: the firm and the work-unit. What motivates a court to lean toward one mode of governance over the other? Why are some courts more firm-like and others work-unit-like? The behaviors of judges are not dictated in any simple way by production or organizing costs, but are broadly shaped by a complex interaction of institutions, politics, economics and culture. To understand the behavioral differences between the two types, one must be aware that courts do not operate in an independent and well-formed legal environment. Courts deal with multiple external constraints. These constraints set limits to when their judges can use the law and when they have to do away with the law. The constraints come from different sources. A reference group includes her colleagues and seniors, judges in higher courts, local political leaders, mass media, and "trouble-making" litigants. Together, these different strands of constraints constitute a court's *institutional environment of judging.* This environment is the context through which judges make their everyday decisions. To use law as a means to resolve social disputes in China is always contingent upon the courts' interactions and shifting relations with other state actors, the public and the mass media, and the litigants.

The institutional environment of judging in China is highly fluid and ever evolving. To put it in sociological parlance, the development of the *juridical field* of China remains at a nascent stage. A field, according to sociologist Pierre Bourdieu (1990), is a well-demarcated social space whose logic of practices is shaped by its own field-specific interests. Accordingly, a juridical field is one that converts direct conflicts between parties into regulated debates between (legal) professionals who accept the rules of the field (Bourdieu 1987:831).[11] A strong field is one in which players can operate in a relatively stable institutional environment – actors have to adjust to the rules of the game, rather than the game having to change its rules on an *ad hoc* basis to adjust to the interests of powerful actors. Powerful actors dominate by playing by the rules, i.e., holding a monopoly over legitimate practices. The legal field of China, however, is limited in its ability to translate social, political and economic conflicts into legal disputes. This limitedness means that legal disputes are often not resolved by legal rules, but have to be dealt with by other rules – for example, as social or political conflicts as well.

It is in this sense that we suggest that the Chinese courts are deeply embedded institutions. We use the term "embeddedness" to describe the open-ended and indefinite character of the institutional environment of judging within which the courts operate. The contingent character of judicial actions is particularly pronounced in the case of China.

The term "embeddedness" is most widely used in the field of economic sociology to challenge the purportedly pure autonomy of economic actions (Beckett 2003; Granovetter 1985; Polanyi 1944; Portes and Sensenbrenner 1993; Krippner and Alavez 2007). We appropriate the term to underline the connectedness between the judicial decision-making process and other spheres of power. In other words, we use the term to describe the leakiness of the judicial field in China. The way we appropriate the concept of embeddedness means that we emphasize both the organizational dynamics and the political economy of judicial decision-making (Zukin and DiMaggio 1990). It refers to the administrative, political, social and economic structuration of judicial decisions.

In line with the sociological literature on organizational ecology (Hannah and Freeman 1977; Hawley 1950; Carroll 1984), we argue that the Chinese courts operate in ways that enhance their survival. Our focus is not literally on the survival of the court as an institution, but on the survival and thriving of a certain *organizational form* that the court adopts. In a superficial sense, as government bureaus, courts always survive. But the dominance of work-unit organization over firm-type organization in some settings, or vice versa, has important consequences in determining the institutional character of a court. Carroll makes this point clearly: "When the environment and the organizational form match, selection is positive and enhances survival. When they do not, selection acts against the organizational form" (Carroll 1990:57).

In so doing, we distinguish our approach from institutional economists who put the foremost emphasis on efficiency. Oliver Williamson (1970, 1981), for example, emphasizes technical efficiency as the single most important selection criterion. Certainly, efficiency has its place in our analysis. As we will see, technical efficiency is more relevant for firm-type courts that operate in a market-like environment. But it is more appropriate in our view to conceive the pursuit of efficiency as one means for survival in the unique political economy of judging in China. Striving to survive by *performing* as a competitive firm is one way. But local courts that do not (and cannot) make enough money by being market-efficient have other survival means – for example, by serving as the chore boys of local governments.[12] As Hannan and Freeman point out (1984:339), "although ... considerations of efficiency have powerful consequences for many kinds of organizations, ... they do not obviously override institutional and political considerations."[13] Our discussion of embeddedness is meant to capture the key social, political, and institutional factors that shape the adaptive process of the courts.

We should also add that all judicial systems are, to various extents, embedded – the idea of a hermetically sealed legal machine that operates on its own is a myth anyway. In the United States, judges sitting on the bench of the most powerful courts are either elected or appointed by an official who is elected (e.g., the US President). Similarly, the majority of the state judges are determined by election, which is a powerful mechanism for enabling public opinions to influence the decision-makers of the legal system (Jacob 1996; Friedman 1998). But these channels through which politics, economics, and other social realms influence legal operations are institutionalized. Institutionalization allows the judicial system to incorporate political consideration into the judicial realm; it marks any influences outside of the established channels as undue.

We emphasize the *immediacy* and *directness* of external influences in China. The Chinese system differs most markedly in that the influences of other social realms are deeply embedded within the bureaucratic process of resolving problem cases. By and large, Chinese courts now follow standard procedures to deal with new, incoming cases at the grassroots level. But Chinese judges are not persistent in applying the law. It helps if one understands how Chinese judges think. For them, when the law fails to satisfy all parties, it becomes the judges' "problem." The case at stake becomes a "problem case" that requires further actions from the judiciary. What these further actions entail all is too-often guided by mixed and complicated considerations, including public reactions, social stability, control over resources, and personal connections. This enigma is well captured by a comment made by a head judge from Zhejiang. The judge said to us during his interview, "Do you know what's really surprising about our laws? China is not a democracy. The Communist

Party can pass whatever laws it wants to make. Who could've thought that carrying them out is so darn difficult?" But if the law is just one among many forms of central policies, it should not be so surprising after all. As Xueguang Zhou points out, "The more uniform the state policy and/or the greater the separation between policy making and implementation, the less the fit between the policy and local conditions, therefore the greater flexibility allowed in the implementation process" (2010: 61). The law is the most uniform of all state policies; as a result, courts are flexible in not just carrying it out, but also deciding when to use it.

The relationship between the judicial process and their contextual contingencies is the focus of this book. The rest of this chapter aims to develop a framework for making sense of the key embedded components that make up this fluid institutional environment of judging. We identify four key types of embeddedness that are most central to judicial decision making in China: *administrative, political, social* and *economic* embeddedness. At the ends of the spectrum of impact for each are the work-unit and firm-type of courts. We briefly discuss each type of embeddedness below.

ADMINISTRATIVE EMBEDDEDNESS

The judiciary is supposed to be a *different* government branch. In a liberal democracy, the court is supposed to be independent, though, as Shapiro (1981) points out, this ideal of judicial independence is often unrealized. At a minimum, the court aspires to follow a relative clear set of rules (the law) in every step of the judicial decision process. This rule-based nature distinguishes judicial decisions from political decisions. Disagreements or blatant mistakes are addressed by referring to the same set of rules through an iterative mechanism of appeal. Administrative embeddedness refers to the high degree of selfsameness between the court and other government bureaus in its decision-making process. Important judicial decisions in China are at least partly based upon some assessment of non-legal factors. Administrative embeddedness can be analytically differentiated into two subtypes: internal and external. By internal administrative embeddedness, we refer to the manner in which the decisions of the Chinese courts are subject to the supervision and collective consensus-creating process of senior judges. The superiors have strong decisional control over their subordinates. In Chapter 4 we will account for how this control is achieved. Suffice it for now to point out that the "administrative" review process of a problem case is structurally porous to such an extent that it becomes almost amorphous at the very top end. A Chinese court follows a decision-making structure that operates like an inverted sieve – as a case is kicked up, the context of consideration expands from one that is predominately (and narrowly) legal to one that is increasingly (and broadeningly) social and political.[14] As it goes up the administrative hierarchy, legal issues become embedded within a larger and larger social and political context of consideration. This "spiraling-over" tendency, as cases move up the hierarchy, is the most emblematic trait of Chinese-style judicial decision-making. Often, a judge cannot decide on her own but must coordinate both internally with senior judges in the court *and* externally with other local party organs and government bureaus, through various formal and informal mechanisms.[15]

This decisional hierarchy is an administrative bureaucracy. It certainly is different from the Anglo-American model of the professional court (Guarnieri and Pederzoli 2002). It also deviates significantly from the judicial bureaucracy in the continental European systems. In a judicial bureaucracy, the law and the rules governing the application of the law are followed as to what has to be done, regardless of who makes the decision. In an administrative bureaucracy, however, rules are only applied as to who should be in charge of making the decision. In other words, rules decide *who* makes the decision, but not so much *how* the decision should be made or *what* the decision should be. Instead, the designated decision-maker often, as in the case of China, actively refers to extra-legal reasons in arriving at her rulings.

While a judicial bureaucracy is designed to defend a juridical space within which officials with specialized legal knowledge can operate, an administrative bureaucracy emphasizes supervision and oversight. This structure is vertically organized in a nested way to make sure that "problems" can be spotted and dealt with as early as possible. Chinese courts, from the very top (SPC) to the bottom (grassroots), from the biggest urban court to the smallest rural one, all share a similar basic organizational structure. Such a baseline structure made up of roughly three layers of supervision – with the collegial panel as the first layer, division meeting as the second, and the adjudication committee as the third. Each layer oversees a bigger pool of cases and holds veto power over the immediate layer below it. Power is distributed according to administrative rank instead of judicial expertise. At each layer, those who occupy senior administrative roles (the president, and to a much lesser extent, the vice presidents, division heads and deputy division heads) have broad powers over their subordinates. These power actors play a dominant rule in the vertical process of supervision. Hence, the degree of professional division of labor in fact descends as one ascends the hierarchy. Those at the top oversee everything.

Chinese courts have not cultivated a rule-centered institutional culture (even though this is changing in some courts). Consistency and predictability, the qualities that define modern legal systems, are not entrenched as core values. Chinese judges in many grassroots courts are at their innovative best for finding ways to resolve "problem cases" without using the law, either by bargaining in the shadow of the law or by getting around the law and resorting to other means (see Chapter 5). In interviews, some Chinese judges acknowledge that it is challenging for them to follow the law if following the law will produce bad social consequences. They cannot just "go with the law" this time and wait for the law to change next time. Judges would not say: "Let's rule by the law even if we do not like the result. Our government will change the law and get the right result next time." Judges are so involved in everyday governance that they would rather find ways to get around the law if following the law would jeopardize governance. Because the courts are expected to achieve immediate responsiveness, they are not inclined to treat like cases alike (and when immediate responses are difficult to give, they tend to stall rather than to rule).

This brings us to the second dimension of administrative embeddedness: the external dimension. External administrative embeddedness refers to the manner in which the Chinese courts and their judicial decisions are shaped by the sometimes converging, sometimes diverging interests among members of local party-state coalition. China's state bureaucracies, including the courts, coexist in a highly complex system of interdependency and competition. Courts, particularly those located in the inland region, work for other, more powerful government branches. The image of a professional court quietly and passively resolving cases fails to convey the sensitive and precarious atmosphere in which many of the courts operate. Courts are expected to provide support to local policies. This is shown, at a superficial level, by judges who are asked to show up in various local political campaigns, from anti-corruption to promotion of public hygiene (see above). More important, courts are expected to support local governance by being "friendly" in judgments involving local government and state-owned enterprises. This has led to the persistent charge of local favoritism among Chinese courts (e.g., Gu 2015; Keith et al. 2014).

A note is in order about our understanding of the state. Similar to our understanding of the court system, the modern political state is not understood as a homogeneous entity. Instead, states comprise an ecology of competitors. As Andrew Abbott (2005:251) points out, "'the state' is in practice neither a single unified thing, nor a complex machine with many parts, nor an aggregate of many individual wills. It is yet another ecology of competitors, albeit one in which some members have their hands directly on the machinery of government."[16] This is even the case for an authoritarian state like China. The local party-state is made up of a congeries of bureaus, each with their own institutional goals and interests. State power shall be and can be studied through the interactions between various authorities at multiple levels and how they interact with assorted social groups (Migdal 1994:14).

As an institution, the court has a dual nature. This dual nature is reflective of the character of the Chinese state as a party-state. The court is both an organ of the local party-state and a unit of the judicial hierarchy. Local party and government officials can influence a grassroots court through the Chinese Communist Party (CCP)'s Political-Legal Committee (PLC). The PLC is composed of senior officials from the local party committee, relevant government branches, the procuratorate, and people's congress. The court president is also a member of the PLC (He 2010:181). She is also a member of the local governance coalition (Diamant et al. 2005). But the committee is usually headed and convened by a senior party member who often serves in the government, such as the head of the police.

By the same token, the court president plays a dual role. On the one hand, she is the head of the court. She and her judges are the officials who apply the law locally. On the other hand, she serves as the vessel to facilitate the flow of information between the court and other members of the local party-state. She is involved in formulating key policies. When the president discusses matters with other core members of the governance coalition, she thinks as a senior bureaucrat. The context of consideration is not merely whether a decision is legal or not. The president has to persuade (and be persuaded) and bargain with other bureau heads. The coalition as a whole must balance the bureaucratic interests of different departments. The outcome of their consideration will depend on their respective political weight and on their ability to demonstrate that a certain course of action that benefits the court is most desirable, in the bigger interests of the party-state and the public.

The necessity of political consideration means that court leaders are chosen from a pool of pragmatic bureaucrats. Certainly, court presidents come in different shades.[17] Some are tigers and some are tabbies. Nevertheless, scholarly intellectuals rarely make Chinese senior judges. These judges are deft, worldly administrators. They play the role of "politician" for their courts. They assess not just the legal, but also the political merits and risks of a certain pending decision. Their risk assessments are crucial for determining the court's decisions on "problem" cases.

Often, the two halves of her dual identity collide. She must therefore tread a fine line between carrying out the law and working with local government officials, who have considerable control over the courts' personnel and budget, and, increasingly, responding to the media and public opinion (Peerenboom 2010:83). Senior judges know the importance of not appearing too subservient to local governments. Sometimes judges have no choice but to apply imposed solutions, but at other times they exploit the power fragmentation of local government in order to allow themselves to exercise innovation at the margins (He 2010; Stern 2013). For example, while weak local courts must restrain themselves from using the law *positively* to defy the will of the local party-state, some are able to *innovatively* decline the use of law to promote the interests of powerful local political players (He 2010).

POLITICAL EMBEDDEDNESS

By "political embeddedness," we refer to the subjection of the use of law to the political goal of maintaining stability. Ever since the Chinese party-state's inception in the 1950s, it has viewed law as a tool to promote social stability and to exercise social control. This instrumentalist view of law means that judicial decision-making is influenced by political policies.

The concept of political embeddedness can be further understood from the macro and micro perspectives. Macroscopically, political embeddedness refers to how broad judicial directions such as the exercise of death penalty, the adoption of suspended sentences, the promotion of mediation and grand mediation and the use of reconciliation are tied to the legal campaigns of the day. The law, particularly the criminal side of it, remains deeply embedded in the broader government operations of stability maintenance and its operations remain directed by government bureaus that serve other, non-judicial functions.

Reforms of the judicial system are always partly legal and partly political in China. They are not simply directed at concentrating enforcement efforts and securing greater compliance with existing law, but are integrally linked to cycles of political and legal reform (Biddulph et al. 2012). For example, by around the early 2000s, stability maintenance had become the publically acknowledged premier goal of the public security system, of which the judicial system is a part (Trevaskes et al. 2014). The promotion of political ideals such as "harmonious society" and "the mass line" (群众路线 *qunzhong luxian*) (Zhao 2014) dominates the discussion of the role of the legal system at the top.[18]

Organizationally speaking, scholars have long characterized the Chinese judicial system as part of the civilian coercive bureaucratic clusters (other parts including the public security system, the prison and forced labor administration, and intelligence/counterintelligence units) (Lieberthal 1992:3). As mentioned, PLCs at each level of government have extensive power to oversee courts and other legal institutions (deLisle 2014:227). They play a leadership role in defining and coordinating law-and-order-related policy goals. The party justifies its coordination of criminal justice organs on the grounds that criminal justice policies cannot be effectively implemented without unified leadership (Trevaskes 2011:335). The courts have traditionally played a subordinate role to two other, more powerful agencies that with the courts make up the so-called three arms of justice. The public security bureaus are responsible for managing the police and performing social monitoring. Their important frontline duties and the sheer size of their establishment easily make them the most powerful entity within the cluster. The procuratorate is given the power both to prosecute and to oversee malfeasance by other government organs, including the judiciary. The procuratorate can use its powers under the Chinese Procedural Law to "supervise" a case. This gives them a superior role over the court. Some criminal judges said that the supervisory power of the procuratorate could become "the monkey over their shoulders" when sensitive cases were tried. In short, Chinese courts have to work alongside other government agencies in maintaining stability. For that reason, criminal cases, alongside administrative cases, are most closely monitored and reviewed in many courts.

At a micro, case-unit level, the constant quest for political stability invites judges to positively take into consideration litigants, interested social groups, and the mass media when dealing with problem cases (Trevaskes 2007). They share a double consciousness that is often contradictory – on the one hand, they see themselves as officials who carry out the law; on the other, they see themselves as bureaucrats who are tasked to maintain social stability and thereby sometimes refrain from carrying out the law. Sensitivity, perhaps even insecurity, to popular opinion and to protesters also contribute to a bureaucratic mentality that privileges mediation and reconciliation. This tendency to placate is particularly pronounced for cases in which larger groups are involved and in cases in which protests may spread to a wider group. Judges are instructed to exhaust all means to prevent the disputes from escalating into social disturbance and "malignant incidents" (恶性事件 *exing shijian*), such as protests, demonstrations, or in more extreme cases, violent attacks upon judges that sometimes end in the attacker committing suicide (Minzner 2009; He 2017). Failure to curb "malignant incidents" will result in political responsibilities and administrative sanctions (Yu 2005; China Daily 2007; Beijing Youth 2013). Courts are also sensitive to media reports. In places where social stability is more vulnerable (some of the economically less-developed inland regions), the environment of judging is so uncertain that it leads to a general aversion to adjudication. Some of the most politically charged cases are never taken up by the courts. For other sensitive or potentially disruptive cases, judges lean on diversionary practices such as mediation in civil trials and victim-offender reconciliation in criminal trials. Their concern is that adjudication distinguishes litigating parties into clear winners and losers. Winner-takes-all adjudicative decisions run the risk of challenges by the losing parties.

Courts in China do not have, to quote the famous phrase of political scientist Davis Easton, "a reservoir of favorable attitudes or good will that helps members to accept or tolerate outputs to which they are opposed or the effects of which they see as damaging to their wants" (1965:273; cited by Gibson 2007). There is always a whiff of suspicion surrounding a court's decision. The degree of institutional legitimacy the Chinese courts enjoy is minimal, if it is seen to exist at all. In other words, courts are not recognized as appropriate decision-making bodies "when one disagrees with the outputs of the institution" (Gibson 2007).

Many cases in which courts in China adjust their outcomes in response to protest are not high-profile cases. As Liebman points out (2011), they are instead routine cases involving a small number of parties. This is because, besides the formal channel of appeal, judges also fear being ruined professionally by persistent litigants. Petitioners often resort to the ubiquitous letters-and-visits system, or *xinfang* (信访), to pressure the courts (O'Brien and Li 2006). In fact, the number of petitions and appeals against judgments handed down by individual courts is a crucial indicator of courts' job performance (Minzner 2009). Hence, contrary to common perception, China's judicial system has become more populist (He 2009a; Liebman 2012; Trevaskes 2010). There is ample evidence indicating that protesting, petitioning, or threatening to do either often is a successful means for litigants to pressure courts to rule in their favor or to alter decided cases (Liebman 2011:269).

SOCIAL EMBEDDEDNESS

Social embeddedness refers to the influences of other social roles a judge holds in his carrying out of judicial duties. Tautological as it may sound, judges are supposed to decide on cases *as judges*. In China, judges do not always perform their official/

professional role alone when they decide cases. Social ties, or *guanxi*, are often seen as operating in juxtaposition to the judicial process in China. As Potter points out, the juxtaposition is illustrated by the aphorism that contracts are agreements between people who do not trust each other – people who trust each other (or are connected) do not need law (Potter 2002:180).

As mentioned, the Chinese court as an institution does not command a lot of trust. There is a widespread perception that all the trappings of procedural rigor are a façade and that one's strong connection is all that matters. Many people, especially those who have used the courts themselves, tend to believe that more seems to take place behind courtrooms than in them (Michelson and Read 2011). It is "know-who" (connections) that matters the most (Ang and Jia 2014). They believe that judges are often asked by friends and family members to use their public power to advance private causes. Yet, though the public and the media in China perceive corruption as rampant, few cases are ever officially reported. In its annual working report of 2015 (Supreme People's Court 2016a), the SPC revealed that courts at all levels found only 721 persons with disciplinary violations or violations of the law against abuse of adjudicatory or enforcement powers. Of these, only 120 were pursued for criminal responsibility. This number is negligible considered in context of the 190,000 Chinese judges nationwide. While underreporting is an issue contributing to the unbelievably low numbers, a more important factor is that *guanxi* runs through the "pores" of laws and regulations (see Chapter 6). Even though bribery and *guanxi* favoritism both deviate purposefully from the exercise of legal reasoning to arrive at preferred outcomes, it is important to analytically distinguish the two. The criminal laws of the PRC (Article 385) focus only on cases that involve monetary bribes. Cases involving the use of social connections to influence outcome, what in Chinese known as 人情案 (*renqing an*), are not discussed in the criminal laws.

Our (by no means systematic) observations are that cases involving the use of social connections clearly outnumber those involving monetary transactions. Many judges whom we interviewed acknowledged this – they were, to a certain degree, influenced by friends and acquaintances. The operative phrase is this vague expression "to a certain degree." We will further address this question in Chapter 6. Here we just want to point out one thing. Existing literature commonly treats *guanxi* as either a synonym or a precursor of corruption (Lü 2002; Li, Ling 2011, 2012; Zhan 2012). Yet the relationship between *guanxi* pulling and bribery is intricate and complex. Strong *guanxi*, characterized by trust and obligation, discourages the use of money. Favors are not paid back immediately, but they are tallied in long-term obligations. Moreover, *guanxi* becomes strong when it spans different personal spheres between a favor- seeker and a favor- giver. The offering of money, a rather impersonal medium of exchange, undermines the personal quality of *guanxi* (Simmel 1990).

Social embeddedness would be an aggregated individual phenomenon if judges were only influenced by their own personal networks. The reality is more complex and sociologically interesting. The complexity arises from the fact that frontline judges are influenced not only by their own friends and relatives but also by the friends and relatives of their superiors and their colleagues. Social ties in institutional contexts work as transitive relations – i.e., if *a* affects *b* and *b* affects *c*, then *a* affects *c*. *Guanxi* can work at one remove or further. It is this transitivity that makes the problem of social embeddedness more extensive than any bureaucracy can handle. *Guanxi* fuses and becomes entangled. In fact, the problem of social embeddedness is that it often acts through the administrative hierarchy of the court. Individually viewed, a judge's social network is made up of a series of egocentric circles, as captured by the famous analogy made by anthropologist Fei Xiaotong: "ripples formed from a stone thrown into a lake, each circle spreading out from the center becomes more distant and at the same time more insignificant" (1992:65). But when the personal networks of judges are put together and linked to each other through the administrative hierarchy, it becomes a form of divergent power that is diffuse but extensive. This is why social ties reach afar in China. Effective ties can be ties that come either directly from the personal networks of a judge, or transitively from the personal networks of his superiors and close colleagues.

Chinese courts, however, are undergoing changes. Social embeddedness turns on the willingness of judges and administrative regulators to base decisions, partially or at times completely, on obligations of personal networks. There are signs that suggest the effects of strong ties, particularly strong transitive ties, are gradually weakening for larger courts that follow a more formal organizational structure.

ECONOMIC EMBEDDEDNESS

By characterizing courts as "economically" embedded, we refer to the fact that court finance is in many ways refractive, if not reflective, of local economy. The mechanism is roundabout, yet the correlation is unmistaken. Court budgets are tied to court revenues, which in turn depend very much on the vibrancy of the local economy. This is the unique political economy of judging in China. Courts in Western countries are non-market organizations that are mostly grant-funded. This financing mechanism puts courts into the category of public bureaucracy, as distinguished from other organizations that generate income by selling their products or services (Beetham 1996:39–40). From the standpoint of traditional political economy, public bureaucracies, including courts, are less concerned with generating revenue from their services or products. They are more interested instead in expanding their jurisdictions in order to grow their establishment to justify a bigger budget (Niskanen 1973). Yet a closer examination of the financing method of Chinese courts suggests a hybrid, two-tier system. Courts that are able to make enough money support themselves by generating their own revenues. The rest that are not able to make enough money fall back on the support of local governments, but with added constraints on their judicial goals and policies.

The financing of Chinese courts is an obvious case of "institutional decoupling" (Meyer and Rowan 1977). Until recently, a given court has been funded by the government of the same level (Zhu 2007). The SPC, for example, is funded by the central government's Ministry of Finance. High People's Courts are likewise funded by provincial or autonomous regional governments, Intermediate and Basic People's Courts in the cities by municipal government, and those in the rural areas by rural county government. A chronic shortage of funds is a problem facing many courts at the grassroots level.[19] This is the case despite the continued increase of supplementary funding from the central and provincial governments to provide the basic-level courts with discretionary financial support for special construction projects and other designated or one-off expenditure (Keith et al. 2014:116–117). The situation has been, ironically, made worse in recent years by the party-state's determination to provide better access to justice. In 2007, the State Council issued a new administrative regulation aimed at encouraging the public to use the courts more. The regulation reduced litigation fees amid a bigger policy of readjusting the structure of court charges (see Chapter 7 for details). It reduced the court fees charged for cases involving small claims, divorce, and labor disputes. The new policy was intended to make sure that working-class litigants would not be barred from litigation because of economic reasons (Zhu 2011:185–187).

Why do many courts operate in deficit? The reason is quite simple – they do not make enough money, and in contradiction to the central policy, how much the courts can practically spend remains tied to how much they make. As early as the late 1990s, the central government publicized the policy of 收支两条线 (*shou zhi liang tiao xian*), literally meaning "two lines in income and expenditure." The slogan visualizes a picture wherein expenditure and income run as two separate lines that are independent from each other.

Yet law is traditionally placed low on the list by local officials. Even today, in the eyes of many local government officials, law is viewed as a "mushy" product, to borrow a term from Lynn Paine (1992), in the sense that it is hard to measure the payoff of the investment of resources in law. Local governments, always with more tangible and pressing needs to address, are most reluctant to give courts more than what they earn. As a result, the fund allocated to a court closely approximates the amount of revenue it generates. The arrangement is a *de facto* rebate system. The court sends its revenue to the local government; the local government then returns most if not all of the court's money back to the court. The more the court turns in, the more will be returned.

The overall result is that allocated funds are still determined by revenues collected, and the policy of separating expenditures from income thus results in a return to the original situation in which expenses and income are linked. The two budgetary lines, income and expenditure, eventually evolve back to one line, or one curved line at best (He 2009c). In a 2007 study of a basic-level court in Guchang of Hupei province, researchers found that the county government of Guchang regularly budgeted the expenditure for its basic-level court at a level about 3 million Chinese yuan. However, half of this amount depended on the expected revenues from the fees and charges collected by the court. The county government normally provided half of the budgeted money at the beginning of the year but then held back the remaining half until the fees and charges of the court were enough to make up that second half of the budget (Court Finding Research Group of the Higher People's Court in Hupei province 2009, cited in Keith et al. 2014:114).

The *de facto* link connecting expenditure and expense means that courts are variably endowed – some with wholesome budgets to invest in new information technology, to construct new courthouse buildings and above all, to offer more generous bonuses to their judges; others with shoestring budgets that make them all the more dependent on the unreliable financial relief that local governments provide, with cutbacks that leave them further behind the wealthier courts. The deciding factor that separates the two groups is the quantity and quality of revenue-generating commercial cases that arrive at their doorsteps. Here lies the irony – for an institution as bureaucratic as the Chinese court, its internal differentiation is predominantly driven by market conditions. The growing sector of "economic cases" in the overall civil caseload is perhaps one of the most overlooked aspects of the changing nature of law in China.

As a group, economic cases have overtaken the traditional civil cases of family disputes and personal injury to become the biggest category of cases in the dockets of Chinese courts. Surely, there are more – in fact a lot more – divorce petitions in China nowadays, as divorce rate in the most urban region of China hit an unprecedented high rate of over 40 percent (Frecklington 2014). But the rapid growth in family cases is dwarfed by the huge volume of commercial disputes unleashed by the expanding market in urban China. Courts now play a crucial role in adjudicating disputes in market exchanges. It is quite clear that economic policies, and economy-related policies more broadly, have been put in legal form to an unprecedented extent (deLisle 2014, 2015; Gu 2015). It is also quite clear that the courts that rule have benefited financially, albeit unevenly, from the growing economy. Many firm-type courts can now be considered a legitimate "economic" bureau. Certainly, compared to the most established market economies in North America and Europe, the role of law in promoting and sustaining economic development is still somewhat limited. Yet it is hard to ignore the bigger role of law in facilitating and regulating economic activities. As recently as the mid-1980s, the entire corpus of the PRC laws could literally fit into a single, slim volume. Commercial litigation was virtually irrelevant in the aftermath of the Cultural Revolution in the late 1970s (Liebman 2012:221). By the early 2000s, just the new input of statutes in one year would make up a tome (deLisle 2014:227; Liebman 2012:220). There are more laws today in China. Many market activities, from simple bank loans obtained by local family businesses to corporations raising capital in the stock market, are now done through law. They are reflected in the growing number of economic cases in purchase and sale, money lending, and contract. Between 1980 and 2001, the number of economic cases increased almost 300-fold (Liang 2008:46). The total claims of the total of economic cases in grassroots courts are closely related to the vibrancy of local economies (He 2007).

The civil litigation rate is clearly on the rise, from 31.5 cases per 100,000 people in 1978 to 435.6 cases per 100,000 in 2010 (Zhu 2011:4). According to the latest statistics released by the SPC, over 63 percent of the cases heard in Chinese courts are civil cases. There are now more than 8.5 million civil cases annually. By comparison, criminal cases made up only 8.3 percent of the total caseload (Zhou 2015).[20]

The growth in number is just part of the story. Civil litigation has not just increased in volume, but more importantly, in its diversity. Anyone who has done fieldwork in the "big-city" courts in China would probably agree that the newer Civil Division Number 2 (民二庭 *minerting*) and Civil Division Number 3 (民三庭 *minsanting*), i.e., courts that deal with commercial and intellectual property disputes, are, economically speaking, where the action is.[21] These divisions are also places in which courts invest the most manpower. There is a clear diversification of commercial disputes into different categories (intellectual property, company, contractual and labor), reflecting the increasingly refined categorization of civil disputes that mimics the Anglo-American system. Contract disputes make up the major category of cases, and other civil cases including personal injury, housing and land disputes, environmental law-suits and defamation claims are growing (Liebman 2012:221).

Cases dealt with today are drastically different in nature from cases dealt with as recently as two decades ago. Statistically speaking, over one-third of the civil cases (if one combines the categories of commercial and civil cases), or a total of 3.34 million cases, were commercial cases (finance cases, private lending disputes, sales contract disputes, intellectual property cases, corporate disputes, maritime cases). On top of these commercial cases are private loan cases not involving financial institutions, i.e., lending disputes between individuals, between a company and an individual, or between two or more companies, which accounted for about another 22 percent of civil cases (Supreme People's Court 2016a). If we add up the two categories (commercial cases and private lending disputes), over half of all of the civil cases are disputes arising from market transactions, either between individuals or among corporations.

Yet economic embeddedness is an uneven process. It is this unevenness that leads to the bifurcation of firms and work-units.[22] In economically developed cities, local courts "profit" greatly from deeper embedding of the law and the market. But in most of the rural hinterlands, small contractual disputes and family cases dominate. The absence of large-claim commercial cases deprives work-unit courts of the ability to generate meaningful revenue from the civil case docket. As a result, courts in the countryside, many of them of the work-unit-type, rely more on fines collected from the convicted in criminal cases to support themselves. Even with the money obtained from criminal fines, these courts are financially vulnerable. They run a money-losing "business." Their budgets fall further behind those of their richer, urban counterparts. Their fiscal dependency on local governments just to make ends meet (i.e., to keep the court up and running, to not reduce the number of staff in the court, to retain more qualified judges) is an inescapable fate. This, as we shall see, invites further administrative embeddedness in the operations of these courts.

LOOKING AHEAD

This book is an attempt to explain the socio-economic dynamics that contribute to the growing heterogeneity of the Chinese court system. We sketch out the four types of embeddedness that contribute to the diversity of Chinese courts today. But the effects of the types of embeddedness identified above differ in scope and intensity. The differences, even discordances, among them produce contrasting judicial (and non-judicial) behaviors. The court system is marked by significant and growing regional variations. Our framework of embeddedness is intended to map out, analytically, the underlying socio-economic and cultural forces that lead to the variant operations of Chinese courts. In the following chapters of the book, we explicate the decision-making processes of Chinese courts in different environments of judging, based on the four key types of embeddedness identified.

In Chapter 2, we start by outlining the daily rounds for frontline judges. We offer a detailed picture of what judges do in a typical work day and how they do it. We do this to present the social world of Chinese judges, a world that is strikingly different from that of Anglo-American judges.

In Chapter 3, we analyze the changing makeup of Chinese courts. We draw from our interviews of judges of different age cohorts from different parts of China. The Chinese court system has undergone rapid changes in the past twenty years. The pace of change is astounding for any judicial system and yet particularly so for a bureaucratic system of this size. Nothing illustrates better this rapid change than the complete overhaul of the mechanism for recruiting new judges during this period. The old generation of demobilized-soldiers-turned-judges is noticeably different from the new, post-1980 generation of college-trained (many of them double-degreed) judges. They are different not just in age and education, but also in their social background, which is reflected, among many things, in their attitudes toward the law. To borrow an old term from legal realist Karl Llewellyn (1960), different generations of judges have their own "period style," they each have their own expectations of their jobs and views about how judicial responsibilities are to be discharged. The importance of cohort effects in understanding the operation of Chinese courts cannot be overlooked for anyone interested in the micro-dynamics of daily judicial operations in China. The next four chapters discuss, in order, administrative embeddedness, political embeddedness, social embeddedness, and economic embeddedness.

In Chapter 4, we discuss in further depth the nature of administrative embeddedness in Chinese Courts. We outline the administrative hierarchy that the court adopts to facilitate vertical supervision, a three-tier structure starting with the collegial panel as the first tier, the division meeting as the second tier, and finally the adjudication committee as the third and top tier. To understand the administrative nature of the hierarchy, we focus in particular on the operation of the adjudication committee.

Chapter 5 turns to political embeddedness. We discuss how adjudication is sometimes avoided in the interest of promoting social stability. Judges and their seniors in courts, work-unit courts in particular, tend to use *less* law to deal with their uncertain environment of judging. We describe how the courts *shrink* from adjudicating problem cases in uncertain environments of judging. This shrinking is accomplished by promoting mediation in civil cases and reconciliation in criminal cases. Highly politically charged cases are also avoided through the screening process of the case filing division. Yet there are also moments when the courts would step up and play the role of mediator between the local government and protestors.

Chapter 6 discusses social embeddedness. We examine the different types of social connections in the judicial context and how they differ from each other in terms of their effects. Our analysis suggests that cases involving monetary bribes are often cases where only weak ties are involved. Strong ties do not require immediate monetary transaction. But the most important factor that contributes to the significance of social embeddedness is the property of transitivity. As we shall see, cases that involve the coordinated exercise of social connections (from various parties) usually can be traced back to a strong tie of a senior judge who uses his supervisory role to pull strings and seek help from his subordinates.

Chapter 7 analyzes economic embeddedness. Economic embeddedness highlights the unique political economy of judging in China. The development of a more elaborated legal framework for regulating economic activities means that the legal system is much more deeply interlinked with the economy. It also explains why court finance is crucial to the day-to-day autonomy of local courts.

This is a book about the changing Chinese court system. As mentioned, the changing Chinese courts have drawn a plethora of commentaries. The basic facts are not in dispute. There is, however, surprisingly little systematic analysis about the precise character of this transformation and the underlying causes of the transformation. Will Chinese courts become more rule-dependent and professional? What are the prospects for the firm-type structure to spread among the courts? What are the obstacles facing courts that would like to get rid of the work-unit structure? And what are the implications for the rule of law in China if the firm-type does become the dominant mode of organization for Chinese courts? We address those questions in

Chapter 8, the concluding chapter. In the foreground of this study is the problem of whether the Chinese court system will resemble its Western counterpart in adopting a more independent mode of operation. The emergence of firm-type courts seems to suggest such a possibility. We discuss the implications of our findings. Underlying this inquiry is a broader concern toward understanding the judicial system of China in its relation to the nature of the party-state and in relation to the changing social, political and economic relations that underpin the arrangements. To the extent that the courts become more professional and rule-dependent, this is produced by means of the process of economic embeddedness. This, we believe, delimits the extent to which institutional independence, or the rule of law, can be carried out.

2

The Daily Rounds of Frontline Judges

The institutional aegis under which Chinese judges work differs palpably from that of a typical courthouse in the United States. The Chinese courts present themselves as part of a government bureaucracy. A typical courthouse would display an organizational chart conspicuously in the lobby, either in the hi-tech form of a digital display from a flat panel monitor or in the more traditional form of a big board with photos hanging on the wall. The chart details the organizational structure of the court. It showcases the senior judges, or in Chinese political lingo, the "leaders" (领导 *lingdao*) of the court. The court president is naturally placed at the top of the chart, followed by the vice presidents in charge of different aspects of the court. The current law places judges into twelve ranks, including the categories of chief justice (首席大法官 *shoxi dafaguan*) (Tier 1), grand justices (大法官 *dafaguan*) (Tiers 2 and 3), senior judges (高级法官 *gaoji faguan*) (Tiers 4 through 7) and judges (法官 *faguan*) (Tiers 8 through 12). For a typical grassroots court, its president is usually a senior judge and its vice presidents are either *junior* senior judges or *senior* ordinary judges. Under them are an establishment of other *senior* ordinary judges (division heads and deputy division heads) and *junior* ordinary judges.

This meticulous system of rankings epitomizes the tiered, bureaucratic character of a Chinese court. It spells out a clear hierarchical order that defines the chain of command for judges to follow. Together with the other two judicial organs (the procuratorate and the police), they make up the public security front of the people's democratic dictatorship.

Frontline judges in many grassroots courts work in offices that resemble anything but the quiet, solitary antechamber of an Anglo-American common law judge. Older courthouses built in the 1980s or earlier are basic and crowded.[1] They were not designed to deal with today's ever-expanding caseloads, which particularly affect the urban areas. The same can be said about courtrooms. Many courtrooms in these older courthouse buildings are remodeled meeting rooms and offices with an awkward layout. They have undesirable acoustics that make hearing from the back of the room rather difficult. The freeing up of office space for extra courtrooms means that judges are cramped together into even more crowded offices. Judges are asked to share offices with other fellow judges, usually colleagues who work in the same division. These offices resemble more the backstage area of a bureaucratic unit. Judges sit and work next to each other. They do their work in the physical co-presence of their colleagues.

The crowded office space, while out of necessity, is also "in character." Steady physical co-presence means that many judges literally have to "work together." The idea is to inculcate within them a work orientation that is more group-based than individualistic. Unlike American courts, Chinese courtroom buildings, even some of the newly built ones, are not designed on the premise that judges work alone. Some new courthouses built in the past decade or so, especially at the intermediate and high court levels, have encountered the opposite (and rare) problem of rooms that are so big that judges there do tend to work alone.

Spatial arrangements in court buildings are designed to promote collegiality, to allow information sharing through informal and personal channels. In the rare instances that we were invited to visit their offices, we found out that most ordinary judges in grassroots courts do not have their own room. In some better-off areas in the Pearl River Delta, two judges share an office. But the more common setup is that three to four judges sit together in a room. Their desks are closely aligned. Judges sitting in the same room can have a lot of interactions if they choose to. They move freely and frequently into and out of each other's workspace. When they call their litigants in their office, other judges can easily overhear their conversations. This kind of "open office" structure is far removed from the idea of "chambers," in which space is designed and allocated to help judges to work privately, without interruption and interference. "I share a space of about 10 square meters (about 100 square feet) with two other judges and our clerk. It's very crowded and there's not much privacy to speak of," Judge Liu from a city in Yunnan said.

The idea of a division, or 庭 (*ting*) in Chinese, looms large in the ways Chinese judges work together as an organizational unit. When we interviewed and asked Chinese judges to describe their work, they almost invariably began by telling us their division. The division determines the types of cases a judge deals with: "I work in Civil Division Number 1 (民一庭 *minyiting*)" or "I work in Commercial Division (商事庭 *shangshiting*)."

The basic divisions of criminal and civil are standard. Within this basic dichotomy, bigger courts would create further divisions to allow more specialized division of labor (e.g., a commercial case division, an administrative case division) and divisions that are akin to the "problem-solving" courts in the United States (labor courts, juvenile courts). A division is the most basic unit through which division of labor is accomplished and different types of cases are assigned within a court. It is a *group* in a sociological sense, as members of a division share more or less the same institutional interests. For a frontline judge, the division is more than a formal structure for the division of judicial labor. It is embodied by the colleagues sitting next to her, a few feet away, and the daily interactions entailed, not to mention the supervision from her division head. The division provides the work context within which a judge conducts her daily business. A frontline judge, especially one in a big firm-type court, may see her court president and vice presidents as somewhat remote figures. She does not talk to them often, if at all, but she regularly interacts with other divisional colleagues and her division head.

The ecology of the workspace of Chinese judges means that, to use the lingo of management literature, they are highly networked (Goffee and Jones 1998). Judges are acquainted with what other judges are doing, and it is not uncommon for them to consult informally with other judges about the cases they handle. When we asked judges under what occasions did they communicate to one another, some of them looked perplexed: "I talk to judges in my division all the time." Judges do not need to assign a specific time to talk to each other because, other than presiding over trial hearings (in a summary setting), they constantly interact with each other. A young judge who works in the city, Judge Zhang, said, "We eat together in the canteen. I share office with other judges. Judges communicate with each other all the time." Despite the formal setups of collegial panels and divisional meetings, judges in fact rely heavily on *subformal* communications within divisions. One might even say that, precisely because of the high degree of interdependence among frontline judges working in the same division, subformal communications are crucial. The physical co-presence of fellow judges is a mundane but consequential feature of a Chinese judge's lifeworld. Judges said it was common for them to consult their trusted colleagues for advice on difficult cases. Most of the judges we observed have their "buddies" in the workplace. It is no exaggeration to say that they spend more time with their colleagues than with their family members. The situation, however, is quite different when we talk about the relationship between frontline judges and their superiors. Vertical supervision substitutes for horizontal interaction. This is especially the case in work-unit type courts.

THE DIVISION AS A BUREAUCRATIC UNIT

On a day-to-day level, judges engage in a lot of divisional activities that are of a bureaucratic nature. Chinese judges are asked to participate in internal divisional meetings and training seminars as a group. With their divisional colleagues, they also attend meetings with other local government officials, including representatives from the police and the procuratorates, on matters related to local law and order. Judges are sometimes also asked to show up in political campaigns to display support and to attend mandatory study sessions to show ideological loyalty.

Within the court, the old collective infrastructure that sees a judge as a member of a bigger unit is still in place. This is so, despite the growing emphasis on individual responsibility. One aspect where frontline judges are most subject to divisional control is in case assignment. Individual judges have little control about which cases are assigned to them. Case management is done through a highly centralized system that is coordinated by division heads. A case is centrally assigned to a specific judge after it is formally accepted by the case filing division (立案庭 *lianting*). For example, a civil suit may be initiated orally by a potential litigant visiting the reception unit of the division or it may be initiated by a written request to the division. Most urban courts now have designated reception counters or rooms to help litigants initiate cases. From then on, Chinese courts adopt what judicial administrators in the United States would call an "individual" calendar system. This system is distinguished from a master calendar system under which different judges may handle various phases of a case (in the United States, such different phases may include arraignments, motions and trial).

In this individual calendar system, a single judge assumes responsibility for shepherding the case to completion. For courts in less-developed areas, senior judges higher up in the management strata are responsible for deciding individuals' calendars. For example, in a civil division, it is usually the division head (庭長 *tingzhang*) who is responsible for case assignment. In courts in more-developed areas, it is said that the cases are assigned randomly to individual judges, usually by using some computerized system.

Case assignment is a highly sensitive matter among judges. It is a potential source of conflicts between senior judges and their subordinates. Judges we interviewed admitted that they cared a lot about which cases were assigned to them as well as which cases were assigned to their colleagues of the same division. There are cases that every judge wants to land on her lap and there are cases that everyone runs away from. In the past, it was common for senior judges to use their power to assign cases as a means to bestow favors to develop loyalty or to nurture personal ties. Some types of cases are seen as hot potatoes because of the reputation of the litigants involved (judges would use words such as "headstrong," "volatile" and "disrespectful" to describe difficult litigants) or because of the nature of the cases themselves. Conflict-ridden housing demolition cases are tough for any judge to preside over. Other types of cases, such as investor's grievances and product liability, among others, are also known for their inherent political risks and the accompanying heightened media scrutiny.

Some cases, on the other hand, are perceived as great "number boosters." For example, cases involving run-of-the-mill disputes about winter heating and utility bills (in Northeast China) are considered by many judges as easy cases, since chances of an eventual settlement are high. Besides, heating bill cases often come in bunches and they share similar facts. A judge is able to resolve a large number of cases in one go, for each individual or family agreeing to settle would amount to one case in the judicial record book. They are able to, as the Chinese would say, kill many birds with one stone.

Getting easy cases and avoiding hard cases makes a real difference for frontline judges. It is particularly important for "climbers" who want to achieve high performance in aspects such as timeliness and output. Senior judges never openly acknowledge that frontline judges seek easy cases and avoid the hard ones, but they are well aware of the reality. Worries about favoritism and sometimes fissures among colleagues have pushed more courts to adopt a system of random assignment. Some use computers to randomly assign cases. Others assign cases by following an alpha-betical list (in *pinyin*) of judges. Still, frontline judges – at least some of them – seem to remain skeptical. There were judges who said in interviews that they doubted if the computerized assignments were totally random!

Impartial as it may appear, random assignment is not without its problems. Judge Qian, a judge from Inner Mongolia, said cases were randomly assigned to different judges by computers in her court. The judge added, " There are some problems with the automated assignment system since the cases assigned may not match the expertise of individual judges. However, this is fairer than the previous system under which a division head distributed cases based on his judgment. That could raise concern about his subjective preferences."

In a non-random system with a high level of trust, the division head can assign cases based on considerations of judicial expertise, matching skills with case com-plexities and other informed considerations. It also makes sense to let experienced judges take on more difficult cases, as they are more equipped to deal with the problems that are likely to follow. However, mistrust is common between "the management" and the frontline judges (see Chapter 4).

WHAT JUDGES DO

As the preceding section shows, judges often work in a group context. Yet, the system is increasingly putting more emphasis on individual responsibility. So it makes sense to understand a judge's work routine from an egocentric perspective. In what follows, we outline the typical work routine of a frontline judge at the bottom rung of the court hierarchy. We offer an account of what the judge does on a daily basis as a way to give readers a sense of what being a judge in China is like. Of course, on an individual level, there is considerably range and leeway on what matters the most and the least. Some judges spend more time on one item (e.g., adjudication) while others spend more on another (e.g., mediation). But these tasks, taken as a whole, define the character of judicial institutions in China. They show us, from an ethnographic perspective, how grassroots courts in China *practice* law. We can further build from these practices the structuring principles that court leaders use to organize and distinguish various tasks of grassroots courts. We pay attention not only to the broad policies and declared functions of the tasks they perform, but also to the way in which policies and procedures are put into practice.

Two caveats are in order. First, as we have emphasized repeatedly, there are great variations for judges in different parts of China. The daily routine of judges in some remote parts of the country is quite different from that in the economically developed coastal region of the country. For example, one judge who worked in Hunlunbuir in Inner Mongolia commuted by a long trip of shuttle bus to her court every day (before shuttle buses were available, judges rode on horseback). The court was located at a place far away from the city area. She also experienced much bigger seasonal fluctuations of workload than other judges working in, for example, Guangzhou. Her court did not get many cases during the long, severe winter of Inner Mongolia.

The second caveat is that our account is about the work of frontline *trial* judges. The term "judge" is understood more as a rank than a job title in China. Among judges themselves, judges who try cases are known as 业务法官 (*yewu faguan*), as distinguished from other judges who serve in other posts within the court organization.[2] But not all judges in China hear cases. When discussing the duties of a judge, Article 5 of the Judges Law writes loosely: "(1) to take part in a trial as a member of a collegial panel or to try a case alone according to law; and (2) to perform *other functions and duties* as provided by law" (emphasis added). These other functions and duties include research, propaganda, liaison, letters and petitions, logistics and other administrative work required of a court bureaucracy. For most grassroots courts, judges who try cases make up the substantial majority. But this is not the case once one moves up to intermediate and high courts (that percentage might drop to as low as 20 percent). Senior judges in China are administrators. Many do not try cases themselves; in fact, some of them have never tried a single case in their career. As we pointed out in Chapter 1, the primary identity of many judges, particularly the senior ones, is still that of a Chinese bureaucrat – that is, part politician, part manager. Interpersonal skills are important; so is the knowledge about how policies are formulated and carried out. Unlike some common law systems, for example that of the United States, where a team of non-judicial bureaucrats is assigned to assist chief judges to *run* courts as administrators (e.g., the Administrative Office of the United States Courts), the Chinese courts lack a clear distinction between judicial and non-judicial personnel.

The Work Day of a Frontline Judge

What tasks do judges undertake in a typical work day? In this section, we outline the daily round of a frontline judge working in an urban firm-type court. As we will see, trial hearings have obviously become the one task that takes up most of their time. We focus on the work day of a judge in the city because it is easier for us to describe her typical day. Her routine is more stable and the scope of her work relatively more defined. For judges working in rural courts, days are less structured and are more dependent upon the reactions of litigants.

Taking a closer look at their routines allows us to get a sense of judges' institutionalized practices. These work practices are important in the sense that they are *translational*. The daily rounds of frontline judges represent how laws and policies from high above are translated into daily practices carried out by judges. They represent how institutional ideals such as adversarialism, or professionalization, or social harmony, are pursued on the ground.

Judges typically arrive at the court at around 8 AM. That gives them about an hour before the morning hearing session begins. Many do not arrive in the courthouse early in the morning because they know they have to stay late. A judge begins her work day by taking a look at the list of cases she will hear on that day. On a day when the judge is going to hear cases, she will spend the first hour reading case files (案卷 *anjuan*) to refresh her memory. The common weekly routine for a frontline judge is to hear cases three or four days a week, freeing up a day or two to write judgments, prepare for new cases and take on other administrative tasks.[3]

Hearings are usually scheduled in the morning. Sometimes, two cases will be heard in a morning, with each lasting for an hour or even less. Some of the trials we observed were as short as 10 minutes (when, for example, the defendant(s) did not show up), but in most cases, the hearing lasted for an average of one to two hours. Judge Chen, a young deputy division head of a grassroots court located in one of the city districts of Beijing, describes how court hearings become part of her daily round: "I hear cases from 9:00 to 11:00 in the morning. If I have two hearings, each session will be kept to within an hour. If there is only one hearing, the session can go beyond an hour to around 10:30."

Judges only allow a second day of hearing for the most complex cases. The norm is to finish a hearing in a single session. They do not like to defer a hearing to another date. Not much new important information comes out from a hearing. A Chinese trial continues to rely heavily on written and documentary evidence. If a judge senses that parties are amenable to settlement, she will devote most of the trial time to persuading litigants to settle (see below). The morning session ends by around 11 AM. After hearings, judges will return to their office to make some quick notes about what just happened, or sometimes to remind their clerk of a list of things to be followed up.

Lunch break is a time that Chinese take very seriously and the judges we observed are no exception. No one skips lunch or just "grabs a sandwich." Most courts set up their own canteens for staff, providing cheap but quality lunch as a benefit. Some judges bring their own lunch or go out with their colleagues for a break from work. One can tell a lot about the social organization of judges by looking at the people with whom they go out for lunch. Younger judges tend to cluster together during lunchtime for chats, with senior judges more likely to be on their own or out for business lunches.

After lunch, many like to grab a nap before resuming work in the afternoon. If there are more cases to clear, judges hold afternoon hearings. This happens in some busier divisions (e.g., Civil Division No. 1) of firm-type courts. The afternoon trial session begins at 2 PM. Judge Chen continues with her account:

In the afternoon, I hear cases from 2 PM up until about 4:30 PM. We'll definitely end before 5 PM. On average, I hear two to three cases a day. But we tally cases on a monthly basis. I typically handle more than 30 cases in a month. So, it's more than 300 cases each year.

By contrast, judges working in work-unit courts do not handle as many cases. For example, judges in a Shaanxi rural court until recently had been allowed to end their work day after lunch.

For judges working in the cities, it is common to stay late into the evening. After-hours work is so common that judges have come up with standard terms to describe their work week. They describe their working hours as "五加二" (*wu jia er*), literally translated as "five plus two," meaning working both on weekdays and weekends and "白加黑" (*bai jia hei*), literally translated as "white plus black," meaning working during daytime and evening.

Judge Gong, a young criminal judge (26 years old at the time of the interview) from another court in Guangxi, said she could only find the time to write judgments in the evening. "Judging requires a lot of time. In my own court, working overtime is very typical," she said. Judge Tan, who worked in a city court in Guangdong for about 15 years, said her case was "five plus one." She worked six days a week, including Saturday: "Our workload is very high. I work till the evening on Tuesdays and Thursdays and I work on Saturday."

Like the young Judge Gong, Judge Chen, whose Beijing court typifies a firm-type court, regularly worked overtime in the evening to dedicate herself to drafting judgments. Evening is the time of day she can be alone and undisturbed. Most days, Judge Chen stays in her office until 9 o'clock.

COURT HEARINGS

Preparing and conducting court hearings constitute a big part of a frontline judge's work day. Chinese judges either preside over a hearing alone by way of summary procedure or attend as a member of a collegial panel. The term "summary proce-dure" (or "simplified procedure") (简易程序 *jianyi chengxu*) is a misnomer. A trial by "summary procedure" is procedurally no simpler than one that adopts the standard procedure (Liang 2008:147). It just means that the trial is presided over by a single judge rather than a panel. Summary procedure has rapidly gained popular-ity in recent years (see below).

What does a trial look like in China? As a symbolic testimony to the unitary nature of the court system, the basic procedures of a trial are highly standardized. In the courts we visited in both northern and southern China, coastal and inland regions, and in our interviews with judges from different provinces, a trial hearing invariably comprises the following stages: court investigation, court argument, court mediation (in civil trials) and decision announcement.

The presiding judge begins a trial with a short announcement that is both formulaic and formal. She identifies the names of the key parties, including members of a collegial panel, the litigating parties (the procuratorate [criminal], plaintiffs [civil], and defendants), the court clerk (书记员 *shujiyuan*), and if present, lawyers representing both sides. The judge would ask if the litigating parties object to the composition of judges in the collegial panel (or the presiding judge in a summary trial). As a rule, litigants can apply to the court that a certain judge be recused from the hearing because of alleged conflict of interests. But the judge does not always have to step down. It is up to the presiding judge to determine whether the application is granted.

The first substantive stage of a trial hearing is *court investigation*. In a civil trial, the plaintiff presents the complaint to the court. Ideally, the complaint is supposed to be a concise summary of the plaintiff's grievance, though this is often not the case, especially when the person is unrepresented. It is also during this stage that the plaintiff submits evidence to support the allegations in the complaint. Each party is supposed to present material documents to the court and opposing parties in advance of the trial. The plaintiff's complaint is followed by the defense of the defendant. The defendant then submits evidence to support his case. Even though evidence must be submitted prior to the hearing for it to be admitted, it is common, in grassroots courts in particular, for parties to produce fresh evidence at the last minute. Some judges would allow that; but a substantial number of judges we observed refused to admit the evidence in question.

This stage of court investigation is supposed to be "adversarial," i.e., parties are allowed to cross-examine the evidence of opposing parties, especially the testimonies of witnesses testifying for opposing parties. But cross-examination remains little more than a formality in the Chinese trial. In our fieldwork, we did not see any trial that came close to the kind of slow, methodical, layered questioning that aims to expose the inconsistencies of a witness's account in a common law trial (see below).

The next stage is *court argument*. This is the stage when parties are supposed to present their legal argument. In most cases, the law is straightforward, and it is common for parties to repeat their viewpoints to the court at this stage. Despite recent reform, a Chinese civil trial remains very much a judge-led procedure. This is particularly obvious in the investigation and argument stages. During the investigation stage, the judge decides who can speak, what evidence can be questioned, and what questions can be asked. In short, she controls the pace and direction of the investigation. In the course of our fieldwork, we often saw judges interrupt the speeches of litigants and their representatives, including some lawyers. This dominant role makes the judge not just "the third party" (Philips 1990), but probably the most important party in a trial. Based on the trials we observed, it was obvious that questions raised by judges during trials had a direct bearing on their verdicts. This means that the interactions between a judge and litigating parties are more important than those between litigants. The power relations that structure legal conflicts are mainly played out in the interactions between the judge and the litigants.

The significance of the judge-litigant interaction becomes even more apparent in the third stage of *mediation*. It is at this stage that the judge, if she sees a possibility, brokers to strike a settlement deal between the parties. The judge's involvement here can be at once facilitating and controlling (He and Ng 2013a, 2013b; Chen, Xuefei 2007). For many routine, non-commercial civil trials in Civil Division Number 1, mediation takes up the most of a judge's time. This is despite the fact that the success rate of in-trial mediation is in fact quite low (He and Ng 2013b). Judges in many work-unit courts are asked to mediate; and for reasons that we will explain in Chapter 4, many of them prefer mediation over adjudication.

The fourth and final stage is *decision announcement*. A decision is rarely announced on the day of the hearing. It is held off to allow time for a judge to do work on litigants. Even in courts that are most adjudication-happy, judges would still attempt to mediate (civil) or reconcile (criminal) after the hearing and before deciding to rule. In work-unit courts that avoid adjudication, "doing work" with litigants after trial takes up even more of the judges' time.

In the late 1990s and early 2000s, major efforts have been undertaken by the SPC to promote professionalism in court operations. The current four-stage structure was put in place during that period. For judges working in big cities, presiding over trial hearings has become their number-one task. That said, a Chinese trial is not as singular and as important as a common law trial. The function of a trial varies, depending on the nature of the court, the personal style of the presiding judge and the complexity of the case. It is more accurate to view a hearing as an occasion for litigants to meet face-to-face and for the judge to raise questions that arise from the documentary evidence to the litigants and their lawyers. In some cases, the hearing is just for show. The presiding judge already knows how she is going to rule based on the documentary evidence provided, or based on some extralegal or policy considerations (e.g., denying a first-time contested divorce petition). In other cases, the trial signals the beginning of a long mediation process. Within this formal framework that is purportedly adversarial and litigant-centered, judges retain plenty of power and discretion. As we will see later, judges still rely on negotiations with individual parties behind closed doors to get the outcome they want.

In some work-unit courts, just asking litigants to show up at hearings is already a challenge. Some defendants just ignore the notice sent out by the court. Some litigants, though willing, do not have the means to get to the courthouse. Judges have to do a lot of "prep work" such as calling the defendants and their lawyers (if represented) or their relatives to remind them and urge them to attend a scheduled hearing. In some cases, it is just easier for judges from rural dispatched tribunals (派出法庭 *paichu fating*) to travel to villages to conduct a hearing on the spot.

"THREE-MINUTE" CROSS-EXAMINATION

Since the 1990s, the Chinese Supreme Court has been promoting "adversarialism" at all levels of trials (Ng and He 2014). It, however, remains misleading to view Chinese trials in the image of the Anglo-American adversarial trial. What is Chinese-style adversarialism in practice? If cross-examining witnesses in a common law trial is a slow boring of hard boards, to borrow the metaphor from Max Weber (1946), it is a different process in a Chinese trial, more like running a short sprint or ordering from a fast-food joint – the person who serves you appears eager to speak to the next consumer. Some judges, as we observed, would limit the number of questions that lawyers could ask opposing witnesses. We witnessed this a few times in our fieldwork. Below is our account of a scene of a case involving sometimes-contradictory accounts of a fight between the plaintiff and another employee of the defendant (the case was for wrongful dismissal). In a common law court, the witnesses' account would be subject to detailed cross-examination. But that was not the case in a Chinese-style trial:

> In one case, in which one migrant security guard sued his employer for wrongful discharge, the employer presented three witnesses, including the chef who fought with the guard and two other co-workers who worked in the company's cafeteria. Both sides agreed that a fight broke out as a result of a quarrel over the quality of the food served. The issue, however, was whether or not the guard initiated the fighting. The three witnesses, including the assistant chef who was involved in the fight, said that the guard ran into the kitchen and launched the first punch. But there were inconsistencies among the testimonies provided by the witnesses. Some said the assistant was hit in the stomach; others said he was hit in the neck. Throughout the process, the lawyer who represented the dismissed guard said nothing. The judge did most of the questioning. He summoned the witnesses, asked most of the questions, and interrupted witnesses freely. Only in the last minutes of the process did the judge ask the lawyer if he wanted to ask a few questions, no more than three to be precise (He and Ng 2013a:303).

Cross-examination in China is rarely about eliciting oral testimonies. Often when lawyers examine, their questions are directed at the authenticity of the written documents produced by witnesses. Hence, even during oral examination, the focus remains firmly on textual evidence. "Textual evidence is gold" – that seems to be the motto held by Chinese judges. Younger, college-educated judges values documentary evidence over oral evidence by a wide margin. "One occupational hazard of being a judge is that you tend not to believe what people say," Judge Lin, a young judge from urban Guangdong, said. "I have been a judge for too long to be able to trust what litigants say to me," she added.

Most judges view uncorroborated oral evidence as useless. The pressure judges face to complete a hearing in a tight timeframe of one or two hours means that they cannot dedicate a long time to allow for the cross-examination of the *contents* of oral evidence. Instead, the common strategy is for lawyers and sometimes judges to undermine the validity of oral evidence, *per se*. Hence, opposing counsel would customarily undermine a witness's objectivity by accusing that the person was testifying *for* the other party!

There are other institutional reasons for judges' valuation of documentary evidence over oral evidence. Part of it has to do with the reliance on the Chinese-style system of discovery (usually the evidence disclosed is documentary). Another has to do with judges' belief that reliance on documentary evidence provides them the best safeguard, should a case be appealed. Judges are keenly aware of the need to protect themselves against possible appeal or petition. We will return to this point in later chapters.

THE DECLINING ROLE OF COLLEGIAL PANEL

Collegial panel (合议庭 *heyiting*) is the basic adjudicative unit, made up of judges and/or people's assessors.[4] Joint judging in the form of a collegial panel is designed to create, for all the participating judges, a sense of team involvement and a stake in its decision, not to mention the enhanced expertise of a panel of judges. It embodies the principle of collegiality that Weber discussed as a means for sharing responsibility and to limiting authority (Weber 1978:271). It is a key feature of courts that follow the civilian model of bureaucratic court (Guarnieri and Pederzoli 2002).

Yet, there is a clear disconnect between theory and practice. Though the Civil Procedure Law of the People's Republic of China (中华人民共和国民事诉讼法 *Zhonghua renmin gongheguo minshi susongfa*) (promulgated by the Standing Committee of National People's Congress, August 31, 2012) does not specify the number of members of a panel, a three-member setup made up of three judges or two judges and a people's assessor is the predominant norm in the Chinese courts.[5] In a typical Chinese three-judge panel, the most senior judge invariably acts as the presiding judge (审判长 *shenpanzhang*). This presiding judge takes on the *symbolic* role of acting as the leader of the panel. He is responsible for conducting the trial (announcing the beginning and the end of various stages of the trial, asking witnesses to testify (if necessary), and instructing counsel of both sides to present to the bench). But there is a difference between the symbolic leader of the panel (which is determined by seniority) and the actual judge responsible for the case, known as 承办法官 (*chengban faguan*), meaning *responsible judge*. The responsible judge is the one who handles and coordinates all the matters related to the case behind the scene. Most important, she is the person who drafts the judgment, and by doing so, recommends how the case should be ruled. She is also the person who takes the initiative to summarize the facts of the case at the panel conference and, if necessary, the divisional meeting and the meeting of the adjudicative committee. The third person who rounds out the panel would be another frontline judge in an all-judge panel. That person can also be a layperson, known as a people's assessor in China.[6]

In both the rural and urban courts that we observed, judges from the same division often work together in collegial panels, far more than do judges of other divisions. In fact, it is no exaggeration to say that the collegial panel is a system that more or less overlaps with the divisional structure. Judges do this for many reasons. Their colleagues within the same division share similar legal professional expertise with them. There is also the familiarity factor. Judges tend to know colleagues of their division much better than those working in other divisions, including how they behave in the setting of a collegial panel. Above all, having a panel of judges who all come from the same division creates a clear line of authority, as they all work under the same division head.

Though a new collegial panel is empanelled for each case, this tendency for judges to look for colleagues working in the same division severely limits the diversity of the panel composition. In many grassroots courts, a typical division has an establishment of no more than four to five judges. It is natural and in fact inevitable that judges of the same division (particularly those in smaller courts) serve together on a *de facto* recurrent basis. Judges must concern themselves not just with the immediate task of resolving the case at hand, but also with preserving long-term working relationships with other judges in the panel. This explains why Chinese judges are consensus mongers. A judge who is considered difficult to work with will not be invited to return as a panel member in the future. The pressure of comity is too obvious to ignore in this kind of "repeated game" scenario. Chinese courts tend to reward judges who are in harmony with this consensus-dominated culture. A judge who performs well is one who gets along with colleagues in a group setting, one who knows how to compromise to achieve consensus. Such an environment is certainly not conducive to producing maverick legal minds such as a Billings Learned Hand or a Lord Denning.

Many frontline judges, especially those working in firm-type courts, acknowledged that the use of the collegial panel bordered on a posture of formality. Judge Tang, who works in an intermediate court in Jiangsu province, offered the following description:

> For normal cases that are straightforward, I participate by showing up at trial hearings. Because this type of case usually can be determined easily, the judge in charge can basically determine the outcome on his own, or he may choose to report his decision to the presiding judge, and if the presiding judge agrees, then all there is left for him to do is to have a meeting with the panel members again to formalize the decision.

Another frontline judge, Judge Xue from Guizhou, said that in ordinary civil cases, it is usually the responsible judge who states his opinion. Then the other members of the panel express their views before coming to a conclusion. He agreed that it was the view of the responsible judge that mattered most. "I'd say the view of the responsible judge becomes the eventual decision in majority of the cases. He is the one who speaks first. And then other members speak."

Some judges who served on panels confided that they did not actually read the files of cases for which they were not the responsible judge: "I'd show up as an extra body. Obviously, the collegial panel system in my court is not operating as well as it should be," a judge from Guangdong said.

Scholars who study the collegial panel system have also identified the cosmetic nature of the collegial panel (Liang 2008; Li 2002; Cai 2014). Liang (2008), for example, pointed out that it was common to see one judge (the responsible judge) who followed and read the case file, and for the other two judges to have no copies of the case file in hand. Liang asked (2008:168):"Without extra copies, how could the other two judges follow the parties' statements?" We saw something that appeared to be different but pointed toward the same conclusion. It seemed common for a third judge (non-responsible) of the panel not to read the case file until during the hearing. And some even read the case file of a different hearing of which they were the responsible judge!

What is perhaps most surprising is that this tendency for other sitting judges to acquiesce to the opinion of the responsible judge has become stronger as the courts have pushed for a system of evaluation that focuses on individual performance. Why do judges other than the responsible judge not take their role as a member of the collegial panel seriously? The new system of individual responsibility has created a perverse incentive for judges to shirk. Let us use a simple three-judge panel as an example. Let us first consider the typical thinking process of the third judge, i.e., the one who is neither the responsible judge nor the presiding judge. Under the current system, the third judge who serves on the panel is strongly disincentivized to disagree. The responsible judge bears individual responsibility for the collective incorrect decision. But if the third judge dissents, he will have to write a separate opinion. The separate opinion will not be issued to the litigants but is filed for internal records (Gu 2015).[7] To the litigants, a judicial panel will always present a united front. It is natural for this judge to think: "Why speak up when all I need to do is to keep quiet?"

Furthermore, the makeup of the collegial panel resembles a bureaucratic hierarchy. The third judge defers not only to the responsible judge for self-preservation, but also to the presiding judge, who is the most senior judge of the group. It is just natural for the third judge to think along the following line: "If someone is going to disagree, the presiding judge will, or at least should; not me." In other words, the presence of a more senior judge further encourages shirking. Judge Ye, who works in a basic-level court in Beijing, described how she would consult her presiding judge first before saying something at a trial hearing in which she is the third member of a collegial panel:

> I pay close attention to what is said during the hearing. During the hearing, I will also respect the president judge's control of the proceedings and won't easily interrupt . . .

If I have any thoughts, I will write a memo and share it with the president judge. It is after the presiding judge approves and gives me a chance to speak that I will ask a question. To me, this is a matter of coordination.

When asked how she would act if her view disagrees with the presiding judge, the young judge responds diplomatically: "As a young judge, I will state my suggestions but I also respect the views of the presiding judge because he may have considered the case more thoroughly."

What about the presiding judge? As the most senior judge of the panel, it seems natural that she assumes a more proactive role than the third judge. This is, to some extent, the case. However, a presiding judge is often not as well versed about the facts of the case as the responsible judge. As mentioned, her role is more symbolic than substantive. Given the emphasis that the Chinese system places on documentary evidence, the responsible judge is most prepared to formulate an informed view on the case. In practice, despite the supervisory role that the senior judge is asked to play, she is also reluctant to contradict the opinion formed by the responsible judge, unless some grave mistakes are made or political risks are at stake. We will explain this reticence of senior judges in Chapter 4. The role of the senior judge is more to push the responsible judge to mediate in difficult cases.

"OCCASIONAL" INVESTIGATION

Sometimes, a judge will spend her non-hearing days to conduct on-site investigation. On-site investigation used to be a primary activity for frontline judges (He 2009a; Huang 2009) when the inquisitorial mode of trial still dominated. But with the turn toward adversarial-style procedures in the 1990s, judge-led investigation nowadays assumes at most a complementary role.[8] Judges, especially those working in large cities, do not and cannot afford to investigate on their own. As Huang (2010:129) and others have pointed out, the old practice of on-site investigation is too labor intensive to be practicable today.

On-site investigation now plays a complementary role in the judicial process. Most judges we interviewed said they spent no more than one day a week to gather evidence. Strictly speaking, the term "judge-initiated investigation" mischaracterizes the efforts undertaken by today judges. When a judge takes steps to collect evidence, she usually does so *at the request of litigants*. There are certain types of documents that are difficult to obtain by private parties in China – documents produced and kept by a government department (e.g., police reports or registration records) or materials that are related to personal privacy or commercial secrets (e.g., bank account statements or medical records).[9] A judge intervenes when litigants have difficulties collecting the required evidence. Seldom do judges collect new evidence without a request from a litigating party. In the quote below, Judge Chen of

Beijing explained how she had to "initiate" investigation sometimes, but her "self-initiated" investigation was, in essence, reactive:

> You know, now our policy is to encourage people to produce their own evidence; but we have a lot of litigants who would come to ask us to produce evidence. They say they cannot investigate the case themselves. And the fact is there are government departments and banks, they won't respond to the requests sent by lawyers. So sometimes we have to investigate ourselves, because if the facts of a case are not clear, it is just impossible for us to rule.

Judge Chen made clear that she would only "investigate" if litigants could not secure certain evidence themselves:[10]

> Even when a litigant asks, I won't immediately investigate. I will always ask the litigant to investigate himself first. Some litigants have this habit – they think the judge should find the facts for them. They want to leave investigation to the judge, but that's not the way we operate now.

CLERICAL SUPPORT

The reluctance of frontline judges to take up investigation is in part due to a lack of clerical support. For most frontline judges, when they initiate an investigation, it means more work to do without any backup research support. In bigger firm-type courts in major cities, a judge may be able to share a clerk with another judge or two. In traditional work-unit courts, judges basically have to do everything for themselves. Besides do-it-yourself investigation, minimal clerical support also means that judges have to take care of pre-trial preparation on their own.

In some courts in the most developed cities, a judge might be able to get help from her clerk in compiling court transcripts, contacting litigants, and scheduling hearing dates. Judge Chen described her work in the pre-trial stage:

> Some cases on the court docket will be sent to me. I will then take a look at the case files to get a grip of the key facts. The next step is then to contact the litigating parties. This is done by the court clerk. My clerk usually contacts the defendant by phone to ask them to pick up the pleading of the plaintiff. And then she will communicate with the defendant to fix a date for the first meeting. The clerk will also contact the plaintiff to come to the meeting. If the case is simple, the first meeting can turn into the formal hearing. But if a case is more complex, the first meeting is for the two sides to exchange evidence. We'll set another date for the formal hearing.

The help that Judge Chen gets from her clerk is envied by judges working in work-unit-type courts. They do everything on their own. Judge Deng, whose dispatched tribunal served a suburban neighborhood of Tianjin (where about a third of the population are farmers), said she made the calls herself:

We share just one court clerk among several judges. And since I'm the most junior of judges, I do everything myself. I contact litigants (before trial) and set up hearing dates. I deal with their inquiries. I prepare court transcripts myself and I of course take care of things such as collecting and examining evidence and conducting investigation.

While a constant subject of complaint from frontline judges, the pre-trial phase in China is not overtly complex and time-consuming. This is the main reason the system does not grind to a halt. The work that a judge has to do before a trial is largely administrative – for example, scheduling exchanges of evidence between parties. The use of interrogatories is virtually absent, even though the Civil Procedure Law in theory allows it (Article 61). Chinese courts use a system of evidence exchange that incorporates elements of disclosure from the American discovery process. In practice, because many litigants are still unrepresented, judges play a leading role in directing parties to exchange evidence that is in either party's possession. Overall, the discovery process is straightforward. A simple labor dispute does not require two sides to present stack of documents. In most trials, parties focus their discussions on a disputed contract or salary slip. As mentioned, the pre-trial stage nowadays is also made simpler by the rarity of judge-led investigations. Judges have taken a more passive role in collecting evidence today.

The idea of a professional "para-judicial" staff is still at a nascent stage in China. In the United States, judges depend on their so-called "elbow" clerk for legal research, to help write opinions and do other clerical work. Many courts also have a sizable team of staff who answer to the chief judge and to the court. But this is absent in China. Judges often lament this. They also see it as a sign of a lack of professional prestige. They attribute their lack of productivity (in terms of the number of cases processed per capita) to the lack of support. Judge Liu, who has practiced for five years in a city court in Yunnan, said:

> You look at us. There are more judges in China. By comparison, there are fewer judges in the US. Why do we handle fewer cases in total? . . . We're talking about two totally different systems. I visited the courts in the US. Their judges have a cast of supporting staff. We don't have that. We're on our own. My clerk doesn't have the time to help me out. If she can help you to file the judgment you delivered, that's already very good. In our case, three judges share one clerk. It is impossible for my clerk to offer me any help. We do everything ourselves.

Budgetary constraints limit the quantity and quality of clerical support judges can get. The lack of clerical support not only makes on-site investigation a costly venture that judges avoid; it also makes in-depth legal research impossible. Many basic-level courts struggle to make ends meet; clerical and research support are considered nonessential.

But financial constraints are just part of the reason. The ideal of socialist popular justice has little tolerance for professional judges who are bookish and pedantic. This is especially the case in work-unit courts. A scholarly judge was for a long time considered too detached from the "mass line." The image did not fit well with the party-state's promotion of judges as "people's judges." Even today, official publications continue to carry profiles of judges who serve the people.

Furthermore, frontline judges are not expected to conduct legal research individually. They work in an institutional environment that emphasizes teamwork and "groupness." Colleagues are supposed to help each other out. As such, legal knowledge is not formalized and systematized in ways that are easily searchable and therefore researchable. Younger judges complained that there was a lack of quality Chinese judgment databases comparable to *Lexis* or *Westlaw* in the United States. Despite the fact that the Internet has now made available some judgments produced by courts in other parts of China, the available corpus of judgments is far from systematic.[11] It is not clear why judgments from some courts are made available while others are not. It is equally unclear why some judgments from the same court are made available while other judgments are not. But judges, particularly the younger ones, are eager to conduct more thorough legal research, even if that means more work for them.

Whether the development of online Chinese judgments and other resources is likely to have significant impacts on the legal development of China remains to be seen. Yet the current situation remains that specific assets, or "personalized" advice from colleagues of the same court, are still far more valued than any judgments a judge could obtain on the internet. Legal databases in China are still developing. Their bare-bones structure limits their usefulness to judges. Judges pointed out that online cases records are difficult to navigate and it is difficult to determine, in the absence of a proper reporting system (the inclusion of headnotes, keywords, and other references), which cases are useful and relevant and which cases are not.

By contrast, personal advice from more experienced colleagues are considered to be more tailored, well-tested and trustworthy. There are a lot of provincial, even county-level variations in the interpretation of law (e.g., labor law) that the central government does not, and indeed cannot, standardize. A more experienced colleague from the same division could say, "Follow this decision. This is how we do things here. It works." The reality remains that, at the level of individual courts, many past judgments are not catalogued in an easily retrievable manner. Inexperienced judges with fewer years of service have to turn to more experienced judges for this type of "privileged" information. Sometimes, older judges would use this "privileged" information to cultivate instrumental ties or to improve their bargaining position. Hence, these decisions have become a form of asset specificity – that is, information that is locally valued.

MEDIATION

Besides court hearings, mediation is the other activity on which frontline judges spend the most time. Chinese judges play a major role in mediation, whether the mediation is in-trial or off-trial. On a day when no hearings are scheduled, the judge continues to work on her remaining open cases. Post-trial liaisons with litigants consume long hours. The end of the trial hearing in China does not confer the sense of finality that it does with a court in the common law system. As mentioned, decision is seldom immediately delivered. The judicial process is, hence, structurally open-ended. Mediation continues after a hearing. On paper, judges are only required to mediate during trial hearings. If litigants fail to reach a resolution, the presiding judge then moves on to adjudicate. But it is rare for in-trial mediation to yield an immediate settlement (Ng and He 2014). As a result, judges buy time by reserving judgment until a later date and then continue to mediate beyond the termination of a hearing.

Judges have limited control of the mediation process; much of what they can do depends on the responses of litigants. On more than one occasion during our interviews with judges, they paused and stepped out of their office to take phone calls from litigants and their lawyers from cases where hearings had already been held. Judge Hu, a young judge working in an urban court in Guangdong, said after stepping out for a phone call during our interview, "I know it's not a good idea to give my cell phone number to lawyers and litigants. But sometimes I just have to. I need to make sure they can find me when two sides are close to reaching a settlement."

Little empirical work has been done to identify the intensity of judge-litigant contacts after trial hearings. A reason for the lack of scholarly treatment on the subject is that it is so difficult for researchers to study. It is an activity that takes place without stage lights, usually in judges' offices or just over the phone. Judges were coy about the time they invested in it when we asked. At interviews, even though judges did not use the word "mediation," some said they spent a lot of time "meeting with litigants" after hearings. Based on what we observed, judges in rural work-unit courts generally spend much more time on post-trial mediation than on trial hearings: "In some cases, I met with the litigants many, many times to persuade them to mediate," said Judge Deng, who worked in a rural dispatched tribunal under a grassroots court in Tianjin.

Without the high costs of adjudication serving as a stick, litigants who go to court are not keen to settle. They settle upon the urging of judges. Successful mediation requires heavy investments of judicial time and energy. In truth, judges play more of an active role than does a mediator in facilitating private settlements (see Ng and He 2014 for a detailed discussion). "Persuade" (說服 *shuofu*), "explain" (解释 *jieshi*), "discuss" (讨论 *taolun*) are the words that judges chose to describe what they do in mediation. We would add that sometimes mediation is a form of soft coercion to litigants, as judges would tell the litigants how they would rule if the latter did not settle. Judges are expected to push for mediation. The extent to which judges are subject to the pressure to secure settlement varies across firm courts and work-unit courts. Some judges working in the big cities do not spend too much time trying to mediate. They take a rather nonchalant attitude toward mediation. They told us mediation was "not a big thing" for their courts. Judge Su from Guangxi, for example, works in a city court that put less emphasis on mediation, and she herself adopts a rather hands-off approach toward mediation. She said that she tended not to initiate meetings with litigants after trial hearings, and that when she did, she organized meetings at the urging of the litigants: "I only mediate when litigants show an interest to settle. Even in those cases, I meet with litigants once or at most twice. I tend not to interfere. Instead, I'll just ask them to negotiate among themselves."

The reality is that firm-type courts have come up with ways to boost their judges' mediation rates that do not require frontline judges to mediate themselves. We will turn to the coping strategies of the firm-type courts in Chapter 3 and 7. Even among judges working in firm-type courts, Judge Su's nonchalant attitude toward mediation is an outlier.[12] For most judges, mediation is preferred over adjudication when problem litigants are involved. If the parties fail to settle after repeated attempts, the judge is left with two choices, and neither is an attractive option from the perspective of the presiding judge. The first option is to stall. Obviously, stalling comes with costs. It means the judge is unable to close the case by the deadline stipulated by the central government. That aside, stalling is sometimes difficult when a litigant is pressuring for an outcome. The second option is to give a ruling. In a vacuum, it seems ironic that a judge would dread judging. But the logic in the irony is plainly visible once we take a closer look at the difficult institutional environment of judging for some work-unit courts, so much so that delivering a judgment is taken as a much-avoided last resort (see Chapter 5).

One noticeable difference between firms and work-units is the extent to which their judges are willing to push for mediation. It is widely known that certain rural work-unit-type courts impose hard targets on judges to boost mediation rates (Liebman 2007). Some judges also acknowledged in interviews that they were under great pressure to mediate, to meet a certain threshold or quota. It is a real burden for frontline judges when they are expected to mediate more than half of their cases. It changes the nature of their job from a judicial official to that of a liaison officer, a counselor, a social worker, a go-between, and of course, a grassroots bureaucrat. Certainly, this is what the party-state expects of their grassroots judges – to know the pulse of the society and to be able to resolve disputes for the people. The problem is that it goes against the self-imagery of judges, especially the younger ones, who are increasingly self-conscious of their professional identity and expertise. We will return to this problem in Chapter 3.

Disposing of cases assigned to them, whether it is by means of adjudication or mediation, is the most crucial duty of frontline judges. Basic-level courts in China derive a large part of their caseloads from civil cases with relatively modest monetary claims – minor contractual disputes, debt actions, divorce petitions, labor disputes, enforcement of judgments and arbitral awards making up the major categories.[13] These are the cases that frontline judges deal with the most. Judges said the laws they apply are not complicated. In fact, cases can look very repetitive from a legal vantage point.

"You feel a sense of knowledge fatigue after a while, because you rule on the same types of cases every day. You don't feel that you replenish your legal knowledge by doing what you do as a judge," Judge Deng, the young judge from Tianjin said.

Official statistics suggest that caseloads are on the rise across the country. Nationwide statistics show a gradual but steady increase of the total cases disposed of by the three levels of courts below the SPC. For example, in 2010, all the lower courts combined handled a total of 10.99 million cases. In 2014, that number increased to 13.79 million cases, an increase of about 25 percent in total caseloads over a period of four years.[14] Though more refined statistics are lacking, judges interviewed are of a consensus that courts in coastal urban areas have been experiencing a sharper spike in caseloads than their rural, inland counterparts. This has led to the emergence of firm-type courts. For a frontline judge working in the civil division of the courts in coastal China (Guangdong, Jiangsu, Shanghai, Zhejiang), hearing more than 300 cases a year is a common feat, which means an average of at least a case per working day, a very heavy load by any standard. For some courts in the Pearl River Delta of Guangdong, the number may go even higher, to about 400 to 500 cases per year, depending on the type of cases a judge deals with. A court in Shenzhen is reported to have an average caseload of 411 cases per judge (Zhang, Zhiquan 2014). A judge from Dongguan is reported to have once disposed of 1,600 cases in a year, which translated to an average of six hearings a day (Lin 2014). It is important to point out that even in the busiest courts of China, not all judges, in fact not the majority of judges, are asked to handle that volume of cases. For reasons we will explain in Chapter 7, some of these numbers are the result of a new, cost-conscious mode of operation in firm-type courts.

Growing caseloads are the key structural reason prompting the "youth movement" in frontline judges, especially among the "firms" in big cities. It is also among the reasons that contribute to attrition among judges. In the course of our fieldwork, we did not see many trial judges over the age of forty.[15] There are judges of this age bracket of course, particularly in rural courts, but many of them have "retired" from the frontline and moved to other departments within the court bureaucracy, such as letters and petition, research, logistics and propaganda. Judges who work in the trenches, so to speak, are young, many of them belonging to the so-called post-'80 generation, i.e., those who were born after 1980 and are now in their late twenties and early thirties. Only younger judges can deal with the unremitting daily grind of long hours and quick work required of a frontline judge. For older judges with family, the hurly-burly of firm-type courts is sometimes hard to bear. "The rhythm of work is fast. My schedule is packed every day," said Judge Tang, who was in her early thirties and worked in a court located in a mid-sized city in Jiangsu. "I worked overtime a lot before the birth of my child. I cut down on overtime because I wanted to spend more time with my family. But my court is now taking on more cases. Our leaders encourage judges to work overtime on weekends. I have to go back to working overtime."

ADJUDICATION AND JUDGMENT WRITING

Though it does not take up as much time as court hearings and mediation, judgment writing is the most solitary of a judge's routine work. Judges describe it as an activity that requires single-mindedness and concentration, an activity that requires, a judge to "settle down" (沉下心來 *chen xia xin lai*) and be alone to do it. Yet, the fast pace of the daily round makes it difficult for a judge to find quiet time. For a lot of judges working in the cities, judgment writing is done in the evening. When asked how long it takes to write a judgment, Judge Chen of Beijing commented, "It depends. Sometimes it takes a week or a few days for a complicated case that requires a longer judgment of more than ten pages (in Chinese). For a simple case, I can finish the judgment in an evening. A simple case is simple because it is similar to other cases."

"In fact, I should say this," Judge Chen continued. "Actual writing is not the most crucial component for the time I spent on judgments. The most crucial component is the time I took to think through the case. Formulating ideas is more important. When I write, I already know what I'm going to say. I already know the focus of the case and the relevant legal rules. But the time it takes prior to the actual writing, the time it takes to sort out the relevant facts and laws is longer."

Other judges acknowledged that they did not spend as much time as they would want writing and rewriting decisions. Many judgments produced by grassroots courts adopt boilerplate templates with minimal changes for specific factual details. This is particularly so when litigants agree to settle and the judgment merely serves as an official record of the settlement reached. The decision spells out the outcome of the settlement. If one party fails to deliver his end of the deal, the other party can refer to the judgment as an official record to hold the party accountable. There is no point for a judge to dive into the details or rule on controversial matters because a settlement apparently takes care of that.

Judgments that come out of grassroots courts, with or without a settlement, are generally terse. In conversations, Chinese judges are typically very articulate and outspoken. But they clearly do not carry their eloquence over to their written judgments. Chinese decisions are stylistically laconic. For a typical civil case from a grassroots court, the judgment is just a couple of pages long. The majority of decisions contain a simple summary of facts and a quick mention of the laws that are applied.[16] But the precise relationship between the two and how the law is applied to the case is not discussed at length. Legal analyses rarely appear in these judgments. Neither do judges respond directly to lawyers' submissions in judgments. Dissenting opinions, if any, are not made public (Gu 2015). Of course, lengthy legal analyses seldom appear in the judgments of any first-instance courts in the United States or other countries, either. But more seems to have been omitted in Chinese judgments. There is usually minimal exegesis of legal doctrines and principles. One does not get a clear view of the reasoning process one would expect to see from a professional judge. Seldom does a judgment, for example, discuss disputed evidence and whether the judge is relying upon it, a point that is in fact highlighted by the SPC in its latest Fifth Year Reform Plan (Supreme People's Court 2015a).

The pressure of heavy caseloads certainly renders long, detailed judgments impractical. But the brevity of most decisions is also in part intentional. In highly contested cases, judges write in anticipation of pending appeals. They are cautious with the way they characterize the litigants and their acts. A judge is particularly cautious with her account of "what happened," as this can become a focus of attention for the appellate court hearing. As pointed out in the previous chapter, an appellate court in China adopts what legal scholars would describe as a "low standard of review" when examining a lower-court decision. Factual findings are generally reexamined.

POST-JUDGMENT WORK

The job of a judge does not end with the handing down of a judgment. Besides the formal channel of launching an appeal, litigants sometimes choose to express their grievances through letters and petitions. In fact, litigants, through letters and visits or the system of *xinfang*, may petition to the court to further review cases that have already been tried twice by courts (a first-instance trial and an appeal).[17] This open-endedness can be traced back to the idea of socialist popular justice from the Soviet system, upon which the Chinese system was built. Placing procedural integrity above substantive justice was considered a gesture of bourgeoisie formalism. The Chinese judicial process is, by design, structurally porous. The reality is that the Chinese party-state has as a policy encouraged this multiple-channel system to make sure there are enough safety valves in place to dissipate social grievances. Hence, as Nathan (2003) points out, the central party-state has encouraged, or at least condoned, a Chinese-style check-and-balance system, encouraging a range of official actors, including courts, the media, letters and visits bureaus, the procuratorates, and people's congresses, among others, to counteract each other.

For many judges today, litigants who "believe in letters and visits but do not believe in the law"(信访不信法 *xinfang bu xinfa*) are a source of their trepidation. Under the so-called "responsibility system," a judge is asked to handle complaints from unhappy litigants who lose a case or for whatever reasons are dissatisfied with the outcome of a case in which the judge ruled. As Liebman (2007:629) points out, judges are under pressure from their own courts and party superiors to resolve litigants' grievances.

Judge Zhang, a young post-'80 judge working in one of the busiest courts in Guangdong, said:

> As a judge, you're responsible for the outcome of the cases you handled. What is that responsibility? Well, it doesn't mean that if you follow the law, then the litigant will

agree with you and say nothing. Some litigants still have a lot of things to say. They say you're wrong. And when you run into a difficult litigant, you can't say "I can't deal with this litigant." It's your case and it's your responsibility to find a way to resolve it.

Judge Sun, a division head of a court located in a small city in Jilin, said that for judges working in his court, meeting with "lowly educated" (文化水平低 *wenhua shuiping de*) litigants was an important part of the job. These litigants had to be persuaded to accept an unfavorable court decision or to be dissuaded from appealing or petitioning to higher authority. Judge Sun said:

> A judge is expected to explain to litigants how legal regulations are applied to their cases. He is also expected to communicate to litigants about what the court finds to be the basic facts of the cases. Finally, it is his job to conduct mediation or reconciliation work. In recent years, I have to say that this type of communication has consumed most of judges' energies. Indeed, outside of the time allocated for hearings, much of my time is spent on interacting with unhappy litigants.

It remains a judge's job to explain and pacify litigants who are not happy with the court's decisions. However, liaison work of this kind is now conducted under an atmosphere that is palpably more tense. In recent years, there have been reports of judges verbally threatened or physically assaulted by disgruntled litigants in China. There have also been reports of judges killed by disgruntled litigants (see Arce 2010). Judge Tan, who has been working as a judge for twenty years in a city in Guangdong, lamented, "We didn't have metal detector and x-ray inspection and all that stuff at the front gate in the past. Now we have to do it. Judges are not very safe now. Some litigants resort to violence."

Some litigants nowadays block the court's entrance, or they mobilize other people to protest. In those cases, the judge in charge is asked to meet with the litigants. Judges have to learn how to do their job amid conflicts. Another veteran judge, Judge Fang, who has worked for twenty-six years as a judge in Shandong, said:

> Litigants nowadays are different from those in the past. Chinese judges face a great deal of stress because, besides adjudicating cases, there are other tasks for them to do, such as mediation, "doing work" to litigants, etc. All of these tasks are quite difficult. Furthermore, the pressure on judges doesn't just come from the cases they handled. Pressure comes from other sources as well. Judges have to deal with many petitions. Judges are asked to assume greater social responsibilities, to resolve social conflicts, to make sure that the same litigants don't come to the court every day . . .

INEFFICIENT JUDGES?

Chinese trial hearings are typically short, half-day events. Surprisingly, the number of cases processed by judges, per capita, is low. On average, Chinese judges handle fewer cases than judges in all Western countries. It is a fact that many Chinese judges are sorely aware of, as they are constantly asked to "speed up." The low efficiency of Chinese judges has also been identified and discussed by Chinese scholars. Professor Zhu Jingwen of Renmin University of China suggested that Chinese judges handled far fewer cases than their Western counterparts (Zhu 2010). By his calculation, Chinese judges handled an average of 22.3 cases per year (2001 figures). In comparison, US judges handled an average of 965 cases per year! German judges, the least efficient judges among Western developed countries, still managed to process a total of 140 cases (2010:196).

The reasons for the low number of cases handled by Chinese judges are mainly two-fold. First, as mentioned, not all bureaucrats with a "judge" title hear cases. Many of them are administrators or research and support staff in courts. This is a phenomenon that the central government sought to address in its latest reforms (Supreme People's Court 2016b). To date, judges in administrative and research units of different courts are still included in the calculation of per-capita average. The average number would have been higher if only sitting judges were included for the calculation.

Second, in countries such as the United States, a full-scale trial is so prohibitively expensive that it has become a rarity (Galanter 2004). Courts have carved out special divisions, such as small claims courts and eviction courts, to resolve cases by adopting abbreviated and informal procedures. More important, the US system imposes a combination of cost barriers (out-of-pocket expenditures and high fees, as well as queues and risk) to induce parties to abandon claims during the pretrial or trial stage. Yet, when tallying up total caseloads, cases withdrawn or settled during the two stages are counted as cases resolved. So just about 3 percent of all the cases filed in the US federal district courts ended with a completed hearing (Administrative Office of the United States Courts 2013). An average Chinese judge in a basic-level court presides over 200 to 300 cases per year, an impressive figure if we compare it to the number of trials a US District Court judge actually presides over.

For many reasons, not least because the courts also function as a stability maintenance apparatus, the Chinese judicial system is not set up to divert cases from the trial process. As a means for social control, it needs to take in *more* cases.[18] Hence, most cases that come to Chinese courts are "heard" by a judge.

Furthermore, Chinese courts view the trial hearing in a different light. As we have seen, it is not a be-all-and-end-all event. It is a stage in the judicial process, an occasion for judges to talk to litigants and persuade them to accept settlement if possible. It lacks the procedural complexity and the sense of finality that a common law trial commands.[19] This difference of institutional purposes is crucial for understanding the meaning of "adversarialism" in the Chinese context. Adversarialism does not mean examinations and cross-examinations of evidence that last for weeks and even months. It denotes a shift from judge-led investigations to litigant-led presentations of evidence.

Once a case is filed and accepted by a Chinese court, it will in all likelihood get to the hearing stage. Ironically, just because most cases in the United States are disposed of before they reach the trial stage, Chinese judges, by comparison, handle *fewer* cases as a result.

PERFORMANCE EVALUATIONS

The quality of judicial performance is difficult to assess. As with all bureaucracies, the Chinese courts do not face their competitors in an output market where they sell what they produce for a price. Performance quality is hence an elusive term and scholars find it difficult to agree on the criteria for assessment. In the United States, quality is often equated with "customer satisfaction." It is common to assess a judge's competence by asking people who deal with judges or are able to observe judges at work – attorneys, jurors, witnesses, court staff, and litigants (Andersen 2001; Brody 2008). In China, this form of user evaluation has not been adopted. Performance evaluation is internal. In other words, judges are evaluated by their superiors, and to a lesser extent by their peers. Much like other government bureaus, courts have adopted myriad assessment standards to evaluate the performance of individual judges (Edin 2003; Kinkel and Hurst 2015; also see Chapter 4). Common targets include the number of cases to be handled each year, successful case closure ratios, and mediation rates (Minzner 2011a, 2011b; Kinkel and Hurst 2015; Cai 2013). But within this broad and encompassing evaluation system, courts differ on the one or two criteria identified as most relevant to fulfilling their own organizational goals. Specific court-wide performance goals are commonly installed in grassroots courts. Courts with ambitious presidents are most eager to get ahead in the so-called "league charts," i.e., charts that rank courts from top to bottom according to specific indicators. It is here that firms and work-units differ on the criteria that they most value. Firm-type courts, for example, put strong emphasis on efficiency, as measured by the number of cases closed per capita. As mentioned in Chapter 1, firms value output. Reduction of delays is a primary goal of court management for this type of court.[20] "The first thing I do when I get into my office is to turn on my computer and check out the cases waiting for me on that day," Judge Tan, who has been working as a judge for twenty years in a major city in Guangdong, said. "Just looking at the case list on my computer sometimes gives me a headache. When the title of a case blinks yellow, it means its deadline is approaching. When it blinks red, it means I failed to close the case before the deadline set out by my court," Judge Tan explained.

Judge Gong, the young judge whom we quoted earlier, said that she "felt bad" about her small caseload in her first year working as a judge in an urban court in Guangxi. She evaluated her first-year performance harshly: "I wasn't efficient. I was inexperienced. My caseload is smaller than other judges. Judges in my grassroots court typically handle 200 to 300 cases a year," she said. In comparison, she disposed of about 90 cases during a period of nine months.

Judges are expected to dispose of the cases that are assigned to them within a certain time period. They are not given much latitude in the choice of case-processing practices and are not free to determine when certain procedural stages have to be completed for a case. Sitting on unfinished cases without reason is strongly sanctioned. The length of a deadline varies by type of case. For ordinary civil cases, that period in most courts nowadays is 90 days. This 90-day limit is a local, court-imposed deadline. The statutory limit specified in the Civil Procedure Law is twice as long, a period of six months.[21] Senior judges who manage their courts want to leave themselves with room to maneuver. The same is true for summary procedure cases: the statutory limit is three months,[22] but in some courts, judges are asked to conclude the litigation process within 20 days.

Division heads know how many and what cases belong to each judge. They make data such as a judge's caseload and comparative data on judges' performance known to all judges within the same division. In many courts, judges receive monthly printouts of cases newly assigned, in process, and resolved. This means that judges can learn of not just their own performance, but that of their colleagues – which of their colleagues dispose of the most cases, and which dispose of the least (Kinkel and Hurst 2015). This is again by design. Peer pressure is built in to push judges to work harder.

Deadlines put pressure on judges to keep the chains moving, to increase output. They fear to be viewed as someone who goldbricks. There is a sense that frontline judges work as the proverbial cog in a bureaucratic machine. It is under this institutional environment that many judges, particularly those working in big cities, feel that they are constantly treading water.

Work-unit courts, on the other hand, put their energy on raising mediation rates. They play a different game. They cannot compete with the firms in caseloads. Instead, work-unit courts emphasize "quality" indicators, or as we said earlier, outcome. High mediation rates are key to achieving other quality numbers. A court with a high mediation rate usually carries low rates of appeal and reversal, since litigants usually will not appeal when they have agreed to settle. Many work-unit courts boost a mediation rate of well above 50 percent. In his study of a basic-level court located in an underdeveloped county of Yunnan, Xiong (2014b) observed that the overall mediation rate of the court was 86.1 percent. To raise the rate of mediation, many courts imposed a quota for the judges and rewarded those who were able to achieve a higher rate of mediation among their cases (Minzner 2011b).

What is common across the two types of courts is that a system of inducements and sanctions is installed to align the pursuit of individual self-interest with the organizational goals. The mode of accountability is unmistakably individual-based, though peer group pressure is sometimes used to "shame" those who lag behind or simply fail to perform. The force of the evaluation system comes from the fact that career advancement depends on judges' demonstrated abilities in checking the boxes. The pressure is most palpable for younger judges who are at the beginning stage of their judicial career. Judges who consistently fall short of deadlines will be subject to

judicial discipline – that is, the court administration to which the judge belongs
would issue a 批评 *piping* (criticism). "The mark of a criticism will certainly affect
career development," Judge Gong commented.

One of the unintentional consequences of the reliance on performance measure-
ment in court management is that the court has become more of an individualistic
institution. Judges have become accustomed to thinking about their own cases and
their own cases only. Judges do not see themselves as working together for the greater
good of the court. *Esprit de corps* is low among judges, as reflected by the growing
number of frontline judges exiting from the judiciary (Chin 2014; Finder 2016).

3

Cohorts of Judges

Structurally, work-unit courts and firm-type courts differ in their modes of govern-ance and operation. But similar divisions and fault lines can also be found when one looks into judges' self-understanding of their role. Judges from different social demographics seem to understand their role differently. This is the question that we turn to in this chapter.

Throughout this book, we have emphasized how Chinese courts vary by locality and region. Yet the recruitment policy for judges is the one area where the central government has been able to impose a uniform policy (with some regional differ-ences). While local party-state has tremendous influences on the appointments of senior officials from division heads to vice presidents and the president, the central government has more to say on what kind of people can be recruited to become judges. Let us cast our minds back over the changes in the Chinese legal system in the last quarter century. The first comprehensive Judges Law, a gesture both sub-stantive and symbolic in contributing to the identity of judges as a distinct breed of bureaucrats, was passed in 1995.[1] Prior to that, there were no requirements for becoming a judge; theoretically, anyone could be appointed to the position. In practice, many appointees who joined during and before the late 1980s received no formal legal training. Majority of them were military officers discharged by the CPC Central Military Committee and sent to work as judges (Wang and Madson 2013:81; Liang 2008). Not only were judges army retirees back then; they also dressed like military officials. Judges then wore a military style uniform, olive green in color, characterized by epaulets, cap and a standing-collar design that made them hardly distinguishable from military officers in appearance.[2] Being a judge, symbolically and substantively, was no different from being a government bureaucrat working in other bureaus in the so-called public security cluster (Lieberthal 1992). The biggest problem facing the Chinese judiciary back then was the overall poor quality of frontline judges. The Chinese party-state's solution to the problem was to embark on a determined path of credentialism and professionalism.

It is hard to exaggerate the changes undergone in the educational level of Chinese judges. Newly recruited judges today are college-educated. Just as recent as 1995, the proportion of judges with a college degree was merely 6.9 percent. Since 2005, over half of the Chinese judges have university degrees (Liebman 2007:625; see also Chapter 4).[3] By most assessments, one of the most significant and lasting achievements of the tenure of SPC president Xiao Yang was the reform to improve the educational qualifications of judges (Peerenboom 2010). During the years when Xiao Yang presided over the SPC, there was a series of promotions to put officials with formal legal training in position to preside over People's Courts at the provincial level (Zhang 2011:256).

The compressed, rapid change to the social demographics of judges has left an indelible mark on the Chinese courts. It makes the idea of generation or cohort (代 *dai*) a very salient category among judges themselves. By judges' own classification, the Chinese judiciary today is made up of three generations of judges – the veteran, the middle-aged, and the post-1980. The categories are no mere crude classification of judicial demography. They refer to the different social and educational upbringings, the habitus, so to speak, of the three generations. In this chapter, we first offer a quick overview of the social milieu that gave rise to the three generations. We then turn our attention to the youngest, the post-1980, who now make up the bulk of the frontline judges in China.

Through interviews and fieldwork, we observed young judges at close proximity. We get a sense of how young judges evaluate themselves and how they are evaluated by their older colleagues. We focus on their sense of bureaucratic ethic – how do they view themselves? What do they see as the key values that guide them through the dilemmas they encounter in their cases?

JUDICIAL COHORTS

A judicial cohort is a socially defined group with which judges self-identified. Education, mode of entry, socialization, career, culture and values all contribute to the significance of a judicial cohort as an identity marker. One unique characteristic of the Chinese judiciary is the significance of the cohort effects in its judicial makeup. Chinese judges can be roughly divided into three cohorts – the veterans who joined the courts during or before the 1980s, the middle-aged who joined the court in the late 1980s and 1990s, and the "post-'80" generation (those who were born after the year 1980) who joined the court in the new millennium. In Europe, judges in some countries are differentiated by the courts in which they serve. In France, for example, there are distinct judicial corps, each with its own functions and experiences, among the judges (Bell 2006:44–102; 360). In China, cohort, along with ranking, is the most salient line separating different groups of judges.

The boundaries separating the veteran, the middle-aged, and the "post-1980" are a reflection of rapid social and cultural changes China has experienced in the past fifty years. But they are also the result of dramatic and wholesale institutional changes made to the judiciary. The distinctiveness of the judicial cohort is based firmly on a range of institutional factors. Within each of the three cohorts, judges share a variety of experiences in all aspects of the socialization process of being a judge, from initial recruitment (but also from training and further education) to placement and promotion.

This distinction is also well known among judges themselves. Judges often talk about the three generations working in courts. When we conducted our fieldwork in courts in southern China, our hosts in the courts we visited typically prefaced their introduction of other judges by referring to the cohort they belonged: "Zhang is a veteran judge. He was among the first of his cohort who received a college degree in law." Or "Liao is a post-'80 judge. She is very energetic . . ." To promote a common culture despite their different training and backgrounds, courts often mix, when possible, the three generations in collegial panels and committees.

THE VETERAN

The English word "veteran" is in fact more suited to describe this generation of judges than the Chinese word 老 (*lao*), which literally means "old." Certainly, the older generation of judges in China have all served many years in courts, the youngest of this generation are in their early fifties, approaching the age of retirement. But many of them are also veterans in another sense – they are retired army officers who began their judicial careers at a time when college education and specialized training were not required for judges.

Early legal education of the PRC in the 1940s and 1950s aimed to train "judicial cadres" (Shen and Wang 2005:398). In 1952 and 1953, four politico-legal institutes (政法学院 *zhengfa xueyuan*) – Beijing, East China (*Huadong*), Southwestern (*Xinan*) and Central China (*Zhongnan*) – were created (Shen and Wang 2005:399). The initial purpose for setting up these institutes was for the training of cadres (政法干部 *zhengfa ganbu*), but they also began to accept undergraduates in the 1950s. According to Zou, "students came from three sources: cadres, judicial personnel who served the Kuomintang regime and needed to be retrained and reformed, and young students directly from high schools" (2006:206).

It was also a period when China's legal system was heavily influenced by the USSR's socialist model (Depei and Kaner 1984). Soviet legal specialists were hired as consultants and lecturers in China. Soviet laws, codes, legal scholarship and curricular materials were extensively translated (Zeng et al. 2012:400–401).

It is obvious that the law back then did not see proper legal training as the primary qualification for judges (Cabestan et al. 2012:711). The Organic Law of the People's Courts of July 1, 1979 stated: "Citizens who have the right to vote and to stand for election and have reached to age of 23 are eligible to be elected presidents of people's courts or appointed vice presidents of people's courts, chief judges or associate chief judges of divisions, judges or assistant judges; but persons who have ever been excluded of political rights are excluded" (Article 34).

Pre-1980s legal education was marked by frequent political turmoil. The growth of the anti-rightist movement in 1957 led to severe setbacks in legal education (Shen and Wang 2005:402–403). Legal education was completely subsumed under political education during the decade of Cultural Revolution. All politico-legal institutes and other institutes of higher learning ceased enrollment of students in 1966. In 1971, the national conference of educational labor declared a policy regarding the adjustment of institutes of higher learning (关于高等学校调整方案 *guanyu gaodeng xuexiao tiaozheng fangan*) that revoked the operation of all institutes of higher legal education except for the law departments of Peking University and Jilin University (Shen and Wang 2005:404). It was not until 1977 that politico-legal institutes and departments of law that had been shut down began to resume operation. Beginning in the late 1970s, more politico-legal institutes and colleges were also set up across the country and student enrollments increased dramatically (see Liang 2008:58–59).

Veteran judges received their on-again, off-again legal education during this politically turbulent period for China. Despite recognition of the importance of proper legal training, there was a lack of quality teachers of law immediately after the long, disruptive decade of the Cultural Revolution (Shen and Wang 2005:406). To wit, this generation of judges are the products of a legal education system set up to train cadres who were proficient in law. Among the three cohorts, the veterans seem to hold the weakest professional identity. It helps to remind ourselves of what the Chinese court looked like when they joined it. Back then, they were referred to officially as "cadres" (干部 *ganbu*), "political-legal cadres" (政法干部 *zhengfa ganbu*) and "political-legal security cadres" (政法干警 *zhengfa ganjing*). The Supreme Court did not begin to refer to them as "judges" (法官 *faguan*) until the 2000s (Jiang 2010:224–225). They saw themselves as government officials working in the courts, not as judges specialized in legal affairs.

Nowadays, veteran judges have mostly retreated from the frontline to work in the research and propaganda divisions of the courts. In the course of our fieldwork and interviews, we did not get to run into too many of them. There is a reverse "age lump" phenomenon among frontline judges in China as a result of the court system having reached its growth plateau only in the last decade, almost twenty years after the veterans joined the courts. The veterans we met were generally not very outspoken. On the occasions when we got a chance to talk to a group of judges, older judges were most reticent. They kept a low profile. They deferred, at least in public, to younger and higher-ranking judges. That might have to do with our identity as outside visitors, but statements from other judges confirm our impression.

Judge Jian, a division head from a basic-level court in Zhejiang, aged 49, said, "Some older judges in my court started working as a judge in the 1970s. You know back then how the law was like in China. Nowadays, the qualification required for becoming a judge has become much more demanding. These veteran judges who were without formal legal training, they have very little to say about legal matters."

For a society where Confucian beliefs still hold sway, educational credential is not merely qualification; it is the single most important status marker. One just needs to take a look at the educational qualifications (some of which might be inflated) of senior judges of the SPC. Even though some of them were career bureaucrats not trained in law, they all have at least their master's degrees in law (many of these are part-time or honorary degrees) on the resume.

Veteran judges are often described by their younger colleagues as "not strong in law" but "good at dealing with people." They are often described as judges who know how to mediate. Judge Liang, a vice president of a basic-level court in Jiangsu, explained how the good people skills possessed by veteran judges is a generational matter:

> As a group, most of our veteran judges did not graduate from college. Some of them came from a military background. They are gradually stepping down from everyday adjudicative work. I interact with many of them. They lag behind in their mastery of legal concepts and professional knowledge. You can say their knowledge of the law is just so-so. But some of them are very good at working the mass. They know how to deal with people. They are good at mediation. They know how to deal with litigants.

Judge Sun from Jilin, who was quoted earlier, made the following comments:

> There is a certain thinking habit that is most commonly found among older judges. Judges of this generation tend to think that they can tell who is telling the truth and who is not by listening to the litigants. They have a tendency to judge based on how well litigants present their side of the story. Younger judges, especially those who are university-trained, they are more receptive of the new legal concepts and they put more emphasis on listening to both sides of an event and then examine the supporting evidence.

This cohort of early post-Cultural Revolution judges is retreating from the frontline. Some of them are still active in rural work-unit courts, but as a group, not many judges older than their fifties still take on an active adjudicative role. Even those who have made it to the position of division head or deputy division head are often asked to make way for younger judges. This is particularly so in firm-type courts. In the city, it is common for judges in their mid-fifties to step down from their administrative roles in the final years leading up to their retirement. Many move to sinecure positions that are more clerical than judicial. Other members of this age cohort have already retired or transferred to other departments.

THE MIDDLE-AGED

Middle-aged judges today received their legal education in the 1980s and 1990s, the decades when legal education became "normalized" again. It was also a period when legal education rapidly expanded and developed. There was a push from the central government for the development of legal education.[4] There was an increasing diversity of institutes offering legal education. In 1988, there were 25 politico-legal institutes and 81 university departments of law, compared to 4 institutes and 4 departments in 1978. The organization of legal education became more structured and rationalized – for instance, by 1987, along with the increased training of lower-level legal specialists, there were 25 doctoral programs and 79 masters programs that responded to the expanding legal system's need for highly skilled legal specialists (Sheng and Wang 2005:406–407). This period also witnessed an increased differentiation of law as a field of specialization. By 1987, nine specialized fields of law – law, international law, economic law, international economic law, labor reform law, criminal investigation, criminology, environmental law and intellectual property law – were recognized by the national education council (国家教委 *guojia jiwei*, predecessor to the Ministry of Education) (Sheng and Wang 2005:406–407).

As Biddulph (2010:264) states, "In 1992, the concept of the legal services market was introduced following the decision of the fourteenth Chinese Communist Party Congress to implement a socialist market economy." Following this decision, the Central Committee of the Chinese Communist Party, together with the State Council, issued the Outline on Reform and Development of China's Education (中国教育改革和发展纲要 *Zhongguo jiaoyu gaige he fazhan gangyao*) in 1993. The outline formed the basis for implementing further reforms in the field of legal education (Biddulph 2010:267).

Most judges in their forties are the product of this period of legal education. More important, they are the transitional generation who experienced first-hand the change from a strict government placement system to a system that allowed some leeway for graduates to choose their own future employment.[5] It is important to point out that not all judges who joined the courts during this period were college graduates. As recent as 1995, only 5 percent of Chinese judges were university graduates (Waye and Xiong 2011:4). There remained a lot of the middle-aged judges who came from a non-legal background; some joined the courts from other government bureaus and some were retired military officials.

Nowadays, middle-aged judges who have a college degree constitute the core of the middle-ranking judges of the Chinese courts. Many of them are division heads and deputy division heads at the courts they serve. They are considered as the cohort with both experience and knowledge. Some of the forty-something members, particularly those who are college-trained, occupy the high ranks of president and vice president.

These judges play an important role in running the bureaucracy. They vet the judgments written by ordinary judges; they put the official court stamp on routine judgments. They are the gatekeepers. Besides supervising junior judges, they also participate in the adjudication committee to discuss difficult cases. They are asked to deal with the increasing pressure upon the courts to be more adroit and responsive.

Middle-aged judges with over ten years of experience are expected to deliver sound judgment and to be able to handle litigants, even the vituperative ones, with tact.

As division heads, their job is primarily administrative. They assign cases to junior judges of their divisions and deal with problem cases under their watch. Their job as superiors for appraisal, promotion, and posting plays an important role in shaping the culture of a judiciary. They identify and promote younger judges who are seen to be the future core of the judiciary; they also supervise and at times chastise judges who do not perform up to par.

Among those judges of this group who have successfully climbed the bureaucratic ladder to become part of "the management," their primary identity remains more that of a bureaucrat. In our fieldwork, we have met some of the successful members of the middle-aged – they are worldly, savvy by temperament and cautious and detail-oriented in terms of their working style. They are also team players. This is important for anyone who wants to succeed as a bureaucrat in China. Even for those who occupy positions of leadership (e.g., presidents and vice presidents), they must know how to work as a group. At the very least, they must not be hated by their peers. A big part of their job is to constantly interact with leaders of other bureaus and party organs. They are asked to establish the authority of the judiciary and to increase the involvement of the judiciary in the decision-making process of different levels of government. Senior judges are also regularly involved in formulating and shaping policies for social harmony and stability. They are involved in "ideological-political" work. In a sense, there is nothing uniquely Chinese about senior judges playing the role of administrator. Outside of the Anglo-American common law system, judges in many civil law countries play significant roles in bureaucratic management. However, senior Chinese judges stand out in the amount of inter-departmental politicking and negotiations in which they engage. As a non-income generating government branch, these judges have to constantly make connections with other departments in order to secure resources. It is this double task of securing resources *and* maintaining the relative autonomy of the judiciary that nurtures the worldly, pragmatic style of the senior judges in local Chinese courts.

That said, judges of this middle-aged generation enjoy greater power than their predecessors. By and large, compared to the pre-2000 era, there has been an increase in the relative strength, autonomy (both administrative and financial) and standing of the local courts. The result of these changes is the growing autonomy of the leadership of local courts, particularly in firm-type courts, with a more defined scope of powers and responsibilities. The singular ability that the leaders of this group show is the ability to manage and to innovate within the parameters specified in the high-level decisions made by the central authorities. From an administrative standpoint, they are asked to be problem-solvers and decision-makers. There is residual discretionary authority given to presidents and vice presidents of local courts under this system. They are often tasked with deriving concrete plans to implement new policy initiatives.

THE POST-1980

The term "post-'80" or "post-1980" is in common use among Chinese judges themselves to describe a new breed. It means more than simply young judges who were born after 1980 and are now in their thirties or younger. The 1980s was a watershed decade, a period of historical and symbolic significance. It marked the beginning of Deng Xiaoping's open-door policy that jump-started the massive industrial and economic transformation in China. "Post-1980" Chinese are a generation who grew up in a China further and further removed from the ideological struggles that defined the era of the Cultural Revolution, in a China defined by an agenda that is post-Mao through and through – modernization and economic growth. In many ways, they are very much the children of a more marketized China. They are also the first generation who grew up under China's famous one-child policy, which was first applied in 1979. Most of these post-1980 judges have no siblings. Unlike the previous generations, they did not grow up in traditional, big Chinese extended family, and they are widely considered by older Chinese as being more "individualistic."

But the term "post-1980" carries more specific significance as a generational label to describe judges. The post-1980 judges are the generation who (1) are college-educated in law and (2) entered the judiciary through the formal mechanism of judicial examination. When judges themselves talk about the post-1980 judges, they consciously distinguish them from the earlier generations.

The 1990s and 2000s were decades of even more rapid expansion of legal education in China. By April 2006, there were 620 institutes of higher learning nationwide offering a law major (Biddulph 2010:266). College education in law has taken on the development of specialization. This was in part reflected by the reorganization of the five traditional politico-legal institutes into part of the higher education system managed by the Ministry of Education (Zeng et al. 2012:410).[6] The 2000s was a decade when legal education in China was heavily influenced by the Anglo-American model of education. For example, the introduction of J.M./LL.M. programs into China (Biddulph 2010). Another program inspired by experience in the United States is the legal clinic. In 2000, permission was granted for seven law schools to establish legal clinics within their law programs: Peking University, Tsinghua University, Renmin University of China, Fudan University, East China University of Politics and Law, Zhongnan University of Economics and Law, and Wuhan University. These became the founding members of the Chinese Clinical Legal Education Network, funded by the Ford Foundation, which applied the United States' model of the legal clinic to the Chinese situation. By 2007, as many as 64 university law schools had already established legal clinics (Biddulph 2010:271). Post-1980 judges are the product of this more professionalized and, some may say, Westernized curriculum of legal education.

The Judges Law issued in 1995 (Article 9) made a degree from an institute of higher education a prerequisite for newly hired judges and procuratorate officials. Internal examination was introduced within the judicial system to improve the quality of newly recruited judges. The central authorities also reworked their annual evaluation system for court presidents and bureau chiefs to place greater emphasis on their success in recruiting individuals with university or even postgraduate degrees (Minzner 2013:348). In 2001, the National People's Congress Standing Committee amended the 1995 Judges Law and Procurators Law to unite and standardize the examinations for judges, procurators and lawyers into the National Judicial Examination (国家统一司法考试 *guojia tongyi sifa kaoshi*) – a move that further professionalized the judiciary (Zeng et al. 2012:411). In March 2002, the first national law examination was held.[7] For more than a decade now, many applicants have been shortlisted through the mechanism of a public examination. Candidates who passed the examination are then interviewed by the courts to which they apply. If recruited, these new members enter at the most junior level of the judge hierarchy.

The examination is admittedly a big step toward credentialization. As Chen (2015:152) observes, "Gone are the days when demobilized army officers were transferred to the judicial system en masse and when the judiciary was one of the professions in which it was most easy for non-professionals to be employed." The examination, dubbed as the "number one examination in China," reminds people of the 科举 (*keju*) examination of Imperial China, for good and bad reasons. Passing the examination is a requirement for anyone who aspires to become a judge, a prosecutor, or a lawyer in China. In recent years, more than 400,000 people took the examination annually (the latest figure in 2016 is 438,000; see Xinhua News Agency 2016), with an average pass rate that fell short of 10 percent.[8]

The examination was criticized by some scholars as too bookish. It also requires students to memorize large amounts of legal information (Biddulph 2010:268–269). Despite its limitations, it is considered relatively meritocratic, as it is a system open to all. It is important to note that even though all takers stand the same chance of passing the examination, not all takers who have passed the examination stand the same chance of being recruited by the Chinese judiciary. The reality is, though fresh college graduates made up less than 20 percent of the examinees who took the examination in recent years, they are the group that are primarily targeted by the courts.[9] The unified examination is a first hurdle for some mature applicants to attain the necessary qualifications to apply to become a judge. But it is not the only hurdle. Senior judges we interviewed made no pretense about their preference for young, single, twenty-something, college-educated applicants who passed the examination. They believe young recruits are more able to withstand the long hours required of frontline judges. Apparently, judges do not believe that just anyone who has passed the examination can be admitted to the court. Passing the difficult examination is a necessary but insufficient condition.

CHARACTERISTICS OF POST-1980 JUDGES

We now turn to this new generation of judges and examine how they view themselves as judges working in this populous and rapidly changing country. We do this for two reasons. The first has to do with our overriding concern about the nature of the Chinese courts as a bureaucracy. Earlier, we discussed the hierarchical structure of the Chinese judiciary. In many senses, frontline judges are bureaucrats who work within the confines of the bureaucracy. Yet, as many sociologists after Weber have pointed out, officials do not blindly adhere to procedures and rules. They do not react to rules reflexively, the way we kick when tapped on the knee. The question of the source of adherence is, for example, a central question in Alvin Gouldner's classic *Patterns of Industrial Bureaucracy* (1954). To paraphrase Gouldner, the question we raise here is this: Do young judges conform to bureaucratic rules reluctantly for fear of sanctions? Or do they conform to those rules because those rules conform to the professional values they hold (i.e., they regard those rules as necessary on technical grounds)?

At a more practical level, the views of young judges are particularly relevant for our purpose because these people constitute the core of the frontline judges working in the 3,500 courts in China. This is particularly true in the big cities. Only young judges can withstand the long hours necessary to deal with the heavy workload of these courts. Judge Yang, a judge who works in a big city in Pearl River Delta, explained: "Our court has about 120 judges. Our average age is 30. We're that young by necessity. You can't have old judges with this kind of workload. All of us have to work overtime." Another judge from Pearl River Delta, Judge Wu, said, "In our court, most of the thirty-something colleagues still want to be a judge. But most of the forty-something colleagues loathe to be a judge."

The use of the unified judicial examination put China closer to the continental European model of public competition among young law graduates who have little or no previous professional experience (Guarnieri and Pederzoli 2002:19; Merryman 1985:103). Judges in China nowadays begin their career at a relatively young age. It is not uncommon to see some twenty-something judges presiding over trials that involve litigants older than their parents. In a sense, the new generation of Chinese judges is more homogeneous than the judges recruited in many European countries. While there is now increasing variety in routes of entry to the judiciary in Europe, the urge to professionalize the Chinese judiciary means that most of the judges are recruited through the unified judicial examination.

One overlooked phenomenon is that the courts are populated by judges who are ranked among the youngest in the world. They are recruited at a very young age, most of them in their twenties, and are expected to gradually move up the ladder within the judiciary. A fresh college graduate at the young age of 23 is eligible to be recruited into a court. After two years of on-the-job training as a court clerk, the young 25-year-old begins to adjudicate as a member of the collegial panel, and more and more often, as the sole presiding judge in routine civil cases.[10] While much has been said about the attrition rates of young judges, there is also the reverse "age lump" in the Chinese courts. As a judicial system, the Chinese court is young. It reached its growth plateau in the 2000s. The cohort of judges recruited during the previous decade has yet to be "aged."

Among the many young judges (35 or younger) we interviewed, their self-descriptions and their characterizations of older judges are surprisingly consistent. There are differences among the accounts of individual judges. Some are more direct and critical of their seniors; others are more diplomatic and circumspect. But the overall themes are consistent. As a group, they share a clear and tangible professional identity.

"WE ARE DIFFERENT FROM OTHER GOVERNMENT OFFICIALS"

A common way for a group to carve out a new identity is through the process of "othering" (Barth 1969). It is through this process of articulating their distinctiveness from otherwise similar groups that people develop their unique identity. Young judges make a distinction between themselves and other government bureaucrats. They see themselves as professionals who possess special knowledge. Among judges, they certainly see themselves as the most professionally qualified group. To be a judge, to them, is to be a professional rather than a bureaucrat. Perhaps for this reason, young judges are more used to calling themselves judges (法官 *faguan*) than adjudicators (审判员 *shenpanyuan*), the former being more a professional identity and the latter an administrative rank.

Most of them described their careers as judicial. They did not frame their decision as a choice to become a civil servant. Instead, they talked about wanting specifically to become a judge. "Judges look very dignified. They uphold social justice. I can also apply what I learned in university," Judge Fu (female), aged 31, of Sichuan said.

A lot of them mentioned Hong Kong-produced courtroom dramas made in the 1990s (depicting counsel and judges working in the common law system of Hong Kong, all dressed in wigs and gowns) as an early source of motivation to become judges: "Funny you asked. Back in those days I watched a lot of Hong Kong TV legal dramas. What're they called? 壹号皇庭 *yihao huangting* (File of Justice). And I thought to myself, wearing robes appearing in court was awesome," Judge Lin (female) of Guangdong said.

Some offered thinly veiled criticisms of what they perceived as the frivolous job nature of officials in other bureaus. "I do solid work for my salary (干事情拿工资 *gan shiqing na gongzi*). There are officials in other government departments who do not get a lot of things done," said Judge Zhou (male), a young judge, aged 28, working in an intermediate court from Shaanxi. Despite the low pay and the hardship, most judges believe they make real contribution to society. This is the one thing that they often brought up in the interviews.

PROFESSIONAL IDENTITY

Post-1980 judges tend to distinguish themselves from their more senior, middle-aged and veteran judges. They see themselves as the first generation of all-college-educated judges. Some described this distinctiveness as possessing a certain legal disposition or a legal frame of mind.

Judge Ding (female), aged 30, from Yunnan said: "I really think there is a difference between college graduates and others from other channels, even though both groups passed the judicial examination. If you take a look at the exam, you'll know the results are in part determined by a person's mastery of exam techniques. But one who masters those exam techniques (and passes the exam) might not share the values of being a legal professional."

When asked to describe how they are different, a few talked about the presence of a certain legal disposition or a legal frame of mind. To these young judges, legal disposition means that one considers the law first, rather than other factors such as expediency and feasibility. Judge Xue (male), aged 30, from Guizhou explained:

> After four years of college education, I think for me and for my peers, we've internalized a certain legal frame of mind. This frame of mind is made up of some beliefs that you hold about the law. You develop a sense about how law should operate. Our generation share this frame of mind. We let ourselves be guided by this frame of reference. Our sense of restraints is stronger than the older generation of judges.

Judge Zhang (female), aged 28, from an urban court in Guangdong made a similar observation: "I think our generation will apply the legal frame of mind by default. We are accustomed to considering matters from a legal perspective, and that's not necessarily the case with the older generation of judges."

The question can be pushed further – what exactly is this legal frame of mind? Is it "rule-following" mentality? Or is it something more specifically jurisprudential? Are judges referring to some broader beliefs in constitutionalism? In other words, is this talk about legal frame of mind a discreet way for young Chinese judges to talk about a full-fledged concept of judicial independence? Answers from the judges seem to suggest the former. A legal frame of mind for these judges means a "law-first" mentality – take legal statutes seriously and follow them as faithfully as possible. The evidence for a belief in constitutionalism is sparse. The term "judicial independence" was rarely brought up by the judges we interviewed. In fact, when they talked about independence, they meant work independence (not being supervised by their superiors) rather than the independence of law.

That said, this law-first mentality is, the young judges believe, what separates them from the older judges. They see themselves as more process-oriented and rule-governed. Judge Ding from Yunnan, whom we quoted earlier, remarked, "Judges of the older generation rely more on common sense. They are more ready to speculate based on what they have seen in previous cases." Judge Gong from Guangxi, aged 26, said that even though senior judges were good at dealing with people from all walks of life, sometimes they did not take formality seriously enough. She said:

> Some observers or defendants may only participate in one court hearing. If formalities are not adhered to, the judge might give off the impression of being lax . . . I think there are certain things that should be strictly observed in court. Even though we might think that procedures are just a matter of formality, yet the solemnity of a trial is manifested by formal procedures.

Judge Xue from Guizhou said that among the judges above the age of 40 in his court, legal procedures and rules were often casually referred to as an afterthought. The most important thing was to resolve the underlying conflicts: "Older judges put emphasis on resolving conflicts regardless of the means. They think that this is most important and as long as this is achieved, they will find a way to convert what they do into legally acceptable forms." Judge Zhang from Guangdong again invoked the legal frame of mind as a distinguishing characteristic of her generation:

> Very different. I think when we [the post-1980 generation] consider a problem, we always approach it first from a legal frame of mind. We approach it first as a legal problem . . . In contrast, the older generation of judges, they lack the professional legal training but they have a lot of life experience. They use their life experience as resources to deal with litigants. The judicial style of the older generation has to do with the historical context in which they came of age as judges. Back then, the litigants were also different and most of them were from the rural society and they were also less educated.

TECHNOCRAT MENTALITY

This "legal frame of mind" is best understood as a form of technocrat mentality upheld by the post-1980 judges in their approach to daily tasks. One tangible expression of the mentality is their preference for adjudication. The post-1980 judges are generally lukewarm toward mediation. Some said they did not dislike mediation; it was just that they were not eager to promote it. A few of them who worked in big cities said they adopted a "natural attitude" (平常心 *pingchangxin*) toward mediation, which was a discreet way of saying that they did not coerce litigants to settle. The most typical response is, "I'll mediate when litigants indicate a willingness to mediate."

Post-1980 judges are quick to point out that they are not "one of those" judges with stellar mediation rates. As we got to know some of them more, it is obvious that they preferred adjudication over mediation; some in fact privately despised aggressive mediation. For most routine cases, if given a choice, they adjudicate. Many post-1980 judges mediate only because they are urged to, or are even instructed by their superiors to do so. For controversial and difficult cases, they also mediate in order to avoid getting themselves into trouble. Otherwise, young judges overwhelmingly prefer to adjudicate.

The most academically qualified "post-'80" judges can be found in the firm-type courts located in big cities. These courts use their better financial resources to hire extra supporting staff (non-judge clerical staff, e.g., judicial clerks) to help their judges. The supporting staff form outreach teams to mediate cases that are not officially accepted by the court's docket. Team members participate actively in many extra-judicial mediation activities, such as helping out at people's mediation committees administered by local villagers and residents committees. They also work with other government officials in the grand mediation setting.[11] Through the work of these outreach teams, firm-type courts participate in cases that are success-fully mediated non-judicially and count them as part of the total number of cases successfully mediated judicially (Li et al. 2016). The outreach teams make the quota for judges. They generate enough "mediated cases" to meet the target without really asking judges to spend long hours mediating. This reserve of mediated cases is a valuable organizational resource. Frontline judges can tap into the reserve to meet their required target. That explains why some judges from firm courts are noncha-lant about their pedestrian mediation rates. They know they are "covered."

The preference for adjudication turns on both practical convenience and profes-sional self-image. Professionally, many of them see adjudication as a judge's primary activity. Judges want to *use* the law, to *apply* the law and to *develop* it into a set of precise and well-defined rules. Adjudication is also relatively easy. This new breed of college graduates, many of them with multiple degrees, are trained to deal with interlocked rules and technical details. Using law is a means for them to display their intellectual and technical prowess. As Max Weber (1978) pointed out long ago, it is the natural tendency for bureaucrats to expand their power. But the method for the post-1980 judges to accumulate power is different from that of their seniors. Senior judges gather power by showing other powerful members of the local party-state that they are in control of the court. Young frontline judges expand their power through a form of knowledge domination. Their jurisdiction as a judge is reinforced through the use of a specialist's knowledge essential to modern legal decision-making.

It is no wonder that one area of practice that the post-1980 judges most wanted to improve is the judgment reference system. This emphasis on research and knowl-edge techniques conforms to the ideal type of a "rational" Weberian bureaucrat. Judge Lin emphasized the need to catch up on legal research:

We don't have a good database (of past decisions). It is nothing like Lexis or Westlaw. I think this is a really big problem. We don't have a good database. And every time when you disagree with your seniors, they could always show you a past decision to which you have no access. We have difficulties even accessing past important decisions of SPC. We can only access those available on the web. But my senior judges, they perhaps dealt with a similar case five years ago, and then they know what the decision was back then.

Implicit in the judge's comments is the belief that the knowledge of past court decisions should be more systematically and openly available. She is taking seriously the idea of law as a professional system of knowledge. China's statutory laws are usually presented as broad statements of principle and do not offer precise guidelines on the fronts of application and enforcement. Local courts often set their own terms, within the broad parameter of the law – for example, on whether a certain act falls within the definition of a statutory term or how specifically a certain fine or compensation is calculated. Unevenness in sentencing practices and statutory interpretation across local courts is common. These "local rules" are not organized and centrally filed. It is a form of knowledge with a high level of asset specificity (Williamson 1981), so to speak, that judges who have more years of experience know and understand. The post-1980 judges' desire for a better legal database is correlated with their want to be more independent at the level of daily operations. Young judges who work in the urban centers of China are those who are most eager to push for better legal research support. They are also the ones who most aspire to work independently. A more developed database would mean that all judges could do their legal research independently, without resorting to personal means for information. "Your ability to be a good judge has a lot to do with your research ability. In my court (an intermediate court in Guangdong), a good judge must be one who is able to conduct good legal research. Your ability to research is directly correlated with your ability to write good opinions," Judge Lin added.

Legal research has become an ever more important area of focus for the group of young judges. In fact, under the policy of litigantism, young judges put more emphasis on the research of law than on the investigation of facts. Judge Lin again:

I don't investigate. I think lawyers are more qualified and capable nowadays. Lawyers are very smart, especially those working in Guangdong. In many cases I dealt with, the lawyers were way more experienced than me. They absolutely were capable of investigating for their clients. If they didn't do it, they had their own reasons.

Young judges give a lot of weight to documentary evidence, material evidence and official records, but tend not to "speculate" on the truth and falsity of oral evidence. Judge Lin explained why she had become less gullible:

I have no "emotional feeling" about what witnesses say. I tend not to believe what they say . . . I don't give a lot of weight to what they say. I think this is not my responsibility (to verify what litigants say). If your judgment is based on what witnesses said to you, a lot of people are going to challenge you. I need to make sure my judgment is a solid judgment. It's an occupational habit. I tend not to trust what people say.

Judge Chen from Beijing, whom we quoted in Chapter 2, concurred:

Documentary evidence and physical evidence are much more important than witness testimonies. If you have a contract, show me the contract. [Interviewer: "What if someone is duped to sign on a contract?"] You can't just say it. You need to prove it to me.

GAP BETWEEN ASPIRATION AND REALITY

It is perhaps ironic that the new generation of college-educated, law-majored judges are psychologically less prepared than the preceding generation of ex-military officials for working as a judge in China. Yet it is the reality. China has devoted a tremendous amount of resources to improving its legal education, and such efforts have worked perhaps too well for its own good (Liebman 2012:227)! The actual content of law classes is strongly borrowed from foreign and, above all, American models. Some law schools, for example, tried out a "case and materials" curriculum based primarily on the Anglo-American common law model. It is hard to argue that legal education, and indeed college education in general, in the past two decades has not moved closer to university education in Western societies, both in form and content. To use a Weberian term, legal knowledge in China has gone through a phase of *intellectualization*. Knowledge is made more coherent by the development of ideas and principles. Post-1980 judges are the product of China's university legal education. The net result of that is that the new judges who come out of this system are by temperament much more inclined to think of law as a set of rules. The development of university legal education has vastly outpaced the professionalization process of the Chinese judiciary, so much so that judges have found that much of what they have learned cannot be applied in Chinese courts.

Those who joined the judiciary in the past ten years are considered the cream of their generation, yet many of them are asking themselves more questions about their career choices. New-generation judges find it difficult to adjust to the fact that law is only a component, and often not even the most important component, of their job, an environment where outside factors beyond their control swirl from all directions. To them, there are a lot of non-legal elements that they need to consider: "letters and petitions" of litigants, supervision of their superiors, and increasingly, the scrutiny of the media in some high-profile cases, not to mention the fact that they are asked to satisfy the administrative benchmarks (caseload, rates of appeal and retrial) used to measure their performance.

Many young judges want their everyday tasks to be more "legal," in the sense that cases can be handled according to some clear, predetermined rules. But that is often not possible for judges working in work-unit courts, and in some cases, in firm-type courts as well. Some cases are delayed because courts are eager to negotiate with litigants; some are put aside after hearings for the same reason; some are reopened for administrative reasons. Typical post-1980 judges do not see themselves as different from professionals such as accountants or medical doctors. They think that years of education (particularly for those who graduated with a law degree) have made them into professionals. Yet the biggest shock for them is that, unlike an engineer or a doctor, whose everyday work involves the exercise of their specialized knowledge, law is not a professional field where they can put their expertise to work day in and day out. The first two years working as a court clerk is meant to get college graduates accustomed to the working environment of the courts. But many have to continue to adjust their expectations after becoming a junior judge in the court.

"There are other things you need to consider. You soon find out that the law is not as certain as you want it to be," Judge Fu from Sichuan said. "To me this is a sacred profession" said Judge Qian, aged 30, from Inner Mongolia. "I admire the solemnity of the law." But the extent to which these younger judges can make use of the law is contingent upon the institutional culture of the courts in which they serve (see Chapters 4 to 7). This limit is clear: in work-unit courts located in the inland rural regions, courts prefer less law (mediation) over more law (adjudication). Certain laws are seen as unenforceable in the less economically developed parts of China (see Xiong 2014a). Working in Inner Mongolia, where litigants often have difficulty just traveling to the courthouse, Judge Qian said she had to learn that applying the law (to adjudicate) was not the only part of her job. She was under pressure to adjust herself to the culture of the court. She reflected on how she had changed since the day she first entered the court a few years ago:

> Perhaps because I'm a bit older, I'm a little different now. When I first arrived, I was labeled by my colleagues as a "college-trained" (学院派 *xueyuanpai*) and an "intellectualist" (学术派 *xueshupai*). In practice, social problems are complex. If you say you just follow the law, then you just resolve a legal problem, but often you do not resolve the fundamental social conflict underlying the problem. The problem will come back in another form ... So I think mediation and adjudication should complement each other. Of course, we should not overemphasize mediation. After all, I work in the court. But they (adjudication and mediation) complement each other, I think.

"WE DON'T GET NO RESPECT"

Young judges lament they do not get the respect they deserve from the public. As a group, they see themselves as those who quietly do all the heavy lifting. They said the bad reputation of Chinese courts was caused by a few bad apples from above. Some young judges said it was demoralizing to see when bad news about court leadership broke out. They expressed a sense of helplessness. They did not engage in those activities, and yet they share the bad reputation. At the time of our interviews, a well-publicized scandal broke out in Shanghai. A group of division heads and deputy division heads from the High Court of Shanghai, one of the most developed courts in China, were caught apparently consorting with prostitutes in nightclubs (Perlez 2013). Judge Fu said:

> Sometimes I got upset when some cases of corruption within the judiciary became so publicized that the public think that all judges are corrupted. All judges take advantage of the plaintiff and the defendant (吃了原告吃被告 *chi le yuangao chi beigao*).

The formulaic expression "吃了原告吃被告" was often used by disgruntled litigants to describe the rapaciousness of judges. At interviews, the post-1980 judges conveyed conviction in their own rectitude. They believed that their generation served the public well, but that they did not get the recognition they deserved. Judge Yang, a judge who worked very long hours at a busy city court in Guangdong, said:

> Sometimes litigants who lost would say to me: "You must have taken money from the other party." Many of them are elderlies. When I had the time, I'd sit down and chat with them. And I'd tell them: "Grandma, we're talking about 3,000 yuan (the disputed claim). You lost and you said I took money from the other party. So, please tell me, how much money did you think the other party paid me to make you lose?"

The judge's point is that the public image of Chinese judges has sunk so low that losing litigants almost reflexively blame judges for corruption, even though the money in dispute was so small that it would not be "economical" to pay off a judge. "We have very little legitimacy. The public does not respect us. It becomes more and more difficult to do our job," he added.

Judge Gong from Guangxi approached the matter from a more personal and sentimental perspective:

> When I leave my office at night, I like to count how many rooms have lights on. And there are many rooms with lights still on, because many of my colleagues work overtime. But when you talk to people outside, they are very surprised when told that judges work overtime. "Why do judges need to work overtime?" They would ask. "Isn't that the case that you make a lot of money?" They would say that all judges are corrupt . . . And then they think being a judge is easy and it is a very stable job. To me, this does not fit with what I see in the lives of the majority of the judges I know . . .
>
> I really think many judges sacrifice a lot, but they feel frustrated by the way they are portrayed in the media.

The post-1980 judges hold complicated and ambivalent feelings toward their jobs. They think working in the court is more meaningful than working in many other government bureaus. Yet they crave more respect. Status disenchantment is widespread among young judges. Judge Fu, who joined the court in 2003, said she became a judge because she thought judges were very dignified and important. But she added, "I realized that being a judge was quite different from what I had thought it would be like . . . Now I realize that in China, being a judge means you have to plant your feet on the soil of reality." Judge Fu refused to elaborate about the reasons behind her disenchantment, but she added that some of her colleagues were doubtful about the future of judging as a profession. "One needs to be able to see the future of a judicial profession to be passionate about her work," she said. Judge Gong shared Judge Fu's ambivalence about their future. She said, matter-of-factly, "It is sometimes just hard to keep going just based on your belief alone."

REVERSE LATERAL RECRUITMENT

The pyramidal structure of the courts means that prospects for promotion are dim for most judges. Low prestige and heavy workloads all contribute to the condition of young judges today being less wedded to the court as their lifelong *danwei*. It is now common for judges to transfer to other government bureaus after working in the courts for a few years. For judges working in urban courts located in large metropolises, there is a widening gap between the salaries of judges and those of lawyers in private practice. This is particularly the case for judges working in the commercial divisions. There have been reports that some of these judges could make a 7-figure (in yuan) annual salary when they leave the judiciary to become a lawyer in a private firm. Judges we interviewed were well aware of their "market value." Judge Wang, aged 40, an intellectual property judge from Beijing, said that a judge with fewer years of experience than he recently quit to become a private lawyer: "He made 800,000 yuan a year."

Some scholars have characterized rising attrition as a looming crisis (Cohen 2016). In our interviews, though, not many young judges talked about leaving. A senior SPC judge wrote that the number of judges who left the court system in 2015 was just over 1,000, or about 0.5 percent of the total establishment (Chen, Haiguang 2016). While this might be an underestimate, we agree that the attrition rate is not high (see Finder 2016).[12] After all, leaving the government is still considered a very risky move by many Chinese bureaucrats today. The shocking part of this news does not come from the absolute numbers, but instead lies in the fact that many of those who chose to leave were the cream of the crop – young judges who were recruited into the most competitive city courts but who then left for private practice. This kind of early departure in big cities was almost unheard of a decade ago. The uncompetitive economic rewards they get, coupled with the political and social constraints that they face (to them, even firm-type courts are not firm-like enough), discouraged some young judges with good credentials from staying in the system. We asked the young judges from Beijing, Shanghai and other big cities if they would leave. Their answers were circumspect. But judges from these courts conveyed a palpable sense of pessimism about the prospects of retaining the best judges to stay within the judiciary. Judge Chen said the judiciary was not well equipped to retain the most capable judges, especially male judges among the group, who are subject to heavier financial pressure in a Chinese society. Limited as they may be in financial rewards, she said there was satisfaction in being a frontline judge in China, though economic pressure was not to be overlooked:

> I can't say for sure [about leaving]. I'm also thinking about how to resolve this problem (laugh). If you think you have some abilities, and if you have expectations about how much money you make, then leaving [the judiciary] is a logical choice. But in my court, I feel that many of us want to improve, want to do a better job. To many of us, money is not the most important consideration. Otherwise, you wouldn't join the court in the first place. You want a decent salary that's enough to support yourself. But the salary cannot be too low; that's particularly the case with men. They have more practical considerations – supporting their family, buying a house, etc. They need money.

The comments from Judge Chen and others suggest that the problem of brain drain is going to be a chronic problem for the courts to deal with. Judge Zhang, who worked in a city court in Pearl River Delta, was also noncommittal about her future. She said, smilingly, "The situation is like I have a boyfriend whom I like. You ask me if I'm going to marry him. It'd certainly make things a lot easier if this boyfriend I like happens to be rich." Of course, *relatively* low pay for judges is not unique to China. In many jurisdictions, judges earn less than lawyers with similar years of experience. Examples include Hong Kong, a special administrative region of China that adopts the Anglo-American style common law system, and European countries such as Germany, which has a system of bureaucratic judiciary comparable to that of China. Two points, however, should be emphasized. First, the rapid expansion of the market economy in China has pushed the salary gap between Chinese judges and lawyers to the extreme. In Hong Kong, a judge may earn a quarter or a fifth as much as a counsel with similar years of experience. In China, a successful lawyer working for a successful domestic Chinese firm or for a foreign law firm in Shanghai and Beijing can easily earn over 1 million yuan a year, but a judge who works in the court of the same region may still earn less than 100,000 yuan a year. And the gap continues to widen. Second, in the Anglo-American system, successful lawyers move laterally into the judiciary to become judges. The importance of autonomy and freedom associated with judicial work is an important factor that motivates judges in the United States and Britain to choose to work in the judiciary (Bell 2006:106), a factor that is absent in China.

SIMMERING INTER-COHORT TENSIONS

How are the post-1980 judges viewed by the senior and older judges? There are certainly tensions between the post-1980 and their seniors. It is a phenomenon that has become increasingly known among the public. A Chinese movie, "Courthouse on the Horseback" (Liu 2006) was made to explore the differences between judges old and young. In a sense, tensions between older and younger officials are common in every hierarchical system. The tensions are created in part by the different positions occupied by the two groups in Chinese-style bureaucratic hierarchy (Walder 1986). But the tensions are even greater in the case of the courts, because many of the young judges are far more educated than their older, more senior colleagues. It is a classic conflict between hierarchy and knowledge (Gouldner 1954).

Senior judges said the post-1980 judges should unlearn and then relearn as a judge. Judge Xiao, aged 40 and now a vice president of a grassroots court in Guangdong, described the adjustment she made as a college-fresh graduate in the 1990s:

> We were shocked when we heard about our professor's lecture on the principle of separation of powers. Our professor very much bought into the Western ideas of judicial independence and talked about the role the judicial played in a political system. Of course, the first day you began to work as a judge, you immediately noticed that the situation was very different. It was just impossible to just practice what you were taught in university.

Judge Xiao advised that college graduates today adjust themselves, as she did back in the 1990s, to work as a judge. But college graduates who join the courts today are facing a different institutional milieu from that faced by their predecessors who joined in the 1990s. Back then, college graduates were the minority, even in courts in big cities such as Guangzhou and Shanghai. Nowadays, the new post-1980 judges are more uniformly well educated. They see themselves as the new standard of the Chinese judiciary. This was pointed out by Judge Tan, a veteran judge who has worked in a big-city court in Guangdong for twenty years:

> When I entered college in 1988, there weren't a lot of college graduates back then. And there weren't many college law graduates recruited by the courts. They were people who didn't have a bachelor's degree, or they didn't study law in college. People were more diverse. Nowadays, in our court, for example, you need to have a master's degree to become a judge. New judges today are way more qualified. They have more professional knowledge. They have a lot of their own ideas. When I worked as a clerk, I was simple. I dared not raise my own opinions. I just followed what the older judge asked me to do. The new judges today, they have personality. They have their own ideas. They would say: "This is different from what I think. I disagree." We didn't do that back then.

Other judges in middle-management ranks are more critical about the "ivory tower" quality of legal education in China.[13] Judge Jian from Zhejiang, himself a division head, had this to say about the post-1980 judges: "New judges today all graduated from college. They received proper academic training but they lack actual experience. Our college education is pretty problematic. New judges know all the legal concepts but their abilities to handle actual cases are surprisingly weak." From the perspective of older judges (aged 40 and above), the new generation of judges is both over-educated and under-skilled. They know legal concepts well, but they do not know how to practice law that works for the greater good of the society. Judge Jian, who has worked in his court for over 20 years, added:

> Some older judges received no formal education. They don't have the necessary professional knowledge. But nowadays many new judges received seven to eight years of legal education, four years of undergraduate education in law and then three more years of master's degree in law. In my opinion, our laws are not that complicated. I personally think that seven years is too long. Many of them have learned too much. A few years ago, my court recruited over 30 judges, 22 of them were women, and 18 of them had a master's degree. And then they would still work as a clerk for a few more years before they could handle cases on their own. The whole process takes too many years. Five years of education would be more than enough to make them a good judge.

Judge Jian's comment also pointed to an interesting phenomenon in the basic-level courts of China. The requirement of college education and the use of the judicial examination have produced a lot more female judges than in the past. While official statistics are lacking, our observations of grassroots courts in difference provinces seem to suggest that more women than men are working as frontline judges. We also heard, during the course of our fieldwork, from some women judges that their courts favored men over women in recruiting new judges, since it was more difficult to recruit men than women.

Other middle-aged judges told us that better credentials do not necessarily make competent judges. "Young judges today are college-educated, yes. But the overall quality of judges is still not so good. We monitor our young judges. We ask old judges to lead our young judges. We need that. Young judges need to be taught," said Judge Liang, aged 45, a vice president at a grassroots court in Jiangsu.

Some senior judges were of the view that young judges should stay in school for a shorter time but spend more time working as clerks before taking up the responsibility of judging. Judge Fang, aged 40 and a division head in his court in Shandong, said the post-1980 judges have too much theory but not enough practice: "Theory and practice should complement each other. Theory without practice is empty." Judge Fang added:

> I think judging is a profession that requires experience. In my view, there is a difference between old and young judges. Back in the old days, before the judicial examination was in place, when I entered the court in 1987, I was a clerk for seven, eight years. I did things like recording, filing, contacting litigants and so forth. I had no right to speak in the court and no power to make decisions. I only did administrative

tasks. But during that time, I was like an apprentice learning from the master. I learned gradually through my working as an apprentice. But after the installation of the judicial exam, you now only need to work (as a clerk) for two years, and if you pass the exam, you can be a judge. Young judges nowadays lack real experience.

When asked what kind of practical experience the post-1980 judges lacked, Fang elaborated: "For example, an old judge may be able to tell if litigants are lying from their demeanor, attitude, facial expressions and bodily gestures. But young judges are not able to discern. They only know how to analyze written evidence. There is a real difference between young judges and older judges."

We have already heard from young judges about why they privilege documentary evidence over oral testimony. What appears to them as a measured approach toward evidence is, in the eyes of one of their seniors, a weakness. Judge Fang thought that China today needed more old judges to stay but not young judges to join: "There are many old judges in the US and Hong Kong. We in China retire judges at 60 for men and 55 for women. But judges are different from bureaucrats in other administrative departments. They are like medical doctors. Experience is important for making the correct diagnosis."

DISCUSSION

A new set of bureaucratic traits is gradually developing among the post-1980 judges. They bring in some normative external criteria, drawing from what they learned in university and from their exposure to how things are done in Western legal systems. Some nascent practices promoted by the post-1980 judge, such as the emphasis on legal research and a deliberate reluctance to pay too much attention to oral evidence, have changed the way judging is done at the grassroots level, particularly in more economically developed urban areas. As a group, the post-1980 judges' beliefs have imposed cultural limitations on the kind of administrative logic that has dominated the Chinese judiciary since its very inception.

This cultural attitude is not to be overlooked. Sociologists such as Bendix (1949), Gouldner (1954) and Selznick (1949) have long emphasized in their classic works that the effectiveness of bureaucratic rules turns on human attitudes toward them. The post-1980 judges' aspiration is to become more professional, in the sense of being dominantly guided by the laws and technically savvy about the law. They question the bureaucratic rules laid down by their senior colleagues.

This cultural attitude comes from a sense of the professional image of a judge that is starkly different from the old bureaucratic image of adjudicators (审判员 *shenpanyun*) or security cadres (干警 *ganjing*). Recall Judge Lin's comment that she wanted to become a judge after watching the performance of a robed judge in Hong Kong dramas. Of course, one might ask, what does this kind of professionalism actually mean? What does it actually amount to? To many of these young judges who inhabit the lowest rung of the bureaucratic hierarchy, adherence to legal rules can be seen as a strategic response to their subordinate role and the many constraints their subordinate role brings. But as we have seen from the responses of judges themselves, there are also intellectual and value preferences in favor of a more principled way of applying the law.

That said, many of the judges do not aspire to become wielders of political power (which is a logical consequence of the upholder of a more expansive notion of the rule of law). In interviews, none of them talked about what the content of the law should be. Their aspiration is to work for a system in which economic, social, and even state behaviors can be regulated by law, whatever the content of the law is. In an important sense, what they say is no different from what we have heard from generations of Chinese leaders since Deng Xiaoping – a stronger authority of the law.[14]

But even this adherence to the formal rule of law (regardless of content) has created tensions for the post-1980 judges with the outcome-oriented management of the courts. At the end of the day, there is a fine but strong line connecting the rule of law and form of governance, a line that many young judges are aware of. Judge Xue from Guizhou, whom we cited earlier, said that this question ultimately is a question of the value of the authority of the law. He suggested that in today's China, the authority of the law is promoted mainly for instrumental reasons. In other words, the outcome-oriented thinking is not only a mentality held by local officials but also a thinking that has been part of the central government's official discourse on law. He made the following perceptive observation:

> There is a balance that we are asked to strike between following the law and promoting social harmony. A certain piece of law can be very definite and clear. If you adjudicate according to the law, the outcome might contradict things that are now promoted by the central – for example, the emphasis on mediation and social harmony.

The responses of the post-1980 judges and middle-aged judges conform to the classic responses of exit, voice and loyalty that Hirschman (1970) famously identified as responses to organizational change. Some younger judges choose to "voice," and some of them choose or contemplate "exit." The middle-aged judges exhibit a much stronger sense of loyalty to the courts, but the major exception in this case is that the two cohorts of judges seem to hold distinctively different, at times conflicting opinions on what is the right direction for the courts going forward. In the long run, as the veteran generation retires and the middle-aged generation gradually fades out, the post-1980 judges will become the core of the judiciary. Their professionalized vision of law is likely to become more dominant, as the even younger, post-1990 cohort share a similar ideal of law. This suggests that firm-type courts, or at least a firm-type mentality, will become stronger in the future. We will return to this question of the future of the courts in the concluding chapter. In the next four chapters, we will discuss the four types of embeddedness that shape the unique character of judicial decision-making in China.

4

Administrative Embeddedness: The Vertical Hierarchy of Control

The court is an institution whose nature is difficult to clearly define. It is in part a government bureaucracy and in part a professional institution (Shapiro 1981). Courts are funded by a government's money. Judges are paid by the government. They enjoy salaries and perks that are on a par with those of other public servants. And, by and large, they have stronger job security, in the form of lifetime tenure. Yet the judiciary is often described as quite distinct from other government departments. Judges are servants of the law. They are bound by legal values that together make up their elusive ideal of the rule of law.

The complexity of the dual character of the court is reflected in the vast literature devoted to specifying the meaning of the tricky concept of judicial independence. Among legal scholars, Shetreet (1985) has proposed a way to distinguish the concept of judicial independence that is discussed in the literature. Shetreet sees judicial independence as involving two key aspects: external and internal. External independence refers to the relations between the judiciary and other branches of government. Internal independence is about guarantees aimed at protecting individual judges from undue pressures from within the judiciary (fellow judges and, above all, superiors) (Shetreet 1985:637–638).

The distinction between external and internal independence is often used to make sense of how Anglo-American courts different from their Continental European counterparts. The Anglo-American model of court views judicial independence primarily through the lens of internal independence (Guarnieri and Pederzoli 2002). Professionally speaking, a typical common law judge works independently, some even say lonely. He probably is appointed after years of practicing as an advocate. He is recruited for a specific position (e.g., a high court judge), and promotions are not widespread. He is his own boss; there is relatively little control of him from high-ranking senior judges, e.g., an appellate court judge. A senior court of appeal judge can of course reverse the decision of a lower court judge, but other than that, the two seldom cross paths in the everyday operation of the court bureaucracy. In fact, Anglo-American courts are commonly perceived as decentralized and fragmented.

In contrast, the Continental European model of court tends to approach judicial independence differently. According to Guarnieri and Pederzoli (2002:66–67), European courts conform to a model of bureaucratic judiciary that has the following defining elements:

1   Selection of judges is made on a technical basis through examinations at a young age, usually immediately after university, with little or no emphasis placed on candidates' previous professional experience.

2   Training takes place primarily within the judiciary.

3   A hierarchy of ranks determines organizational roles. Advancement up the career ladder is competitive, and promotions are granted according to formal criteria combining seniority and merit. Hierarchical superiors have wide discretion in determining merit.

4   There is a generalist approach to work performance and role assignment. Judges are supposed to be capable of performing all organizational roles associated with their rank (for instance, to be able to adjudicate criminal, bankruptcy, family law, and fiscal cases, or to act as a public prosecutor), and at the same time to compete for higher positions. Judges are therefore recruited not for a specific position but for a wide set of roles, and in the course of their careers judges will tend to change jobs often. This in turn makes guarantees of independence more problematic because of the influence that hierarchical superiors (or in some cases the government itself) have over these moves.

As a result, individual or internal independence tends to be weaker in a Continental court. As members of the bureaucracy, junior judges are subject to more control by their superiors.

What about Chinese courts? Where are they situated in the spectrum, i.e., with Anglo-American at one end and Continental European at the other, as defined by the courts in liberal democracies? Chinese courts clearly conform more to their European than to their Anglo-American counterparts. Not only is the independence of individual judges de-emphasized in China, the decision-making process is in fact designed to deter the making of decisions by frontline judges alone. Decisions are made collectively through the work of the bureaucratic hierarchy. The dominance of the bureaucracy is a shared attribute between the European and the Chinese courts. But there the resemblance ends. There are important differences between two; one cannot simply describe the Chinese model as "Europe-lite." At the most basic level, for those who have seen Chinese judges at work, it is fair to say that their styles are different, and their habits and practices are quite at odds with the stereotypical European bureaucrats that one might have in mind.

In Chapter 2, we discussed the daily rounds for frontline judges. We identified, in other words, the job components of frontline judges. In this chapter, we go further to explore not just what these components are, but how they relate to each other. To do so, we need to see how their daily work is linked back to the institutional structure of the court. We employ Weber's concept of bureaucracy as a benchmark for heuristic purposes. We do not suggest that Chinese courts conform to Weber's concept; no actual, existing bureaucracies do. Weber's conceptualization of bureaucracy sees it as the archetypical modern institution (1978:1111). And the concept allows us to see in what aspects and in what ways the Chinese courts deviate from this rational model of organization. In his writing on bureaucracy, Weber identified a list (or lists) of key features common to formal systems of administration. The relative importance of these characteristics and their relation to one another has stirred much debate (Markoff 1975). The difficulties of exhaustively defining bureaucracy are well known. What we are going to do is highlight the most important aspects of Weber's conception of bureaucracy in order to specify schematically how the Chinese judicial bureaucracy operates. We confine ourselves to the key items that we consider most relevant for our study.

What follows is a discussion of the mode of governance of the Chinese courts. The discussion provides a clearer view of why the Chinese courts are embedded in different networks of power, and at times, caged into particular authority relationships.

1 HIERARCHY OF COMMAND

Hierarchy is among the most distinctive features in Weber's conception of bureaucracy. It is also the most commonly discussed feature among sociologists who adopt the concept of bureaucracy in their research (see, for example, some of the foundational works in Constas 1958; Hall 1963; Stinchcombe 1959; Udy 1959; see also Albrow 1970; Beetham 1996). For Weber, a bureaucracy is superior to traditional forms of organization (e.g., collegial bodies or kinship networks) because of its ability to break down complex problems into manageable tasks coordinated under a centralized hierarchy of command (Bendix 1977). Each official is answerable for his/her performance to a superior (Beetham 1996:9; Blau 1968).

Like the Weberian bureaucracy, the court emphasizes hierarchical control and supervision. This should not come as a surprise. The court is the quintessential hierarchical authority structure. The appeal system central to all modern judicial systems is the prototypically hierarchical mechanism: higher courts are capable of reversing decisions by lower courts. But for Chinese courts, the appeal system plays only a secondary role in the institutional hierarchy. Hierarchical authority is manifested primarily through the court's internal administrative structure. This administrative structure is a tight, interlocking hierarchy made up of rank (级别 *jibie*) and job position (职务 *zhiwu*). A judge of higher rank occupies a job position that supervises a judge of lower rank. It is built in a pyramid shape, with clear, distinct layers of judges that make up the hierarchy. The hierarchy is set up to relay decisions from the top to the bottom. Vertical supervision is the designed goal.

TABLE 4.1 *Basic Three-Tier Vertical Hierarchy of Supervision*

Collective organ	Highest-ranking officials present
Collegial panel	Presiding (most senior) judge
Divisional meeting	Division head
Adjudication committee	President/vice president

Formalized structures are devised for sifting information from below to senior officials higher up in the hierarchy.

A three-tiered reporting system is in place in every Chinese court to oversee judicial decisions. As shown in Table 4.1, at the lowest level is the collegial panel. As the basic unit of adjudication, it occupies the first rung of the ladder of vertical supervision.[1] As mentioned, there is the presiding judge (审判长 *shenpanzhang*), the responsible judge (承办法官 *chengban faguan*) and a third judge who plays a usually passive, at times merely cosmetic role (see Chapter 2). The presiding judge is the most senior judge in the panel and the one who supervises. The responsible judge is the one who actually prepares for the court hearing and drafts the case ruling. For cases that are routine and straightforward, the responsible judge is expected to rule on his own. In that case, the panel conference becomes a formality. But if, by his assessment, the case is not progressing as smoothly as he expects, or if there are potentially controversial issues that emerge in the course of adjudication, the judge is obligated to report the case to the presiding judge. The reporting system is set up to ensure that a judge engages his presiding judge (usually a deputy division head or division head) as early as possible. Even if the responsible judge fails to report, the presiding judge is supposed to monitor the situation and alert the responsible judge.

For problems that are potentially more serious, the presiding judge will report the case to the more senior judges in the next tier up the structure (see Table 4.1). This is done either through direct reporting to the head (庭长 *tingzhang*) of the division or at a divisional meeting, which is made up of all judges in a division. Divisional meetings are not part of the official organizational structure, but are found in bigger grassroots courts. Cases that deserve attention are discussed at the meeting, with the input of division head and deputy head, as well as judges with more years of experience. It is also at the divisional meeting that judges decide if a case should be reported further up the hierarchy. Divisional meetings play a more important role in determining which *civil* cases will be reported up the chain. With criminal cases, many are still vetted by the adjudication committee. That is particularly the case in work-unit type courts.

The adjudication committee (which is made up of the president, vice president and other senior judges of a court) is the highest decision-making body of a court. The problem cases that deserve the most attention are reviewed by the adjudication committee.[2] Gauging or anticipating the controversy a case might potentially generate is a matter of political judgment rather than legal analysis. It is an exercise that senior judges are keen to monitor, particularly if the responsible judge is inexperienced or has a tendency to want to make decisions on his own. Courts in general prefer to deal with problem cases early and prevent them from escalating. As judges reported in interviews, the idea is, "Don't let small disputes grow to become big disputes."

Table 4.1 presents the basic structure of monitoring for the courts of China. This three-tier framework by no means exhausts the hierarchical nature of supervision and control within the Chinese judiciary. Vertical monitoring goes beyond the bureaucratic establishment of the grassroots court to that of the intermediate court and the high court in the hierarchy. A superior court may initiate independent general inspections and also review of specific cases (Grimheden 2011:109). But within a single court, this three-tiered structure makes up the basic hierarchy that supervises and controls the decision-making process. This is the structure that Chinese courts at all levels share, from the SPC down to the basic-level courts in districts or counties. Reporting and monitoring also stretches beyond the judiciary. There are consultations between the court and other local party-government officials, including members of the police and the procuratorate, as well as the local CCP's Political-Legal Committee.

How far a case goes up the hierarchy depends on a wide range of factors, including those in the following, non-exclusive list: case type (administrative and criminal cases are more likely to be reviewed than civil cases), claim size (the bigger, the more likely), litigants' makeup (Is the litigant prone to disruptive or violent behaviors? Is an influential state-owned enterprise (SOE) or the local government involved?), protest element (Does one party use the case as part of a social campaign?), media coverage (Are the media all over the case?) and the nature of the dispute (certain topics, e.g., land-taking, or environmental protection, are more conflict ridden; see He 2014; Stern 2013). It bears repeating: just like other courts in the world, a great majority of the cases handled by the Chinese courts are routine and straightforward. The use of "summary procedure"(one-judge format) has become the dominant mode of trial for many grassroots courts in the country's different regions (Cai 2014; Yan 2013). Routine cases are commonly tried by a single judge and the decisions are final (see Chapter 2).

2 PROFESSIONAL EXPERTISE

Bureaucracy, in Weber's ideal-typical description, bases its recruitment and promotion upon technical competence. This distinguishes bureaucracy from other organizations that recruit by means of personal retainers, unpaid amateurs, and elected officials (Weber 1978:973). A bureaucrat is a person who is duly skilled at the domain of knowledge in which she specializes. She is credentialed. To what extent is the Chinese judiciary made up of personnel who are professionally competent? We can examine the question by looking at two things: firstly, the recruitment system for new judges; and secondly, their system of internal promotion.

As Peerenboom points out, for a long time, judges' lack of technical competence was a more serious problem for the courts than were limitations on judicial dependence (Peerenboom 2002:289). The system has made great strides in raising the educational qualifications of its new judges. We discussed this at length in Chapter 3. Here a summary will suffice. Within a relatively short span of two decades, the judiciary has put in place a much more professionalized body of judges serving in frontline positions. In 1979, there were about 59,000 judges in China, most of whom were drawn from the military and communist party with minimal educational qualifications. In 1995, the Judges Law went into effect. The law required that new judges have either a law degree or a university degree with special legal knowledge. It also required that acting judges who were army retirees without formal education receive extra legal training (Liang 2008:65).

The Judges Law of the People's Republic of China was further amended in 2001. All newly recruited judges are required to "have obtained the qualification through the uniform judicial examination of the state and are best qualified for the job" (Article 2). For nearly two decades, new judges recruited into the judiciary have passed the uniform judicial examination. On top of the uniform judicial examination, they are all required to pass the civil service examination, which was reinstated in 1994 (Yang 2014).[3]

This double-examination requirement substantially raised the qualifications of judges. By 2005, there were more judges who held college degrees than did not (Liang 2008:206). Yet while the recruitment and training of judges have become more professionalized on paper, there remain complaints about judges' lack of expertise in more technical areas of law (e.g., commercial law, see Gu 2009). Judges' expertise also varies greatly across different regions, a point we alluded to in Chapter 1 and will return to later.

Making judges more qualified is the first step toward building a professional officialdom. The next step is to promote the best among them based on the criteria of professional competence. Here, the system's resemblance to the Weberian ideal is more limited. Promotion of lower-level judges is now more merit-based. When a vacancy is available in a promotion grade, it is openly advertised and qualified judges can apply. The courts adopt a system of promotion that is based on competitive examinations and assessments of judicial work (based on evaluation by senior judges). The rules for appointment, promotion and conditions of service are similar to those of other government bureaus.

When it comes to the promotion of senior judges, the selection process is murkier. "Senior judges" are judges with administrative power in the court, including court presidents, vice presidents, and division heads. Chinese courts do not follow a straight and exclusive line of promotion from within. Moving in and out of the judiciary is rather common for those who move up the ladder. Many of the most senior judges in the system today have worked in other party-state organs before returning to, or simply landing in, a senior position. This is one of the biggest differences between the career path of Chinese and European judges. Both are bureaucrats, yet European judges follow a well-defined and exclusive career path that is not seen in their Chinese counterparts. The socialist tradition of law sees law and politics as going hand in hand. In the CCP's view, this is shown by the coupling of politics (*zheng*) and law (*fa*) in the party committee – hence, the powerful Political-Legal Committee (Saich 2015). The idea of an exclusively judicial career is inchoate in China.[4]

Furthermore, if we compare the European and Chinese models of judicial appointment, the latter lacks the institutional organs that, to various degrees, carry out the self-government of the judiciary in personnel matters, institutions such as *Conseil Supérieur de la Magistrature* in France and *Richterwahlausschuss* (judicial selection committee) in many parts of Germany. Judges of a Chinese court are appointed by the corresponding local people's congress (Balme 2010; Gu 2015). Article 11 of the Judges Law states that while the presidents of the people's courts at various levels are elected or removed by the people's congresses at the corresponding levels, the other judges, including the vice presidents and members of the judicial committees, shall be appointed or removed by the standing committees of the people's congresses at the corresponding levels, upon the suggestion of the presidents of those courts. Given the symbolic role played by local people's congresses, this means that, in practice, the appointment of senior judges is in the hands of local political leaders. Hence, the nomination of the president is normally determined by the general secretary of the local party committee (Keith et al. 2014:106–107).

In the game of judicial promotion, the higher the rank to which one is promoted, the less professional credentials matter (Zuo 2010, 2014; Wang 2015). Though the central policy is to promote professionalism, professional credentials are not a necessary qualification for appointing the leaders of the courts. The Judges Law stipulates that the president and the vice president, the two "leader positions" of a court, can still be selected from people who have not taken the uniform judicial examination or have not been legally trained.[5] At the apex of the system, political consideration trumps professional qualification, as reflected by both the design of the appointment system and some actual appointments made. One obvious example was former SPC President Wang Shengjun. Wang, who presided over the highest court of the country from 2008 to 2013, received no formal legal training but spent most of his career as a senior bureaucrat in the CCP Political-Legal Committee. The part-professional, part-political appointment system is a lens through which to view and understand the mixed, at times contradictory character of the Chinese judicial system. The judiciary has become more professionally competent, yet at the same time it has to remain politically dependable. Its recruitment and promotion systems create a hybrid mobility regime that takes both political capabilities and technical expertise into consideration (Walder et al. 2000). As seen in Chapter 3, one consequence of the Chinese-style appointment system is the creation of a judicial personnel system wherein frontline judges are professionally more qualified than their supervisors, and those supervisors are in turn more qualified than their own supervisors. This, as we argue, has become a source of tension inside many Chinese courts.

There is also a growing gap in educational achievement and placement test performance among applicants for probationary judgeships in different parts of China, between firm-type courts in big cities and work-unit-type courts in rural hinterlands, though, formally, both are grassroots courts at the bottom of the hierarchy. Many grassroots courts located inside the major cities of China – Beijing, Shanghai, Guangzhou, Chongqing, Nanjing, Tianjin, and others – now require, as a rule, that applicants for the deputy judge post (the entry position) have a master's degree on top of a bachelor's degree. In other words, a fresh college graduate is not even qualified to *apply* for the job.

The situation is starkly different for work-unit courts located in the inland and less economically developed parts of China. Courts there constantly fall short of their recruitment targets. There are not enough qualified candidates who pass the judicial examination, despite the lowered passing marks set by the SPC for candidates there. These courts largely adopt the policy of 先进后考 (*xianjinhoukao*), recruiting yet-to-be-qualified candidates and then hoping that they will be able to pass the examination within a couple of years after joining the courts.[6] Yet the policy does not seem to have achieved the desired result. In the province of Shaanxi, none of the early recruits from seven grassroots courts were able to pass the examination (Wang and Zhong 2010).

The use of a single nationwide examination has created a perverse incentive that galvanizes the most qualified candidates to work in big, firm-type courts and drain people away from the peripheral provinces. Drawing from his study of grassroots courts in southwest China, Xiong (2014b:17) makes the following remarks:

> [The] so-called improvement of the qualification of judges seemingly does not benefit southwest rural China. On the one hand, in the underdeveloped regions of China, the fact remains that qualified judges are still very scarce. For example, in P County Court, there are only six judges who have graduated from formal law schools and around ten staff members who have passed the judicial examination. On the other hand, the uniform judicial examination may even worsen the judicial human resource situation in southwest China. That is because a successful candidate, who passes the uniform judicial qualification examination, will be awarded a certificate that is nationally valid. This certification will open another door to young judges and clerks newly graduated from universities, allowing them to pursue their dreams of practicing law in the modern cities where they may have more opportunities and a higher income. This may worsen the unbalanced distribution of legal human resources between urban developed China and rural underdeveloped China.

The gap in the credentials of judges working in the two types of courts has grown bigger in recent years and will likely continue to do so under the existing policy (Liang 2008; Xiong 2014b). While the proportion of legally qualified judges already reached 77 percent in Guangdong in 2001, some local courts in Shanxi province did not have one single judge who held a college degree in 2003 (Liang 2008:206). This is a problem acknowledged by the Supreme People's Court in its annual reports. Yet no easy solution is in sight.

3 PROCEDURAL SPECIFICITY

Allegiance to specific procedures and rules is another hallmark of bureaucracy (Weber 1978:220–226). A bureaucracy develops well-established procedures for dealing with various work situations and clear, albeit sometimes cumbersome rules covering the responsibilities of positional incumbents (Weber 1978; Hall 1963). To what extent is the Chinese court bureaucratic in this respect? In the above section on hierarchy of command, we talked about how Chinese courts adopted a three-tiered reporting system to carry out hierarchical control. Here we revisit the tiered system with a different question in mind: What are the procedures and rules that guide judges to determine which cases to report?

Not all cases are subject to extensive scrutiny. In a typical, basic-level court, the procedure before finalizing the outcome of a case depends much on the responsible judge's recommended action. A judge is almost always welcome to ask litigants to settle or withdraw in civil cases or to reconcile in criminal cases. These outcomes do not require reporting to superiors. Mediation and reconciliation are safe because by definition, they require the consent of the litigants. But if a judge decides to adjudicate, she is obligated to report the case to the presiding judge of the collegial panel or to her division head. In work-unit courts, it is common practice for superiors to sign off on a judge's ruling before issuing it to the litigating parties.[7] If necessary, the case is discussed in the divisional meeting. If a case is a problem case that requires further review and consideration, the responsible judge and her division head will send it up to the adjudication committee.

Judges who face an unpredictable institutional environment of judging tend to report decisions on touchy cases to their superiors, who in turn would further report them to their own superiors. This process of kicking the can down the road, or up the bureaucratic ladder, is intended to make sure that potentially contentious decisions are sufficiently reviewed. Frontline judges also want to make sure they are not the lone person responsible, should litigants protest against the outcome. The shared desire for reporting among frontline judges and their seniors suggests that institutionally, the Chinese judiciary is agnostic to the idea of internal independence.[8]

In an intermediate court, the rules governing to whom a responsible judge must report are even more intricate, since its decision is, purportedly, final. The operation of an intermediate court reveals most clearly the complex bureaucratic rules required for different possible outcomes. Judge Lin, from an intermediate court in Guangdong, describes what she does:

> I will first write a preliminary opinion based on my analysis of documents and the proceedings. This document is called an adjudication report (审理报告 *shenli baogao*). After the report is written, I will then find a time to discuss the case with the two other judges on the panel. Ideally speaking, I will probably give the other two judges the adjudication report and other case-related documents two days before the meeting. When I give them the documents, I will briefly state what is being disputed in the case. They will then have about two days to read the materials before discussing whether to agree with my opinion. For cases that are not too complicated, our discussion usually takes about one hour or even shorter. But, for complicated cases, we will have to hold several discussions. For instance, the other judges might tell me that some of the facts are not clear and need to be further clarified.
>
> When a consensus or a majority opinion is formed, I will draft the judgment. I will then submit the draft to the presiding judge of the panel. If my decision affirms the opinion of the basic-level court and a consensus is established in the panel, the presiding judge will just sign off on the document and the ruling will be issued. But, if the presiding judge thinks that the monetary stake is large, he might choose to consult the deputy division head to review the case, even if our decision affirms the original judgment. The deputy division head can sign off on it if he agrees that the original judgment should be affirmed. If the prior decision is affirmed, the deputy division head will typically not send the case to the division head.
>
> But, if there is a reversal, that is, a change is made to the judgment of the first-trial court, or an order for retrial, the case must be presented to the division head. This is specified in the internal regulations of our court. These regulations dictate which kinds of cases need to be sent to the deputy division head, division head, and vice president, or presented to the adjudication committee for discussion. Sometimes the vice president may be swamped with cases. In that case, a member of the adjudication committee may help review cases before they are sent to the vice president.
>
> Currently, for cases that are sent back for retrial, they are typically signed off by the vice president. The vice president may even bring the case to the adjudication committee. This is because a retrial order means that the lower court judge has made a "serious mistake" in handling the case. These cases have to be reviewed by the vice president to show that the higher court takes this very seriously.

Judge Lin's account outlines the complex reporting mechanism adopted by her intermediate court. The mechanism is complex because it is outcome-dependent. For a typical case, a judge has four options before her: affirm a decision, modify it, reverse it, or send it back to the first-trial court for a retrial. Affirmation is routine. It happens to the majority of the decisions (higher for criminal cases than civil cases;

TABLE 4.2 *Decisional Outcomes and Levels of Review for Appeal Cases in Intermediate Courts*

Nature of pending decision	Seniority of the judge who signs off
Retrial	Vice president
Reversal/modification	Division head
Affirmation (large sum of money at stake)	Deputy division head
Affirmation	Presiding judge

see Zhu 2011). An affirmation is procedurally simple. The presiding judge is authorized to sign off on her own. If substantial money is at stake, the deputy division head may have to sign off on the decision to affirm. Modification and reversal are not as routine. In official statistics, the two are often lumped together as "amended decisions." To modify or reverse the decision of the lower court carries an element of adversity to the original decision. The person to approve, this time, is of a higher rank. Not the presiding judge, but the division head is asked to sign off on a reversal or modification. The most adverse option is an order for retrial. A lot of judges described that as "a slap in the face" of the first-instance judge and his superiors. Such an order is not to be given lightly. It is to be signed off by an official near the top of the hierarchy, a vice president, or in some cases the president. And the person entrusted for making the decision has to weigh the risks involved. If the risks are too great, she might decide to send the case to the adjudication committee. Table 4.2 shows that how far the collective consultation process has to go depends primarily on the nature of the pending decision.

The judge's account offers a fine-grained picture of the various procedures that a judge follows before issuing a certain decision. Does the complexity make Chinese courts a legal bureaucracy that is procedurally meticulous? The courts are clearly bureaucratic in terms of their procedural elaborateness. The question is whether this is a *legal* bureaucracy. Judge Lin's account highlights the use of vertical hierarchy. How far up a case should go is governed by rules that differentiate cases from an *administrative* rather than a *legal* standpoint. What triggers the sending of a pending ruling to a vice president rather than a presiding judge? It turns on the administrative impact of the pending decision. Of course, there is nothing wrong with being more prudent when dealing with adverse decisions. However, the legal nature of a case – e.g., whether a novel legal argument is involved or a new factual situation is dealt with by the law – factors little into the process. Not once in her detailed account did Judge Lin mention legal technicality as a factor in determining whether a pending decision should be further reviewed.[9] It is the potential repercussion of a decision, not the complexity of the legal argument on which it is based, that determines what bureaucratic procedure to follow.

Within this administrative system, appeals have assumed a strong disciplinary quality not found in the similarly bureaucratic European courts. No judges like to have their decisions appealed or reversed. However, from an institutional standpoint, the appeal mechanism serves as a channel for introducing some self-correcting elements into the judicial system. Appeal is also a means for promoting coherence and uniformity across different levels of courts. Other judicial systems with a structure as centrally hierarchical as China's re-examine a substantial portion of lower court decisions (Damaska 1986; Shapiro 1981; Guarnieri and Pederzoli 2002:81). By comparison, the rates of appeal in China are noticeably low. Over 90 percent of cases do not progress past the trial of first instance (Zhu 2007). The low numbers for review are less a reflection of the overall quality of the rulings than the tremendous efforts made by judges to avoid appeals at all costs.

The disciplinary nature of appeals is reflected in the fact that appealed cases are subsumed under the heading of "incorrectly decided cases" and are a criterion for performance appraisal (Minzner 2011a; Zhu 2011:55–60). A reversed decision is the second-most severe form of administrative sanction (second to an order for retrial). To avoid reversals and retrial orders, judges engage in the practice of advisory request, or 请示 (*qingshi*) in Chinese, to proactively solicit the views of higher courts. Judges may request advice formally in writing, but more often do so informally, by phone. *Qingshi* has been a common practice for decades. Even today, it is informally practiced by many lower court judges, despite the stated policy of the SPC that consultation should be infrequent and should be made formally between one court and another court (Minzner 2011b; Zhu 2011; Liu 2006:93–94). Sometimes judges would choose to consult senior party-state officials outside of the judicial hierarchy for truly politically contentious cases (see Zhang, Hongtao 2014).

So, is judicial decision-making in China governed by procedures and rules? On the surface, it appears so. But the Chinese courts are different from a legal bureaucracy in two crucial ways. First, rules and procedures are primarily administrative; they are created and used for administrative reasons. The driving motivation for an internal vetting of a pending decision is risk management. Though the Chinese court is procedurally specific, its bureaucratic logic is governed by administrative concern rather than legal consideration. The legal-technical quality of the process is further undermined when informal *qingshi* is used to minimize the use of appellate review. Legally speaking, the higher court is in a position to review the decisions of a lower court, but *qingshi* remains primarily a type of *subformal* or *personal* communication that "can be easily withdrawn, altered, adjusted, magnified, or cancelled without any official record being made" (Downs 1967:113). It undermines the legal purpose (and enhances the administrative nature) of an appeal mechanism if the lower court makes it a habit to informally consult higher courts for every controversial case.

ADJUDICATION COMMITTEE AS A BUREAUCRATIC ORGAN?

Our first order of business was to examine the Chinese court as a bureaucracy. The analysis above suggested mixed results. Our next task is to closely examine the adjudication committee, widely known as the "cabinet" of the Chinese court. The adjudication committee is by far the most powerful organ of any Chinese court. Decisions on important and controversial cases are without exception reviewed by the committee. Yet it is quite secretive in its operation. It is a court within a court. How does the adjudication committee operate? What rules and procedures, if any, does it follow? Is the coordination between senior and junior judges regular and routine? Most important, does it operate like the apex of a bureaucracy that bases its decisions on rules, or does it operate more like the papal conclave, whose decisions turn on networks and powers? Examining the decision-making process of the adjudication committee gives us a sense about how senior judges assess the decisions made by frontline judges and what factors matter most in given situations.

Let us present a fuller list of the key attributes of a bureaucracy as identified by Weber. The characteristics or dimensions that are typically ascribed to the concept are useful diagnostic tools for evaluating the institutional nature of the adjudicative committee. A bureaucracy tends to operate with the following key features (Weber 1978; Bendix 1977:132; Hall 1963):

- clear hierarchy of authority that defines the power of each member, which is defined by his/her position within a bureaucracy
- scope of power of the bureaucracy clearly defined, often prescribed in written regulations
- work of a bureaucracy fits its declared purpose
- clear division of labor
- separation of office from incumbent, in the sense that the employee does not own the "means of administration" and cannot appropriate the position
- appointment and promotion are rationalized, in the sense that expertise is emphasized and officials are picked according to merit
- impersonality, i.e., work is conducted according to prescribed procedures that minimize the degree of arbitrariness or personal influence
- rules are set up to govern behaviors of incumbents and to minimize influences that deviate from the organizational goal of the bureaucracy
- developed filing system and written records to allow decisions to be reviewable
- clear procedures for decision-making

Understandably, no actually existing bureaucracies conform fully to the list above. This list is better viewed as formulating a series of dimensions, each in the form of a continuum (Hall 1963). In comparing the adjudication committee to Weber's list, we can get a clearer idea about how it fits or deviates from the characteristics that are typically ascribed to bureaucracy.

The adjudication committee exists in the courts at all levels, from the highest Supreme People's Court to the grassroots courts at the basic level. The genesis of the committee can be traced to the 1930s, in the communist settlements in rural China during the revolutionary period. According to historical records, the committee was set up because adjudicators at the time had little professional training and because policies, guidelines, directives and statutes were difficult to apply. To ensure the quality of justice, it was better for a committee to make a collective decision based on majority rule (Wu and Liu 2005:19). The committee was later incorporated into the judiciary of the PRC as the decision-making body for important and difficult cases (Article 10 of the Organic Law of People's Courts).

The Organic Law also describes the operation of the adjudication committee (or "judicial committee," in the official translation) as a practice of "democratic centralism" and says that its task is to "sum up judicial experience and to discuss important or difficult cases or other issues relating to judicial work."[10] While the specific role of the committee is never quite spelled out in the three major procedural laws of the PRC (the Criminal Procedure, Civil Procedure and Administrative Procedure Laws), it is no secret that the committee reviews and rules on the most complicated, controversial and significant cases (Cohen 1997, 2006; Su 2000). A typical adjudication committee is made up of senior judges of a court, including president, vice presidents, division heads, the local procurator and sometimes some specialist committee members.

BACKGROUND

The court we studied is located in Shaanxi, an inland province located in the western part of China. About a third of its 430,000 residents live in the countryside. The economy of the region grew during the initial stage of the reform period, but by 2008, the income per capita for rural and urban residents had reached only around 4,000 and 14,000 yuan, respectively. Since 2006, the courts have heard about 3,000 cases annually, most of which were civil, criminal and enforcement. Overall, the jurisdiction of the court is of medium scope for China's lower-level courts (see Zhu 2007:218).

We examined the minutes of the court's adjudication committee. The minutes offer a rare first-hand look at its actual mode of operation.[11] Our report here was based on careful examination of two handwritten volumes from 2009 that contained the minutes of deliberations on all the reviewed cases.[12] At the time of the research, this was the most recent year in which the grassroots court had already processed most of the cases of the year. Some of the decisions were being appealed. The minutes were intact. Page numbers ran continuously and were consistent with the table of contents. It was clear that no cases had been removed because of their sensitivity or other concerns. Compiled manually and threaded together through punched holes, the minutes were supposed to be kept indefinitely. For each case, there was a cover page, the upper half of which recorded the time, venue, attending members, reporting judge, and recorder. It was followed by letter paper of the court if the other half of the cover page could not accommodate the discussion content. The poor quality of the letter paper reflected the court's limited financial resources.

For each of the cases discussed by the committee, the minutes invariably included the following: the subject matter of the case, the draft opinion provided by the responsible judges, and the committee's decision whether to affirm or overrule the opinion. They also recorded the speaking order of the case discussion, including the persons who concluded. But they were not a verbatim report. Indeed, as we learned from subsequent interviews with judges, the committee members seldom read the minutes after meetings. The purpose of the minutes was mainly to record the decisions taken by the committee.

Attending members did not sign on the minutes individually. This seemed to conform to the principle of collective responsibility. Individual signatures assume individual responsibilities. But if the decision is viewed to be of a collective nature, participating members are not held individually responsible. Nor were voting records included in the minutes. According to the Organic Law of People's Courts, the decision of the committee shall follow the majority rule, so one would expect to see voting records. The fact, however, seems to be that the committee rarely formally voted. As shown in the minutes, most decisions were reached by consensus, even though in some cases, there were debates right up to the moment when "consensual" decisions eventually emerged. As we will explain, this was only possible because of the hierarchical nature of the committee membership. To put it bluntly, the president always has the final word. A "consensus" would invariably form around his view, which then made formal voting superfluous.

COMPOSITION OF THE COMMITTEE

Let us take a closer look at the composition of the committee. The committee makeup deviated from that of a typical professional bureaucracy. The committee was made up of the president, the vice presidents and the division heads of the major adjudicative and enforcement divisions; it also included the disciplinary inspector of the local party (纪检组长 *jijian zuzhang*). The inspector was appointed because he represented the local party leadership (党组成员 *dangzu chengyuan*) who were treated as *de facto* court leaders. Its composition showed that it was no different from other party-state institutions, blending political personnel with bureaucrats. Another deviating feature was its indefinite terms for the members, which suggested there was no strict separation of office and incumbent (Weber 1946:196–198). Indeed, the terms of these judges are usually for life, and replacements have been rare. Once appointed, a judge would not be removed except for illness, retirement or leaving the court. One original head of Civil Division Number 1, for example, kept the appointment when he was transferred to the enforcement bureau as the vice director, a position not typically associated with the committee membership. Another division head also kept the appointment after retiring from the position. For the adjudication committee we studied, membership has become an individual's power asset.

SCOPE OF REVIEW

While the adjudication committee is said to review significant or complicated cases, there are no statutory definitions on the meanings of "significant" and "complicated." This arrangement leaves the individual court to have much discretion on its own list of reviewable cases (see, for example, Pengzhou Court Net 2004).[13] In the case of this Shaanxi court, it interpreted "significant" and "complicated" cases broadly, a common tendency found among work-unit type courts. A non-exhaustive list of cases that fell within the definition includes cases that a judge or panel could not resolve through consultation with immediate superiors, cases that the president or the vice presidents regarded as needing further discussion, cases involving local institutions or powerful figures, bankruptcy cases and administrative adjudication cases. In addition, the following types of criminal cases were reviewed: cases involving suspended sentences, exemptions from punishment, acquittals, monetary fines, institutional crimes, corruption and serious criminal cases that might invoke ten years or more of imprisonment. Among civil cases, the list covered those involving government agencies, mid- and large-sized enterprises, foreign-invested enterprises, class actions, migrant workers, newly emerged cases and disputed amounts of money in excess of 3 million yuan. Finally, there is still the catch-all provision – "other cases or questions the adjudication committee regards as necessary." Procedurally, there are two routes through which a case is selected for review: one is direct determination by the court leaders, including the division heads and the (vice) presidents; the other is initiation by the collegial panel or the responsible judge.

From 2008 onwards, the court has required that the judge who reported a case submit a written report prior to the meeting. The report describes the basic facts of the case and the recommended action (or verdict) of the judge or her panel. The reporting judge is asked to join the meeting when her case is discussed. She is there to present the case report; in particular, she is asked to justify her proposed decision. She also answers questions, but does not participate in the discussion.[14] She leaves the meeting as soon as the discussion of her case is over. Once a decision is made by the adjudication committee, the reporting judge will photocopy the relevant part of the minutes and attach the copy to the case file as an appendix. The appendix is for internal records only. It will not be made available to litigating parties or the public. The minutes are classified as adjudicative secrets (审判机密 *shenpan jimi*), which are archived in separate dossiers known as 附卷 *fujuan* (cf. Li 2012:861). Her

TABLE 4.3 *All Cases Reviewed by the Adjudication Committee in the Shaanxi Court* (2009)

Types of cases	No. of cases handled by the court	No. of cases reviewed by the committee	Upholding rate	Modified rate	Opinions sought from higher courts	Others	Ratio of the type of cases to all reviewed cases
Criminal	375	363	54.52%	40.77%	0.55%	4.13%	84.42%
Civil	1,401	48	58.33%	8.33%	14.58%	18.75%	11.16%
Administrative	8	5	60%	20%	20%	0%	1.16%
Enforcement	716	14	57.14%	0%	42.85%	0%	3.26%

Note: Upholding means that the committee upheld the suggested (majority) opinions of the adjudicating judge or the collegial panel.

TABLE 4.4 *Suggested Opinions Modified by the Committee in Criminal Cases*

Cases changed	Main penalty changed	Supplementary penalty changed	Both changed
148	30 (24 increased)	51 (monetary; all increased)	67 (46 increased)

judgment will reflect the committee's decision. For the court we studied, a judgment that comes from the adjudication committee always begins with the standard line "According to the decision of the adjudication committee of this Court."

CASES REVIEWED

In 2009, the committee held 47 meetings, almost one each week, of which 46 discussed cases. In total, it reviewed 430 cases. In most situations, the meetings lasted for a morning. Most cases were handled relatively quickly because the committee discussed, on average, more than nine cases in each meeting. On average, each case was discussed for approximately just 20 minutes.

As shown in Table 4.3, the vast majority of cases reviewed were criminal, with a modest number of civil cases. The committee also reviewed all of the administrative adjudication cases and some enforcement cases. But, similar to what Liu (2006) documents in another lower-level court in northern China, only a few administrative cases were filed, reflecting the tremendous difficulty of administrative litigation in China (Pei 1997; Peerenboom 2002). Amongst these few administrative cases, even fewer survived the stage of formal adjudication. Many were withdrawn or settled due to the pressures of the government agencies and the efforts of the court in persuading both parties to compromise. When some of them (five in the year) eventually made it to the committee, the issues were more procedural than substantive. It usually involved the approval of the committee, for example, of the government decision on compulsory housing demolition, which invoked little discussion. Similarly, enforcement cases were mostly reviewed by the committee for formal procedural reasons. The core components of the committee's work were the criminal and civil cases, to which we now turn.

CRIMINAL CASES

Criminal cases constituted the overwhelming majority of the cases reviewed by the committee (84.4 percent). The dominance of criminal cases in the committee was even more extraordinary, considering that criminal cases were a minor category compared to civil cases, which made up the bulk of the court's caseload.[15] In fact, for the court we studied, almost all of the criminal cases on its docket (96.8 percent) were reviewed by the adjudicative committee.

The practice of reviewing virtually every criminal case is not merely *pro forma*. The committee modified almost 41 percent of the suggested opinions of the adjudicating judges, a much higher rate than the equivalent for civil cases (8.3 percent). The committee tended to increase the penalty, and especially the fines for the defendants (Table 4.4). Among the 51 cases in which only supplementary penalties were changed, all of the fines were increased (by 1,000 to 10,000 yuan). The same pattern could also be found in the cases with suspended sentences. For the 103 cases suggested for suspended sentencing, the committee upheld 96 percent of the suggestions, but changed 42 percent of the cases on supplementary penalties, including the probation period, suspended duration and fine. Once again, the changes for fines were generally unidirectional; more often than not, they were raised.

Contrary to official expectations, the committee did not focus on developing generalized rules or principles for its judges to follow. Instead, it became a regularized component of the adjudication process, reviewing cases that were by conventional standards routine, even trivial. What the committee did was a form of quality control. It made fine adjustments. This can also be inferred from the duration of discussion on each case: it seems improbable for the committee to have engaged in in-depth lengthy debate of legal points within an average time frame of about 20 minutes per case.

Second, among criminal cases that were modified, the committee's changes clearly skewed toward heavier punishments or greater fines. In one injury case, for example, the collegial panel suggested a three-year sentence, but suspended for four years. Three members agreed with the suggested ruling, but another three believed that, since the injury was severe, a suspended sentence should not be adopted. The final decision followed the suggestion of the president: "In my personal view, it is okay to award suspended sentence. For this sort of case, settlement (between the defendant and the victim) shall be encouraged. In this case, the defendant already compensated the victim, and it just reaches the standard of severe injury. It is fine to lengthen the suspended sentence to five years."

From our interviews, we gathered that this almost unidirectional raise in punishment was in part economically motivated. Underfunded courts have an interest in raising fines. Indeed, insufficient funding has been a chronic problem for courts in less-developed areas. We will return to this in Chapter 7. Suffice it to point out here that the court made it a policy to fine convicts whose offenses did not mandate imprisonment. In one case, the minutes recorded what the president said: "The defendant gets a penalty below the stipulated sentencing level, so he shall pay some fines. If he does not pay, eight years will be imposed; otherwise six years."

If the court wanted to impose heavier monetary penalties to increase its income, wouldn't it be easier to for the president to directly instruct frontline judges to do so? The answer goes back to the hierarchical mode of supervision that has been the *modus operandi* of the work-unit type court. The adjudication committee – or, more precisely, the senior bureaucrats of the court who made up the committee – was keen to know what disputes and conflicts transpired in criminal cases. Grassroots courts are most concerned about social unrest in the district or county under its watch. Input from the highest level is part of the regular process of monitoring from above. Leaders do not want to get "blindsided." This type of micromanagement serves as a survival strategy for senior judges facing an uncertain environment of judging.

From the standpoint of individual members of the committee, any effort to increase the penalty of the defendants is seen as clean, above-board, and thereby safe. The criminal trial has long been an area in China that is susceptible to bribery and corruption. Some criminal defendants or their family members are willing to offer bribes because of the prospect of imprisonment. Meanwhile, the court has greater room to maneuver because victims in criminal trials do not have a direct stake in the punishment decisions, at least in less-serious cases where life imprisonment or the death penalty is not involved. In most cases, a victim is not particularly concerned whether a defendant receives a shorter imprisonment of two years as opposed to three years, or a fine of 5,000 yuan as opposed to 10,000 yuan (Li, Ling 2010:218). The situation is different in civil cases, however.[16]

CIVIL CASES

The committee reviewed 48 civil cases in 2009, among which only four suggested opinions were changed. In other words, 8 percent of the civil cases reviewed had their suggested opinions changed. The committee also decided to seek written instructions from upper-level courts for seven cases. The committee upheld the suggested opinions of the responsible judges in the majority of the cases (58 percent). Very few of these cases involved intricate points of law.

Compared to criminal cases, the committee took on a more discerning approach when reviewing civil cases and ordering changes. This was related to the nature of the civil cases that were sent to the committee. The adjudication committee reviewed, by comparison, a small set of civil cases. These cases can be broadly grouped into two categories. The first were "significant cases," that is, cases that involved external influences or pressures from powerful parties. Judges would tell us that they know a significant case when they see one. One example was a straightforward "breach of contract" dispute. The plaintiff, a local enterprise, had the support of prominent political leaders. He refused to settle with the defendant, which was a company based in X province. The plaintiff was absent from several court hearings.

The responsible judge went to his office and begged him to sign the court documents. When the committee reviewed the case for the first time, the court leaders, already under heavy external pressure, urged the judges in the collegial panel to return a decision for the plaintiff. But the plaintiff remained unhappy with the proposed decision. When the case went up to the committee for the second time, senior judges made a further compromise to placate the plaintiff by agreeing to change the judges who served on the panel.[17]

The second category was made up of cases that the adjudicating judges requested for committee review. There were cases that were, in the view of the responsible judges, simply risky to adjudicate. They were cases in which, as reported by Yang (2010), "the facts are complicated, the litigants are emotional, which may lead to adverse social consequences." Responsible judges sent these cases to the committee, not because they held different opinions from their immediate superiors nor because the legal issues were too complex for them to decipher, but because they were concerned about what would happen *after* the ruling was issued. Regardless of who won and who lost, litigants from either side would likely appeal, and petition or even protest.

A bitter case of divorce illustrates this kind of judicial Catch-22 scenario dealt with by the committee. A wife filed for divorce. Her husband contested it. The relationship between the two turned rancorous. The wife left home; the husband looked for her throughout the city. He became mentally unstable. While the wife said she would die for a divorce (死也要离 *si ye yao li*), the husband said he would die if divorced (离了就死 *le li jiu si*). The law was clear and straightforward on the subject: the court would grant divorce to couples whose emotional relationship was broken. But the law offered no help to deal with the emotional standoff of this couple. The responsible judge denied the petition when the wife filed for divorce for the first time, but she filed again six months later. While divorce would customarily be granted for a second-time petition (He 2009a), the adjudicating judge felt uncomfortable with the prospect of doing so.[18] She sent the case to the adjudication committee, alongside her recommendation for a rare second denial. The committee upheld her proposed ruling. Nobody wanted to take the blame if the husband committed suicide.

The case highlights a few things common among civil cases submitted to the committee: they are legally and factually straightforward; in terms of money, not much is at stake, for this court at least; litigation parties are often dead-set on their demands. In this case, it would be emotionally ravaging to either the wife or the husband to be the losing party. It would be difficult for the court to enforce judgment against either one. Forcing the issue might provoke violent behavior. Judges are well aware of the predicament. In submitting their cases for review, they are not looking for better solutions or additional insight. They are buying political insurance.

Political insurance comes in two forms. First, having the case reviewed by the committee offers the responsible judge a modicum of protection by the principle of collective responsibility. At the very least, her responsibility would be, in part, shared by other committee members who endorsed her proposed judgment. A judge said in the interview, "If a decision is made by a single judge, he or she is 100 percent liable for the decision. If it is made by the collegial panel with three judges, then only one-third for each." As we will see, there is a limit to how far the collective principle can take the heat off a responsible judge, especially now that frontline judges are supposed to assume "lifelong responsibility" for the cases they decide (Zhang, Xinbao 2014). Nonetheless, while the presence of committee review does not completely banish risks, it does offer some form of insurance. Second, the act binds the senior judges of the court. If things go wrong, these judges could not just throw the responsible judge "under the bus" and say, "Look, she should have approved the divorce."

The difficult and uncertain nature of the civil cases reviewed is the main reason the committee rarely disagreed with the rulings proposed by responsible judges. Senior judges on the committee are playing cat-and-mouse with their subordinates. One who advocates for a new solution puts himself "on the hook." If the new solution backfires, the member assumes the hot potato from the responsible judge. In contrast, endorsing the recommendation proposed by the responsible judge involves lesser risk: the responsible judge is the first one to fall (see Chapter 5). Finally, unlike criminal cases, civil cases in most work-unit courts involve much less opportunity for judges to benefit from the litigation parties, a fact understood well by everyone in the court. Subsequently, the committee members do not need to "prove" that they are clean.

WHOSE OPINIONS COUNT?

Existing studies suggest that the discussion of the committee follows a set pattern: first, the responsible judge reports, then the report is followed by members' questions. The president does not speak until the end (Wu 2006; Su 2000). This sequence has also been stated in some court documents (e.g., Supreme People's Court 2010). It is a procedure designed to allow the president to evaluate the discussion without prejudicing it or influencing the views of individual members.

The minutes, however, indicated that this supposedly standard procedure was not always followed. Many cases were decided without much group discussion. The president just decided. We identify a few sequences in discussions that were held. In some cases, the head of the relevant division spoke first, followed the vice president who supervised the division. In other cases, the president or vice presidents spoke first. So there was no standard about who spoke first. What was common across these varied sequences was that once a leader (the president or the vice president of the division) proposed a solution, other members would concur and the discussion was virtually over. One judge said in the interview, "The rule is that the president shall keep silent until the end, but there is no way to enforce such a rule. When the president wants to have control, he'll simply speak first to set the tone. Can any other member stop him from speaking? Of course not." Another judge who has more than ten years of experience reporting cases to the committee agreed: "Even if the president speaks last, but when other members realize that his opinions differ from theirs, they would try to amend their positions to stay with him."

Analyzing the committee's decisions shows clearly the extent of the influence the president has over the process. Taking the criminal cases as an example,[19] among the 148 criminal cases in which the suggested opinions of the adjudicating judges were changed, 135 (91 percent) were changed largely according to the suggestions of the president, 11 (7 percent) were changed according to the head of the criminal division. Only 1.3 percent were changed based on suggestions by other members. It is clear that the president was the one who, to use a Chinese expression, 拍板 *paiban*, literally meaning "slaps the table" to signify a final decision.

The law states that the committee shall follow the majority rule and every member has an equal vote in the committee. Many adjudication committees hold roundtable meetings, a setup that symbolically suggests that members are of equal status.[20] In reality, the adjudication committee does not abide by the principle of collegiality (Weber 1978). The superordinate-subordinate status distinction is strongly reflected in the decision process. Who decides? Answer: The president and, to a much lesser extent, vice presidents.

Some more examples can be used to underscore the weight that the president's opinion carries. In a property dispute, the plaintiff sold her right to buy a work-unit-sponsored apartment to her colleague for 10,000 yuan in 2000, which was more or less the market price then.[21] But housing prices had tripled over the decade after the transaction. Relying on a law forbidding such transactions, the plaintiff asked the court to invalidate the transaction. Both parties, however, agreed that they had voluntarily engaged in the transaction that sold off the right. There were no clear rules on how the dispute should be decided. Both parties had connections with the committee members. The plaintiff, working part-time as a people assessor and well connected in the court, had support from all committee members but the president. When the committee reviewed the case, these members expressed their support for the plaintiff. If the majority rule was to be observed, the discussion should have ended with a verdict for the plaintiff. Then the president spoke. The president, who was connected to the defendant, refuted the others' position. He argued that invalidating such a transaction that was harmless to others and that had been completed a decade earlier was pointless and would have serious negative social consequences. He suggested seeking instructions from the intermediate-level court. That was the committee's final decision.

Table 4.3 shows that the percentage of cases that ended up with a decision to *qingshi* some higher court was not insignificant. The frequency with which this committee sought instructions from the intermediate court deserved further explanation. As we found out, seeking instructions from the intermediate court was a discreet way for this president to take control without appearing to be autocratic. From interviews, we learned that the president, before he assumed the current position, had worked as the head of the criminal division of the intermediate court. There were subformal and informal channels through which he could influence his former colleagues at the intermediate court that were unavailable to his subordinates. Soliciting the views of the court above was a roundabout way for this president to get the decision he wanted.[22] The move deflected the resulting resentment at his decision, as it was not exactly *his* decision. This tendency to "defer" to the intermediate court was, however, not followed by the president's successor (the current president), whose background was different. With no formal legal training and few connections in the court system, the current president preferred to have more decisions made by the committee. Despite the different procedural routine adopted, the new president shares with his predecessor the intention to steer the committee toward decisions that conform to his assessments, and in some cases, interests.

THE REPORTING PROCESS

The decision of the committee is based on the report given by the responsible judge. From interviews, we learned that many responsible judges devoted considerable time to preparation for their appearance at the committee's meeting. For those with the ability, it is an opportunity to articulate ideas in front of their superiors. They hope to show to their seniors how thorough and careful they research the material facts, apply the relevant law and consider relevant policy matters in the course of making a recommendation. They also want their suggested opinions adopted. If a judge's suggested opinions are frequently reversed, it is a vote of no confidence in the person's abilities. But frontline judges also understand well how the adjudication committee operates – it is dominated by the president and vice presidents. Some career-minded climbers tailor their opinions in anticipation of the outcome preferred by their superiors. This tendency to lay a brick path that leads to the president's desired destination further undermines the role of the committee as a professional collective decision-making body.

The long agenda of the meeting and the limited time the committee can afford for each case raise doubts about the quality of the discussions. Some judges might not be able to articulate the issues and facts of some complicated cases accurately. As observed by Wu (2006) and Yang (2010), sometimes even decisions of the committee may not be accurately reflected in the judgments.[23] Meanwhile, some judges complained that the questions raised by some members, especially those who had never adjudicated, were not professional. One of the judges interviewed said, "The only function of reporting is to educate some members." Another judge who often reported cases said, "I always hope that my case is placed at the end of the sessions. By then the minds of the members are muddled because they have been discussing cases for hours. So they will not raise many questions about my case and my suggested opinions are more likely to be upheld." Some reporting judges thus have taken advantage of this arrangement to manipulate the outcome (Yang 2010, Wu 2006:198–199).

ADJUDICATION COMMITTEE AS AN INSTITUTION

We are now in a position to offer an assessment of the institutional character of the adjudication committee. Table 4.5 summarizes how the adjudication committee fares against the benchmark of Weber's ideal type.

The adjudication committee, and by extension, the court itself, adopts a rigid structure of authority, one that is layered and hierarchical. Indeed, it is this aspect that makes the adjudication committee a bureaucratic organization. But in other aspects, the committee does not resemble a legal bureaucracy. Its operations do not adhere to the stated procedures. Voting seldom took place and decisions were usually unanimous, a testimony to the extent of the influence of the president. Some decisions that clearly defied due process were left out of the scrutiny of the committee. A judge with twenty years of working experience in the court said, "The most outrageous situation that I have encountered involved local protectionism, where I was asked by the court leaders to release the assets of a local enterprise already frozen by the court, upon the request of a Shanghai petitioner in an enforcement case. Such behavior was

TABLE 4.5 *Adjudication Committee as a Partial Bureaucracy*

Dimensions of bureaucracy	How adjudication committee fares	Remarks
Hierarchy of authority	Yes	An incumbent's rank determines his/her power.
Scope of power clearly defined	No	Committee reviewed more cases than one would expect from reading the law, but some cases were, interestingly, left out.
Work fits its declared purpose	No	Committee does not develop general principles and rules, but review cases on a broad but *ad hoc* basis.
Division of labor	Limited	Divisions oversee different areas of law, but president and vice presidents oversee operation.
Separation of office from incumbent	Limited	Members have indefinite terms.
Technically competence among participants	Limited	Senior judges are more administrators than professional judicial officials. Some local party officials are also members.
Clear procedures for making decisions	No	Actual practices indicate the principle of collegiality is displaced by monocracy.
Rules governing behavior of incumbents	Limited	As indicated in the minutes, extralegal consideration is often given in the deliberation process.
Emphasis on written record	Limited	Minutes did not give a clear account of deliberation process. They focus on outcome.

outright illicit, but the president, vice president in charge of our division, and the division head had all signed the release order and I had to follow suit." When asked why the issue had not been reviewed by the committee, the judge replied, "Those illicit requests are not appropriate for formal discussion."

Its composition also belies its publicized function of a legal decision-making body. The division heads are experienced adjudicators, but they have taken up so much administrative work that most of them are more court administrators than judges at this stage of their career. The situation is worse for presidents and vice presidents, some of whom parachuted in from outside to the court and have no adjudicative experience themselves. At the time of the study, among the eleven members of the committee, only four continued to adjudicate as judges.

The minutes also reflected that the committee paid more attention to the potential social and political repercussions of a contemplated outcome. Seeking instructions from the intermediate court and communicating with the local government and the party were frequent. Legal interpretation is an iterative process, involving interlinked cycles of lawmaking, interpretation and implementation, and reinterpretation based on the principles developed in the previous round of interpretation of implementation. But the committee does not contribute to general principles and rules that frontline judges can follow, despite the generally poor professional quality of its frontline judges.[24] In fact, developing general principles and delegating the authority to decide to individual judges would undermine the committee's *de facto* function of monitoring most of the criminal cases that arrive at the doorstep of the court.

Also lacking is a well-established mechanism to disseminate the committee's decisions to frontline judges.[25] The minutes show the decisions, but not the rationale behind them. Matters pertinent to the decision-making process are often classified. As such, the minutes are seldom checked and referred to by judges because they lack precedential value. The reasoning process of the committee remains opaque, not just for outsiders, but even for frontline judges. It is clear that the committee sees day-to-day supervision and risk management as more important than developing general principles and rules for judges to follow in the future. All of this suggests that the adjudication committee is more an *administrative* bureaucracy that turns on the power of rank rather than on the authority of professional expertise.

The adjudication committee is purportedly a legal-cum-professional bureaucracy. Ideal-typically, a professional bureaucracy is a structure of its own: officials are so conditioned as to confine themselves willingly and with technical competence to the decision-making process and the implementation of its decision (Bendix 1977:140). Prominent Chinese legal scholar Su Li (2000) certainly sees the committee as professional. He argues that the committee contributes to consistency in adjudication within a jurisdiction by bringing the specialized knowledge and experience of the committee members to bear on complicated cases. Su also suggests that the committee system creates a united front against external pressures and thus preserves the independence of the judiciary as an institution (Su 2000).

Yet our study shows that quite a number of the committee's decisions were made as a result of political influences from without. The minutes, as an internal document, were faithful enough to record traces of political influence, to show how local government and party officials influenced the judicial process. In many cases, the committee gave in to external influences, sometimes bending over backward to cater to the government and the party. For example, in housing demolition cases, a court approval is required before the government authority can enforce demolition without the owners' consent. In discussing one request by the local government, the president, as recorded in the minutes, said, "The compulsory enforcement is granted; prepare the decision, but wait for further instructions from the district party committee before delivering to the parties." A judge later explained to us: "This is to see if the party committee has a different opinion over the issue." From the political discernment he made, together with his many *qingshi* to the intermediate court for instructions, it is clear that the court's president played the role of a bridge linking the court to the local party-government coalition.

The priority of political over legal consideration explains why the committee reviewed 97 percent of criminal cases but only 3.4 percent of civil cases. For a system with a relatively straightforward set of procedural laws, criminal cases should not present many legal puzzles. The numerous reviews undergone by the committee were clearly motivated by the fact that this court, like most basic-level courts in China, examined criminal cases with a vigilant eye and was on the lookout for potential social unrest.

The motivation for frontline judges to report is similarly administrative. Judges report not so much because they do not know the law, but more so because they do not know what to do with the litigants. As observed by Wu (2006:196), many judges, when asked when a case would be submitted for review, responded, "When I need it [the committee] to share responsibility with me." If the committee upholds the ruling recommended by a responsible judge and that decision is later proven to be wrong (i. e., something goes wrong), her responsibility is somewhat mitigated because of the committee's endorsement (Yang 2010). A shared, and thus reduced, responsibility gives judges the incentive to not decide difficult cases by themselves (Balme 2010:156). Contrary to the intended function of improving the judicial skills of the adjudicating judges, the existence of the committee has in fact discouraged judges from improving themselves, or at least discouraged them from taking on responsibility.

MONOCRATIC STRUCTURE

Power is highly disproportionate among members of the adjudication committee. If one has to fit it into a subtype of Weberian bureaucracy, it would be the *monocratic* bureaucracy in which a "chief" enjoys supreme authority over his administrative staff (Weber 1978:272–277). A monocracy, in Weber's view, represents the negation of the principle of collegiality. The institutionalization of collegiality came in two historical forms. The first form is realized when a group of incumbents share the common power of veto. As we have seen in its actual practice, this is not the case of the adjudication committee. The president, as a monocrat, holds the veto power exclusively. The second form is more common and is how the adjudication committee is supposed to operate: when decisions are "produced by the cooperation of a plurality of people according to the principle of unanimity or of majority" (Weber 1978:278). More recent authors have argued that the collegial form is the dominating form of organization in professional organizations, universities and above all, courts in the Anglo-American context (Sciulli 1986; Waters 1989).[26] Perhaps one could say that the adjudication committee operates by the principle of unanimity. In the committee we studied, consensus was virtually the outcome in all of the cases covered by the minutes. Yet unanimity in this context was a reflection of the president's dominant power. Like other work-unit-type courts, the president holds great sway over his subordinates on things big and small, from getting a key to the court's car (to share with other colleagues) or being given a more capable clerk to being promoted to become a deputy division head or being allowed to move to a bigger intermediate court for career development. What we have identified in the work of the adjudication committee confirms a well-documented operating principle that permeates every level of organization of the court: administrative rank trumps expertise and collegiality.[27]

The monocratic character of the adjudication committee further lends weight to the argument that the court is a part of the local party-government coalition. The president is at once a member of that coalition and the leader of the court. His dominance means that political and economic considerations that dominate the agenda of the local governance coalition are factored into the judicial decision-making process. Yet the president is a prudent monocrat – that is, one who prefers to exercise his power judiciously. It seemed that his will was never defied. But the reverse was arguably true. He rarely overturned the recommendations of his subordinates. What he did was to tinker at the margins in most criminal cases. Among the criminal cases, even though the committee modified 40 percent of the recommendations by responsible judges, those modifications were not of a fundamental nature. As mentioned, most of the changes were made to raise the amount of fines or to extend the period of the order suspending a convict's sentence. Similarly, while it is customary for the committee to add a little to the period of a suspended sentence, it is rare for the committee to fundamentally question whether a suspended sentence is appropriate in a given case.[28] Seldom did the committee overrule a responsible judge's recommendation.

What leads to this stable state of affairs in the adjudication committee? Perhaps before formal discussions commenced, his subordinates have already anticipated what the president would want to do with many cases. They were either socialized into the president's way of thinking or had already been told of the president's preference through informal communications with other senior judges. The president was also keen to maintain this façade of collegiality. As shown, in cases where he preferred an alternative outcome, he would ask his subordinates to seek instructions from the intermediate court rather than push them through unilaterally (which he could easily have done). It is in everyone's interests, from the president to the responsible judge, that the principle of collective decision is "followed." That veneer of consensus offers committee members and responsible judges some protection. A member could claim that it was a decision collectively made, should things go wrong, though, as we will see in later chapters, frontline judges get less protection from this mechanism than do senior judges.

In any case, the role of the president is more of a gatekeeper. The president seldom overturned his subordinates' recommendations. He and other senior judges were clearly cognizant of the fact that they did not know a case as well as the responsible judge. Only in sensitive cases where the dissemination of information was differentiated by the hierarchy of ranks did the president need to explicitly make his intention known, as in some of the administrative cases discussed by the committee. He used his excessive power most sparingly so that it would not appear that he had an excess of power.

Finally, there is an element of a certain "clique culture" in the committee. The regular members of the committee constitute a power clique around the president. The clique culture fostered around the president contradicts the kind of impersonal systematization that bureaucratization is supposed to achieve. In some courts, such ties often blur the boundary between work and life in the Chinese context. Senior judges forge ties in dinners and social occasions with other local government officials. Some of them are badminton or tennis pals who share an easy camaraderie over their morning session before work. They are the "repeat players" in the game (Galanter 1974). In contrast, though frontline judges are not the classic "one-shotters," they are the outsiders looking in. The difference between the two groups in terms of one's ability to adopt optimal strategies and bargaining credibility makes the adjudication committee all the more a top-down administrative hierarchy.

PROTECTION OF THE ADJUDICATION COMMITTEE: VIEWS FROM FRONTLINE JUDGES

How do frontline judges react to the layered mechanism of reporting described above? This was the question we often brought up to judges we met during the course of our fieldwork. The question is understandably a rather sensitive one. Some judges talked about the topic in general terms. A typical answer would be along the following lines: "I think there is some merit to the mechanism." Some judges, particularly the younger ones, are more willing to discuss the issue. They are not shy to point out the problems.

Frontline judges deal with the bureaucratic practice of layered reporting to superiors on an everyday basis. From the perspective of the Anglo-American professional model of courts, the most obvious reason for objecting to hierarchical control is that it takes away individual independence. Judges working inside the hierarchy cannot rule on their own. But frontline judges in general do not resist the concept of supervision *per se*. Their grievance came mainly from their concern that sometimes supervision was not done in good faith. Younger judges also want more independence and that has become a source of tension within some courts, as seen in Chapter 3. Chinese judges, particularly those with more years of experience, see themselves as part of a bureaucracy. They are socialized into the idea of judging as a collective work. They accept this is the way Chinese courts operate.

Many of them however are realistic, some even cynical, about the integrity of the mechanism of reporting to their seniors. Some frontline judges believed there were glaring problems in the reporting mechanism. In a system where power is heavily skewed toward the top, even the most conscientious superiors can only offer protection for mistakes made up to a point, and for some less well-meaning superiors, abandonment is a convenient option.

As insurance, the extent of the protection offered by endorsement from senior judges and the adjudication committee is structurally undefined and at times quite limited. What an endorsement from the adjudication committee means is that the responsible judge would be given some leeway, and sometimes help, to deal with the party made unhappy by the decision the responsible judge recommends. It remains the job of the responsible judge to placate the disgruntled litigant. And if the person eventually decides to petition further or to appeal the case, it will be the responsible judge who bears the consequences. The case will become the proverbial strike that counts against him. It will be *his* perfect record of no appeal that is broken. It will be *his* yearend bonus that is deducted (though his colleagues in the same division might be affected too). If more serious fallout ensues, the responsible judge will be the first one to take responsibility. Surely if the backlash is strong enough to rattle the court as a whole, for example, when the public protests or when regional government officials complain, more people will be asked to go. Yet, the bottom line is, if things go sour, the responsible judge is the first to go. Judge Lin, who described to us how the collegial panel worked in practice, remarked: "Whoever approves the decision, the responsible judge is still responsible for the outcome of a case." In this aspect, the Chinese court operates in ways that are not that different from American corporations: blame moves from the bottom up, while credit flows from top down (Jackall 1988).

If we take a look at some of the cases that attracted a lot of public attention in recent years and see what happened to the judges who were in charge of these cases, it is not difficult to understand why frontline judges have no illusion about the limits to the protection that their seniors and the entire court system can offer. In the famous, or infamous, case of *Xu Shuolan vs. Peng Yu* in 2006, also known as the case of the "Unfortunate Good Samaritan," Xu Shuolan, a 65-year-old grandmother, stepped off a bus in Nanjing and fell to the ground. While others passed her by, Peng, then a 26-year-old student, rushed to her aid, accompanied her to the hospital and even offered 200 yuan to help cover the cost of hospital fees. Ms. Xu, the injured senior, returned the man's kindness by suing Peng for personal injury compensation, claiming he caused her fall. The Nanjing court found for Ms. Xu and held Peng liable for damages and awarded Ms. Xu 45,876.36 yuan (approximately $6,076 at the time) as compensation. This verdict received widespread media coverage, engendering public outcry over the controversial decision. The case was commented upon then by people as high up as Chinese Vice President Li Yuanchao, who was then the CCP Secretary of Jiangsu. The case was eventually resolved through the mechanism of grand mediation (Young 2013).

Much controversy was about the decision of the presiding judge, a Judge Wang. His published judgment was widely criticized by scholars and the media. After the fallout of the Peng case, Judge Wang was promptly transferred out of the court to a small "judicial office" nearby, which practically signified an end to his judicial career. Certainly his judgment had been reviewed and approved by his superiors, given the way the courts operate. But he was the one, at least according to public reports, who paid the price for it.[29]

The protection of the adjudication committee is also undercut by the complex game-theory-style considerations that individual members in the committee go through in order to minimize the risk they would bear. Indeed, one of the most surprising findings of our case study is that the committee we studied rarely changed the recommendations of responsible judges in civil cases. This contradicts the findings of earlier research that responsible judges cannot follow their own recommendations in controversial cases, and if they do, they put their careers at risk (see, for example, Zhang 2003:84). Our study of the adjudication committee in Shaanxi suggests that judges put their careers at risk by being asked to carrying out their recommendations in difficult cases. Whoever proposes an alternative shifts the burden of responsibility to himself. The person runs the risk of becoming the "fall guy." Even for a case of Peng Yu proportion, going along with the opinion suggested by the responsible judge is apparently the safe option. If the solution suggested by the adjudicating judge is later proven bad or wrong (as in the case of Peng), it is the judge who takes the blame.

As we have seen, this game of risk avoidance is also practiced by powerful court presidents and vice presidents. They too have to secure power against possible fallout. In controversial cases such as the well-publicized case of Li Chungkui's homicide in Yunnan, strong, emotional, vitriolic attacks were directed at the judges who made the controversial decision, but also at senior judges who came out to defend the court's decision (see Wang 2012). The lack of a strong tenure system is a reality that senior judges have to face. Senior judges know that their grip on power is perilous. "It takes just one real bad mistake to destroy a career," one senior judge in Guangdong said.

All in all, blame is first assigned to low-ranking judges (Liebman 2012:217). But frontline judges needs no reminders. At interviews, frontline judges take a very realistic view of the protection offered by the reporting mechanism within the court structure. Most of them do not detest it; but they understand very well that the protection offered by the reporting system extends only up to a point. They are still the ones who deal with the messy complications of difficult cases. And if those complications cannot be dealt with satisfactorily, they take the blame.

SIGNING-OFF OF DECISIONS BY SUPERIORS

The presence of administrative hierarchy goes beyond the official reporting mechanism that culminates in the decision of the adjudication committee. In many work-unit courts, other means of vertical control exist beyond the reporting mechanism. Cases that do not reach the committee are still subject to the monitoring of senior judges. This is done through the "signing-off" mechanism. The signing-off mechanism is an internal administrative practice that is not mentioned in the three procedural laws of China. It is, however, commonly found in work-unit courts. The practice requires a responsible judge to ask his superiors (usually the division head and the president) to sign off on his judgment before releasing it. The official release form is not included as part of the formal judgment when it is made public. Hence, litigants do not know who signed off on the judgment. In Chinese, the form is known as 司法文书审签笺 (*sifa wenshu shenqianjian*). It is a form that responsible judges use to get the signatures required to release their judgments. When the judgment is released, it is the responsible judge who alone has his signature on the decision. That means he alone is responsible. The internal, often unwritten nature of the process of signing off means that senior judges can often hide in the dark despite their strong influences on the outcome of a case.

The form is a single-page document made up of two halves. At the bottom half is a short summary of the case drafted by the responsible judge. The top half is further divided into two parts. On the right upper quarter are the comments and signature of the division head. On the left upper quarter is the signature of the president or sometimes the vice president of the court. The signature of the responsible judge occupies the right lower quarter, at a position below the case summary. Again, the hierarchy of authority and power is materially manifest in the layout of this simple, one-page form. The signature of the president occupies the most prominent space of the upper left quarter.

In some work-unit courts with strong hierarchical control, signing off is more than a matter of formality. A judgment drafted by a responsible judge has to be signed off by both the division head and the court's president. Even though the president would just write down a simple Chinese word 发 (*fa*), meaning release, it is a required procedure that senior judges in this type of court take very seriously. Some presidents revert back to the traditional character, i.e., 發, which appears to be more authoritarian. If anything, it has more strokes, which makes for a more complicated, and usually bigger character. If the judgment were not released straightaway, then the president would recommend that it be reviewed by the adjudication committee instead.

Insofar as administrative hierarchy involves supervision by and submission to superiors, its introduction undermines any solidarity that might have developed vertically among judges of different ranks. This seems to be particularly the case for work-unit courts in inland provinces, where hierarchical control is most rigid and entrenched (Balme 2010). The lack of trust is reflected in the fever of enforcement that some senior judges show when signing off on judgments they receive from subordinates. These senior judges approve their documents not just by personal signature, by but the use of a paging seal (it seems to be a practice common in Chinese societies), that is, a seal is stamped across the margins of each page of a document. The idea of putting the seal on the margins is to prevent a judge from replacing certain pages of a judgment without approval. The practice is indicative of a lack of trust among senior judges and the subordinates they supervise. It is also a practice that can easily become a source of nepotism and power abuse. At the very least, this practice can become a source of tension between frontline judges and their superiors. Judge Zhu, a deputy division head who worked in a base-level court in Shaanxi, said, "I had a colleague who did not get along with his division head. He submitted his draft judgment but the head sat on it for two months. Later, he came up with a record book himself and asked his division head to sign upon reception of his draft judgment. The head of course refused."

Sitting on a judgment for two months causes a case that was on pace to close within the target deadline of three months to become "late." The example shows that superiors hold great sway over the constitution of the performance-related numbers of a judge. This kind of discretionary power gives superiors the "chips" with which they could bargain to secure cooperation from frontline judges, particularly for those who are mostly concerned about how those numbers affect their performance evaluation. It also provides the superiors with the power to punish insubordinate judges if necessary.

BLUE PENCILING

Some senior judges do not just sign off on the judgments; they exercise what journalists would call the "blue pencil." The extent of blue-penciling varies. Some superiors were sticklers for perfect grammar. They would perform the job of a copy-editor, fixing typographical errors and grammatical mistakes. Other superiors were overly careful. They would double-check the law for their subordinates, making sure that the right law was cited.

But in some cases the extent of blue-penciling goes beyond fixing clerical mistakes. Some judges said their superiors had made substantial changes before agreeing to sign off on a judgment. Based on what we gathered from interviews, it seems to be the case that when these changes are needed, senior judges often choose to communicate their intent verbally. They avoid making the changes on record. Communication of this kind defies the boundary separating formal and informal communications. Its content is formal but its form is discreet and circumspect. It renders the process of blue-penciling even more invisible, since it leaves no traceable paper trail.

Frontline judges said they were often "instructed" discreetly by their seniors. Once a case gets beyond the level of collegial panel and gets the attention of the people higher up in the hierarchy, the advice that they receive is always intricate and often obscure. This is particularly so with difficult civil cases. Judge Zhou who worked in an intermediate court from Shaanxi, said:

> My boss tends to say things in a rather circumspect way. That is the Chinese way. Of course, that doesn't mean he has no power. He's way up there. He's like a king. He could have been direct. He could have been blunt.

Judge Sun also said senior judges seldom issued direct and clear instructions. He said, "In my years working as a frontline judge, I never heard my leader say 'You should do this' or 'You should do that.' They won't say that. They would just tell me: 'Handle the case prudently.'"

The coded expression "Handle the case prudently" requires some elaboration. It is a classic way for the senior judge, or in fact any boss, to push down details to protect the privilege of authority to declare that a subordinate has made a mistake when necessary. Robert Jackall, in his study of the world of corporate managers, noted that corporate CEOs tended to give similarly vague instruction to their subordinates: "Give me your best thinking on the problem with [X]" (1988:20). The use of oblique language attenuates the responsibility that a senior has to bear if things go wrong. The senior could come back and tell the responsible judge, "You didn't handle your case prudently enough." In short, when a responsible judge and her seniors disagree on how a case should be ruled, this process of blue-penciling potentially puts the judge in a double-bind. If the junior judge should disagree, she would not get the signature required to issue her judgment. But if she should agree, it would be a judgment under her name, even though it is not exactly *her* judgment. The responsible judge is thus set up to be "sandbagged" should something go wrong, to be the one who takes the heat for others' decisions. After all, the rule of thumb is: the responsible judge is responsible for any consequences. We can see how this process can be open to abuse. When judges talk about interventions from their superiors, invisible blue-penciling is the most extensive kind. The judge from Shaanxi recalls a rare, candid, direct quote from her superior that is all but discreet: "I once heard a division head say the following in a division meeting: 'When you sit on a trial, you report to me, I report to the president. We always report to our superiors. Don't try to think that since you're the judge, you can make the decision. If that's the case, what's the point of having me as the head?'"

Judges are under pressure to maintain a reputation for being team players. They have to choose between the hard-won trust of the management of the court and insistence on their decisions. Other judges conceded that it would be difficult not to be "open-minded," not to be "flexible." "It is very difficult to insist on your own opinion when your division head or president asks you to reconsider. Very few people can do that. If you insist, you'll be left on your own," said Judge Zhu, the judge from Shaanxi.

But there is a minority of judges who said they considered insisting on following the law to be the better option. Judge Liao, a deputy division head who dealt with civil cases in an intermediate court in Yunnan said, "If a decision cannot be legally right and socially desirable at the same time, I choose following the law. I'll let my superiors decide if they want to violate the law." The judge added, "You know, I do this because this is my means of survival. If I violate the law and the social reaction is still bad, I'll be the one who will be hung out to dry. If I rule according to the law, I can at least say I follow the law. A leader can leave tomorrow; what he said to me, there will be no records. But if I rule against the law, it is on record and people know."

Judge Liao's response, rational as it sounds, might be perceived as "insubordination" or "uppityness." The judge believed he paid a price for his decision though: "I have been a deputy division head for eight years. I should have received a promotion. And that was because I did not follow my leader in some cases."

Other frontline judges we interviewed also brought up unnecessary interventions from their superiors. When judges refer to "unnecessary interventions," they point to interventions that are unrelated to consideration, even from the standpoint of administerization. These interventions have little to do with concerns about the well-being of a court. Instead, they arise as a result of other factors that contribute to the influence of social embeddedness: patronage, *guanxi* and corruption.

Judges often talk about their degree of independence in the form of a percentage. A judge would say, "I am 70 percent independent." To outsiders, this seems to be an odd way for judges to describe their job nature. For example, one judge from Guizhou, Judge Xue said he could be 65 percent independent. As we gradually came to understand, when a judge said he was 70 percent independent, that means about 70 percent of his cases were decided by him alone, without the input of the superiors. As for the remaining 30 percent, they were either sent to divisional meeting or adjudication committee for discussion, or were "blue-penciled" by his superiors.

It is ironic when judges describe their independence in terms of percentage. On the face of it, they seem to suggest "70 percent ain't so bad. Most of the time I'm on my own." Yet the answer suggests the contingent nature of their independence under the control of the administrative hierarchy. Perhaps one of the most poignant findings of our study is that judges' self-assessment of the culture of their own courts is not strongly legal-oriented at all. Chinese judges do not see their courts as particularly legalistic. Most of them believe that the law is just one among many factors that their superiors consider when making decisions. Of course, as we will see, frontline judges are sometimes perpetuators of social embeddedness themselves. Judges, as members of the Chinese society, are subject to socio-moral persuasion or peer-group pressure to mete out favor or to reciprocate. Trading their legal power for other social obligations and personal favors has been a persistent problem among frontline Chinese judges, as scholars have pointed out (Zhang 2003). The Chinese party-state acknowledges as much, as the Standing Committee of the National People's Congress repeatedly pointed out in its examination report on the implementation of the Judges Law and the Public Procurators Law that judicial incompetence and corruption were major concerns (Zhang 2011:256).

In fact, the signing-off mechanism described above was set up in part to address corruption at the grassroots level. But, as is often the case, a policy designed to address nepotism and power abuse would gradually, over time, become part of the problem itself. In organizational studies, this is the question of "guarding the guardians." For grassroots courts, it turns into a question of the abuse of one's supervisory role. We return to the problem in Chapter 6.

TRUNCATED HIERARCHY

Signing-off assumes a less prominent role in big, urban, firm-type courts. Judges from the busy courts in the big cities said in their courts, presidents and vice-presidents seldom signed off on judgments (unless cases were discussed by the adjudication committee). In fact, it was difficult to get them to sign off on a decision. They are too busy to do that. Some divisions require the division head to sign off. But it is also common for judges to sign off on their judgments themselves. "I'm the only person who signs on a judgment. I don't have to ask my division head to sign off on it before I release it," said Judge Yang, a frontline judge working in one of the busiest courts in Guangdong.

Judge Yang admitted that his division head was of the trusting kind, and he had a good track record at the court. But in Judge Yang's court, even if another division head signed off on their subordinates' judgments, the whole exercise was done more fitfully and perfunctorily. The process is truncated when compared to the layered signing-off process that is still practiced by work-unit courts in inland provinces. The judge said, "I know in some inland courts, a case that involves say 100,000 yuan is a very big case already. A case like that would require the court president to sign it off. But in my court, a simple loan case might already involve a few million yuan. The president will not have time to go through all these cases and sign them off. They won't do that." He further explained, "Our president and vice president never sign off on judgments that are not discussed in the adjudication committee. They don't have the time."

The truncated use of the vertical hierarchy is found in other firm-type courts. Judge Zhang, aged 30, who worked in another busy city court in Pearl River Delta, said, "The number of cases handled by one single judge in my court exceeds the number of cases handled by the entire staff of some courts in the inland region." She said an average judge in her court processed more than 400 cases a year. "My seniors won't bother to sign off on my judgments. I have to sign off on them myself," said Judge Yu, who works in another busy city court in Guangdong.

The primary reason contributing to the flattening of the hierarchy is the sheer volume of cases that firm-type courts handle. With bigger workloads also comes the reduction of vertical oversight and control that we saw in the more controlling type of work-unit courts. Firm-type courts still retain the vertical bureaucratic structure, but they create latitude within bureaucratic structures to promote efficiency. Senior judges in these courts cannot afford to devote the time needed to go through all the cases done by their subordinates.

CONCLUSION

Chinese scholars have pointed out the lack of distinction between the Chinese judiciary and other state bureaucracies. Among Chinese scholars, this is often characterized as the problem of administerization (行政化 *xingzhenghua*). The term itself, even in Chinese, is a rather awkward one. For historical reasons, it is, however preferred over the more obvious choice of 官僚化 (*guanliaohua*), the original translation of the English term "bureaucratization." As Whyte (1989:237) points out, the Chinese term 官僚化 or 官僚主义 (*guanliaozhuyi*, literally translated as bureaucratism) has long been viewed as politically incorrect.[30] The term was historically avoided for ideological reasons. Yet, it turns out that the term "administerization" captures, in a serendipitous way perhaps, quite accurately how the Chinese court deviates from a professional bureaucracy. This chapter shows how administrative considerations are built into the decisional hierarchy of the court, with the adjudication committee as its apex. This form of administrative bureaucracy resembles in some ways the kind of judicial bureaucracy found in civil law countries, in which judges enter by examination and ascend in the ranks according to seniority and merit (Abe 1995; Guarnieri and Pederzoli 2002; Solomon 2007). The judiciary operates like "a hierarchically organized civil service, more or less cut off from private practitioners, and with relatively close affinities and connections with the rest of the higher levels of the career government bureaucracy"

(Shapiro 1981:156). Junior judges' decisions are held accountable by judges higher up in the hierarchy through a system of close monitoring and evaluation.

Yet, what sets the Chinese model apart from the civil-law model is the embeddedness of the court in the local party-state governance coalition. Administrative calculations are an integral part of the judicial decision-making process. When deciding a case, the court does not simply apply legal rules.[31] In many cases, the following of legal rules is not the primary consideration.[31] Judges assess the risks of various options in the process of deciding the outcome of a case. The risk of a potential option is reflexively factored into the decision-making process. This mechanism of administrative assessment is layered and its distribution of power is unmistakably top-heavy. Formal procedures and rules are circumscribed at many points by the concerns and interests of external, powerful parties, the most important of which is the local party-government. As aptly put by Liu (2006:94), "[i]t is through the internal power structure within the court that external influences are capable to control the outcome of cases." In fact, from our perspective, to describe the local-government coalition as an external party fails to really capture the hand-in-glove relationship of the two. As shown, the president plays a dual role as at once the head of the court and an integral member of that coalition.

What distinguishes the Chinese court from the civilian bureaucratic judiciary is the extent of the day-to-day interactions between the judiciary and other party-state institutions in the case of the former.[32] The Chinese judiciary is openly part of the local party-government and is heavily involved in a lot of state actions, even before a litigant takes his case to the court (e.g., in the case of grand mediation). This is natural for a system that has traditionally valued mediation over adjudication. The primary function of the Chinese court, until the 1990s, was to resolve disputes through non-adjudicative means. When facing organized social protests and petitions, the party-state expects local courts to help by resolving disputes (Su and He 2010). Sometimes, the party-state wants to borrow the court's legitimacy to help "judicialize" an administrative process. This is the case in any administrative cases of compulsory enforcement, the majority of which are housing demolition cases.[33] The court is subject to the financial and personnel control of other, stronger institutions. Many local courts, particularly those of the work-unit type in inland regions, have no choice but to agree to deliver. Making decisions according to the stated law (which is more a product of the central government) is difficult because of the constant interactions between the court and other components of the local party-state coalition, a concern that the central government openly acknowledges. There have been some signs of change in the big, firm-type courts in China. In Chapter 7, we explore changes that indicate that there are now cracks in this top-down hierarchical structure found in courts in the big cities.

5

Political Embeddedness: Courts as Stability
Maintenance Agencies

The previous chapter analyzed the Chinese court as a bureaucracy of a special kind. The court is constituted of a hierarchy of judges created to respond to a range of policy goals set out by the party-state. What distinguishes the Chinese court from its Euro-American counterpart is that many of these policy goals are explicitly and immediately political. There is an inherent tendency in the setup of the administrative hierarchy to exceed its purportedly narrow judicial role because it is taken to be a political tool. The Chinese judicial system is therefore a strange animal. On the face of it, it operates very much like a modern bureaucracy. Underneath the bureaucratic goals, however, are political drives that respond to the sometimes long-term, but more often short-term needs of the party-state. In this chapter, we further examine how politics influence the courts.

In a recent annual report, SPC President Zhou Qiang boasted of a total of more than 19.51 million cases that local courts at various levels had handled. The courts concluded 1.1 million criminal cases, convicting 1.23 million people (Supreme People's Court 2016a). Like many other bureaucracies, the SPC puts an emphasis on the "output" of its courts. It is important to note that this output is defined according to internal criteria. A bureaucracy, unlike a market enterprise that buys and sells, justifies its own work within a certain demarcated policy space by referring to the *internal* criteria it sets out to measure its output – hence, the number of cases received and concluded. The underlying premise is that by handling more cases this year than last, the courts have made the society better. This is, of course, a debatable assumption, as one might say that a good society should have fewer lawsuits, not more.

But even this discussion of output is not apolitical. The SPC is known for highlighting different sets of statistics to support changing policy priorities. It is through picking which numbers to report and which not to that the SPC and its subordinate courts manipulate perceptions of their performance. This has become a constant source of frustration for scholars of the Chinese judicial system, as statistics released in the SPC annual work reports often are not comparable across the years. For example, the mediation rate was one of the key statistics highlighted during the tenure (2009–2013) of Wang Shengjun, whose reign was marked by a heavy push for mediation across all levels of courts, which fitted well with the ideology of "harmonious society" promoted by then-party chief Hu Jintao. The national average rate of mediation headlined Wang's annual reports. But that changed abruptly when Wang was succeeded by Zhou Qiang in 2013. Since the beginning of Zhou's SPC presidency, the number has not been brought up again in the annual reports.

There is the more important distinction between "output" and "outcome" that characterizes the political nature of the Chinese courts. Output is about quantifiable numbers – numbers of cases accepted, cases heard and cases concluded, among others. Internally, among the party-state leaders, the significance of "output" is dwarfed in comparison with the weight that the party-state, both at the central and local levels, put on "outcome." Outcome is about effectiveness; it is about whether the work of a bureau matches its policy objectives (Pollitt 1986). It is clear here the Chinese courts are viewed differently from the judiciary in a liberal democracy. Political considerations dominate what make for the right outcome. Are there threatening protests and demonstrations under a court's watch? Are there discontented litigants who complain to the mass media or make a scene in public? Are there bitter appeals and petitions? Are there violent behaviors?

Political embeddedness refers to the instrumental nature of law in promoting the broader government operations of stability maintenance. Strict adherence to legal rules is not an end in itself. Law lacks the kind of institutional integrity that insulates it from immediate political considerations on a day-to-day basis. The embrace of law is conditional on the benefits of following the law outweighing the risk of escalating instability. In socialist lingo, the courts are "weapons" of the people's democratic dictatorship. As the Chinese courts have become more professionalized, they have never abandoned this instrumental, law-as-means mentality. In one of his annual reports to the National People's Congress (NPC), Zhou Qiang said that the judiciary is "for the people" and that it will follow the law "to strive to maintain national security and social stability" (Supreme People's Court 2015d). The same "socialist rule of law" theory was emphasized by senior Chinese officials. Luo Gan, then head of the CCP's Central Political-Legal Committee, stated that the goal of the committee was to guarantee the political system's "political color" and loyalty to the party, the nation, the people, and the law (Liebman 2007:628).

THE INSTITUTIONAL ARRANGEMENT OF POLITICAL EMBEDDEDNESS

The courts are institutionally put in a position of greater responsibility toward the party-state than toward general promotion of the law. Since the establishment of the PRC in 1949, the exercise of law has always been bound up with political concern. The courts of China have long been subject to more direct and intense political influences than their Western counterparts. In the highly politically charged period of Maoism in the 1960s and 1970s, formal procedures and regular rules were abandoned in the midst of waves of campaigns for mass-line politics and political re-education (Zhu 2007; Huang 2010).

The reemergence of Deng Xiaoping in the ensuing two decades and the open-door policy he and his handpicked successors pursued reined in the influence of political campaigns to an important extent. Nowadays, politics do not come in the form of explicit ideological struggles or mass campaigns. Instead, political concerns come in the form of promoting stable governance. In practice, politics influence the judicial system in four ways. First, the judiciary is, institutionally speaking, supervised by the people's congress of the corresponding administrative level. Article 16 of the Organic Law of the People's Court states that the standing committee of a local people's congress supervises the work of the people's court at the corresponding level. Article 16 further states that the SPC is answerable to the NPC and its standing committee. The SPC reports on its work to the NPC and its standing committee. Judges who are responsible for political propaganda and communications spend an inordinate amount of time each year preparing for the court's annual report to the congress. Courts at various levels are accountable to their local people's congresses. Political intervention from people's congresses sometimes come in the form of 个案监督 (*gean jiandu*), or "supervision over individual cases." In certain cases, a local people's congress will order the court it supervises to deliver a certain verdict or to amend existing verdicts (Keith et al. 2014:109). Supervision of individual cases was at its peak in the late 1990s. Many Chinese legal scholars considered this form of supervision from without as blatant political intervention (Li 2014:41; Keith et al. 2014:110). If non-legal authorities can second-guess what the judiciary says about the law, it is difficult to see how the institution of law is empowered by the process. Other political institutions at the local level, including local governments and local party committees in practice also play a role in supervising the decisions of the courts. Besides supervision of individual cases, the NPC has in recent years stepped up its scrutiny of the work of the judiciary. It has become more critical of the annual reports given by the SPC and its sister bureau of the procuratorate (Saich 2015:132). In March of each year, SPC President presents the judiciary's work report to the annual session of the NPC held in Beijing. Although an SPC report has yet to be disapproved, some have received low rates of approval (by the NPC standard) in recent years. In 2013, the last year of Wang Shengjun's reign as SPC President, the approval rate of the judiciary's annual report declined to an alarming level of 75 percent (Li 2014:47)!

Second, the Chinese courts take part in and even take charge of dealing with a set of stability-related problems that in the eyes of most Western courts fall squarely outside of the realm of law. For example, some courts are asked to play a coordinating role in the consultative and administrative process of "grand mediation" (Hand 2011). It is not entirely clear what is included under the banner of grand mediation, but it appears that some local courts are asked to play a key role in facilitating inter-bureau, multilevel consultation on stability maintenance. They coordinate and manage cases that involve the input of more than one bureau, particularly in incendiary situations that may turn into mass protests. Other courts that assume a less prominent role in local governance are still expected to "show up" and participate in various forms of local campaigns, from wide-ranging themes that include anti-corruption, birth control, respect for the elderly and street cleaning. There are also asked to participate in economic campaigns such as soliciting commercial investment and eradicating poverty, among others (Keith et al. 2014:105).

Third, politics sometimes dissuades courts from exercising a legal determination of the issue put before them. This may sound unbelievable, since the party-state makes the laws that the courts are supposed to carry out. But the Chinese party-state is far from monolithic. The difficulty with implementing the law reveals the tensions between governments at the central and the local levels in China. Law represents the policy directives of the central government. Beijing uses the law to break up cartels of local interests, but often the interests of local governments and businesses are tightly intertwined. There is a popular saying among Chinese officials: "The policies of Zhongnanhai do not leave Zhongnanhai." Zhongnanhai is where the headquarters for the Communist Party and the state council are located. The saying refers to the enormous obstacles encountered by the central government in trying to break up the power of the regions. Indeed, generations of Chinese leaders have devised different plans to ensure local compliance with central policies.[1] While there is a grain of truth in the saying, it is important to note that central-local relations are themselves pluralistic and evolving. The laws are observed, applied, and interpreted with varying degrees of poetic license, followed loosely in some places but promoted heavily in others.

Fourth, the impact of politics goes beyond making courts take up extra-judicial duties and set limits on the exercise of law. Politics is in fact embedded in the everyday practice of law. We are referring to the inherent openness of judicial boundaries. The penetrating influence of politics is most manifest in the parallel structure of the *xinfang* office, literally translated as the "letters and visits office" within the formal organization of every court in China. While court-related letters and visits offices are usually located within a courthouse and staffed by judges and other judicial staff, they are, institutionally speaking, not part of the judiciary. *Xinfang* constitutes a second and parallel mechanism, on top of the judicial channel of appeal, through which unhappy litigants can challenge judicial decisions.

For the rest of this chapter, we examine how political embeddedness leads to a unique behavior for the Chinese courts – "shrinking" – and how it impacts the everyday operation of the courts. We then examine a few key areas where political embeddedness is most immediate and manifest: the petition system, housing demolition cases and bitter divorce cases. We also examine how the courts deal with politically charged cases when shrinking is no longer possible.

SHRINKING VIOLET SYNDROME

In the literature of organization and bureaucracy, Anthony Downs (1967:217) describes the "shrinking violet syndrome" as a bureau's deliberate policy to dial down its activities or narrow down its actions to avoid sanctions. We use the term "shrinking" to refer to an aversion to adjudication for some Chinese courts. Sometimes the law is better left unused in China, many judges believe. Political embeddedness goes beyond the meaning of politics affecting some judicial decisions. It means politics affects the triggering of the judicial process (or not).

Adjudication is chiefly avoided by two means. First, a court can refuse to accept a case. This is the *de facto* role of the case filing division (立案庭 *lianting*). The division performs an active vetting function. It is the first department that handles a claimant's complaint within the judicial process (Liu and Liu 2011). In theory, the division was set up to filter disputes for resolution through other channels, thereby reasonably reducing the caseload of a court. In practice, the division often pushes off controversial cases based on political considerations (Ying and Xu 2009). This explains why some incendiary incidents that would have produced class action cases in the United States never made it to the courts of China. In 2008, for example, the China dairy giant Sanlu Group produced the contaminated milk powder that caused many babies to develop kidney stones, with some cases resulting in death. Yet those cases did not result in product liability cases due to overriding concerns with regard to political stability (Liu and Liu 2011:317).[2]

The second, more common way of avoiding adjudication is by resorting to mediation as a substitute. Mediation is heavily promoted among work-unit courts, where adjudication is risky and can easily backfire for a variety of reasons, either because disgruntled litigants have little regard of the legitimacy of the law or because local officials see the courts as a subordinate branch. In fact, for many rural courts, mediation is more than a complementary mechanism of adjudication. It is the *primary* mechanism. These courts regularly boast a mediation rate of over 50 percent. So common is mediation in these courts that adjudication is relegated to a complementary role (Wayne and Xiong 2011). The high volume of mediated cases is indicative of the strong institutional preference to offload the risk of adjudication. Judges working in these courts are asked to settle, through mediation, a certain percentage of the cases they handle. The ratio of cases with a mediated settlement has become a criterion in assessing a judge's performance (Minzner 2011b). Some courts even claim that their goal is to achieve zero adjudication, meaning that all the cases processed by a court are settled through mediation (Henan High Court 2014; see Peng 2011).

It is in this sense that the Chinese judicial system is populist. As public relations and political repercussions are factored into the assessment of judicial performance, Chinese judges, in comparison to their Western counterparts, are driven less by the need to maintain the integrity of internal processes and are more willing to resort to different administrative means to accommodate changes in the broader external environment (Peerenboom 2002:280–343; Fu 2003). The overwhelming and immediate political concern with stability maintenance and the desire to avoiding bitter grievances in a society that has become increasingly conflict-ridden means that the ideal of fairness and justice is politically reframed as a promotion of the Chinese notion of "middle way" (中庸 *zhongyong*), a broad and eclectic philoso-phized notion of the idea of "balance."

SYMPTOM ONE: PETITIONED CASES

The petition system embodies the checks and balances to which Chinese govern-ment bureaus, including the courts, are subject. This system serves as an outlet for popular grievances and as a mechanism by which the party-state can check on the performance of a bureau (Liebman 2011:274). Petitioned cases provide important information about how well the courts perform in resolving social disputes and alleviating grievances. They are there to keep the courts from becoming sclerotic.

The existence of a letters and visits office inside the court, however, blurs the boundary between law and politics (Minzner 2006). Institutionally, the office is both an organ of the judiciary and part of the state's petition system, which burdens court officials with the political concerns of the state as well as the judicial normative referents of the law (Minzner 2006:103). In interviews, some judges described the court petition office as an organ that undercuts the court's own mission. Judges who work in the petition office often see their job as a 苦差 (*kuchai*), i.e., a tough assignment. On the one hand, they find many petitioners' claims to be without merit (or at least without legal merit). From the perspective of these judges, many petitioners simply want financial compensation for claims that have no legal basis. And many try to use the law to deal with social issues that the law is not equipped to deal with. In these cases, the court becomes a haven for some litigants to voice political demands (Su and He 2010). Judges who work in petition offices are reluctant to bend, for yielding to a petitioner begets more petitioners. On the other hand, their job is to assuage petitioners so that their petitions will not turn into something more damning to social stability – for example, escalating into mass protests or high-profile suicides that draw the attention of the media. Judges also come under pressure from local political leaders or their presidents to resolve complaints that petitioners take to Beijing.

This is especially the case during periods when the state has heightened concerns over social stability. For example, when national events with significant political impact such as the NPC annual session are scheduled to take place, courts are on high alert. In some places, all the court staffs are mobilized to watch over the most disgruntled petitioners around the clock (Feng 2015). On the eve of those important political events, some courts asked their judges to station themselves in rural villages day and night to pacify local petitioners and dissuade them from petitioning to Beijing. Similarly, during the period when big events are held in China, such as the Olympics or the World Expo, the courts are asked to stamp out petitions.

In some cases, when petitioners insist long and hard enough, they succeed in making the courts yield (Feng 2015). It is difficult to tell how many petitions end up with tangible results. Some scholars seem to believe that petitions have forced the courts to change its decisions quite frequently, leading to them to describe the Chinese judicial system as a "populist" one that defies its authoritarian image (Liebman 2011; Trevaskes 2010). According to Liebman (2011:269), protesting, petitioning, or threatening to do either often is a successful means for litigants to pressure courts to rule in their favor or to alter decided cases.

This is an area where evidence is mostly sporadic and anecdotal. Official statistics offer very little help except to outline the broadest trend. They provide no breakdown on the number of decisions changed as a result of petition, or of courts agreeing to rehear a case because of a petition. From what we are able to glean from official statistics, it seems to suggest that since the beginning of the early years of the new century (2002), the total number of adjudicated decisions has outnumbered the number of petitions received and processed by the court, but that before that, petition cases persistently outnumbered adjudicated cases (Zhu 2007:25). Yet, while the total number of petitions has slightly declined or plateaued in recent years, courts still receive a large number of petitions every year. It is just unclear how many of these petitions have led to changed decisions or retrials.

If anything, we suspect that the number of petitioners who have their decisions reversed or their cases retried is very limited. More likely, the requests of petitioners, if addressed, are dealt with through administrative means. Basic-level courts of China, for example, have allocated relief funding to help petitioners. It should also be pointed out that the most persistent and diehard petitioners of the country are those who are, but for resorting to the means of constant petitioning, powerless. Their petitions lack legal merit, but this does not alter the fact that many of them suffered in conflicts caused by demolition decisions, state-owned enterprise lay-offs or private loan frauds.

Petitioners are generally told that their petitions would not work, or that the system of petition is not designed to rectify the decisions made by the courts! This is all part of the standard technique deployed by judges to temper expectations. Yuqing Feng (2015), who has done excellent ethnographic study of Chinese petitioners, described how petitioners were often told by judges in the letters and visits office that petitioning was futile. Below is a conversation between a petitioner named Luo and a judge in Beijing that Feng (2015:89–90) observed (the petitioner wanted the court to reconsider its decision on her land-taking case):

OFFICIAL: Petitioning is not a lawful procedure. It has no legal consequence.
LUO: But it solves problems.

OFFICIAL: Nor does it solve problems.

LUO: You just said that it could not solve problems. Then why did you let us petition?

OFFICIAL: Yes. I could only say you have some information for us to know. Yes, you should not petition at all. Look at the foreign countries with better rule of law. Do they have a petition system like ours? If you are dissatisfied with court decisions, you have plenty of remedies, such as to appeal.

The system is set up to reward only the zealots who are determined to trample all obstacles thrown their way, so much so that successful petitioners are often not considered "normal." They are labeled by officials as unreasonable, vexatious, sometimes even mentally unstable (He and Feng 2016). These petitioners were able to get the courts to yield partially to their requests. But they often paid a high price to climb the petitioning pyramid (e.g., quitting their job and becoming a full-time veteran petitioner; see Feng 2015).

Why do the courts shrink from cases that are likely to be petitioned? Obviously, dealing with petitioners is, as mentioned, an unpleasant "chore." But the reason is also deep-rooted in political embeddedness. As Downs (1967:218) explains, *shrinking* or retrenchment is most probable when a bureau's power setting provides fast and powerful feedbacks. This idea of *immediacy* is rendered clearer if we compare the Chinese courts with their Western counterparts. It is important not to absolutize the power of courts in the liberal democratic setting. While an Anglo-American court is usually able to provide a final legal determination of a dispute, such a determination does not necessarily mean that the issue behind the legal dispute is always settled or resolved. It is not uncommon for a party to a dispute to carry on arguing about the matter in defiance of the court's decision. Sometimes, this kind of persistent effort can lead to reform of the law. For example, in the United States, many victim-led movements in high-profile cases have led to tougher criminal laws (Garland 2001). In Britain, cases of domestic violence have similarly led to legal reform on the defense of battered woman syndrome (Cownie et al. 2005:30).

In contrast, the Chinese petition system provides faster, albeit less systematic, feedback than the channel of legislative amendments. Petitions are able to create *immediate* negative feedbacks. It is at root a complaint system distinguished by its narrowness of focus (one specific case). The difference between the Chinese and the Anglo-American courts is that continuing efforts from the disagreeing parties in the former system push for reversals of specific decisions, not changes to the laws behind those decisions.

This explains why Chinese judges loathe petitions and often shrink from adjudicating cases that are likely to be petitioned. It is a system designed to blame the officials who *implement* the law, not the law itself. The looming threat of petitions casts a long shadow over the everyday decision-making of many frontline judges. Some local courts discipline judges based on the size and scale of citizen petitions from their jurisdiction to higher-level authorities (Minzner 2011a:88). As a result, judges deliberately hold back on adjudication. A formal ruling runs the risk of challenges by the losing parties.

SYMPTOM TWO: BITTERLY CONTESTED DIVORCE CASES

Divorces have become more common in China today. Official statistics report a national average that hovers between 2 and 3 percent. According to the official data released by the Ministry of Civil Affairs, a total of 3.63 million couples applied for divorce in 2014 (Ministry of Civil Affairs 2015). That translates to a divorce rate of 2.7 percent. It is clear that the divorce rate in China has been on a steady rise in the past two decades. A national average divorce rate of 3 percent might seem low, but as Saich (2015) points out, for a society coming out of the Mao years of enforced social conformity and repression of sexual desire, rising divorce rates, however moderate, are seen as a "disturbing" trend. The low national average rate conceals the fact that in the most urbanized part of China, divorce rates are much higher. According to a National Public Radio (NPR) report in 2010, about 40 percent of marriages in Beijing ended in divorce (Lim 2010). The quick marriage and divorce of famed Chinese hurdler Liu Xiang, the first, and to date the only Chinese man who has won a gold medal in Olympics track and field, epitomized the new attitude toward divorce, especially among the younger urban population. Liu and actress Ge Tian started to date in May 2014 and married in September of the same year. They divorced in 2015 after less than 10 months.

Just about thirty years ago, back in the 1980s, it was very difficult to divorce in China. Repeated and prolonged mediation was a prerequisite for any divorce petition to be seriously considered by the government, and it was common for an application to be delayed for months, even years in some cases (Parish and Whyte 1978:193). Divorce petitions that finally reached the courts were mostly mediated (Huang 2010). Petitioning couples were repeatedly cajoled to reconcile. More often than not, they had to confess their "mistakes" and "naïveties," and reach a so-called reconciliation with the other spouse (Huang 2010).

Nowadays, uncontested divorce applications are routinely approved in China. The new "Regulations on Marriage Registration of the People's Republic of China" that came into effect on October 1, 2003 removed many of the old impediments to divorce (Zhu 2003). Though once mandatory, couples seeking divorce are no longer required to wait for one month of examination. They are no longer required to obtain "reference for divorce" from other people such as superiors at work, thus eliminating the involvement of the state-owned work-units. Under the new system, a majority of divorce petitions are handled by local civil affairs departments. According to the latest statistics released, of the 3.64 million couples who divorced in 2014, civil affairs departments handled 2.96 million, or over 80 percent of the cases. The courts handled the remaining 0.68 million applications in which couples could not reach agreement on either the divorce decision or details related to the divorce (such as child custody, alimony or property division).

Even though most couples who sought divorce through the courts cannot arrive at mutual agreements, the courts have since the 1990s taken a more accommodating and pragmatic approach toward handling these petitions.[3] In practice, the courts generally adopt a no-fault rule: as long as the petitioning party is persistent in seeking a divorce, he or she will get it, regardless of whether or not the disagreeing party has been found at fault (Huang 2010:204–208).

This routine way of dealing with divorce petitions is however overridden when dealing with "problem cases." What are problem cases? They are those that pose palpable threats to social stability because of the antagonism displayed between opposing litigants. Judges have to decide whether the dispute has the potential of escalating into malicious incidents. As mentioned, one of the "outcome" targets for performance evaluation of local officials, including judges, is their performance in maintaining social stability. An incident that gains the attention of higher-level authorities costs a demerit or the loss of bonus for an official (Saich 2015:220). The goal of the court is to ensure that "small problems do not leave the village, large problems do not leave the township, [and] conflicts are not passed up to higher authorities" (Zhou, Yongkang 2010; cited by Minzner 2011b:938).

While the concern for social stability is not explicitly written into the Marriage Law, it has shaped the ways in which the courts, particularly work-unit courts facing an unpredictable environment of judging, deal with problem cases. What has emerged is a mediation process that on the surface looks similar to the traditional mode. However, the goals, discourses, procedures and outcomes are different.

Interviewing litigation parties is the judge's first task in both modes of mediation. When taking on highly contested divorce cases today, judges are expected to form an assessment of the litigation parties' mental state and their potential reactions if the court were to rule against them. This looks similar to the traditional mode of mediation, but with a different focus. In mediations, judges identify the underlying cause of the deteriorating relationship through interviews. However, in the current mode, judges are expected to discern whether the litigants are mentally stable, whether they are able to peacefully accept an unfavorable decision, and whether they may react explosively. This has become a key to success in today's mediation: to uncover parties' genuine requests and feelings. Only if a judge effectively assesses the litigants' mental status can she propose a solution acceptable for both parties, hence minimizing malicious incidents of any kind.

The following cases were observed in a typical work-unit court in the rural hinterland of a western province, a region with a low level of economic development. In one case in which one of us sat, the wife, a doctor in her mid-30s, wanted a divorce. She broke down in tears when talking to the judges, and during both the trial and the mediation process, constantly turning her face away from her husband. But the husband was determined not to give in. During the court hearing, he made a remark that was a red flag for the judge: "I will cut off her feet if divorced." The hearing became the pivotal scene of a bitter breakup. The determined wife indicated that she would commit suicide if her petition was denied. Yet the threat to resort to violence by the husband was realistic. After several interviews with both parties, the judge was still unsure about what they would do if the verdict did not go their way. She decided to stall. As documented by He (2009a:102), some judges "would never grant a divorce if the defendant is suicidal or homicidal, no matter how many times the plaintiff might file a divorce petition." This is because, as one of our informants said, "For 1 percent of recklessness, we will be held 100 percent responsible." Judge Gao, a deputy division head with 20 years' experience in handling civil cases said:

> Handling this type of divorce case is not a test of a judge's ability to master the law or to apply the law. It is more of a test of a judge's ability to solve problems. In this process, I did not consider whether "the mutual affection still exists" as provided in the law. My standard is to avoid the malicious consequences that might result from a divorce decision. I would not approve the divorce petition even if "the mutual affection between the couple had already been broken down."

In another case for which the presiding judge decided to exercise caution, the husband did not threaten to use violence. The man, in his 50s, was once a proud worker in a big state enterprise. But he was recently laid off and was uncharacteristically quiet during the trial. The wife, in her 40s, was once financially dependent on her spouse but has now built a career as a successful saleswoman. She was eager to divorce. She rushed to the court president's office for what she saw as the court's delay to her petition. She cited incompatible personalities and her husband's failure to take care of the family as the main reasons for her petition. But she was the socioeconomically superior party in the relationship – younger, more educated, with a stable job and income. The wife said she would kill herself if the court denied her petition. But the judge believed she was deliberately putting pressure on the court when she said so. The man was in fact unpredictable. The judge, working in this part of China, has seen many men like him.

The resentments generated by changes in circumstance between the man and his wife were dangerous. The man personified a growing demographic of laid-off workers from state-owned enterprises. Moreover, a laid-off worker working part-time for less than 1,000 yuan a month, the man had a remote relationship with his son. Losing his marriage would be a big blow, the judge said. In difficult divorce cases like the present one, the court tends to prioritize the welfare of this group of laid-off workers, for fear that they, if left without a family, would become a source of unrest. It seemed to the judge that the husband struggled to cope with the divorce process.

Despite the wife's threat to commit suicide, the judge told her the petition would not be approved. The judge later spent much time trying to persuade the plaintiff to withdraw her petition. The judge said the wife could return to file another divorce petition if she so chose. The husband was the more vulnerable among the two, the judge reasoned. The disapproval decision informed the husband that the court sided with him this time.

At times, this concern with stability comes at the cost of promoting gender inequality, as "angry men" are perceived to be more socially threatening. In one case in which the wife sued for divorce for the first time, the plaintiff complained that she was physically abused. She said her husband fought over trivial issues with her almost every night. But the husband's family was broke. The man had a disabled brother and a mentally ill mother to care for. Without much hesitation, the judge denied the wife's petition. She explained her decision to the wife's lawyer in her office:

> No way will this marriage persist, but this time they cannot get a divorce. We must honor the husband's dignity. At this moment we cannot wipe out the hope of his whole family. We have to maintain this marriage. This is to give the husband's family some time to be psychologically prepared for losing this woman.

This perpetuation of gender inequality was again visible in another case handled by the same court, where the wife sought a divorce because of her husband's displayed violence toward her and her family. The defendant was emotionally volatile. He and the plaintiff fought against each other before the judge at the first court hearing. At the second hearing, the husband threatened that he would kill himself at the judge's home should the judge agree to his wife's petition. The presiding judge, succumbing to the man's threat, denied the wife's petition. Six months later at the court hearing when the wife filed another petition for divorce, the husband attempted to beat the wife again. He was taken into custody at the detention center for three days. He told the center's guard during his detention: "I have lived long enough! Just leave me alone!" Other male defendants would make similar threats: "I will die in front of the courthouse if you render a divorce decision." Or "Now that my life is destroyed and I do not want to live, I will make hers miserable for the rest of her life" (He 2017). As resistance, these threats are similar to suicidal protests (Lee and Kleinman 2000). In the Chinese political context, judges who choose to dismiss these threats as posturing do so at their own peril. In this case of the violent husband, the judge again denied the petition. She feared that the husband might "go off the deep end." When the wife's mother, through connections, asked a veteran judge from the same court why there was still no divorce after the petition had been filed five times, the judge responded circumspectly, "You'd better find ways to compensate the other side and then try to get a settlement."[4]

SYMPTOM THREE: HOUSING DEMOLITION CASES

Public law is another area where the footprint of political intervention is most noticeable. In theory, public law is a principal means to address official behaviors that threaten to undermine government policies. For example, under the Administrative Litigation Law, citizens bring challenges in court to state decisions that affect economic interests, ranging from land rights to government benefits and fines to enforcement of business regulations. Similarly, China's new property law regime made it a priority to restraining expansive state behavior. Constitutional amendments were introduced to impose public interest and compensation requirements for the taking of private property, regulations on land registration, tenure, expropriation, and reclassification of land from rural to urban. Other amendments were also made to clarify the scope of court jurisdiction over land disputes and over litigation (administrative litigation challenges to state eviction orders) and protests by citizens ousted from their homes or farms (deLisle 2015:264–265).

In practice, courts have openly refused to accept politically sensitive or socially controversial cases, an ultimate acknowledgement on the part of the courts that law is of no use in these cases. As mentioned, the case filing division of a court serves as a *de facto* screen for politically sensitive cases. Peerenboom (2009) describes this phenomenon as the "dejudicialization" of cases that are too politically sensitive or socially controversial for the courts to cope with. Many judges privately acknowledge that there are cases related to sensitive topics such as land disputes, housing relocation and enterprise reform that cannot get past the gatekeepers in the case-filing division of a court. These cases touch on topics that are so intimately related to the material interests and political authority of the local party-state that, in most cases, courts cannot decide them on their own. Another category of cases that reveals the fight between central policy and local government is environmental litigation. In 2007, the SPC called on local courts to set up environmental courts and to encourage public interest litigation. The environmental courts are empowered to hear administrative, criminal, civil, and administrative enforcement cases. Yet most scholars agree that the environmental courts failed to take on a significant caseload. Instead courts tend to guide cases away from formal adjudication against local governments and state enterprises (Wilson 2015:145–176).

The embedding of political consideration in everyday judicial practices means that judges are highly discriminating in their application of the law. The decision to litigate is not a decision made by litigants and their lawyers alone. It is a decision in which judges also play an important part. Within the setting of liberal democracy, the court is often described as a passive institution, in the sense that it is up to litigants to bring their own cases to the court (Neubauer and Meinhold 2012). In China, not all cases that arrive at the doorstep of the courts will be heard. Ironically, sometimes the courts proactively solicit potential litigants to file cases, particularly for cases with large claimed amounts. The courts thus play an active role in deciding whether more or less law is used.

If bitterly contested divorced cases are treated with caution because of their *potential* to undermine social harmony, housing demolition cases are already a prototypical form of *political protest*. With the rapid pace of urbanization in China, large amounts of agricultural land are being put to new use and old buildings are being demolished, frequently against the will of those whose livelihoods depend on their entitlement to land and a home. As in other sectors, China has aspired to regulate land-taking through the use of "the rule of law." Starting in the 1980s, the state promulgated a series of laws and regulations governing relocation and redevelopment. For two reasons, however, the laws provide little protection for original homeowners, who are thus often unsatisfied. First, while the laws and other related regulations provide procedure and compensation for land-taking, they often have serious deficiencies. Some legal procedures are unclearly stipulated and the rights of the original homeowners are only vaguely defined. But even these poorly drafted laws are being improperly followed or ignored because of the strong incentive of local government officials in favor of taking land. Economic development and local GDP have always been crucial criteria in the assessment of the performance of top local officials. For most cities in China, real estate has been the engine for economic development. Putting agricultural land to industrial use or replacing old buildings in urban areas with luxury complexes or shopping malls will attract large amounts of investment and bring about plenty of job opportunities. Moreover, local government officials can often benefit themselves by colluding with business developers in these processes. Farmers and homeowners receive only a fraction of the small sum that is their legal due; all too often, the local government and its corrupt officials take the bigger slice. The gross disparity between the affected individuals' losses and the gains of the real estate developers and city officials only exacerbates the dissatisfaction. These are all reasons for the growing number of often-violent "mass incidents" in China (see generally Upham 2011:257–260).

Litigation has become an important means of collective action, as the courtroom is considered a safe haven for protesters to stage their opposition (O'Brien and Li 2004; Liebman 2011). For the protesters-cum-litigants, the Chinese courtroom has become a public space in which the resistant voices and practices of lay people can be expressed. Negative political labeling is avoided by going to court because such an activity is "institutionally indecipherable" (Ewick and Silbey 2003:1337), that is to say, it is impossible for the state to say that going to court is politically subversive or incorrect. This is the paradox – right at the center of the house of power comes a space of relative discursive freedom. This paradoxical practice harkens back to a rich and long tradition of dissent in China. What often happens in China is that the government's template of control is turned into the protesters' instrument of resistance (Wasserstrom and Liu 1995). This explains why legal appeals and social protests often go hand in hand in China. Going to court is as much about winning as about making a point (Clarke 2009). Similar to the environmental justice campaigns in the United States (Marshall 2006:174–175), many of the protests occur in the context of the public hearings required by the law and held by government agencies, but more often they occur during court hearings. Individuals facing the demolition of their homes have filed both civil and administrative cases for reasons ranging from outrageous unfairness and the due process of law to government information disclosure. In a case documented by Erie (2012), the plaintiff filed thirteen cases in fighting against the demolition of his home.

In some high-profile housing demolition cases we observed, litigants were highly organized. They wore the same style of clothes or clothes with the same color as a display of solidarity. They chanted the same slogans in and outside of the courthouses to voice out their discontents and demands (Chongqing Municipality 2010). Some organizers are simply people affected by the demolitions, whereas others are seasoned activists. Some have been involved in the opposition to the demolition process and have thus accumulated experience of resistance. Some are simply friends or family members. Seasoned protestors solicit and persuade families to participate in the efforts to obtain a favorable settlement from the developers; in exchange, they receive a percentage of the settlement or a flat fee (cf. Liebman 2012). Some of them have even set up consulting firms dealing with housing demolition issues (CCP News Net 2010; Chongqing Municipality 2010). Organizers coordinate with other affected households, put together protests inside and outside the courtroom, educate families on the laws and policies related to urban housing demolition, feed the media with stories, and help hire experienced lawyers. Some seasoned protestors go as far as either to coach the plaintiffs affected by demolition directly or to act as their representatives themselves, thus improving the performance of the plaintiffs in the litigation process.[5]

Undercompensated by the government or government-supported developers, homeowners have employed various forms of resistance that clash with the state actions. According to one estimate, of the 180,000 collective actions in 2010, the number caused by forced evictions was greater than that based on all other causes of action combined (Jacobs 2011). Official statistics show that the number of collective litigation cases over land-taking has also skyrocketed. In some courts, such cases make up more than 20 percent of all administrative litigation cases (Liaowang Newsweek 2006). In these cases, the plaintiffs are hundreds, if not thousands, of farmers from several villages or residents from a block in an old city district. They defend their rights collectively through both legal and extralegal means.

While some grassroots courts continue to shy away from housing demolition cases (Wang and Yin 2010), others understand that dodging and stalling work only to a certain extent. For petitions with a strong actionable case, an outright rejection might lead to an appeal to the upper-level court. The higher court is in all likelihood going to send the case back to the basic-level court. Even for other petitions that are legally flimsy and unlikely to prevail, the local government would still want the courts to take off social pressure from this kind of "legal" protests (Su and He 2010).

COURTS AS POLITICAL ACTORS

The coordinated nature of some housing demolition cases means that judges cannot follow their standard playbook. In fact, the court's approach is to handle these cases not so much as court cases but as political campaigns to be engaged on all fronts. The first task they face is to not aggravate the political-charged atmosphere. Chinese judges play a dominant role at trials. Chinese trial remains a judge's show (see Chapter 2). In protest-supported litigation, however, judges have become extremely cautious about interrupting the litigants for fear of aggravating the crowd. Supporters often believe that judges are in the same position as the powerful, or at least they protect the powerful. Grassroots litigants accuse the judges of colluding with the developers and the demolition authorities and believe that the judicial process is a sham. Some threaten to commit suicide (Chongqing Municipality 2010). According to one judge with plenty of experience in hearing this type of cases, the cardinal rule is to not interrupt the representation of the litigation parties. As a result, non-legal discourse, such as moral and political arguments, is tolerated in the trial process (He and Ng 2013b). Since the court debates and arguments are often made public by the media, the courts have to, in their decisions, deal with these non-legal arguments.

The second task is "crowd control." One common strategy among organizers is to floor the presiding judge with a surprise show up of supporters. In one case in the Luqiao district of Taizhou municipality in Zhejiang province in which three holdout hard-nail households – those families who rejected the compensation arrangements and refused to move out – fought against the district government because the government had allegedly adopted an outdated compensation standard, the overall audience number reached more than 400, with people coming from all over Taizhou municipality. The hearing venue had to be changed three times due to the overwhelming turnout of supporters, which entirely exceeded the court's expectations. Obviously, the organizer played cat and mouse with the court. They had deliberately kept this arrangement from the court, lest the court limit the audience number. In an administrative licensing case in which nineteen affected individuals sued the government in Nantong, Jiangsu province, more than 200 affected individuals and human rights advocates showed up in a courtroom built to accommodate twenty people. The court thus kept most of the supporters out of the court building; enraged, the excluded supporters immediately blocked the gate to the building, preventing the passage of motor vehicles. The court then had to make concessions and allowed the supporters to audit the trial. Due to the small size of the venue, the defendants and the supporters were not clearly separated, despite concerns that the supporters might physically harm the defendants. Some supporters stood behind the plaintiffs and some stood in the corridor; as a result, the courtroom doors remained open. The room was so packed that the plaintiffs did not have seats during the whole hearing process and other litigation participants had to sit in the seats designated for the audience.

To maintain courtroom order in open trials packed with supporters, some courts have deployed all available bailiffs and, when this proved inadequate, sought help from the local police. Sharing his experiences, a veteran judge said, "The key is to choose a courtroom which is large enough to accommodate the supporters. This will prevent the supporters from turning emotional and getting out of control. A corresponding number of court bailiffs should be present so as to establish a psychological deterrent against the supporters." Other courts across the country have broken plaintiffs up into smaller groups, provided spokespersons to meet with them, and encouraged conciliation, settlements and even withdrawal (Chen and Xu 2012; Li, Li 2011). To dissipate the politically charged nature of housing demolition cases, courts often act as a third party (albeit not entirely neutral) in the chess game between protestors and the government. In many of these cases, the interest of the courts does not always align with the local land and housing bureau or the developers they back. The courts do not benefit, at least directly, from demolition policies and activities. They are not the decision makers who approve the projects and determine the compensation plans and prices. They may not even have anything to do with the demolition activities or the developers; but they are responsible for doing the most difficult part of the job when conflicts arise. In cases involving the mishandling of demolition projects, the courts are there to face the music. In short, the housing demolition authorities reap benefits, but the courts take the brunt of protesters' anger. As one judge put it bluntly in an interview: "We are clearing the shit left by the demolition authorities and the developers! They take away all the carrots, but we are asked to use the sticks and bear the responsibility in case of incidents."

Yet housing demolition authorities are strong and grassroots courts are weak. The latter alone are incapable of restraining the decisions of the former. Since the local party committee holds the highest position in the governance coalition, the first thing that the courts usually do is to seek party support. In Nantong, Jiangsu province, for example, the court lobbied the party committee to strengthen the administrative litigation system by emphasizing its impact on social stability. In a letter to the committee, the court stated: "With the deepening of reforms, various social contradictions become salient and state-society conflicts have become a crucial factor contributing to social instability . . . Taking the initiative in sharing the worries of the party and in bearing social responsibility for the government, the courts have already resolved and settled many state-society conflicts and this effort shall be further beefed up" (He 2014).

The court's request was met with a positive response: both the vice chief of the municipal party in charge of law and political affairs and the municipal mayor, who was another vice party chief, endorsed the letter and forwarded it to all the government and party agencies in the region. The endorsement stated that "the administrative agencies being sued shall fulfill the duty to respond to the litigation, enforce the judgments of the courts, and shall not unlawfully interfere with administrative litigation" (Du 2007).

The backing of the municipal party meant that the court could present the housing bureau with specific requests. The court could ask the chief official of the bureau to take the stand in trials. The required appearance of the chief official in administrative litigation has markedly facilitated the process of administration in accordance with the law. The arrangement means that not only the presiding judge, but also the leader of the agency, have to come out and face the music.

As seen, some courts are adept at playing politics from the inside. They do not defy the agencies openly. They exploit the institutional fluidity and ambiguity that defines the "negotiated" nature of the local party-state (Saich 2015:189). They "nudge" behind the scene. One example of nudging by the courts is to make use of internal judicial suggestions to rectify the agencies' unlawful behaviors (He 2013). Unlike letters to the local party committee, judicial suggestions are informal opinions sent by the courts to litigation participants on matters that may not be addressed by way of judgments. Such a suggestion will not only expose the flawed administrative practice, but also still exert pressure on, and provide guidance for, the agencies to make adjustments. The court points out in the suggestions that the administrative practice that is unlawful. A judicial suggestion involving housing demolition licenses, for instance, states that the authorities, in violation of Article 47 of the Administrative License Law, did not inform the affected private parties of the hearing before issuing the land planning and demolition license and thus have infringed their lawful rights. With all the facts and related legal regulations clearly specified, the onus is on the agencies to comply.

In some cases, although the courts rendered a decision in favor of the government, they pointed out what should have been the right action of the government. In a case dealing with the demolition of a public hospital located on the site of a cultural relic, a judicial suggestion provided explanations for the case outcome: "Considering the fact that the demolition applicant has reached agreement with the majority of the affected individuals and the local government has sought approvals from upper-level government with regard to the demolition of the public hospital, this court rejected the petition of the appellant, largely due to the concern of social stability. But with regard to the cultural relic, your Bureau must strictly follow the reply of the Jiangsu Provincial Government" (Nantong Intermediate Court 2008). Underlying the message was the warning that such future cases would be struck down.

The courts must tread a fine line when dealing with politically charged cases such as the housing demolition disputes described here. While in many of these cases the courts still support the housing bureaus, it is clear that the courts are keen to keep a distance. In one case involving thousands of plaintiffs and several petitions in May 2001, an intermediate court in central China delayed handing down a judgment in favor of the government after the hearing. It worked hard to convince other government agencies to provide additional remedies for the litigants in advance. These remedies serve as pre-emptive measures to lower the potential of further mass protests (Liaowang Newsweek 2006). Obviously, politics complicates and prolongs the judicial process. Delays are common with these cases. Many of them took the courts two to three years to resolve, which is well beyond the statutory adjudication period of six months (see Chapter 2).

About three decades ago, Susan Finder described (1989) filing an administrative lawsuit against the powerful in China as throwing eggs against a stone. The country has experienced momentous changes in the ensuing three decades. While there are more administrative cases in the urbanized regions, there has only been a gradual but modest increase in the overall caseload of administrative lawsuits (Li 2013).[6] But the court is more malleable than a stone. In fact, the courts are at their innovative best when they play the role of a go-between, playing the housing bureaus off the protestors, and vice versa. That said, the occasional successes of the courts turn on their ability to act as a savvy political actor, not an impartial judicial actor. If the promulgation of administrative procedural law in China in the 1990s was aimed at providing a rules-based check on the unruly behavior of administrative cadres, this goal remains aspirational.

Courts can sometimes turn the tables on more powerful bureaus; they do so not by drawing from the strength of the law, but by riding on the pressure waves built up from social conflicts (Ginsburg 2008; He 2009d). The party-state's position toward a more independent and empowered judiciary has always been ambivalent. In the midst of its rhetoric in building the rule of law comes the state propaganda that the Western notions of separation of powers and judicial independence are not applicable to China (People's Net 2011). This instrumental view of law, as we suggested, is the source of political embeddedness.

CONCLUSION

This chapter explores how the concern of political stability casts a shadow over judicial decision-making. Petitions, contested divorces, and housing demolition cases are just a few of the problem areas that courts tend to shrink. Of course, the scope of political embeddedness goes above and beyond the types of cases we used as examples. Scholars have identified the role of politics in, for example, labor cases (Su and He 2010), environmental litigation (Stern 2013), court petitions (Liebman 2007) and criminal cases, especially cases involving the use of death penalty (Trevaskes et al. 2014). What characterizes political embeddedness is its mercurial nature. Routine cases can quickly become political when the parties involved turn violent and the media becomes interested.

Courts in many parts of the world are influenced and constrained by political power. Yet the Chinese case is distinguished by the extent to which the efforts for safeguarding public security and promoting political stability are prioritized. That is particularly the case for work-unit courts in less-developed regions. For many of these courts, their judicial work is not premised on legal rules on the book. Instead, judicial decision-making often goes hand in hand with political discernment.

Applying the law is one of their works; others include propaganda, community building, promoting social harmony, and conflict resolution in the "grand style" (i.e., in non-trial setting).

There is, however, a risk that this populist streak of the courts that has worked so well for three decades has nurtured a culture of extremism among litigants. Some litigants take advantage of the court's aversion to conflicts and instabilities in order to obtain a ruling in their favor. They resort to threatening words and violent behaviors. Although judges make avoiding malicious incidents their foremost priority, such incidents continue to occur and seem to be on the rise.[7] In 2016, Ma Caiyun, a young woman judge who worked in Beijing, was shot to death by a litigant of a post-divorce property settlement case that the judge heard (Chen, Te-Ping 2016).

There are more obvious tensions between promoting political stability and applying the law judiciously today than in the past. The Chinese society is changing. Urbanization has undercut the very social fabric that made the conciliatory form of control so effective and pervasive in the past. While courts are asked to promote stability, the bureaucratic tendency to equate an absence of petitions and appeals with social stability incentivizes judges to sweep social problems under the legal carpet. For example, in courts that aspire to have more civil cases mediated than adjudicated, "settlements" are often precarious. They are made as a result of intense, judge-brokered negotiations among parties. With the increase in the settlement rate come more settled cases that require compulsory enforcement (Fan 2005). In theory, a settlement agreement does not need the court to enforce it because both parties have agreed to and accepted the deal. But the reality is clearly different. A study (Jiang 2010) conducted in an intermediate court in an inland province concluded that more than 40 percent of settled cases ended up requiring compulsory enforcement. Of these, 41 percent of the petitioners refused to deliver the payment in accordance with the settled agreement, despite being capable of doing so; another 29 percent of the noncompliance resulted from the unclear or illegal elements in the settled agreement (Jiang 2010). If, as its name suggests, a settlement is a solution agreed upon by all the litigation parties, why did some litigation parties not voluntarily fulfill the duties they agreed upon? The worrying numbers of noncompliance indicate that some of the settled cases might involve an element of coercion from frontline judges who were eager to close cases. The stronger pressure put on judges to attain higher settlement rates seems to have led to more reported incidents of inappropriate tactics.

Some frontline judges are not oblivious to the question of justice. They question the appropriateness of pursuing a high mediation rate and have argued that a high settlement rate does not necessarily indicate the success of mediation (Li 2008). If the primary goal of mediation is to make a society less litigious, the overly aggressive use of mediation might eventually lead to even more disputes or lawsuits. While the central policy of stability maintenance remains unchanged for courts in different parts of the country, there are unorganized and yet visible signs of pushback from grassroots judges in urban cities. As analyzed in Chapter 3, the party's emphasis on professionalism added to a wholesale reform of the system of judicial recruitment. It brought in younger judges with much better credentials and legal education. These judges view themselves more as officials who exercise their professional expertise than as "people's judges" who promote stability. We will return to this question of pushback in Chapter 8.

6

Social Embeddedness: Ties from Within and from Without

Administrative embeddedness and political embeddedness are concepts derived to identify the sources of constraints experienced by Chinese judges in using and following the law. From the perspective of judges, this sense of a lack of freedom comes almost exclusively from the pressure they experience from local party-state and sometimes litigants who petition to their superiors. In this chapter, we flip our perspective and examine how judges and their superiors act as the vessels through which courts become socially embedded.

The concept of social embeddedness, as we adopt it here, refers to the effects of social ties, or in Chinese, 关系 *guanxi*, on the decision-making process of a judge. These ties are personal and particularistic. The effect of social embeddedness turns on the willingness of judges to base decisions, partially or at times completely, on obligations of personal networks rather than the requirements of law. The idea of social embeddedness underlines the fact that Chinese judges do not often operate in their official/professional capacity alone when they decide on cases. They bring their obligations of their everyday lives, as husbands and wives, parents and children, friends and relatives into their role as judges. This co-existence of identities is particularly consequential in China because of the nascent status of the legal professional: the professional identity of being a judge does not take precedence over other social identities. As a result, the line separating the formal and the personal is porous.

Indeed, one of the oft-cited justifications for imposing strong hierarchical control in the Chinese courts is the varied quality of frontline judges. There is a lack not just of legal expertise, but a strong professional ethic that makes abuse of judicial power a real threat. Hence, so the argument goes, vertical supervision is necessary as a form of judicial quality control (Su 2000). But it is misleading to treat social embeddedness as an individualistic phenomenon. The effects of social embeddedness work through the veins of the vertical hierarchy that we identified in the previous chapters. Impactful social ties sometimes come directly from the personal network of a judge, but often it comes indirectly from the personal networks of a judge's superiors and colleagues. In fact, superior ties (i.e., ties that come from the network of a superior) are often the most potent and consequential.

AN INSIDE-OUT APPROACH TO STUDYING SOCIAL EMBEDDEDNESS

The dual mission of grassroots bureaucrats and judicial personnel means that Chinese judges are in general much more visible than their Western counterparts. In some newer urban courthouses, judges are beginning to enter and exit the court building through a separate designated entrance. But this is only to be found in the biggest urban courts. Traditionally, the boundary separating the social role and the professional role of judges is often blurred. Even today, and particularly for judges working in inland areas, when they interact with litigants (e.g., where judges investigate the circumstances of disputes before them), they do so in a "socially embedded" way. For example, when judges visit litigants at home to conduct an investigation, they are often invited to stay for a banquet with litigants (Yang 1994; Potter 2002). Many scholars studying the Chinese legal system, including ourselves, have seen and reported the practice of judges meeting over dinner with disputants and their counsel to talk informally about business related to the case (Potter 2002; Balme 2010; Ng and He 2017). From a formal legal perspective, this kind of socially embedded encounter seems to blatantly violate the protocols of *ex parte* meetings common to many Anglo-American and European jurisdictions. But there is palpable pressure for judges to conform to the boundary-blurring social norms so prevalent in a networked society such as China.

Yet, while scholars generally identify social embeddedness as a problem with regard to judicial institution building (Gold et al. 2002; Potter 2002), little is known about the mechanisms of social embeddedness. We examine the operation of *guanxi* from the understudied perspective of the favor giver – the judge. Specifically, we asked judges how they deal with 人情 (*renqing*, meaning sentiment), 关系 (*guanxi*) and 金钱 (*jinqian*, meaning money) cases – the so-called three types of cases (三案) in the lingo of the Chinese judiciary. We focused on cases in which the judges were centrally involved, usually as the responsible judge (承办法官 *chengban faguan*), or cases in which they participated in making the decision, since in these cases they were in the best position to understand the impact of *guanxi*. We analyze the character of the *guanxi* involved, the nature of the requests from their *guanxi* sources and the means through which requests were conveyed. We also problematize the relationship between the *guanxi* source and the target judges, the responses of the target judges, the outcomes of the efforts, and the means of compensation (gifts, banquets, money or other non-monetary compensation).

In our interviews with judges, we asked them to evaluate the role of *guanxi* in their career development, and the risk entailed. We asked them, if possible, to give some examples they encountered, either from their personal experience or from their close colleagues. We asked how they viewed their superiors and how they character-ized their relationships with them. We also asked them how they reacted to such requests (if they were asked for a favor). Additionally, we asked them if they would have handled certain cases differently had there been no *guanxi* involved. Questions we asked judges include: "What was your relationship with the person who asked you for favor?" "Did you feel pressure?" "Did *guanxi* affect the outcome of the ruling?" "Why did you turn down the request? (in cases that *guanxi* had little influence)" "Was there any favor in return?" "Was money involved?"

Some of our informants talked about their own cases. Others talked about cases of their colleagues that they saw or were involved indirectly. Our informants usually came to know the cases from discussions in division meetings or in private conversa-tions, or from both. A majority of the judges we interviewed were frontline judges. A few of them were division heads and deputy division heads. Some were former frontline judges who at the time of interview have moved away from frontline judging and worked in the research department of their courts.[1] In short, our reports were from insiders. We did not, and could not, observe directly the dealings that influenced the outcomes of the cases we report below. Since few judges would be likely to make up their "dirty laundry" and their accounts were more consistent than not, we believe our data present a fairly accurate picture of how *guanxi* is at work inside the courts. We did check reliability by asking the same question (or the same question in slightly rephrased form) at different times during an interview to make sure that judges' accounts were consistent.

Cases used to illustrate social embeddedness came from two basic level courts: one a work-unit type court located in the rural region of an inland province where the GDP per capita was only one-third that of the developed coastal areas; the other a firm-type court in the south, one of the most affluent areas of the country. The locations of the courts allow us to identify the effects of the market economy on the judicial process, a topic that we will address in greater depth in the next chapter.

CONCEPTUALIZING THE ROLE OF SOCIAL TIES IN THE CHINESE JUDICIAL CONTEXT

As Gold et al. (2002) characterize, there are two prevailing views on *guanxi* in the literature. The first, the institutionalist perspective, sees *guanxi* as the structural consequence of an authoritarian state filled with powerful officials in a society with weak internal controls. It treats *guanxi* as a strategic resource and a form of institu-tional soft power. Specifically, it argues that *guanxi* is instrumental for navigating uncertain institutional environments in the reform economy (Guthrie 1999; Wank 1999; Xin and Pearce 1996; Keister 2002; Smart and Smart 1991). Exemplifying this institutionalist thesis, Walder (1986) describes the relationship between superiors and subordinates in traditional work-units as a form of patron-client relation. In a centralized command economy, *guanxi* mattered when powerful officials were in full control of scarce necessities such as housing, promotions and other non-wage benefits.

The second view, commonly known as the cultural thesis, sees *guanxi* as a broad, diffused, and deep-rooted phenomenon of Chinese culture. According to the well-known thesis of famed Chinese anthropologist Fei Xiaotong (1992), Confucian ethics are a form of tiered social ethics: familial relationships, long-term friends, classmates, schoolmates, in-laws, colleagues, business partners or acquaintances. Society is composed not of discrete individuals and organizations but of overlapping networks of people linked together through differentially categorized social relationships. Each individual is at the center of an egocentric network with no explicit boundaries, always involving *guanxi* of varying magnitudes. Furthering the cultural thesis, Bian (1994) and Yang (1994) study how individuals cultivate and utilize their *guanxi* to advance personal interests. In return, those benefiting from *guanxi* are obligated to assist the connected (Bian 1994:972). For example, in assessing the relative efficacy of network ties on job searches, Bian (1997) argues the need for "bringing strong ties back in."

In debating about the nature of *guanxi*, the two theses are often presented as oppositional – *guanxi* is *either* institutional *or* cultural (Gold et al. 2002). This precludes the possibility of treating the two as analytically distinct dimensions that differentiate types of *guanxi*. Here we treat the two distinct dimensions as super-imposed on each other. The first dimension deals with the degree of direct control or supervision a favor seeker has over the favor giver. We ask whether or not a connection comes from the supervisors of the judge who decides, and whether ties can be classified as superior and non-superior. This is where vertical hierarchy comes into play. A judge is under pressure to deliver in a court with a strong, tall hierarchy if she is approached by a superior – that is, someone who is ranked higher than she. Such pressure is weakened if the favor seeker does not occupy such a superior position. The term "superior" goes beyond the immediate boss of the judge; it includes any officials who are empowered to assess the performance of the judge and thus affect her welfare and career prospects. For a frontline judge, "superiors" thus refers to the division heads and the vice presidents and presidents of the court. Often, her superiors also include the senior judges who work in the corresponding division of the appellate court. Though some of those judges are not ranked higher, they are empowered to determine whether the judge's ruling should be reversed or remanded, a criterion adopted for assessing the performance of the judge. "Superiors" can even go beyond the establishment of the court and include local party leaders who have much say on the staffing appointments. As discussed in Chapter 4, local party-state officials are *de facto* responsible for the appointment and removal of court officials. Local officials in charge of powerful bureaus in the economic sector and the people's congresses also occupy "superior" roles, as they have *de facto* control over the court budget and staffing decisions.

Favor seekers are non-superior when they do not have as much power and influence over the judge's career development. These include court colleagues of equal or lower ranks, as well as judges from neighboring courts that are not in a supervisory position to the court. Non-superior *guanxi* may also involve contacts with persons outside of the court and the local government, such as a judge's classmates or schoolmates or her former colleagues. They may also include her relatives or friends. As will be shown, whether a relationship is superior or not makes an important difference in influencing the decision-making process.

The second dimension is about the strength and intensity of *guanxi*: whether a social tie is strong or weak (Granovetter 1973). A tie between two individuals can be strong or weak depending on the time spent in interaction, emotional intensity, intimacy or reciprocal services (Granovetter 1973; Marsden and Campbell 1984). Strong *guanxi* is also multiplex. Multiplex ties exist in multiple contexts (Kapferer 1969) and are more likely to extend to a new setting, playing the role of a "bridge" (Bian 1997). Analytically, multiplexity can be defined as the degree of the overlap of roles, exchanges or affiliations in a social relationship (Verbrugge 1979). *Guanxi* that appears in many settings is harder to resist, and is likely to extend its effects to new settings. For instance, judges have many colleagues in their courts, but only with those in their inner circles will they spend time together over the weekend or share family vacations. Only with those who are in a given personal circle will a judge share her experiences and opinions on the difficult cases she deals with. The same applies to the relations between a judge and her friends. The relations between a judge and her family members are strong because familial ties straddle across different settings. This is the innermost circle of Fei's original thesis of differential modes of association. The relation of a judge with her old classmate may also be strong if they see each other frequently and assist each other in many aspects. On the other hand, uniplex *guanxi*, i.e., ties that are based on one type of relationship, are relatively weak and often superficial: their ties do not extend beyond that setting. Of course, the line between close and superficial is fluid and is sometimes hard to draw. Our framework nonetheless provides a perspective for examining the impact of *guanxi* (Table 6.1).

Influence is most intense when *guanxi* comes from a relational point that is both superior and strong. The relationship between the favor seeker (higher) and the favor giver (lower) is both formally hierarchical and multiplex. This relationship is mostly found in bureaucracies when hierarchical control is strong. Walder (1986:170–175) has attributed this as a form of patron-client relation that mingles personal loyalties, institutional assessment on performance and material interest. The patron offers not only advantages of official bonuses, raises and promotions to their clients, but also informal "goodies" such as better housing allocations and scarce commodities unavailable on the market. Under this circumstance, the target judge is under pressure to fulfill the requests of the patron in order to show that she is both capable

TABLE 6.1 *A Typology of* **Guanxi** *and Its Influence on Judicial Decision-Making*

	Strong tie	Weak tie
Superior	Strong impact, a judge's help may go beyond the scope of discretion. Neither money nor gift is offered.	Significant to moderate impact, judge helps by exercising discretionary power. Non-monetary gift or no gift is offered.
Non-Superior	Significant impact, judge's help usually within the scope of discretion. Non-monetary gift offered.	Uncertain impact, judge's help, if any, is within the scope of discretion. Money and gift offered.

and loyal. She regards the matter raised by her superior as her own business in order to show personal allegiance.

The intensity of influence subsides when the connection is superior but weak. This kind of *guanxi* can be found between a superior and a subordinate in more impersonal types of bureaucracies. The relationship is formal and narrow. It does not span a broad range of settings. The target judge still complies with the requests from the superior, but she adopts a more detached and cautious attitude. She may not want to risk her career, and is hesitant to go against the law in order to satisfy the superior. The third type of *guanxi* is strong but non-superior. Since it is non-superior, the target judge does not worry about how the favor seeker can affect her position in the court. This person may not even be a part of the court. But the *guanxi* is strong, meaning that it calls upon the judge's obligations in other social capacities, as son/daughter, sibling, relative and friend. Compared with the first type of *guanxi*, this type with non-superior but strong ties also has significant influence on the favor giver. However, the extent of the influence seldom goes beyond the scope of her discretionary power. Her superiors are not "in" on the exercise. To protect herself, the judge who offers such favors will much prefer to work within the confines of the law. Usually no immediate favor is needed.

The influence is the weakest when *guanxi* is non-superior and weak. This is, however, the most available form of *guanxi*. This type of *guanxi* lies on the periphery of a judge's egocentric network; ties of this type are so numerous that they are easily replaceable. This type of *guanxi* is also uniplex. It does not straddle across settings. The judge approached is prepared to "harden her heart" and is reluctant to bring weak *guanxi* to her job setting. Furthermore, since this type of *guanxi* is not superior, the target judge is not concerned about the feelings of the favor seeker. The judge has little incentive to make efforts, not to mention break the law. She may only reply to questions for which the other party could also get answers from official websites or published documents, or may offer a "personal take" on what the party could do, without promising anything. In short, she only provides information without exerting influence (Granovetter 1973, 1974, 1995).

SUPERIOR AND STRONG TIES

Few judges are able to turn down the pull of *guanxi* when it is superior and strong. In small work-unit courts, the court leaders who occupy superior positions retain broad and substantial power. Their subordinates are heavily dependent upon them in more ways than one. As mentioned, presidents of smaller work-unit courts would review decisions (criminal cases in particular) drafted by their frontline judges. More important, court leaders have tremendous power over the promotions, job postings and fringe benefits that subordinates are entitled to receive.

The following case was told by a veteran judge who worked in the civil division of an inland grassroots court. A woman was injured at work in a big brick manufacturer. Workers there had been used to heating up drinking water by putting a kettle on the top of the kiln. One day, when the woman tried to climb up the kiln to heat up another pot of water, the top collapsed and she fell into the kiln. She was pulled out of the kiln immediately, but a large part of her body was burnt. The accident left her in critical condition. She survived and made a recovery, but only after a long series of treatments and multiple skin grafts. Her medical expenses totaled 190,000 yuan, an enormous sum by the local living standard. She filed a civil lawsuit against the brick manufacturer for damages (*Case of the Collapsed Kiln*).

The court stalled the case for five years. No judgment was rendered. The brick manufacturer was one of the biggest enterprises of the region. The owner was a delegate of the local people's congress. His relationship with local officials was well known: when the local government had claimed the manufacturer's land for redevelopment, it was rumored that the manufacturer had been overcompensated by millions of yuan. The owner had had a close relationship with the vice president of the court as well as the senior officials in the intermediate court of the region. The ties were so strong that the responsible judge was asked to directly report the case to the vice president.

The counsel for the manufacturer requested to include more defendants. They argued that the manufacturer had contracted the construction of the kiln to a work team and thus should not be held liable for the injury. In informal meetings with the judges on the case, the vice president would not approve of any rulings that held the manufacturer liable for damages. On the eve of the 2013 Spring Festival, the responsible judge and her division head proposed that the manufacturer pre-pay 10,000 yuan for the victim as temporary relief, a small fraction of the incurred medical expenses. The vice president was angry. In the presence of the brick company owner, he scolded the responsible judge and the division head. The vice president did hint at the meeting that the owner could offer some help to make the case "go away," but added that it would be completely at his discretion. Over the five years, the injured employee received 5,000 yuan compensation from the defendant. Emboldened by his *guanxi* with the vice president, the defendant refused to settle. Matters did not change until five years later, when both the vice president and the president were replaced.

The relationship between the vice president and the responsible judge was not only superior but also strong. The vice president treated the responsible judge as his protégé, a relationship reminiscent of the "patron-client" type (Walder 1986:170). This explained why the vice president admonished her in front of the defendant. The vice president expected the junior judge to take care of his business as if it were her own business. The responsible judge had already done her part to protect the interests of the owner, but the owner insisted on offering no compensation. The pressure on the judge was intense and she obliged. The case was stalled indefinitely.

The strength of a superior tie is much affected by a court's institutional makeup. Superiors who hold *broad* power foster strong *guanxi*. They can reward junior judges if pleased and punish them if offended. Thus, the subordinates are willing to heed their superiors' needs, even if doing so might apparently contradict their own beliefs and short-term interests. "Helping out" a superior is a common way for the supervisee to demonstrate her abilities and loyalty. The following is another case handled by a close colleague of an informant.

In a small, low-stakes civil case that took place in a hinterland province, the plaintiff filed for damages of 3,000 yuan for his stolen motorcycle. He alleged that the bike had been stolen from the defendant's parking lot located in a residential complex. But he could not produce the receipt to prove that he had parked the motorcycle in the lot at the time when the alleged theft had occurred. What he had, however, was a handwritten statement from the management office of the residential complex that the motorcycle was missing. To make matters more interesting, at the hearing, a staff member from the management testified that statement was fake (*Case of the Stolen Motorcycle*).

The case had proceeded routinely until the responsible judge sought the approval for his draft judgment from the court president. The president returned the draft with a terse, circumspect comment: "This case shall be handled carefully." As it turned out, the plaintiff was a relative of the political leader in charge of political-legal affairs at the municipal level. This leader was thus the immediate superior of the court president. Organizationally, the court is a bureau of the local government. Soon the judge was summoned to accompany the court president to report it to the political leader. Major and influential cases are reported to senior local party-state officials so that they could decide which cases to keep a closer eye on. The judge was surprised that he was asked to report his small case. From a legal viewpoint, the case was a simple contractual dispute in which the plaintiff failed to produce the contract in dispute (the receipt). Our informant, who was not present at the meeting, could not suppress his gibes at the political leader and the court president.

If I were the leader, I would rather commit suicide. A leader at the municipal level, and the one in charge of political legal affairs, he summoned the court president and the responsible judge to report on such a trivial case! The sole purpose was to inform us of his expectation. In my eyes, he was worth little more than the 3,000 yuan!

The judge continued, "Now I know that it is not easy to be a court president. He looks like a king inside the court. But he was a nobody in front of the municipal leader. I can't really describe how my president was chewed out by that leader."

Within days, the responsible judge had a new judgment ready to be endorsed by the president: the defendant should compensate 3,000 yuan for the loss of the motorcycle. In the judgment, the statement of the management office was admitted as authentic, and their countering oral testimony that the statement was fake was ruled invalid for an overtly technical reason: the 30 days limitation for the submission of evidence had passed when the oral evidence was filed.

The judge and his court president acquiesced to the request of their political patron without putting up much resistance. The judge admitted his ruling was weak from a legal standpoint, yet that was the ruling he made in the face of the pressure from strong superior ties. The judge seemed torn between satisfying his superior and despising himself for the judgment. Though not keen to seek promotion, the judge told his colleague that he needed the job to support his daughter for her college education. Other judges we interviewed said for this type of cases, judges are pushed to create a legal opening not available under normal circumstances. Cases of this kind are opportunities for court leaders to nurture their ties as they perform acts valued by political leaders because those acts serve their interests. The leader owed the court president a favor, and the two grew closer as a result. The favor in return does not have to be of a private nature. It can be a willingness to raise the total appropriations of the court next time. In fact, it is this blending of institutional and individual interests that make ties from a close superior so powerful and appealing.

A shortage economy and weak legal infrastructure were the main reasons why *guanxi* became widespread in the early stage of the economic reform (Gold et al. 2002:14–16). The influence of *guanxi* may have declined among bigger and more professionalized firm-type courts. Legal infrastructure there is more developed. Judges who work in those courts, many of them located in coastal urban cities, are able to pursue more goods from the market. They are also subjected to greater scrutiny both from within the party-state and from the media and public. To a certain extent, this seems to be the case. We find that in developed areas, judges and their superiors are more cautious in dealing with *guanxi*. Nonetheless, the influences of superior and strong ties remain substantial.

A judge in her early thirties who worked in a coastal city told us about the appellate case she handled. Four persons were charged with selling bootlegged cell phones worth more than a market value of one million yuan. The trial court determined that a young girl in her early 20s was the gang leader. She was sentenced to three years in jail. The other three defendants were given suspended sentences for their subordinate roles. The trial judge found the girl in charge of the financial transactions and marketing arrangements of the illegal operation. However, one defendant testified: "She is not a boss, but only a wage earner." Our informant concluded from the court hearing that the girl was an agent for the real boss behind the scene. However, the girl was insistent in her refusal to disclose the man's identity.

The division head to whom our informant reported was connected to the girl. He asked our judge to "consider the case carefully, and to display not just legal skills but also skills in social relationships." The division head had been the mentor of the responsible judge for many years. The responsible judge appreciated his help.

But under normal court practices, unless there are defendants at large, the court should designate a leading role to one of the defendants. No defendants were at large. None had taken a more prominent role than the girl. When the judge indicated to the division head that treating the girl leniently would contradict standard practices, the latter responded, "Why not? Shouldn't doubtful cases be treated leniently?"

The judge, however, was reluctant to heed her superior's request. She was concerned about the repercussions to the three other defendants. If the girl was not the leader, then they all played equal roles. Suspended sentences would be out of the question. The three defendants would be sentenced to three years in jail, the minimum penalty according to the law. Such an elevation would violate the practice of "no penalty added in appeal."

The judge went back to study precedents on selling counterfeiting goods. She consulted colleagues who specialized in criminal trials. At the end, she decided to keep the part of the verdict that ruled the girl to be the leader. But she went on to argue that the case of the girl was "serious" but not "very serious." This allowed her to fine the girl in lieu of imprisonment. The three-year sentence was changed to a suspended sentence. To justify the change, she asked the girl to pay a heavier fine. Her counsel did so promptly.

When she proposed what she wanted to do to the division head, the latter was upset. He was concerned that asking the defendant to pay a heavier fine was in its own way legally inappropriate. In a routine divisional meeting, the director requested that the responsible judge and the other members of the collegial panel deliberate the case in front of other judges in the division. The head seemed to want to show to his division that it was a decision initiated by our informant.

This case shows that judges in developed areas are more cautious in handling *guanxi* related cases than their hinterland counterparts. The responsible judge did not blindly heed the head's plead for leniency toward the girl. To the judge, the facts indicated that the girl had taken a leading role among the four defendants. She wanted a legal cover and she got that by raising the fine. The division head was also careful about how the case would appear to other judges. He was concerned about the legality of his subordinate's imposition of a heavier fine. He also did not want any trail of *guanxi* left. He requested the collegial panel to deliberate before the division members in order to show "due process." From the outcome, however, the superior and strong *guanxi* from the head remains impactful. At least in this case, while the means are circumspect, the tie remains consequential in determining the outcome.

A judge's relationship with her immediate superior remains a strong tie in many Chinese courts. The judge reports directly to this immediate superior. One interviewee said, "If a judge of the Supreme People's Court (SPC) wants to influence a case at a basic level court, she would not directly contact the responsible judge. Instead, the SPC judge would contact a judge at the high court, who would then contact another judge at the intermediate court, who would eventually contact the responsible judge. In this way, a remote source influences a trial judge through a chain of immediate superior *guanxi*. The chain is so long that the responsible judge may have no idea where the source of *guanxi* comes from." This holds true also for senior judges trying to influence their frontline judges in big courts, where the president and vice presidents do not necessarily know all of their judges personally. A judge we interviewed in Guangdong said, "Court presidents rarely instruct their frontline judges what to do, unless their relationship is close. Rather, they first contact the division head, who will then contact the frontline judge." The reach of strong *guanxi* in China is long and can overcome umpteen degrees of separation. Favor seekers and their targets, originally disconnected, are bridged through intermediaries to whom both are strongly tied (Bian 1997).

SUPERIOR BUT WEAK TIES

Weak ties are weak in the sense that their reach is not as long or as encompassing as that of strong ties. A weak tie is distinguished from a strong tie for its delimited, uniplex nature; i.e., the influence comes from the person's office rather than from her person. Often, the superior acting as a favor seeker is not the immediate supervisor. When *guanxi* comes from a person in a superior position but is itself weak, the force of the pull from *guanxi* is abated. The target judge understandably would not offend the superior. But this type of request is different from the request from a patron. What the target judge will do is to give "face" to the superior. One judge said, "I would take it seriously but make sure that my handling follows the law."

A middle-aged Guangdong judge told us that she received a call from a head of another division to immediately withdraw a case she handled. One of the involved companies in that case was scheduled for review by the securities regulatory authorities the next day. This was the last step before its public offering. It thus needed to clear all related litigations. Normally such requests are not approved, since a filed claim can only be withdrawn after a definite period of time. But an early withdrawal is allowed if the court has already undertaken some preliminary examination by taking testimony from the plaintiff. The head therefore suggested that the judge take testimony from the company.

By law, the judge could have just ignored the request, since it was the company that first filed the claim and she had other urgent matters at hand. The judge was not a close friend of the division head – the latter was transferred from another court. Nonetheless, it was possible that he could become her immediate supervisor some day due to internal reassignments.

The judge set aside all work. She did the preliminary examination and collected testimonies from the company on the same day. She then quickly drafted a decision approving the company's withdrawal of the claim and presented it to her own division head in the afternoon. But she did not inform her supervisor of the call from the other division head. She said to us, "I did not want to mention anything. I did not want my supervisor to suspect that I had any interest in it, which I did not. If he approved, that was his decision. If he did not, it would be out of my control." Her supervisor reviewed the application that day and a decision for approval was issued as requested. The other division head was evidently pleased.

The help offered by the judge was procedural in nature: the withdrawal would have been issued without the judge's help, but it would have taken more time if it had been prepared by following standard procedures. The judge helped by doing what was required for an early withdrawal. She set her regular work aside but she did go out of her way to urge her supervisor to approve the withdrawal. Frontline judges rarely turn down requests from their superiors. The bureaucratic personnel evaluation system empowers any superiors who *may* become a future supervisor of the target judge. It is possible that this person may affect the judge's chances for improving her position in the future. But the intensity of interaction is much less than for interactions between the judge and the immediate supervisor. It remains the fact that the immediate supervisor has the greatest influence on the judge's next promotion. The judge was wise not to show her supervisor that she has done a great favor to the other division head, as this could raise a question of loyalty toward the judge's immediate boss.

In some cases there is even resistance from a target judge facing pressure from superior, but weak, *guanxi*. One informant from an urban court in the coastal region recalled a case in which she participated as a member of the collegial panel. It was a trademark transfer case. Prior to the date of the hearing, the parties presented a settlement application, stating that the defendants would pay the 20 million yuan as requested by the plaintiff. The judges on the collegial panel found the litigation suspicious, and questioned whether it was phony – that is, whether the genuine intention was to facilitate a legal transfer of properties between the plaintiff and the defendants. The judges disapproved the settlement application as a result.

Before the judgment was announced, however, the plaintiff filed a motion to withdraw the case. This only confirmed the judges' suspicion that the litigation was phony. Alongside the filing of the withdrawal motion came a request from a vice president of the court, to whom the judge had only an indirect and lukewarm relationship. The superior wanted her to "carefully consider the withdrawal application." The responsible judge found herself in a dilemma: she wanted to deny the withdrawal application and to rule on the case, but the vice president had spoken. Eventually, she employed a subtle tactic that, according to our informant, had been widely used to divert *guanxi* requests in that particular court: the panel reached a non-unanimous decision. The responsible judge did not follow the suggestion by the vice president; she voted instead to disallow the withdrawal. But the other members of the collegial panel held a different opinion and voted to allow the withdrawal. Their votes constituted the majority opinion. Since a non-unanimous decision would need to be approved by the division head and vice president, the judges' "agree to disagree" decision shrewdly protected them if a formal investigation was conducted – the responsible judge followed the rules and voted against the withdrawal. But the collegial panel still approved the application.

The influence from a superior tie may be further discounted if the target judge is not keen to plan for her next promotion. In a case in which a married-out woman sued her village committee for land compensations, the issue was whether the woman had indeed been "married" – she had not obtained a marriage certificate, but had hosted a wedding banquet for the relatives of the two families, a ceremony regarded by the locals as getting married. The vice chief of staff at the court, obviously related to the married-out woman, sought out the responsible judge for help. The vice chief had not been a direct supervisor of the judge; neither had his post provided him with any substantial power over the judge. However, the vice chief could be transferred to a position superior to the judge.

The responsible judge, a colleague of the informant who told us the case, could have offered some help. She could have helped bolster the plaintiff's case by collecting evidence to prove that there was no marriage certificate issued for the woman and information about the amount of compensation money distributed to other villagers. But at age 52, the judge was to retire in three years. It was unlikely she would suffer any future losses if she offered no help. Without any desire to be promoted or transferred to a better position, she chose not to help. The judge went ahead and suggested the married-out woman to withdraw the case.

NON-SUPERIOR BUT STRONG TIES

In a relational society like China, strong ties do not come only from superiors inside the court. As with officials working in other government units, ties also come from colleagues, friends and family members (Feng 2010). Strong but non-superior ties of this kind hold sway over the decisions of Chinese judges (Hwang 1987). If superior ties represent vertical influences from within the bureaucracy of the court, non-superior ties represent the horizontal pushing and pulling from outside. Judges are government bureaucrats, but they are also members of what the Chinese call a "society of acquaintances." For judges located in the inland rural regions of the country, even though they can *buy* more of the previously scarce items on the market now, personal networks and the practice of favors and reciprocity remain crucial in help getting things done – obtaining a bank loan or sending children to preferred schools being prime examples.

Many judges feel obligated to members of their personal inner circles. They offer help to those members who pull strings, sometimes to repay a favor owed, and sometimes to put the person in *renqing* debt, i.e., by bestowing a favor to be reciprocated later. What distinguishes non-superior ties from the two earlier types we covered is that the judge has to act without the help, and sometimes even the consent, of her superiors. It is harder and riskier for the judge to offer help, because any deviation from the formal rules and practices of the court is subject to the scrutiny of her superiors. Instead, the *modus operandi* for providing help for this type of tie is to maneuver the grey area of the discretionary power that the judge holds.

The case we used to illustrate non-superior ties came from a work-unit type court located in an inland province. It was a personal injury case centered on a traffic accident. An elderly man in his mid-seventies was hit by a pickup truck (*Case of the Jaywalking Man*). The traffic police determined that both parties had been negligent. The man jaywalked when he crossed the road hastily. But the pickup truck shared bigger responsibility, as it failed to slow down. The man's daughter, the director of an administrative bureau in the local government, contacted her high school classmate, our informant, for help. The latter was a middle-ranked judge at the court. They were close friends. They had kept in touch for two decades since graduation. Upon being asked by her friend, the judge contacted one of her closest colleagues, who was in charge of the initial filings of new cases. This colleague offered some astute advice. For example, originally the plaintiff intended to file a request to impound the pickup truck. The colleague advised the plaintiff to directly file a lawsuit instead. This saved the man 3,000 yuan for the impounding fee. The court formally accepted the case in the afternoon of the day it was filed. The acceptance decision was made while the plaintiff was still submitting documents required for filing. In addition, the filing judge also "randomly" assigned the case to a judge with whom our informant also had a close relationship. That judge started working on the case as soon as it arrived on her desk, whereas normally it took several days to prepare for a case before a hearing was scheduled.

The plaintiff did not hire a lawyer. As the judge indicated to us, it was unnecessary. The responsible judge offered detailed legal advice throughout the process. At the end of the trial, the judge ruled in the plaintiff's favor. It was not a surprise ruling, as the plaintiff had a strong case. But the judge worked within the rules to push up the damages for the plaintiff. For example, the judge awarded 2,000 yuan to the plaintiff for consulting medical experts, but this kind of fee was usually excluded from the calculation of damages under Chinese law. Yet, it was included under the heading of "transportation fees." Another 3,000 yuan was awarded for outpatient medical costs. This was again normally inadmissible, but the judge labeled it as "nutritional fees." The judge also generously included in the damages the cost of hiring two helpers to tend to the injured man, though normally the court allowed for one helper. The difference of including an extra helper, a decision that was subject to the judge's discretion, was more than 3,000 yuan.

The judge found the plaintiff 20 percent at fault for his own injury. This, again, deviated from the usual practice, by which a 30 percent liability was assigned to a jaywalker. Our informant said that the judge had originally ruled that the man was only 10 percent at fault, but eventually changed her mind. A 10 percent liability for the minor party in a comparative negligence case would have been too exceptional, and would have aroused the attention of her superiors. To get the extra 10 percent in damages would require the tacit approval of the division head.

From the way the judge talked about the case, the final outcome was much affected by the strings that she had pulled. The plaintiff saved time and money by opting not to impound the truck from the other party. This had been done based on the advice offered by the filing judge. The case was expeditiously processed. Some procedural requirements were generously forgone. Then the plaintiff received a favorable verdict. Perhaps the one area where the use of *guanxi* was most consequential was in the calculation of damages. It was the area where the discretion of the trial judge made the most difference.

The encompassing effects of strong outside ties show the porousness of the Chinese courts as an institution in two ways. Some judges do not seem to draw a clear line between work and personal life. Judges are also able to exercise so much discretion that, to an important extent, it influences the substantive outcome of adjudication. Close *guanxi* matters, even when the actions affected by *guanxi* seem to follow the law. In the example above, the favors were done by more than one judge exercising discretion to favor the party with connections. Had the case drawn the attention of the division head, or had it been appealed, the responsible judge could have accounted for her decisions by referring to relevant legal provisions and established procedural rules. While the spirit of the law is violated, no law was explicitly violated.

One might argue that work-unit type courts are located in more networked communities where it is hard for judges to turn down requests from their closest family members and friends. Yet many firm-type courts in big cities are not immune to social embeddedness. One judge with eight years of experience in a Shenzhen court said, "I have friends, fellows from the same home town, and classmates too; so does everyone. They may contact me for procedural convenience or substantive favors. But overall, the requests are reasonable and I will try my best. In most situations no money is involved in return." In other words, although a frontline judge may be willing to resist the requests from her superiors, she still has to deal with strong ties from her own personal network. Another young judge from Shanghai said, "In some cases, I have to tilt toward a particular party because they are friends of relatives or friends of friends. This kind of 人情案 (*renqingan*, meaning cases involving connections and human sentiment) will not disappear overnight."

A male judge in his mid-thirties who worked in an intermediate court in Guangdong told us about a rape case. The case was handled by the basic-level court in the same county. The victim invited the two defendants to her rental apartment after a late dinner. The rape occurred when all three were playing with an iPhone in her bed. The second defendant helped the first defendant in the crime.

The parents of the second defendant approached our informant judge through his father. The two families went way back, as they were from the same village. Since the case was not handled by the intermediate court in which the judge worked, he told his father that he could not do anything until the case reached the trial stage at the lower court. The second defendant hired an experienced lawyer who allegedly advised the family to send 30,000 yuan to the prosecutor. The case was still prosecuted, but the prosecutor recommended a jail sentence of a year and a half. The lenient recommendation suggested that the bribe money worked. After the hearing, the responsible judge hinted to the lawyer that a suspended sentence was unlikely.

Our informant then sought the help of a colleague in the same court who was close to the responsible judge at the lower court. Both the responsible judge and his colleague told him that a suspended sentence was difficult because it usually required the approval of the division head and even the adjudication committee of the court. However, the responsible judge said that he would propose a suspended sentence. It turned out that the proposed sentencing was approved – possibly the conditions for the suspended sentence had all been met. To express his gratitude, the male judge sent his colleague and the responsible judge each a bag with 1,000 yuan inside (a small gift, given the cost of living of the city).

In this case, the *guanxi* was non-superior but strong. Our informant could not turn down the request from his father. However, what he could do was limited, as he was not officially involved. He told the relatives of the second defendant outright that he could not offer any help until the case reached the trial stage. Even at that point, he could not control the outcome. But he found the right person to get to the responsible judge, who eventually proposed a suspended sentence. Had the proposed suspended sentence not been approved, he could have provided little further help to change the verdict.

NON-SUPERIOR AND WEAK TIES

The situation differs when *guanxi* is neither superior nor strong. Weak, horizontal *guanxi* from the outside means little to judges. This type of tie has no impact on career development. Judges are not obligated to act when approached by a member outside their personal network. A judge has little reason to defy the law. What the judge is sometimes willing to do is to offer some convenience within the scope of her discretionary power, and she has little reason to defy the law.

Our informant is a colleague and personal friend of the head of a dispatched tribunal head in a hinterland court. A dispatched tribunal is an outreach or satellite unit of the court, usually located in the countryside. Its purpose is to enhance access to justice for the rural population. Organizationally, it is a division of the court, but it is a unit that is physically separated from the court to which it belongs. In this case, the matter was a robbery case that involved three young adult defendants, the second and the third of whom were related to the tribunal head (*Case of Three Young Robbers*). There was no clear, undisputed leader among the three. Under normal circumstances, none of them would have been given a suspended sentence. Four judges of different seniorities were involved as decision-makers: a junior judge who was the responsible judge, a more experienced presiding judge who chaired the collegial panel, the criminal division head, and the vice president of the court overseeing criminal cases.[2] With few exceptions, cases involving suspended sentences had to be reported to and thus determined by the adjudication committee (He 2012). The tribunal head wanted to get a suspended sentence for the two to whom he was related. He also wanted to avoid having the case reported to the adjudication committee, where the court president had the final say and his own influence would be virtually nonexistent. Among the four judges, he was an acquaintance of the presiding judge. His relationships with the junior judge who handled the case and his two senior bosses – the division head and the vice president – were further distant. They were colleagues, but he had no personal ties to the three.

The tribunal head, being a judge in a small division (the tribunal) within the court's establishment, held no supervisory power over the judges he had tried to influence. By official ranking, a tribunal head ranks not only lower than the vice president, but also lower than the head of the bigger and more powerful criminal division. His actual power and influence are also limited, as he is, literally and figuratively, away from the power center. To approach the presiding judge and the responsible judge, he treated the two to a fancy dinner. During the meal, the two judges suggested that he should hire a lawyer for the defendants. A lawyer could help build a case that the two defendants were accomplices to the third defendant in the robbery. Then, using the wedding of the son of the vice president as an excuse, the tribunal head sent 5,000 yuan to the judge as a gift, well above the going rate of 200 yuan for a casual friend. Two days after the wedding, the tribunal head revealed his relationship with the two defendants to the vice president. He also made known to the vice president that he hoped that the two could get suspended sentences and that the case would not be sent to the adjudication committee. Similarly, 3,000 yuan was sent to the criminal division head and 2,000 to his not-so-close acquaintance, the presiding judge of the collegial panel. The latter initially refused the money and said it would be difficult to recommend suspended sentencing for the two, given the facts of the case. The tribunal head nonetheless convinced him to take the money by telling him that both the criminal division head and the vice president had agreed.

The eventual decision, however, was disappointing for the favor seeker. The case was sent to and determined by the adjudication committee, and only one of the two defendants connected to the head was granted a suspended sentence. The other defendant was sentenced to three years in jail and a fine of 6,000 yuan. This defendant was eventually granted a suspended sentence in the appellate court. The money spent, to quote the tribunal head, was "beyond imagination," according to what was retold by our informant. Apparently the remaining defendant and his family were outraged by the decisions. They believed that the three young men participated equally in the crime.

Weak, non-superior ties contrast starkly with superior *guanxi*. In this case, the tribunal head had weak *guanxi* with only one judge and virtually none at all with the other three. Our informant said, "If the defendants had had direct *guanxi* with the court president or other major local political leaders, the process would have been much different. In that situation, the responsible judge and the collegial panel would have suggested suspended sentencing. This would have been readily approved by the criminal division head. Even if it were sent to the adjudication committee, every member would endorse the suggestion tacitly. The suspended sentences would have been lawfully confirmed." Besides the strength of *guanxi*, it makes a difference whether it is from a superior, or in this case, someone who can potentially occupy a supervisory role in the future. Indeed, the junior responsible judge was the only official not monetarily compensated, though he directly handled the case. Perhaps the dispatched tribunal head believed he could pull rank on the judge. However, his actual power was dampened by the location of his position, being far removed from the center.

SUMMARY

One informant summarizes her viewpoint on *guanxi*: "*guanxi* helps, but it must be rock solid (硬)! Shallow and indirect personal ties exert little impact on a case. The so-called *guanxi* may serve as an introduction. But to affect the case outcome, you have to resort to money." What the judge describes as "rock solid" is the *guanxi* that we have analyzed as strong, either from a close superior who supervises the target judge and plays a crucial role in affecting her chances for promotion and better benefits or from a close member of the judge's private circle to whom she feels trust and obligation. Another judge in his early 50s from an urban court said, "I feel both obligated and obliged for requests from my supervisors. If I cannot satisfy the requests, it seems that I did not do my job well. But if I do, it is good for me and my development. For requests from my strongly tied friends, I feel bad if I cannot help."

Guanxi is informal, private and often not open to view (Bian 1997:371). Obtaining influence from *guanxi* is illegal, or at least it is publicly disapproved of. Both the favor seeker and the favor giver must know and trust each other to minimize the risk of *guanxi* exchanges. In reality, the risk of exposure is not high. Scholars have pointed out that a large number of people are involved in such activities and evidence of bribery is hard to come by (Li 2012). But the potential risk for exposure does exist, especially since the current leadership of President Xi Jinping has made anti-corruption its top priority. Being exposed for engaging in *guanxi* transactions taints a judge's reputation and career prospects. Moreover, criminal indictments aside, the favor giver will likely face accusations from non-connected parties. The *guanxi* has to be strong enough to make the favor giver feel obligated to overcome the perception of having performed some unprofessional and socially disapproved activities.

As a malleable form of social power, *guanxi* comes in different strengths and types. Our typology aims to explain the nature and character of social embeddedness in the Chinese courts. The stronger the *guanxi*, the more influence it brings. There is certainly a utilitarian aspect in nurturing *guanxi*. The *guanxi* pull from an immediate superior is strong because the person is in control of resources and opportunities that matter to the subordinate. Precisely because of its informal, rule-deviating and private nature, there are few better ways for a subordinate to show *personal* loyalty to his superior than to answer his call of *guanxi*. Yet the strength of strong ties is not just attributable to their utilitarian functions. For the favor giver to bend over backward to help, there needs to be a sense of trust, where the favor giver feels protected by the favor seeker. This is why strong ties come from family and close friends. This same sense of trust can also come from a superior with whom the subordinate identifies, not just out of self-interest, but also because of shared histories, common goals in work or similarities in temperament and style (Downs 1967:79–91). On the other hand, the limited influence of weak ties is not just attributable to the favor giver's sense of not feeling equally obligated to offer help, but also to his uncertainty as to whether the favor seeker can be trusted. This means the judge would rarely agree to engage in activities that would put him at peril.

GUANXI AND MONEY

In the existing literature, *guanxi* is commonly treated as a precursor of corruption (Lü 2002; Li, Ling 2011, 2012; Zhan 2012). However, social embeddedness is a related but different phenomenon from bribery. To wit, strong *guanxi*, characterized by trust and obligation, *discourages* the use of money. Favors are not paid back immediately; they are tallied in long-term obligations. *Guanxi* becomes strong when it spans different personal spheres for the giver and the seeker. This seemingly paradoxical finding explains why the most influential *guanxi* is often the most elusive and untraceable. The vice president in the *Collapsed Kiln* case did not offer his subordinates any money or favors in exchange. He did not need to. It was understood that he would return the favor in due course.

Neither is money needed when the *guanxi* is non-superior but strong. In the *Case of the Jaywalking Man*, the plaintiff only treated the three involved judges – her classmate, the judge at the case filing division, and the responsible judge – to a dinner. Strong ties rarely require monetary exchange – the ties are too multiplex and resilient to require an immediate and exact repayment. Again, favors will be repaid in the long run.

When the ties are weak, favor is returned immediately (Bian 1997:372). Calculation is one-off (*quid pro quo*) and is more exacting. Money becomes the medium for this delimited type of exchange. This is true for a superior using weak *guanxi*. At the least, he is expected to offer some non-monetary compensation. A gift or a nice meal serves to repay the personal debt. As we have seen, the judge in the married-out woman case refused to help when the deputy chief of staff, without offering gifts, sought help from him. The judge expected an expression of gratitude, since the *guanxi* was not strong enough to make the request obligatory. The gift was also an acknowledgment that the superior was "in debt" to the frontline judge who had offered help.

When *guanxi* is neither superior nor strong, money exchange is all there is. The function of weak connection is mostly to pave the way for monetary transactions. In the *Case of the Jaywalking Man*, if the judge were to have gotten the approval of the division head for 10 percent, the *guanxi* source would have needed money to open doors, since the head was outside the judge's trusted personal network.

With weak or no *guanxi*, money serves as a risky substitute for the affectively charged relationships created by reciprocal favors and gifts (Yang 1994:167). This is where the practice of *guanxi* shades into the crimes of corruption and bribery. As Li (2012) demonstrates, in order to get things done, a tactic for favor seekers is to first form relationships with the target favor givers. Personal *guanxi* builds trust and makes it somewhat safer to offer and accept money.

The effect of money is nevertheless limited in cases involving weak and remote *guanxi*. While our evidence here is sketchy, it seems that the offer of money some-times has little impact on judges' actions. If the request comes from someone in a lower position of power, then the favor seeker is often at the mercy of the target. The target person might vaguely respond, "I'll see what I can do." Money may make the pleading more earnest, but it never reaches a point where the judge feels obligated. The actions of the target are unpredictable. This distinguishes this type of *guanxi* from the strong affectively charged relationships. As seen in the *Case of the Three Young Robbers*, the judge who sought help offered substantial money to the three senior judges. Yet he did not get the desired decision, leading him to spend more money in the appeal process.

THE LIMITS OF *GUANXI*

The influence of *guanxi* on judges is not without limits. Although they want to and may favor their connected parties, judges are also constrained. Due to the structure of litigation, most cases have at least two parties, and both parties may have *guanxi*. The judges involved thus have to balance them.

In a work-unit court we studied, there was a case between a local credit union and a state-owned enterprise (SOE) responsible for a water reservoir and irrigation project. The credit union wanted the SOE to repay a loan before the stipulated term expired. The SOE leader had *guanxi* with the court president, who instructed the responsible judge to deal with the case promptly. The credit union had *guanxi* with the division head, who instructed the responsible judge to take his time. The two sides had been clashing when the legal representative of the SOE accused the division head of being arrogant and uncooperative. The division head gave in as soon as he realized that the SOE had *guanxi* with the court president. Eventually the court president orchestrated a settlement agreed to by the parties.

In another case from the same court, there was a criminal case resulting from a traffic accident. A car knocked a couple off of their motorcycle. The man was lightly injured, but the woman died. It turned out that both the car driver and the injured husband were related to the judge. In this type of cases, the defendant usually wants a suspended sentence and the relatives of the deceased want economic compensation. The judge walked a fine line. He was polite and thoughtful to both sides. He explained to them in detail each step of the trial process. The judge managed to satisfy the request of the man on economic compensation, but also informed him that this meant no jail time for the defendant. Both sides were satisfied. Did *guanxi* influence how this case was handled? Yes, from the way the judge treated the litigation parties. But the answer is more ambiguous if judging from the outcome. The case would have been decided more or less the same without *guanxi*. The priority of the judge was to settle the case. He would have wanted to get both parties to agree to criminal reconciliation anyway, if no *guanxi* had been involved. In this case, the *guanxi* of one cancels out the *guanxi* of the other. The judge is caught between the two connections. He could not favor one party at the expense of the other.

The second limit is the law. In many cases, the judges have not committed what the law explicitly disallows. They are careful and pragmatic. Rarely would they risk their careers for *guanxi*, however strong the bonds are. They are also cautious when engaging in unusual practices that may draw the attention of their superiors. In the *Case of the Jaywalking Man*, the allocation of responsibility for the plaintiff was set at 20 percent rather than 10 percent because the latter percentage would have been too far out of line from established practices. Even in the *Case of the Stolen Motorcycle*, under the pressure of a strong superior tie, the judge still presented a legal pretext (on technical procedural grounds) for his unjust decision. Similarly, in the *Case of the*

Collapsed Kiln, the judges deferred the case indefinitely, attributing the delay to procedural reasons. Despite the pressure from the vice president, the judge did not render a judgment against the plaintiff. Even for a case of strong superior ties, in which judges have more room to maneuver and sometimes are emboldened by the protection of their superiors, they remain cautious. Self-protection is a paramount concern.

Judges are also wary of the suspicions of the other parties when they offer favor. They do not want to invite petitions or appeals. In the *Case of the Stolen Motorcycle*, for example, three men and three women confronted the responsible judge right after the judgment had been handed down. The judge who described the case to us recalled, "They were related to the defendant, the old superintendent who took care of the motorcycles. They yelled, 'On what basis did you make the judgment?' 'On what basis did you decide that the motorcycle was in the parking lot?' 'The judgment made our father sick to the stomach. He fell ill because of this judgment. Unable to pay the medical bills, we will take him to your court instead of the hospital!' 'Is not the court a place for reasoning?'" The responsible judge explained that they could appeal, but asked the protestors to calm down. As they became more agitated, it appeared that they were about to physically assault the judge. One of them said, "Is it still a time for law? At this moment, only economic compensation and the fist can talk." With sweat over his forehead, the responsible judge took out a statute book and explained the meaning of the statute of limitations, as well as the procedure to appeal, to the agitated men and women. The judge answered all of the questions the six raised. Thirty minutes later, the petitioners left the court.

The judge's explanation by no means addressed the defendant's grievances. However, he did have the law to fall back on, and was not in an indefensible position. It would have been difficult for him to do so without appealing to the statute of limitations. Certainly, in the eyes of the legally trained, the judge's appeal to a legal technicality appears strained. When determining what to do for the connected party, a judge usually take into consideration the other party's level of knowledge and resources. Whether the other party is legally represented, for example, is also a key consideration. A competent lawyer is able to identify practices that look legally justified but are in fact problematic, which can lead to either appeal or petition. In civil cases, judges also evaluate the likely reactions of the party without *guanxi*. The help can backfire if a favorable decision to the connected party leads to escalated petitions and protests from the losing party. That seemed to explain the stalling tactic of the judges in the *Case of the Collapsed Kiln*.

This risk assessment plays a more prominent role in civil cases (see Chapter 4). In criminal cases, as long as the court does not acquit a defendant, the prosecutor usually will not protest. In the *Case of Three Young Robbers*, for example, the judge was determined to get a suspended sentence for the two connected defendants, despite his unsuccessful initial attempt for one of them.

The third risk is the concern for social instability, i.e., the counterinfluence of political embeddedness. Judges are mindful of the possibilities of protests or petitions in making decisions. As shown in the *Case of the Stolen Motorcycle*, a protest to the decision was hard to deal with. The following example illustrates this further.

The plaintiff sued its tenant, a 62-year-old retired worker, for unpaid rents in a rural court (*Case of the Poor Retired Worker*). The court decided that the tenant would pay approximately 10,000 yuan for the rent and 1,000 yuan for the litigation fees. Nothing was wrong with the decision itself except that the lawyer representing the plaintiff was the former vice president of the local people's congress. The defendant petitioned against the decision on the basis that the court had allowed the vice president to represent the case. Our informant said,

> The defendant said that the people's congress was to supervise the work of the court, and this vice president often visited the court to assess the performance of the court. "How could the court allow such a person to be the lawyer representing the case? How could the court be neutral?"

To make matters worse, the defendant had a mentally disabled son and a mother in her late eighties. Economically, her family was in a dreadful situation. They were left with only "four empty walls," as is said in a Chinese idiom.

In petitions, she took her aging mother and disabled son to the court. Her acts captured the attention of a major political leader in the region, who asked the court to resolve her problem by all means. The court then (1) persuaded the plaintiff to forfeit half of the rent and to compensate the other half from the fund of special remedies, (2) forfeited the litigation fees and (3) provided more than 50,000 yuan from the court's remedial fund to support the livelihood of the defendant. Furthermore, the court had already given 1,000 yuan to the defendant during her petitions. The only beneficiary in this case was that vice president of the local people's congress. He received fees for representing the plaintiff; the court, however, had paid a heavy price for this *guanxi*.

CONCLUDING REMARKS

Through analyzing the informal ordering based on *guanxi*, as opposed to formal ordering based on laws and rules, this chapter deepens our understanding of the extent of the influences of social embeddedness. Favor-giving is a form of power abuse by frontline judges, as the analyzed examples show. Does that justify hierarchical monitoring in Chinese courts? The answer is complicated. It is the hierarchical nature of the Chinese court that makes superior *guanxi* so forceful in affecting the decision-making process. Structural positions matter. A direct hierarchical relationship between the favor seeker and the favor giver creates an extra dimension of power, one that is absent from horizontal relationships. Strong superior ties may either reward or punish the target judge – a supervisor is able not only to promote a supervisee, but also to make her life miserable. This dimension is so dominating and prevalent in China that the variations between work-unit courts and firm-type courts should be viewed as a matter of degree. In the latter, judges are more discreet and sometimes are reluctant to reciprocate. Some frontline judges have also become increasingly resentful of demands from above. Judge Yang from one of the biggest grassroots courts in Guangdong said, "Connections are a source of conflict between some younger judges and their superiors in my court. There are some division heads who are not happy with our generation of judges. They think we are too individualistic."

That said, social embeddedness remains a prevailing phenomenon, not just for work-unit courts but for firm-type courts as well, despite the weakening of the hierarchical structure in the latter. Social embeddedness is at once a *cultural* and an *institutional* phenomenon. The cultural thesis suggests that horizontal personal ties in one's inner circle are difficult to resist for frontline judges. "When you received a phone call from an old teacher who taught you everything, not picking up the phone would be considered morally unacceptable," said Judge Du, a division head in a firm court in Guangdong.

Certainly, in more open, bigger coastal cities, judges, politicians and enterprise officers face greater scrutiny, as litigants are generally more knowledgeable and are more sensitive to any suspicious behavior on the part of judges. The presence of anti-corruption investigators, muckraking journalists, social media-users and foreign investors brings with it more "need" and "demand" for law (deLisle 2014). Meanwhile, the professionalism to which frontline judges aspire may become a value that discourages favor giving.

Yet, judges working in the richer and more prosperous coastal regions are subject to greater temptation in other aspects. The cases they handle, especially in the civil division, are of considerably larger financial stakes (see Chapter 7). Based on what has surfaced in media reports, insolvency cases, a category of commercial case that is much more numerous in urban than in rural courts, for example, attract a high volume of bribes. In the 2000s, two of the national pilot program sites for the then-new bankruptcy law, the Shenzhen Intermediate Court and Tianjin High Court, both faced high-profile corruption scandals (Li, Ling 2010:208). More empirical studies are needed to identify more precisely the different patterns of social embedd-edness in work-unit and firm-type courts. It seems that non-superior ties play a bigger role in firm-type courts, as the decline in vertical supervision there may allow for more freedom among frontline judges, especially for routine, low-stakes cases. Based on what we heard from the judges in different areas, it would be a gross exaggeration to characterize social embeddedness as solely a phenomenon of work-unit courts.

The examples we examined explain why the public and the media in China perceive corruption as rampant, even though few cases are ever officially reported. In the SPC's annual working report of 2016, courts at all levels found only 721 persons with disciplinary violations or violations of the law that prohibits the abuse of adjudicatory or enforcement powers. Of these, only 120 were pursued to fix criminal responsibility. This number is low and does not match the popular perception that judicial corruption is common. While underreporting may be an issue contributing to these very low numbers, the bigger issue is that *guanxi* runs through the "pores" of laws and regulations. The operation of connections is hard to detect because it is often covered by a legalized mantle. Reciprocity in strong *guanxi* is long-term. There is virtually no time limit on repayment (Yang 1994). Long-term and multiplex, strong ties make any concrete offer and acceptance of bribery superfluous. While many connections operate within the stated bounds of law, they contradict the spirit of law and amount to "the abuse of public office for private gains" (Li, Ling 2011, 2012).

7

Economic Embeddedness: The Political Economy
of Court Finances

This chapter turns to the question of economic embeddedness. We explore the interactions between local economies and the financing of grassroots courts. The goal here is to identify the key factors that shape the unique *political economy* that grassroots courts face. "Consider the political economy of judging," means that we consider the activities of the court primarily from an economic point of view. Typically, this form of analysis does not apply to a government bureaucracy. Like other government bureaus, courts are grant-funded and do not operate within the market environment in the sense that they do not finance themselves by the sale of their products on the market. However, as we will see, because of the chronic shortage of funds in many grassroots courts, the pursuit of revenue in a "market" that courts basically monopolize has become a substantial dimension of interaction in the puzzling political economy of the Chinese courts. To understand the full story, we need to first understand the relationship between grassroots courts and their local governments.

One of the key reform initiatives Deng Xiaoping undertook to transform the post-Mao Chinese state was the policy of decentralizing decision-making authority. Deng's policy, which is to a large extent still followed today, was to allow governments at each level to control their own bailiwick. As scholars point out (Shambaugh 2000; Lieberthal 1992; Manion 1985; Shirk 1993), the policy of decentralization had the far-reaching effect of lessening the central-level party's influence and control. Since the 1990s, provincial governments have been giving the authority to determine the tax rate and to reduce taxes within their domains. Decentralization was aimed at accommodating a growing market economy and making the bureaucratic system more responsive to an increasingly complex society (Eger and Schüller 2007; Zheng 2004:83–108). It streamlined government organs, reduced overlapping functions and substantially lessening bureaucratic interference over a wide range of economic and technical policy arenas. Yet, at the same time, as Shambaugh (2000:174) writes, "The withdrawal of the state has only reinforced the 'cellular' and protectionist nature of much of China's political economy, and has stimulated widespread variance in commercial, agricultural, and internal trade practices." We can also add legal practices and the role of the courts to that list.

Administratively, the Chinese party-state is disaggregated into four levels: central, provincial/municipal, county, and local. For our present purpose, most basic-level courts deal with the government institutions at the county and local levels. Revenues for local governments come predominantly from taxes on enterprise profits. Local officials are allowed to keep their money after having divided some of the proceeds with the provincial and central governments. With its share, the local (city or county) government then funds its different units to provide for social services, public works, and infrastructural projects (Walder 1992).

As we have emphasized in this book, the idea that the judiciary is a separate branch of the government that performs a monitoring and corrective function has yet to take root in China. Legal policies in China are guided by instrumentalism, in which the courts are treated as among a set of coordinated means available to achieve substantive ends, such as economic growth and strong governance (deLisle 2014). In fact, the Chinese judiciary cannot even be described as being subservient to the executive, in the way that some European courts are (e.g., France, see Guarnieri and Pederzoli 2002). It *is* part of the executive, and above all, a weak executive branch. Traditionally, it has been the weakest of the three public security bureaucracies, maintaining a close symbiotic relationship with the more powerful police and the procuratorate. In Chapter 5, we also talked about how some grassroots courts are asked to participate in local social and economic campaigns far removed from their judicial function, such as public hygiene and promoting commercial investment.

CHINESE-STYLE FISCAL FEDERALISM

Since the 1980s, the central government has been encouraging local government units to become more self-supporting through bureaucratic entrepreneurship (Lieberthal 1992:9). This has been the case ever since the implementation of the fiscal policy called "eating in different kitchens," pertaining to the central and local governments in the early 1980s (Young 1989; Oi 1999; see He 2009c for a fuller discussion). County and local governments are free to acquire funds beyond those allocated through the central budget. Yet this process of decentralization of financial authority also means that courts became more dependent on local party governments, as direct funding from the central budget had dwindled.[1] Local governments, however, often do not see a need to offer more money to their courts. The courts do not build new highways or suspension bridges, nor do they generate much revenue by selling their products or attracting new investment (though this, as we will see, is changing in some places). Many inland courts were handicapped by their inabilities to generate revenues to sustain themselves. As a non-economic bureaucracy, the judiciary was left out in the cold.

It is under this broader background of central-local fiscal "federalism" that the work-unit model, i.e., the model of administrative bureaucracy, has become the dominant model of governance among Chinese courts. Court presidents lack economic resources to bargain with government bureau leaders in the economic and industrial sectors. They have become ever more dependent on local governments for economic resources. The greatest asset that grassroots courts can "sell" is information. As Barry Naughton (1992) observes, a party's strength in the Chinese bureaucratic bargaining process is determined not just by its control of resources but also by its access to information. What court presidents lack in economic resources, they partially make up for by gathering social intelligence through vertical control of information. Basic-level courts now serve as an important safety valve for a widening range of popular complaints (Liebman 2007). Earlier chapters have already shown how stability is promoted through the work of the courts and their adjudication committees (see Chapter 4 and Chapter 5). A court president keeps a close eye on potential sources of local unrest by monitoring the cases her court handles. This intelligence-gathering function also explains why criminal cases are the most extensively reviewed by the adjudication committee. Judges have even gone beyond the four walls of the courtroom to engage street protestors at the grassroots level (Su and He 2010). Judges need to be "on the ball" to be aware of potential problem cases that may develop into full-blown social conflicts.

With civil cases, sometimes it is too risky for senior judges to leave the matter of making decisions completely to their subordinates. Here, senior judges closely supervise the decisions of their subordinates for a range of reasons: sometimes to make sure that a decision is rightly made according to the law, but at other times to avoid political fallout or to protect local interests. Courts tend to render judgments that favor local parties and interests (Balme 2010:162; Liu 2003; Xu 2010). Once again, this can be traced back to the limited autonomy that local courts have as a weak member of the coalition of bureaus that make up the local government.

Judge Ding, a young criminal judge from Yunnan, was forthcoming when she discussed what many judges see as the rogue controlling power that local government officials have over the courts: "[Sigh] This is the dream of almost everyone in my court. But it remains a dream. You say you want the court to adjudicate independently. But this is impossible. Someone else decides how much money the court can get. The power to promote people is also held by others. How can you rule independently? Your promotion decisions have to be endorsed by others. Even pay raises are decided by someone else. How is it possible for you to rule independently?"

What Judge Ding lamented are problems that the Chinese party-state readily acknowledges: some courts are strongly influenced by their local governments through control of the financial budget and influence on promotion decisions. But to fix the problem is easier said than done. There are two conflicting goals at stake. On the one hand, the central government does not want to revert to the sort of centralized regime that characterized the era of high Maoism. They want to preserve the power of local governments to promote vitality. On the other hand, delegation of powers, fiscal power in particular, at the local governmental level often means less autonomy for the courts.

"DUAL-TRACK" POLICY

As a bureaucracy, courts mainly receive funding from the local government. The "dual-track" policy of separating income and expenses (收支两条线 *shou zhi liang tiao xian*) was first proposed by the central government in the early 1990s as a way to rectify overreliance on court fees as a source of income under the policy of "eating in different kitchens." But it was not until 2001 that it was adopted as the new official policy governing court finances (Zhu 2011). The goal of the policy is simple. It attempts to steer the court away from a revenue-dominated mode of operation. Under this policy, courts are not required to be fiscally self-sustaining. Local governments cover the courts' expenditures with their own revenues. All courts, with the sole exception of the SPC, are considered as a part of their local government. Access to courts is not contingent upon market principles, but is to be financed through local government funding. The idea behind the policy is a familiar one to any students of modern government – certain public goods should be provided independently of the profit mechanisms that determine the dynamics of the market.

While the policy has succeeded in providing cheap access to court services, it has also created a financial double-bind for many local courts and tribunals. On the one hand, courts are not allowed to charge fees at a level that covers costs. Easy court access is the policy, and the courts are asked to charge fees at a low level that is affordable for the working class. On the other hand, many courts found that providing broad access while sticking to the SPC's mandated fee schedule was a costly venture. Local officials often do not see enough tangible good to justify their budgetary commitment to their grassroots courts. As a result, courts are at the mercy of local governments for money to make up the deficits between rising costs and declining revenues. This stark reality of financial shortage means that the "people's court" has come close to being the "lieutenant of its local government" for protection of its territorial interests (Zhang 2003:71). Judicial salaries and the funds for court operations come mostly from local government budgets and are subject to the threat of reduction whenever court decisions adversely affect local interests (Zhang 2003:81). Senior judges are also elected, appointed, and removed by people's congresses at the same administrative level, although, in practice, these powers are often in the hands of local officials (see Chapter 4). Courts, particularly those that do not make enough money themselves, remain weak institutions among the coalition of local party-state institutions.

"MATTHEW EFFECT" IN COURT BUDGETING

The making of the court budget crystalizes the sharpening contrast between work-unit and firm-type courts. Until recently, the budget of a typical grassroots court has been composed of two parts: the budgetary funds provided by the government at the same administrative level (in the case of a grassroots court, it would be a county or township government) and extra-budgetary funds, derived mainly from the administrative income of the courts. This administrative income comes from litigation fees charged to and judicial fines imposed upon relevant plaintiffs and defendants (He 2009c; Oi 1999). The budgeting mechanism provides the context for understanding the "Matthew effect" (Merton 1968) in judicial budgeting. According to official policy, the budgetary funds are declared to be the main source of the courts' income, with the extra-budgetary income generated from fees and fines being supplementary. Yet in rural and inland areas, many local governments turn their back on the courts' requests for budgets based on operational costs, which routinely exceed the revenues the courts are able to generate. By some estimates, over 80 percent of grassroots courts have been experiencing chronic budgetary deficits (Guo 2004:339–340). Local governments can always tell their courts, "We can't give you more money than you make because we also have a hard time making ends meet."

Table 7.1 ranks the public security expenditures of all provinces and direct administrative municipalities and regions. Official statistics at the countrywide level are patchy. The Chinese government does not release figures specific to judicial expenditures. Public security expenditures cover a much broader category, and provides us here with only a crude measure. Besides judicial expenditures, it also includes the expenditures of the police and the procuratorate. But the numbers offer us the best rough approximation available of the variations in judicial expenses across regions, since judicial expenses correlate with expenses of the police and the procuratorate.

The numbers in the table are interesting on a couple of levels. First, there are obviously wide disparities across provinces. Courts in coastal provinces in general enjoyed bigger budgets than courts in the inland provinces. Second, the gap between the rich and poor provinces in public security expenditures seems to have been further widened. Surely, some of the least economically developed provinces such as Guizhou and Yunnan received subsidies from the central government. Other provinces, including Tibet and Xinjiang, received additional funds for stability maintenance. But the rich courts got their big slices of the pie, with Guangdong, Zhejiang, Beijing and Jiangsu all ranking among the top ten. Guangdong and Zhejiang occupy the top spots in the chart. The biggest anomalies are the cities of Shanghai and Tianjin. Both seem to spend less on judicial expenses in comparison to the developed status of their local economies.

In general, wealth seems to beget more wealth: the courts in the richest parts of the country tend to have the biggest budgets, not only in absolute terms, which is expected, but in percentage terms as well. Guangdong tops the list by spending more than 7.62 percent of its provincial budget on public security expenditures. If Guangdong's expenditures had simply tied with the national average rate (5.51 percent), it would have already given its courts and police departments a handsome

TABLE 7.1 *Regional GDP and Public Security (including Judicial) Expenses (China Yearbook 2014)*

Region	GDP per capita (in thousand yuan)	GDP per capita ranking	Total government expenditures (in billion yuan)	Public Security expenditures (PSE) (in billion yuan)	PSE/Total ratio (%)	PSE/Total ranking ratio
Beijing	99.1	2	452.5	28.0	6.18	4
Tianjin	103.7	1	288.5	13.9	4.83	20
Hebei	39.8	18	467.7	24.8	5.31	10
Shanxi	35.0	24	308.5	16.1	5.21	15
Inner Mongolia	70.9	6	388.0	18.0	4.65	24
Liaoning	65.2	7	508.0	23.6	4.64	25
Jilin	50.2	11	291.3	15.5	5.31	11
Heilongjiang	39.2	20	343.4	17.1	4.97	17
Shanghai	97.1	3	492.3	25.1	5.10	16
Jiangsu	81.8	4	847.2	47.4	5.59	8
Zhejiang	72.9	5	516.0	37.1	7.18	2
Anhui	34.3	26	466.4	18.0	3.85	31
Fujian	63.2	9	330.7	19.2	5.80	7
Jiangxi	34.6	25	388.3	17.6	4.53	27
Shandong	60.7	10	717.7	38.1	5.30	13
Henan	37.0	22	602.9	27.4	4.55	26
Hubei	47.1	13	493.4	25.9	5.25	14
Hunan	40.1	17	501.7	24.6	4.91	19
Guangdong	63.2	8	915.3	69.7	7.62	1
Guangxi	33.0	27	348.0	19.2	5.52	9
Hainan	38.8	21	110.0	6.7	6.16	5
Chongqing	47.7	12	330.4	16.0	4.83	21
Sichuan	35.1	23	679.7	31.9	4.70	23
Guizhou	26.4	30	354.3	18.8	5.31	12
Yunnan	27.2	29	443.8	22.0	4.95	18
Tibet	29.0	28	118.6	6.9	5.85	6
Shaanxi	46.9	14	396.3	16.1	4.07	30
Gansu	26.4	31	254.1	10.7	4.23	28
Qinghai	39.5	19	134.7	5.6	4.13	29
Ningxia	41.6	15	100.0	4.8	4.76	22
Xinjiang	40.4	16	331.8	22.2	6.70	3

budget of 50.43 billion yuan. The actual rate of spending for Guangdong, as shown in the 2014 figures, was almost 2 percentage points above the national average. Why did the courts in Guangdong get more? Not just more money in absolute terms, but also in the sense of a higher percentage? Why was the provincial government of Guangdong willing to allocate about 8 percent of its budget to public security expenditures, of which the judiciary was a component?

Courts in rich provinces such as Guangdong and Zhejiang receive more money for two reasons. First, they get more money *because* they make more money. Court presidents and vice presidents who have been involved with the budgeting process for their own courts explained in interviews that the policy of "separate income and expenses" is better understood as the policy of "getting more money than you've made." Ideally speaking, the grants received by a court, i.e., its total expenditures allowed, should be greater than the revenues it generated from fees and other sources of income. The policy would be a punishment if the separately calculated budget given to a court were less than the revenue it generated. Though rare, some local governments were known to impose a "tax" on judicial revenues by imposing fees on their courts (Zhu 2011:175). But the more common practice is that a local government gives back what the court makes (He 2009c; Wang, Yuhua 2013). Hence, the court's budget is still tightly correlated with the revenue it raises. Yuhua Wang (2013:50) mentioned a response by a senior judge in a small, basic-level court in Jiangxi that is typical of the responses we heard from other judges in different parts of China: "The 'dual-track' regulation is never enforced here: the city government always returns 100 percent of what we hand over, and that's it; they give us no more!" Sometimes a factor would be used to calculate a court's budget (based on its revenue); sometimes a basic deduction would be taken out by the provincial government as a form of tax (Zhu 2011:175).

For all the publicity about separating income from expenses, the two are in fact linked. With expanding caseloads, particularly in the civil sector, the courts in the urban regions of wealthy coastal provinces – many of which are bigger, firm-type courts – get more money because they actually make more money from their court fees. At a minimum, local governments have to return what the courts have made.

But there is more to the accumulation of wealth for firm-type courts. There is that crucial transition of quantity to quality that alters the role of the courts in the economic sphere. There is a gradual but unmistakable shift of institutional character as courts move from working in small, less-developed local economies to bigger, more-diversified economies. Scholars who study government bureaucracy make a distinction between "servicing bureaus" and "delivery bureaus" (Dunleavy 1991). Servicing bureaus provide services to other government bodies. Delivery bureaus directly *deliver* services to the public. In smaller economies, grassroots courts play the role of a servicing bureau to the local party-state, providing services to the government by protecting the economy against any "adverse" legal interference. Inland economies tend to be inward-looking and protectionist. Local protectionism can be understood as a set of related governmental practices that allow a few local dominant enterprises to compete on more favorable terms. Big state-owned enterprises or government-supported businesses (政府扶持产业 *zhengfu fuchi chanye*) that dominate a local economy are shielded from market competition. In other words, courts there are asked to act as the local sheriff. Judicial rulings are to be intervened with if unfavorable decisions seriously hamper major local businesses. In bigger and more diversified economies, courts have more opportunities to direct their services to the public instead. The courts there play the role of the delivery bureau. They directly undertake the production of services (law) for the public. They uphold the agreed-upon rules of the game. This changing nature of the character of the courts entails a changing relationship between the courts and their local governments. Courts are under less pressure to provide services to local governments in order to "get paid." The effect of the dual-track policy between judicial income and allocated budget is thus doubly ironic. While the policy was established to help out those courts that are unable to support themselves with court fees and charges, it ended up adding wealth to those courts that are already self-sustaining. In practice, the dual-track policy is *only* fully carried out in the most economically developed parts of China, where the credibility of a trustworthy legal system has become a significant factor for promoting further economic growth (Barro 1997; Haggard et al. 2008; Henisz 2000). Courts there are asked to orchestrate a framework of rules that guarantee the integrity of contracts and the validity of the monetary system. For a few economically well-developed cities in China, local governments are willing to give more to their courts, on top of the revenues these courts are capable of generating themselves – "For unto every one that hath shall be given, and he shall have abundance" (Gospel according to Matthew, 25:29).

Let us illustrate the extent of the "Matthew effect" by examining more closely the finances of the 157 courts in the province of Guangdong, the most populous and economically developed province of China. It is important to note that within the province of Guangdong itself there remain considerable variations in the level of economic development. The network of cities that make up the Pearl River Delta has overtaken Tokyo as the world's largest urban area (World Bank 2015). Yet there are counties in other parts of Guangdong that are less well off and less developed. According to an internal study conducted by Guangdong Provincial High Court in 2012, courts in the most developed Pearl River Delta, i.e., those in Guangzhou, Foshan, Dongguan and Zhongshan, were those that had the dual-track policy "fully implemented" that year. This is just a roundabout way of stating that these courts received even more than the considerable revenues they generated from fees and other sources of income. Table 7.2 presents the per-judge expenditure of courts (2011 figures) in the four regions of Guangdong, juxtaposing the most-developed Pearl River Delta with the other three regions: Guangdong East, Guangdong West, and Guangdong North. Unsurprisingly, courts located in the Pearl River Delta, a region with a per-capita GDP about three times that of the rest of Guangdong, also enjoy the highest per-judge expenditure – 203,100 yuan per year. Not only are the judges in Pearl River Delta better remunerated, they are also better supported, as reflected by the higher per-judge equipment and running costs (52,200 yuan). The report also acknowledges that in less economically developed parts of the province, court budgets were still very much tied to incomes generated by fees and fines (Guangdong High Court 2014).

That this expenditure gap exists among courts located in Guangdong, one of the wealthiest provinces of China, should not be overlooked. One can only surmise that

TABLE 7.2 *Per-Judge Court Expenditures across Four Regions of Guangdong (in Yuan)*

Court location	Total per-judge expenditure	Personnel costs per judge	Equipment and running costs per judge	Material costs of services per judge	GDP per capita
Pearl River Delta	203,100	107,700	52,200	43,200	77,637
Guangdong East	125,400	58,800	20,700	45,900	21,850
Guangdong West	125,900	61,900	24,600	39,400	27,485
Guangdong North	141,000	63,900	33,600	43,500	22,205

Data from Guangdong High Court 2014; GDP per-capita figures from Guangdong Statistical Yearbook 2013 www.gdstats.gov.cn/tjnj/2013/directory/20-01-0.html

the gap would be much more pronounced if we were to compare courts across provinces, as suggested by the public security spending (Table 7.1).

The SPC is allocating more funds to reduce the deficits of grassroots courts and to narrow the gap between the rich and the poor. There has been more funding from the central and the provincial governments. Yet, up until the latest judicial reform, much of the money received by grassroots courts still came from local governments at the same administrative level. According to a report conducted by an SPC research team (Tang et al. 2011), the total funding received by the Chinese courts in 2009 was 46.78 billion yuan, of which 7.98 billion yuan, or about 17 percent, was from the transfer payment funds (转移支付资金 *zhuanyi zhifu zijin*) from the central government. Another 2.7 billion yuan, or 5.8 percent, were supporting funds (配套资金 *peitao zijin*) from provincial governments. The remaining 36.1 billion yuan was local money not controlled by the SPC and the provincial high courts. In other words, local government funding still made up more than three-fourths of the total funding received by the courts. In his study of the finance of a cash-strapped grassroots court, Zuo (2015) arrived at very similar numbers. The court that Zuo studied was located in a county that was designated as a "poor county" (贫困县 *pinkunxian*) by the central government. It was situated in a populous inland province. About 20 percent of the money received by the court in 2007–2009 came from the "higher up" governments. The remaining 80 percent was local money.

One of the most radical proposals of the latest judicial reform involves the fundamental restructuring of the ways grassroots courts are funded. Since the reform is still underway, its full impacts on court finance remain to be seen. We offer a preliminary analysis at the end of this chapter.

THE REALITY OF ECONOMIC EMBEDDEDNESS

The long-term financial sustainability of a court is largely dependent on the "financial quality" of the various types of civil cases that make up the bulk of its caseload. Since the beginning of the reform period in the 1980s, the courts have been playing an increasingly important role in resolving economic disputes (Long 2010). Resources devoted to developing a legal infrastructure for the expanding Chinese economy have also increased greatly during the same period. Economic policies, and economy-related policies more broadly, are increasingly put in legal form (deLisle 2015).

Here are some basic numbers to remind us how much the "stuff" of litigations has changed in China. In 1978, right after the end of the Cultural Revolution, the total of civil cases and criminal cases of the then-revamped legal system were more or less the same, with civil cases making up 52 percent of the total caseload and criminal cases making up the remaining 48 percent. In 2009, civil cases represented 86 percent of the total cases handled by the courts, compared to 12 percent for criminal cases. But it is not just the sheer increase in the quantity of civil cases. More important is the changing quality of civil cases. Back in 1978, most of the civil cases (73 percent) were family cases. But in 2010, family cases made up just a mere 23 percent (Zhu 2011). In 1978, contract disputes made up a meager 1 percent of the total. In 2010, contract and rights infringement cases made up 53 and 24 percent, respectively. The "drop" in family cases did not mean a gradual decline in the numbers of family cases. Quite the contrary, family cases grew at a steady rate of about 6.4 percent annually over the three decades between 1978 and 2010. But this steady growth was dwarfed by the massive expansion in the categories of contract and rights infringement cases.[2] On average, the number of contract cases grew a stunning rate of 30 percent per year during the period, reflecting the much tighter connection between the economy and the law (Zhu 2011:2–5). Besides contractual disputes, there are also personal injury cases, housing and land disputes, environmental lawsuits, defamation claims and a small number of discrimination cases (Liebman 2012:221).

There are many reasons that led to the growth of the civil caseloads. The growth in the number of commercial disputes is one. The malaise of urbanization is another. The courts are asked to deal with many more social conflicts nowadays. And the courts are asked to provide access to make sure that anyone who wants to use the court to deal with their grievances can easily do so. In 2006, the SPC reduced court fees to provide greater access to courts for working-class litigants. In Chinese, it was promoted under the slogan of "judiciary for the people" (*si fa wei min*). The goal is to encourage more litigants, especially working-class litigants, to use the courts to resolve social disputes. Finally, it is noteworthy to point out that despite the constant push toward mediation, the Chinese court system adjudicates more cases now than before. In the 1980s, mediation rates hovered around 70 percent (Zhu 2007:225)! By comparison, the nationwide average mediation rate for civil cases was 57 percent in 2014. This figure already reflected the input of the deliberate efforts by courts to promote mediation under the state policy of building a "harmonious society" (Fu and Cullen 2011). As the percentage of commercial disputes grows in the civil docket, it is going to be difficult for the courts to keep up this 50 percent rate until some further restructuring is introduced (e.g., by drastically raising the court fees to disincentivize litigants, which is unlikely).

The net result of the two countervailing causes – first, the expansion of a diversified market economy, and second, the rise of disputes in a more conflict-ridden society – is that the growth of civil caseloads among Chinese grassroots courts has been remarkable but also remarkably uneven. All courts have experienced some growth. But only some experience a significant uptake in revenue-generating commercial disputes. Official statistics are too sketchy to be of use for comparison, as they do not offer the provincial breakdown of civil caseloads. Several provincial high courts have reported the aggregate claim total for the civil disputes processed by their court system. In Guangdong, the amount far exceeds that of other large provinces with comparable populations. In 2012, that amount was 681.6 billion yuan (Guangdong High Court 2013). As a comparison, the yearly total of inland Sichuan in 2011 was 46.3 billion yuan (Sichuan High Court 2012). The Sichuan High Court did not release its annual total figure in its 2012 report (Sichuan High Court 2013); it only mentioned that the five-year total was 228.9 billion yuan (which produced a yearly average of 45.8 billion yuan), just about a third of Guangdong's total for one year. The annual figures for Henan, another populous inland province, was only 58.4 billion yuan (Henan High Court 2013).

Comparing the current schedule of court fees (passed in 2006 and effective since 2007) with the preceding schedules provides hints about why there is a growing gap between the haves and have-nots. Table 7.3 compares the three fee schedules imposed by the central government after the resumption of work of the legal system in the 1980s. In the first period, before 1989, China basically adopted a no-fee or nominal fee system. It was replaced by a fee schedule in the 1990s that critics said put too much financial burden on litigants, given the limited degree of economic development at the time. The schedule was revised again in 2006. The Litigation Cost Payment Act (诉讼费用交纳办法 *susong feiyong jiaona banfa*) that became effective on April 1, 2007 modestly raised the general fees for different types of civil cases, including divorce, property cases, bankruptcy and rights infringement cases. But it reduced the initial levels in the staggered tier structure that the court used to determine court fees in cases that involved disputed money or property. In civil cases where monetary compensation is sought, the court charges a court acceptance cost based on staggered tiers of rates ranging from 0.5 to 2.5 percent.

The aim of the Act was to promote access to justice. The goal was to allow the working-class people, most of whom would not seek compensation of more than 100,000 yuan, to pay lower court fees. But the changes made to the fee schedule have further widened the gap between the rich and the poor courts. Courts in the poorer regions of the country are most impacted by the policy of charging less for fees on cases with smaller claims (Wang, Yuhua 2013; Zhang, Lijun 2010). For example, according to the old schedule, for cases involving disputed property of a value between 10,000 to 50,000 yuan, courts would charge a fee of up to 4 percent of that property. But the new schedule lowers that to 2.5 percent. And for property

TABLE 7.3 *New and Old Court Fee Schedules Compared*

Case type	1980s and before	1990–2006	2006–
(1) Divorce			
General	10–50 yuan	10–50 yuan	50–300 yuan
Surcharge on the portion of split property with a value between 10,000–200,000 yuan	No surcharge	1%	No surcharge
Surcharge on the portion of split property above the value of 200,000 yuan	No surcharge	1%	0.5%
(2) Infringement of name rights, title rights, honor rights		50–100 yuan	100–500 yuan
Surcharge on the portion of damages with a value between 50,000–100,000 yuan		unspecified	1%
Surcharge on the portion of damages above the value of 100,000 yuan		unspecified	0.5%
(3) Other non-property cases	5–20 yuan	10–50 yuan	nil
(4) Property Cases (based on disputed property value)			
Less than 1,000	30 yuan	50 yuan	50 yuan
Surcharge on the portion of disputed property with values between 1,000–10,000 yuan	1%	4%	50 yuan
10,000–50,000 yuan	1%	4%	2.5%
Between 50,000–100,000 yuan	0.6%	3%	2.5%
Between 100,000–200,000 yuan	0.6%	2%	2%
Between 200,000–500,000 yuan	0.6%	1.5%	1.5%
Between 500,000–1,000,000 yuan	0.3%	1%	1%

(continued)

TABLE 7.3 *(continued)*

Case type	1980s and before	1990–2006	2006–
Between 1,000,000–2,000,000 yuan	0.2%	0.5%	0.9%
Between 2,000,000–5,000,000 yuan	0.2%	0.5%	0.8%
Between 5,000,000–10,000,000 yuan	0.2%	0.5%	0.7%
Between 10,000,000–20,000,000 yuan	0.2%	0.5%	0.6%
Between 20,000,000–50,000,000 yuan	0.2%	0.5%	0.5%
Over 50,000,000 yuan	0.1%	0.5%	0.5%
(5) Intellectual Property			
General		50–100 yuan	500–1000 yuan
With disputed property		Based on the value of the disputed property	Based on the value of the disputed property
(6) Administrative Cases			
Public Safety Administrative Case		5–30 yuan	50 yuan
Patent		50–400 yuan	100 yuan
Others			
General		30–100 yuan	50 yuan
With disputed property		Based on the value of disputed property	No surcharge
(7) Labor Disputes		30–50 yuan	10 yuan
(8) Bankruptcy		The same as property cases (based on the value of bankruptcy)	Half of the fees of property fee (based on the value of bankruptcy, if the value is less than 300,000 yuan)
(9) Fees on execution order			
Executed value below 10,000		50 yuan	50–100 yuan
Surcharge on the portion of disputed property with values between 10,000–500,000 yuan		0.5%	1.5%
500,000–5,000,000		0.1%	1%
5,000,000–10,000,000		0.1%	0.5%
>10,000,000		0.1%	0.1%

valued at less than 10,000 yuan, a flat fee of 50 yuan applies. How much has the new fee schedule reduced the revenue of courts whose civil caseloads are mainly made up of small, individual disputes? Once again, official statistics are sketchy. But the central government is clearly aware of the problem and has allocated more direct funding to courts in the central and western parts of China to offset the revenue loss (Wang 2010). Inland work-type courts that had already struggled with lighter case-loads and few commercial cases became even more financially dependent on their local party-government.

While the new schedule also applies to urban, firm-type courts, the adverse impact of lower fees is countered by the raise in rates of the upper-tier categories. The new structure, in fact, raised the rates that a court could charge on cases with disputed property valued more than 1 million yuan (see Table 7.3). The rate was a uniform 0.5 percent on the pre-2007 schedule. The new staggered structure allows the court to charge a higher 0.9 percent in some cases. For courts located at the richest parts of the country, the money "lost" from charging the lower rates of initial tiers can be in part made up with the money "made" by charging higher rates at the top tiers. Judge Yang, who works in one of the richest courts in Pearl River Delta, made the following observation: "The monetary limit of our court is 50 million yuan. I know for many inland courts, the number is purely academic. They just don't get cases with that kind of claims. But that's not the case for us. A typical loan case between two private individuals can involve a few million yuan. That's very common."

To recap, the number of civil cases has been growing at a faster pace than criminal cases in all of China, but it is exponentially so in the economically developed coastal provinces. The new stream of revenue is sufficient to give courts in the most developed parts of urban China a degree of financial independence that courts that are struggling for financial survival deem a luxury. Figure 7.1 reproduces a public announcement made by a township government in Dongguan of Guangdong. For two consecutive days, the government published a public notice in *Dongguan Daily*, a semi-official local newspaper, railing against the basic-level court's decision to "unilaterally auction a piece of local land" (China.com 2015). The township government chided the court for approving "illegal" use of the disputed land. At first sight, the public notice seems to indicate a typical meddling by the local government with its grassroots court. But this type of meddling is seldom open to public view. That it took the form of a public notice is an indication that the court has defied the former by acting against its will. This defiance could only happen in a region where the court has acquired a good level of fiscal independence. More conflicts between grassroots courts and their govern-ments have come out into the open in the coastal south. It is also perhaps no coincidence that it was the Guangzhou Intermediate People's Court (a court with strong firm-type traits) that made the first-ever ruling against an administrative mono-poly in a decision, ruling against the Guangdong Department of Education for requiring a particular brand of software in a contest (Clarke 2015).[3]

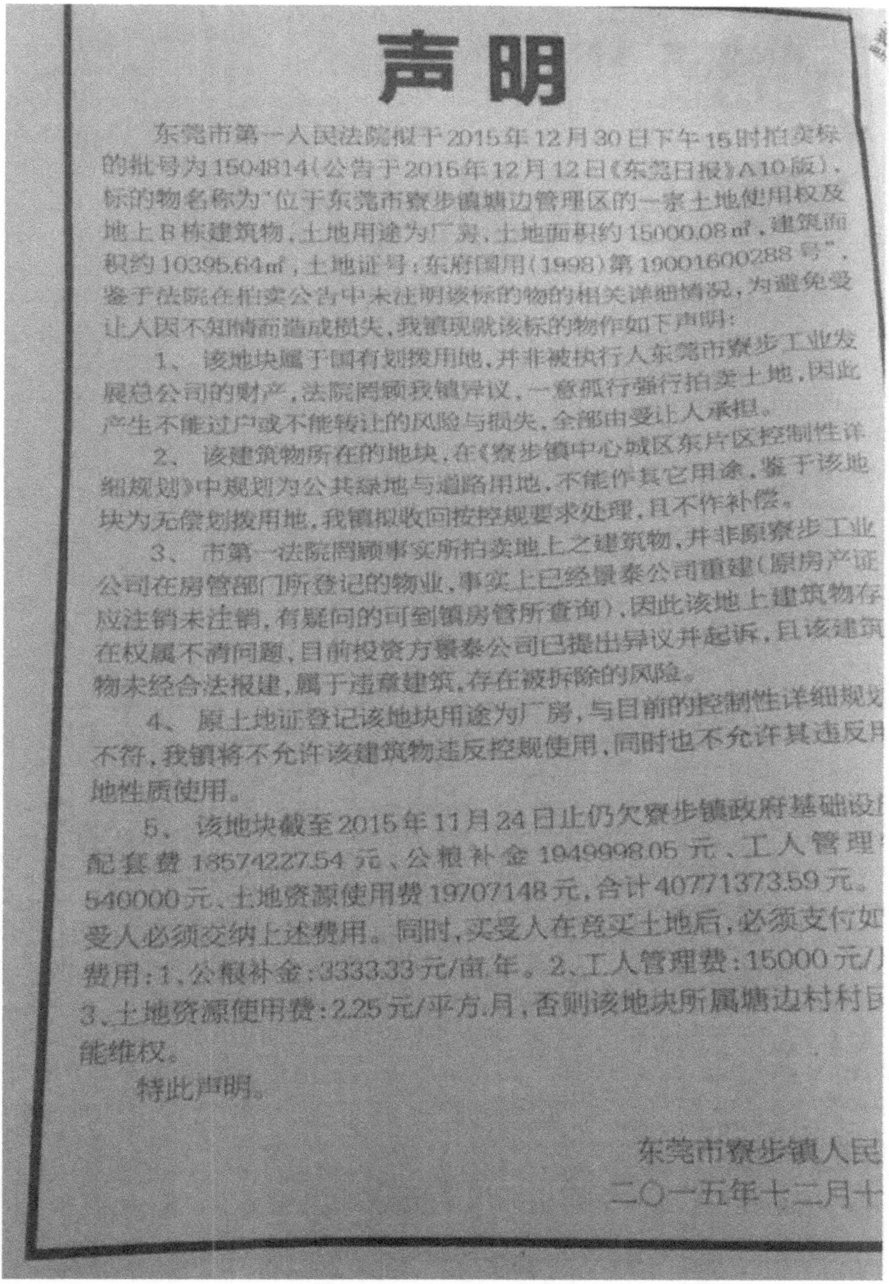

声 明

东莞市第一人民法院拟于2015年12月30日下午15时拍卖标的批号为1504814(公告于2015年12月12日《东莞日报》A10版)，标的物名称为"位于东莞市寮步镇塘边管理区的一宗土地使用权及地上8栋建筑物，土地用途为厂房，土地面积约15000.08㎡，建筑面积约10395.64㎡，土地证号：东府国用(1998)第19001600288号"，鉴于法院在拍卖公告中未注明该标的物的相关详细情况，为避免受让人因不知情而造成损失，我镇现就该标的物作如下声明：

1、该地块属于国有划拨用地，并非被执行人东莞市寮步工业发展总公司的财产，法院罔顾我镇异议，一意孤行强行拍卖土地，因此产生不能过户或不能转让的风险与损失，全部由受让人承担。

2、该建筑物所在的地块，在《寮步镇中心城区东片区控制性详细规划》中规划为公共绿地与道路用地，不能作其它用途，鉴于该地块为无偿划拨用地，我镇拟收回按控规要求处理，且不作补偿。

3、市第一法院罔顾事实所拍卖地上之建筑物，并非原寮步工业公司在房管部门所登记的物业，事实上已经景泰公司重建(原房产证应注销未注销，有疑问的可到镇房管所查询)，因此该地上建筑物存在权属不清问题，目前投资方景泰公司已提出异议并起诉，且该建筑物未经合法报建，属于违章建筑，存在被拆除的风险。

4、原土地证登记该地块用途为厂房，与目前的控制性详细规划不符，我镇将不允许该建筑物违反控规使用，同时也不允许其违反用地性质使用。

5、该地块截至2015年11月24日止仍欠寮步镇政府基础设施配套费18574227.54元、公粮补金1949998.05元、工人管理费540000元、土地资源使用费19707148元，合计40771373.59元。受让人必须交纳上述费用。同时，买受人在竞买土地后，必须支付如下费用：1、公粮补金：3333.33元/亩.年。2、工人管理费：15000元/月。3、土地资源使用费：2.25元/平方.月，否则该地块所属塘边村村民能维权。

特此声明。

东莞市寮步镇人民
二〇一五年十二月十

FIGURE 7.1 A public notice in *Dongguan Daily* published by a township government in Dongguan denouncing the local court over its decision to auction a piece of "public land." The statement is reproduced from China.com (2015).

FIRM-TYPE COURTS

The dual process of economic growth and regional differentiation has reached a point whereby urban courts in the developed regions operate under a different political-economic logic of judging, one that is less politicized. Marketization raises the demand for litigation. More litigated cases, in turn, enhance the courts' capacity to finance themselves, so long as the courts are able to deal with the cases efficiently. Financial reward motivates efficiency. High-stakes commercial cases are by-products of a vibrant economy. They make the courts less dependent on the local party-state for financial resources. But their renewed sense of independence also comes from the competitive pressure of the market. The courts are restrained to practice local favoritism, as the economy of the big coastal cities has now become more diversified. It is less easy for one or a few major local companies to dominate in a more diversified economy (He 2009b; Peerenboom 2011). American, Japanese and European companies, as well as companies from Hong Kong, Macau and Taiwan have established a strong presence in coastal China. In more open and prosperous areas, potentially wayward officials and enterprise officers face greater scrutiny and demands for law-conforming behavior from the mass media, foreign investors and an increasingly activist social media community (deLisle 2014:243).

Gechlik (2005:108), referring to the lower withdrawal rates for administrative cases, argues that the Shanghai judiciary is subject to less interference from party members and administrative officials. Her conclusion is also supported by a survey of 800 randomly selected Shanghai residents that the author commissioned. Approximately 44 percent of respondents agreed or strongly agreed that local protectionism is least serious in Shanghai in comparison with other places in China, compared to 28 percent who disagreed (Gechlik 2005:113). Other studies confirm this correlation between the presence of law and the degree of economic development. Urban residents are more likely to litigate and are more likely to be satisfied with their experiences in court than rural residents (Michelson and Read 2011). Studies of the issue of enforcement of judgments also show a lesser degree of local protectionism in urban areas. Scholars have pointed out the difficulty with enforcement of judicial decisions in China, but recent studies have identified significant improvements in wealthier urban areas while poorer rural areas continue to experience persistent problems (He 2007; Gechlik 2005). He (2009b) conducted in-depth interviews with the plaintiffs of sixty-six randomly selected economic contract cases in the Pearl River Delta. The result showed that local courts were reasonably successful in enforcing judgments, and that local protectionism was not a significant barrier. Those courts were located in places where the local economy has become more complex and diversified. The fate of a single company is less important to the local government in a diversified economy, and that local government now has a broader interest in protecting its region's reputation as an attractive investment environment.

Basic-level courts that are located in the most urban part of the country have adopted a different model of operation, a model that operates, to a significant extent, as a firm. The analogy draws on the fact that a firm is characterized by a looser relationship between its frontline judges and senior judges, in a way that resembles relationships in a business firm. Greater emphasis is put on work efficiency (not just how it comes out in official statistics, which can be cooked) and legal expertise. There are bigger and more rapid changes in the litigation markets that require the law to renew itself quickly and the courts to innovate in response. One can see it in the ways many firm-type courts are set up and present themselves. In the petition filing division, which serves as the first stop for a litigant, many firm-type courts in the coastal area spend considerable amounts of money to put the division in a brightly lit, air-conditioned room that is comfortably furnished. Litigants get the background information needed for filing a case through a computerized inquiry system. More electronic panels on the counters display the specific locations for petition filing and the telephone numbers for registering complaints. The counters and desks for registration, payment, refunds, petitions, and complaints are well staffed. Together, these arrangements give a well-run, businesslike image that firm-type courts present to their litigants.

The established vertical hierarchical structure gives way to more fluid contract-like arrangements that offer a wider scope for individual initiatives in everyday operations, with authority residing in result rather than position, and lateral communication playing a more important role than vertical instruction. Senior judges of firm-type courts are more interested in "maximizing profits," i.e., by producing as large a difference between what courts spend and what they receive from fees. Paradoxically, because of this concern about maximizing output, they have to give up part of the power traditionally vested in the vertical hierarchy.

WORK-UNIT TYPE COURTS

In comparison, civil cases generate less revenue for work-unit courts in rural China. The regional economy in which these courts reside is less developed and diverse. Their civil case dockets are stacked with traditional civil cases such as divorce petitions and inheritance disputes, minor contractual disputes, and some personal injury cases (Gao et al. 2009; Ding 2014). Other categories of cases that made up the stable of urban courts, such as intellectual property rights, securities, bankruptcy, and personal rights (privacy, portrait, and reputation), are virtually nonexistent.

The lack of a vibrant economy means that local governments are cash-strapped. Work-unit courts are accustomed to surviving with budgets that are far below (less than 50 percent) the amount necessary for normal operations. Table 7.4 is the progress report that Court H, a work-unit court located in an economically backward inland province, compiled. It was obtained in an earlier study that showed the growing discrepancies between court finances of courts located in different parts of China (He 2009c).

TABLE 7.4 *Income Progress of Court H (October 2004)*

Division	Task set at the beginning of the year	Litigation fees taken for the month	Accumulated litigation fees	Returned litigation fees for the month	Accumulative returned litigation fees	Accumulated income of fines and penalties	Total	Progress
Criminal Division	400,000	0	1,800	0	0	306,100	307,900	77.0%
No. 1 Civil Division	290,000	15,757	192,070	-1,000	-11,650	0	180,420	62.2%
No. 2 Civil Division	300,000	22,500	221,240	-600	-4,000	0	217,240	72.2%
Administrative Division	276,000	29,050	101,198	0	-1,200	2,000	101,998	37.0%
Enforcement Bureau	500,000	35,890	173,226	-1,200	-1,500	10,800	182,526	36.5%
Dispatched Tribunal 1	100,000	10,000	64,350	0	-800	0	63,550	63.6%
Dispatched Tribunal 2	60,000	7,400	50,450	0	0	0	50,450	84.1%
Dispatched Tribunal 3	50,000	3,600	27,900	0	0	0	27,900	55.8%
Dispatched Tribunal 4	50,000	5,400	53,500	0	0	2,000	55,500	111.0%
Dispatched Tribunal 5	50,000	2,700	49,450	0	-1,450	1,000	49,000	98.0%
Total	2,076,000	132,340	943,874	-2,800	-20,600	321,900	1,245,174	60.0%

We reproduce the report here to illustrate how poor courts make ends meet. The court received a budgetary fund of approximately 1.3 million yuan in 2003, which was less than half of the 2.7 million yuan of its operation costs. To make up the gap, the court put pressure on its judges to explore new and old sources of revenue. The report was compiled to put pressure on every division of the court (excluding the petition filing division) to exhaust all means to alleviate the financial burden (He 2009c:470). If some divisions were behind schedule, the presidents of the court and the division heads met to identify new solutions, and to put pressure on their junior judges. Some judges were asked to urge or even cajole potential litigants to file lawsuits!

It is typical for a work-unit court to mobilize its vertical hierarchy to put pressure on frontline judges to solicit cases. One common administrative measure is the use of a quota system. Each court division has maintained a progress report on this matter. Judges are asked to solicit new cases to add to the court's docket. This is a unique phenomenon of Chinese courts (see also Chapter 5). Courts do not follow the typical *passive* role that is assigned to them and wait for cases. Rather, judges are to, as they themselves said, 找米下锅 (*zhao mi xia guo*) "finding their own rice to cook" (Liao and Li 2005:327). When money is really short (some courts were unable to meet payroll obligations in time and had to hold up the salaries and bonuses of judges until they fulfilled their assigned quota), judges exhaust all means to put new cases into the docket (He 2009c).

Judges in work-unit courts are sometimes required by their presidents to pluck cases from other sources to bolster their caseload. In the rural environment, the preponderance of the civil cases fall within the category of domestic relations, and many are handled through different channels, for example, through mediation by a people's mediation committee or by public security stations (Fu 2011:315).[4] The urgency to identify and create new cases means that some work-unit courts are incentivized to provide more legal goods than the public needs or demands. In some areas of law, budgetary pressures and performance appraisals provide perverse incentives that contribute to the excessive supply of law. But in some other areas, courts shrink and refuse to take on cases (see Chapter 5).[5]

Shady practices involving random over-charging of fees above the amount specified in the fee schedule announced by the SPC, or double-charging enforcement fees from both the petitioner and the petitionee, sometimes occur in courts located in counties and villages that are economically underdeveloped (He 2009c:472). On the rare occasion that the courts come across a civil case with a claim that exceeds their jurisdictional limit, they will exhaust all means to take on the case, sometimes by artificially splitting the case into several cases of smaller claims (Woo and Wang 2005:924).

But big civil cases are few and far between for work-unit courts, a reality acknowledged by the central government. The SPC is fully aware of how the local economy affects the composition of the civil case dockets of courts. For this reason, the SPC

TABLE 7.5 *Differential Jurisdictional Limits in Civil Cases Across Provinces (2015)*

Tier level	Province/Special Administrative Region in which a court is located	Jurisdictional limit of disputed claim (in million yuan) High court	Intermediate court
First Tier	Beijing, Shanghai, Jiangsu, Zhejiang, Guangdong	500	100
Second Tier	Tianjin, Hebei, Shanxi, Inner Mongolia, Liaoning, Anhui, Fujian, Shandong, Henan, Hubei, Hunan, Guangxi, Hainan, Sichuan, Chongqing	300	30
Third Tier	Jilin, Heilongjiang, Jiangxi, Yunnan, Shaanxi, Xinjiang	200	10
Fourth Tier	Guizhou, Tibet, Gansu, Qinghai, Ningxia	100	5

Data: Supreme People's Court 2015b

differentiates the claim limits of the provincial high courts and intermediate courts into a four-tier structure (Supreme People's Court 2015b; see Table 7.5).

For work-unit courts in economically undeveloped and inland regions (i.e., as a rough approximation, those located in Tiers 3 and 4), civil cases generate very lean fees for work-unit courts. Domestic disputes and individual-to-individual contractual disputes do not involve large monetary claims.

A more direct way of visualizing the growing gap of court funding is to compare the total disputed amounts of the civil cases handled across provinces. Court fees and charges are calculated based on the disputed amount of a case. The total disputed amount handled by the courts of a province is a good proxy for gauging the revenue generated from the courts' civil docket. Table 7.6 compares the civil caseloads and total disputed amounts of eight selected provinces. Comparing numbers at the provincial level is inevitably a rough estimate for our purpose. As mentioned earlier, the numbers fail to take into consideration the intra-provincial differences between urban and rural regions. That is particularly the case for some of the bigger provinces. Yet, a provincial-level comparison serves the purpose of outlining the economic differences across regions dominated by firm-type courts (the coastal east) and regions dominated by their work-unit counterparts (inland).

A few points can be made. First, the numbers confirm our observations made about firm-type courts throughout the book. Firms are "volume" courts that deal with a lot more cases, as reflected by their growing caseloads that set them apart from work-unit courts. Most provincial high courts report only combined annual totals of civil *and* commercial cases. But we believe that commercial cases make up a bigger part of the civil caseloads for firm-type courts. In the case of Jiangsu, where a

TABLE 7.6 *Comparing the Civil Caseloads and Total Disputed Amounts in Eight Provinces (2015 Figures)*

	Tier level by SPC classification	Civil caseload (rounded to the nearest thousand)	Total disputed claims (in billion yuan)	Population (in millions, based on 2010 census)
Jiangsu	1	886,000	349.9	78.7 m
Zhejiang	1	663,000	289.2 (only commercial cases)	54.4 m
Fujian	2	370,000	161.3	36.9 m
Anhui	2	443,000	146.2	59.5 m
Heilongjiang	3	259,000	47.3	38.3 m
Jiangxi	3	188,000	47.8	44.6 m
Gansu	4	158,000	20.1	25.6 m
Guizhou	4	205,000	46.4	34.7 m

Data gathered from the 2016 annual working reports of the high courts of the six provinces

detailed breakdown of types of civil cases is offered, family disputes only made up 13 percent (117,860) of the civil docket! The bulk of civil cases are contractual disputes (506,655), making up 57 percent of the docket (Jiangsu High Court 2016b). The sums of disputed claims also span a wide range. A gap is opening up, splitting courts in Tier 1 (Jiangsu, Zhejiang) and Tier 2 (Fujian, Anhui) regions from their counterparts in Tier 3 (Heilongjiang, Jiangxi) and Tier 4 (Gansu, Guizhou) regions. That many grassroots courts are in a fiscally perilous state is a problem that the central government is well aware of. Some of the inland courts are deeply in debt to their higher courts or to local banks. The poorest are not even able to pay judges' remuneration on time (Guo 2004). Since 2007, the central government has been earmarking more funding for grassroots courts (Zuo 2015). Yet, as Keith et al. point out (2014:117), this is more a measure of evolutionary incrementalism than a structural breakthrough. It slows down (to a limited extent), but does not reverse the trend that sets firms and work-units further apart.

With the scarcity of big commercial cases, work-unit courts lean more on criminal cases to make up the gap between budget and expenses. Criminal fines are an important source of revenue. At the discretion of judges, minor criminal offenses such as physical assaults, thefts and traffic-related crimes are punishable by fines instead of imprisonment. The length of imprisonment for drug-related crimes such as possession and trafficking of drugs in small amounts can be significantly reduced if fines are paid. Economic crimes such as fraud are another category in which judges have room to maneuver in sentencing. "The sentencing ranges for both drug-related crimes and economic crimes are large and flexible. We can reduce a twenty-year sentence to fifteen or shorter," Judge Zhu, a deputy division head in a grassroots court in Shaanxi, said.

The option of paying criminal fines in exchange for lighter punishment is commonly offered by courts that are strapped for resources. A judge must sentence within the range specified by the law, but judges acknowledged in interviews that they would sentence a defendant who paid fine to the lower end of the range. Judge Gao in another grassroots court in Shaanxi said, "It was back to the early 90s when we found out that the criminal division could generate income. A tribunal in our county, for half a year, collected less than 100,000 yuan in litigation fees. But one criminal defendant was willing to pay this amount. When we came across a case like that, judges in the criminal division almost felt like celebrating." As documented by He (2009c), cash-strapped courts in China asked their criminal divisions to meet a quota in generating income. The situation is different for firm-type courts, whose operational budget is not tied to their income. We asked the same judge (Ng and He 2017), "What is the situation of your court now?" Judge Gao said, "The district government never allocates more funds to us and we never hand in what we collected. The only difference is that back in the 1990s, the required annual quota for the criminal division was 20,000 yuan, but now it is one million yuan."

Other judges from inland provinces also reported the similar use of criminal fines as subsidies for their operational budgets. A judge who was the vice president of an intermediate court in Yunnan, a southwestern inland province bordering Myanmar, told us, "We differentiate defendants in terms of the fines we charge. For a poor farmer who is caught for drug trafficking, we might ask for no more than 100,000 yuan, for this might be all he could pay. For an official who is involved in economic crimes, we will ask for one million yuan or more, especially if his lawyer takes the initiative in approaching us." It seems that in order to maximize their income, these courts adopted a strategy akin to what economists describe as "price discrimination." In other words, they expect the defendants to pay according to the best of their abilities (Ng and He 2017). "Do you always impose a lighter sentence when a defendant agrees to pay criminal fines?" we asked Judge Gao. "Yes we do," replied the judge.

Criminal cases that involve offenses against official capacity and economic fraud also sometimes bring valuable assets into the courts through confiscation of criminal proceeds. For work-unit courts with meager budgets, confiscated assets are a godsend. But that also raises the temptation to fabricate more cases for the economic benefit of the courts rather than to pursue law and justice (Li 2014; Xu et al. 2015).

Finally, some work-unit courts, at the request of their cash-strapped local governments, perform the most direct form of economic embeddedness – i.e., by asking prominent local businesses to *invest* in the courts. On the face of it, local businesses "invest" because better public security and a law-abiding environment help businesses. Yet, as Ding (2014) reports, sponsorship from local businesses comes with a cost. Court officials are fully aware of the *quid pro quo* quality of this exercise.

THE LATEST JUDICIAL REFORM: TOWARD RE-CENTRALIZATION?

The new funding mechanism proposed in the latest judicial reform (Supreme People's Court 2015a, 2016) represents a significant departure from the trend of the devolution of fiscal power that has been the trademark of reform since the 1980s. More central funding administered by provincial-level governments is among the key proposals that headline the latest, and arguably the most sweeping judicial reform of this decade. The latest policy promises that the central government will fully guarantee the funding of the local courts. Grassroots and intermediate courts will submit their budgets to the provincial government, and budget funds will be appropriated by the centralized payment system of the national treasury.

This model, if fully carried out (always a big "if" in China), should significantly loosen the grip of local government control on grassroots courts. It would place local court budgetary processes more firmly in the hands of the central government. It is too early to gauge the full effects of the new financing mechanism. If history is any guide, the resiliency of Anthony Downs's "laws of counter-control" (1967) should not be underestimated. In the context of China, the greater the effort made by the central government to control the behavior of the local government, the greater will be the efforts made by the locals to evade such control (Zhou, Xueguang 2010). How the new financing model is going to affect the routine operations of grassroots courts remains to be seen. Here we can only pose a few questions.

In theory, the new centralized funding mechanism should significantly reduce local protectionism. It is supposed to reduce the control of local governments over their courts. But this is a plan that tries to resolve the problem of administrative hierarchy (one that is embedded in the local coalition of governance) by expanding the administrative hierarchy vertically (one that gives the SPC and provincial high courts more control). It is a model of a "vertical leadership system" that some Chinese jurists have proposed (Qiao 2004; Keith et al. 2014). It remains the case that grassroots courts are managed as a government bureau within a hierarchical structure. From the standpoint of liberal democracy, the fundamental problem has not been resolved, and that fundamental problem is the lack of thick institutional boundaries separating the courts from the rest of the political system.

Again in theory, central and provincial funding should help alleviate the budgetary plight experienced by poor grassroots courts. But in some of our latest interviews since the announcement of the latest reform, we have already heard complaints from some senior judges in grassroots courts that local officials now consider themselves "off the financial hook." At the end of the day, more central money may not produce as much of an increase in overall funding for grassroots courts as intended. Specifically, while central funding creates a more stable source of revenue for judicial salaries and other recurrent expenditures, grassroots courts still rely on local governments for major capital projects such as new court buildings and investments in new technologies.

Some are concerned that judicial budgetary shortfalls work like a water balloon – if one squeezes it in one place, it sort of pops out in another place. This model of recentralization of fiscal power also turns on the loyalty of provincial governments. To some degree it reverts back to a pre-1980s conception of provinces – "disseminating Beijing's policy directives and monitoring subprovincial compliance with state plans" (Chung 1998:430; cited by Saich 2015:163).

On the other hand, this centralizing strategy, if indeed fully implemented, would give substantial fiscal power to the SPC and provincial high court senior judges, to an extent that they have never enjoyed before. Presidents of courts at different levels are poised to play a much bigger role in budget preparation (Zhang, Hongtao 2015). Is this going to change the relationship between the SPC and its subordinate courts? Are we going to see the kind of budget-maximizing strategy that public-choice scholars such as Niskanen (1973) warn about? Will senior judges focus on expanding their line-item funds rather than promoting the efficient use of financial resources? Centralized budgeting affects not only the operation of cash-strapped work-unit courts, but more affluent firm-type courts as well. Firm courts thrive from their embeddedness in the urban economy, which offers relative financial independence. Will the presence of central subsidies subsume firm-type courts into another hierarchy with layered vertical control? No budgeting system is immune from politics. The new system might curb the political influences of local governments over the grassroots courts. However, the internalized bureaucratic politics within the judicial system will likely increase (Hazard et al. 1972:1300).

The disparities created by the phenomenon of economic embeddedness are unlikely to disappear. If history tells us anything about the policies implemented by the central government, it would be that things seldom go as planned. Given how actual practices deviated from the original intent of the policy of separate income and expenses, we expect to see new forms of inequalities emerge under the policy of "central funding." As explained, economic embeddedness has been a dominant force that shapes court finances. The long-term financial sustainability of a court is largely dependent on the "financial quality" of its civil cases. A central financing model is not likely to alter this reality. As we have seen in the state courts of the United States, a shift from county to state funding is not a cure-all for the problems of fiscal inequalities (Hazard et al. 1972; George 2005). But it might give senior judges expansive power over the courts and lead to the consolidation of a new judicial power center of senior judges and party officials.

8

Conclusion

In this book, Chinese courts are analyzed as embedded institutions that adapt to the external environment in which they operate. The various forms of embeddedness identified in this book complicate the picture of judicial operations, so much so that it deviates significantly from a rules-first judicial institution. The palpable variations between firms and work-units suggest that the behaviors of the Chinese courts are not defined by the law that they are supposed to implement. The law is uniform, but the institutional behaviors are varied. This suggests that courts are institutions shaped by different social forces that are embedded into the nascent legal field.

As we have identified them, these social forces are administrative embeddedness, political embeddedness, social embeddedness, and economic embeddedness. The concept of embeddedness emphasizes duality in different aspects of the court's operation. Administrative embeddedness captures the central/local duality of the court. The judicial system is asked to carry out the law, and law is an extension of the policies of the central government. But the senior judges who lead the courts are often themselves members of the local party-state coalition.

Administrative embeddedness refers to how senior judges themselves are embedded in, and, in fact, embody, the local network of governance. Their administrative agenda and priorities guide the everyday action of the courts through the vertical hierarchical structure that we have described.

Political embeddedness refers to the duality in the purported function of the courts. On the one hand, the court is a legal institution that is supposed to carry out the law. But on the other hand, it is a political institution that is meant to uphold social stability. As a result, judges often exercise restraint in the administration of law. They speak a language of practical politics. The exercise of justice must be adjusted according to the nature of the situation.

Social embeddedness refers to the duality of official and personal interests. It is the result of the mingling of competing commitments originating from other social roles over the impersonality and impartiality required of a judge. Obligations from the outside compete with their professional duties as judges. As a result, the judicial process is not as rule-governed as it appears.

Economic embeddedness refers to the *de facto* duality between the court as a state bureaucracy that is fiscally sanctioned by local governments and a legal institution that is self-supported. Courts that are embedded in the growing urban economy make enough revenue to support themselves. Financial independence, as indicated, is consequential in shaping the working style of the courts as well as the way everyday, routine decisions are made in a court.

Our analysis set its sights beyond big policies from the top, focusing instead on the environment of judging that grassroots courts face. As government bureaus, they are subject to various social forces from outside of the nascent legal field. In identifying the characteristics of the courts, we have analytically distinguished two types of Chinese courts – the work-unit and the firm.

Table 8.1 summarizes the key differences between the two types. Our unavoidably schematic comparison highlights the differences between the two. As with any real-life institution that has survived various policy regimes in China, there is an element of eclecticism to the basic structure of the courts. No single Chinese court nowadays operates in complete conformity with either model.

As ideal types, however, they represent two different types of bureaucracy, each with its own behavioral patterns. They each carry their own distinct action plan in dealing with their everyday businesses, regulating the flow of adjudicative activities, defining modal decisions, and dealing with problem cases. There is a trade-off between the flexibility and efficiency of the firm and the supervision and control of the work-unit.

The four types of embeddedness are not disparate. They are at times mutually reinforcing, and at times constraining of one another. Social embeddedness and political embeddedness point to elements that complicate the use of law in China. Political embeddedness refers to the fact that instrumental attitudes toward the law remain dominant. Firms and work-units share the same concern with political stability, but they differ in their degree of risk aversion. Firms are more inclined to use the law. They only enter the non-law mode of "firefighting" if a case creates strong feedback from external parties including litigants, mass media, and local government. Bigger constituencies and more complex interdependencies between economy and politics give courts more room to apply the law. In comparison, work-units are more law-shy and are more prepared to choose to resort to non-law means of resolving conflicts.

Social embeddedness results from a lack of boundary in the role duties of judges. The diffused power of *guanxi* is reflected in some judges' willingness to use their official power as private assets for favor exchanges. This willingness can be found in both firms and work-units. *Guanxi* is a diffused social power (Mann 1986); judges can enhance their joint power over outside parties by taking advantage of their official roles. This is especially the case with superior ties, as senior judges abuse their power by coercing junior judges into abusing their powers. Social embedded-ness can only be countered by another form of "diffused power" – emerging

TABLE 8.1 *Firms vs. Work-Units*

Embeddedness	Focus of difference	Work-units	Firms
Administrative	How often is law used?	Low volume of adjudication; spend considerable time on cases either too trivial or too thorny to be dealt with by law; emphasize outcome	High volume of adjudication; emphasize output
	Role of vertical hierarchy	Police patrol	Fire alarm
	Culture of consultation with superiors	Strong	Frontline judges are more on their own
Political	Concerns with social stability	Very high; law is often sidelined in the name of promoting social stability	Very high; but sometimes the politically safest option is to follow the law
	Use of mediation	Extensive; courts also engage in extra-judicial forms of mediation	Less extensive; frontline judges prefer adjudication over mediation; special staff are deployed to "mediate" enough cases
Social	Patron-client relationship between senior and junior judges	High	Declining
	Court as a *total* institution to judges	Still binds judges by an encompassing network of relationships stretching across work, home, neighborhood, and social life	Judges treat working in courts as a job, albeit a demanding one; courts have to compete with the growing private sector of law.
	Extent to which judges are influenced by their social ties	Superior ties remain influential; ties from top judges can easily influence frontline judges because of patron-client relationship	While the influences of superior ties fade a bit, judges remain susceptible to the influences of non-superior ties
Economic	Role of professional knowledge	Low; political considerations prevail; people skills and ability to placate litigants remain of paramount importance	High; political considerations persist in problem cases, but more cases are resolved by law; courts are more specialized; judges in certain divisions, e.g., IP, take pride in their legal expertise
	Degree of fiscal autonomy from local government	Low; courts remain heavily dependent on local government's funding	High; cost control and efficiency are important considerations for achieving financial autonomy

professional identity among judges. Professionalism is growing in China, but it has yet to nurture a set of accepted practices that are regarded as natural and core.

Administrative embeddedness and economic embeddedness countervail each other. They represent the pull and push forces that determine the degree of vertical hierarchy adopted by a court. Firms and work-units differ in their degree of administrative embeddedness. Work-units are organized institutionally as a vertical hierarchy. Supervision and control from the top down are tight and extensive. In work-unit courts, judges are accustomed to ask before making any consequential decisions ("When in doubt, just ask."). The law is bureaucratized, or to use a term adopted by Chinese scholars, "administerized" (行政化 *xingzhenghua*), by iterative consultations. In contrast, firm-type courts have a flatter, scaled-back vertical hierarchy. The size of a court also is a factor. Firms are generally bigger in their establishment. The problem of authority leakage is more salient in firms. Frontline judges are freer, and are, consequently, held more accountable. In terms of the forms and conventions of social relations within the court, judges are more "on their own" in firms. If they ask their superiors for advice, it is more out of their initiative rather than as a result of the constant supervision of their superiors.[1]

Another dimension that clearly distinguishes the two types of courts is economic embeddedness. A growing litigation market, particularly on the civil front, is the determining force that frees those grassroots courts in urban areas from the sanction of their local governments. A bigger market creates the need for courts to be more efficient and specialized, hence making it necessary for them to scale back on the extent of hierarchical control. As we have mentioned in this book, the efficient form of organization for a given judicial market is a function of certain properties of the institutional environment of judging: uncertainty, technical complexity, knowledge expertise, asset specificity, market size, looseness of local government coalition and frequency of disputes. Implicit in our analysis is that a different environment of judging is the key factor that alters the institutional form of the courts. Cities, with their more diverse and also more fragmented populations of urban dwellers, allow courts to favor adjudication over other means of dispute resolution. It is under such an environment that firm-type courts are given the space to favor adjudication over time-consuming options such as negotiations, mediation and reconciliation, among others.

THE FUTURE OF CHINESE COURTS

If we look at the big policies developed by the SPC, the central government is clearly pushing for greater legitimacy of law within an instrumentalist framework. To accomplish this, policies are derived to create a more professionalized court infrastructure, to flatten its bureaucratic hierarchy (and to lower its head count), to make individual judges more accountable and perhaps better paid and to establish clearer lines of authority and responsibility. The courts are going to have a more independent identity from other bureaus. They are also going to have more authority conferred by the central government to counterbalance the power of local authorities. This policy direction is clearly reflected in many of the important proposals suggested in the latest judicial reform effort, which is far-ranging in scope and ambitious in the goals it has set out to achieve (Supreme People's Court 2016). The question remains: Is the latest judicial reform likely to succeed?

Prediction is perilous, particularly when made on a subject as complex as the Chinese legal system. But we understand that this very topic is no idle matter, of interest only to academics. What we offer here are speculations, but speculations based on the implications of the embeddedness thesis we have presented. For readers who have followed the arguments in the previous chapters, it should come as no surprise that we are skeptical of the extent of the effects of the latest round of judicial reform pushed by the SPC. Our study was shaped by the sociological literature on institutions. The title of the book suggests that we see the environment of judging as most consequential in shaping the behaviors of a court. We doubt the effectiveness of top-down measures to make the courts more firm-like. Instead, courts are embedded in an institutional matrix and are therefore subject to pressure from their environments. Rule of law was hailed as the central theme of the Fourth Plenary Session of the 18th party congress in 2014. What we have seen since then are changes that are better characterized as piecemeal and incremental rather than sweeping and foundational. "Enhanced" central and provincial funding are offered to grassroots courts. Yet it is not clear if the fiscal hardships suffered by the poorest courts in inland regions have been alleviated. Urban courts continue to get capital funding to upgrade their infrastructure and research support, pulling them further away from the inland courts. The latest judicial reform aims to reduce the total establishment of judges. But what we have seen is that it has proven more difficult to remove non-judging "judges" who have owned the title for years than to stop appointing more new judges. What the policy does is block the career pathway for many young and college-educated court clerks who would have been promoted to judges after a few years of training under the old system. Would that lead to further professionalization of courts? Perhaps – but if that happens, its effects are going to be gradual and slow, as grassroots courts have to wait out the retirements of a large contingency of non-judging judges scattered in different parts of the country. In the short term, the policy risks losing more young judges who are frustrated with their dimming prospects for promotion.

Another problem area that is unlikely to have a quick fix is the all-powerful adjudication committee, the pinnacle of the bureaucratic hierarchy for every court (see Chapter 4). Despite the Communiqué of the Fourth Plenum that called for reforms of the adjudication committee, it continues to play a central role in deciding the outcomes of important cases in many grassroots courts. Some reform measures have been launched, such as the introduction of the subcommittee system. Civil, criminal, and commercial subcommittees now convene separately. The idea is to instill a greater sense of professionalism. But we do not know the extent of overlapping membership, particularly in smaller courts. In any case, the reforms proposed have not altered the monocratic and secretive nature of the committee's decision-making process. The committee decides cases behind closed doors, with the court president dominating the process.

The effects of judicial reform are most immediate in areas where violations are open to view. For example, during our visits to a couple of courthouses after the judicial reform was announced, we found some large offices left vacant. We asked judges we interviewed why precious space was left unused. In one case, the judge offered an embarrassed smile upon hearing our question. He said the room used to be his old office. But he was "only" a division head. The room was too big for a judge of his rank. He had to move out, lest he risk violating the government's rules. The judge moved to a smaller office and left the room unused. At the time of our visit, it was designated as a common area for all the judges of the same division, though it was left unused most of the time. As judges said to us privately, there was no way to hide violations of this kind. A visit by someone from the top with a laser measure could doom the violator. But slight non-conformities, deliberate leakages, veiled resistance to policies and offstage deviance from rules with respect to judicial decision-making are more subtle and difficult to detect (see examples in Chapter 6). The topmost officials of the SPC are keenly aware of these problems. Their solution is to create new structures of their own to counteract the "bad behaviors" of the lower courts. This is reflected in the growing number of new circuit courts that the current SPC President Zhou Qiang has erected during his tenure. Four more circuit courts, located in Nanjing, Zhengzhou, Chongqing and Xi'an, were inaugurated at the end of 2016, on top of the two circuit courts in Shenyang and Shenzhen that were already in action. The six new circuit courts now cover the entire country. On the face of it, they represent a nascent tier of courts resembling the circuit courts of the US federal system. However, institutionally speaking, these circuit courts are not new separate courts; they are subdivisions of the SPC and are staffed by SPC judges. It is clear that the SPC is trying to extend itself to create a group of overlapping courts to counter the forces of local legal protectionism.[2] Redundancy and overlapping devices have long been the means for the party-state to monitor lower officials. In this sense, the circuit court should be understood more as an administrative mechanism of internal monitoring than as a presage of a jurisdictional differentiation that would lead to a dual, federal-state judicial system. Future reforms may turn the circuit courts into appeal courts on matters of law only. At the time of writing, it is too early to tell.

If we had to summarize the goal of the latest judicial reform in one phrase, it would be this: to make work-unit courts more like firms. Yet the environments facing urban and rural courts remain starkly different. While official statistics suggest that the rural-urban income gap has slightly narrowed, the discrepancy remains striking. The annual average per-capita disposable income in rural China was 10,489 yuan ($1,693) in 2014. In urban areas, the average per-capita disposable income was 29,381 yuan in the same year, which suggests a ratio that still hovers around 3 to 1 (Yang 2015).

Despite the stated goal of the central government, institutional culture, local practices, and immediate concerns on the ground are more determinant in shaping the work of the grassroots courts. It is unlikely that the new rules that promote individual responsibility will have any immediate tangible effects. Instead, judges will find ways to adapt to the new rules of the game. The policies initiated by the SPC, as always, will be observed nominally, but whether they will be followed in substance remains an open question.

There are some structural factors that favor the *gradual* growth of firm-type courts in the next few decades. The one macro-level factor is clearly the continued process of urbanization in China. In 2011, for the first time, over half of the country's population lived in urban areas. The party-state estimated that by 2020, 60 percent of the population would live in cities (Xinhua News Agency 2014). China's country-side is shrinking and will continue to shrink in the foreseeable future as the country transforms its economy. It is not only that more courts are going to be situated in cities. More important, for the process of urbanization to proceed in an orderly manner, effective legal regulation is a much-needed component. As Saich (2015:236) points out, the success of the Chinese urbanization program revolves around effective resolution of three interrelated challenges: developing effective financing vehicles, reforming the household registration system and dealing with the question of land ownership and land-use rights in the countryside. A clear demarcation of land rights definitely helps to minimize potential conflicts inherent in the urbaniza-tion process.

So, while professionalization is going to be slow and gradual, the Chinese courts are heading toward that direction. That brings us to an important but difficult question: Supposing that firm-type courts become the dominant type of courts, what would that mean for the rule of law in China? Will the rule of law finally be in place if courts are more professionalized, independent and rule-governed?

As we have said repeatedly, firms use the law more. The propensity to use the law will increase in a system dominated by firm-type courts. However, social embedd-edness prevails not only in work-units but also in firms. Judges are imbued with the values of the wider Chinese society in which they are placed. Close, personal ties, or *guanxi*, find ways to influence their judicial decisions. It does seem that social embeddedness is less of a tangled web in firms, in the sense that its influence comes in more frequently through non-superior, personal ties among frontline judges, again as a consequence of the weakening of the vertical hierarchy. While individual judges might be more "independent" in firm courts, that does not necessarily translate into a collective sense of greater trustworthiness and legitimacy in the eyes of the public.

In the long run, it is possible that courts will develop a rule-based culture that puts precedence on legal professionalism. Many of the young Chinese judges we talked to express an aspiration to work like Western judges. They do not want to be treated "like another bureaucrat." They know that their demonstrated ability to decide against their non-professional social role obligations for the sake of legal correctness is crucial for winning the public trust. Newer college graduates also see a judge's primary responsibility as adjudication. It is an activity that fits with and promotes their self-image of being a professional. They want to use the law, to apply the law, and to develop it as a system of well-defined rules. Adjudication is preferred for this new breed of college graduates. We see some signs in the biggest firm courts today. New and younger judges seem more reluctant to yield to external and internal extralegal demands. The evidence is hardly conclusive; but it provides some signs about how the courts may develop – with the flattening of vertical hierarchy, it is not unrealistic to expect the Chinese courts to develop an institutional culture that is more resistant to personal favoritism and social connections.

What about political embeddedness? At present, the political priority of social maintenance looms large in both work-units and firms. The whole character of political maintenance takes its tone from the authoritarian nature of the state. Stability maintenance is the premier goal of all government bureaus, including the courts. Perhaps in terms of percentage, the portion of cases perceived to be politically threatening is much lower in firm courts. Yet when social stability is at stake, they are as ready as work-unit courts to set aside the law for political goals. Following the law is not a strong value in itself; judges will deviate from the law if the occasion demands.

Will this change in the future? Will emerging professionalism make the courts less a tool for the party-state to maintain stability? To what extent can separate interests and power be claimed on the expanding basis of legal expertise exhibited by younger judges?

The answers to the questions turn on how the idea of "professionalism" is understood by Chinese judges. It is natural for this new generation of college-trained judges to develop a greater affinity with some version of the rule of law. In Chapter 3, we described the mentality of young Chinese judges. To wit, when judges liken themselves to the professional identity of a judge, they refer to the following things:

- to become more expert in the law
- to be able to formulate judgments based on one's knowledge of the law
- to be more skilled in evidence analysis and judgment writing
- to have more support in the form of legal research and clerical help

One can easily understand why professionalism is so appealing to many younger Chinese judges. With regard to those above them, judges want to have a layer of protection against the commands of the leaders of the local and central governments. As we have seen in many Western examples, the development of expert knowledge presents obstacles to those who do not share that expertise (Beetham 1996:54). With regard to those below, they hope the development of professionalism can become a steady source of authority, which is sorely lacking at present.

This notion of professionalism is also confirmed, albeit obliquely, by the criticisms levied against young judges by some older judges: that new young judges stay in the ivory tower of law, that they are not interested in the lives of the ordinary people (老百姓 *laobaixing*), that they are not *with* the people, or in the Communist lingo, are "divorced from the masses." Older judges who did not go to college see a streak of elitism running through the younger generations' "noble" pursuit of law. Sociologically, the schism between old and new judges is a schism between two status strata. Older and younger judges were recruited from different backgrounds: the former were a mixed class of retired military officers, transferred civil servants, and some college graduates, many of whom had prior backgrounds in non-legal government work; the latter are a class predominantly made up of law graduates selected by means of a nationwide, specialized examination. While the older generation's charge of elitism is unsympathetic, the quest for higher social and occupational prestige is indeed commonly cited by young judges as a reason why they want to stay close to the law.

We brought this up because the way professionalism is understood by Chinese judges can easily lead to misunderstanding if approached from the standpoint of liberal democracy, where the rule of law is an integral component that facilitates the separation of powers. And therein lies the problem, in our opinion, with the limited nature of the notion of professionalism in the Chinese context. It is an apolitical pursuit of professional expertise. In a liberal democracy, there is more to legal professionalism than just the mastery of a body of expert knowledge. This goes back to Max Weber: bureaucracy in the Western sense is not merely an institution; it is also a social force with interests and values of its own (1978:990–994). "Judicial professionalism" means a commitment to a definite judicial role, defined as a set of expectations, values and attitudes about the way judges behave and should behave (Guarnieri and Pederzoli 2002:68). It is, analytically speaking, made up of two elements: the first is the acquisition of relevant expertise and credentials; the second is adherence to a certain set of professional ethics that are shared by members of the profession. It certainly takes a great deal of commitment, and even courage, for some Chinese judges to decide according to their legal expertise. Professionalism, however, also refers to a commitment to some fundamental values that are not explicitly written into the law. For judges and lawyers, it refers to a commitment to the rule of law, understood more expansively in the Western context than the narrow concept of legality. Does the commitment of younger Chinese judges to follow the law portend a possible embrace of a broader notion of the rule of law, one that entails liberal ideals of freedom, a more encompassing notion of justice and perhaps proto-democratic aspirations?

Our analysis, however, suggests that the possibilities here are limited. If the Chinese legal system succeeds in becoming more professionalized, judges as a group are much more likely to become a special group within the state, or, in Weber's terms, a specialized officialdom. Younger judges as a group crave higher status. Professionalism is the pathway to attaining higher status. Their view of professionalism is apolitical and strictly technical. Judges we interviewed seldom approach matters "constitutionally." That is, they seldom question whether the bigger principles behind the law are right, or, dare we say, righteous. If anything, they complained that their laws have made the courts too accessible, as evidenced by the low court fees charged for labor cases. It is difficult enough for them to apply the law as it is, and it is important to not make light of the tremendous courage and noble sacrifice that some judges have to make in order to faithfully follow the law. But for most judges, questioning the underlying principles of the law seems like an exercise far removed from reality.

For many outsiders who hope to see the Chinese legal system embrace the ideal of the rule of law, it is tempting to equate the younger generation of judges' longing for professionalism with a rights-centered ideal of the rule of law – that is, the judicial equivalent of liberal democracy. But the two pursuits are, in our view, quite different. We do not find many activist judges who work in the frontline openly championing the rule of law. In interviews, judges are most outspoken in their disapproval of populism. Many of these judges have to deal with difficult and sometimes abrasive litigants. Combined with this sentiment is the judges' pride in being capable interpreters of the law.

Institutionally, the limited nature of the concept of professionalism in China is a reminder that it would be a mistake to conflate the firm-type court with the Western concept of an independent court. Firm-type courts achieve relative operational independence in routine cases as a result of a confluence of factors, none of which can be equated with constitutional commitments or a culture of value-based professionalism, at least not just yet. As we have shown, these courts exhibit a much greater propensity to adjudicate by law. But this instrumental appropriation of law is motivated by efficiency rather than a commitment to values. This means that the use of the law is going to be calculating, and therefore selective. The SPC clearly tries to push local courts to have a greater sense of operational independence, but like a lot of things in Chinese politics, there are bottom lines. There is obviously greater capacity for the law to be applied in the civil and commercial cases, but less so in public security and administrative cases.

The aspiration to *follow* the law is an aspiration intended to make judging easier and more efficient at both the level of the individuals (judges) and of the institutions (courts). This goes back to our focus on the institutional environment of judging. Following the law, or not, is primarily a matter of institutional adaptation. When dealing with stability-threatening cases, firms still lean on the vertical hierarchy of control. This is the essence of the "fire-alarm" system. Firm-type courts see political stability as a prerequisite for them to pursue their financial independence; they have, themselves, imbibed the conservative attitude of the state, adopting the attitude that stability matters most.

So it seems more likely that China will develop a partial "rule of law" that mimics the ideals reflected in the Singaporean "dual-state legality" model. Among scholars who study the Singaporean judicial system, the dual-state thesis portrays Singapore's legal system as two-sided (Jayasuriya 2001; Tey 2011; Rajah 2012). There is a clear bifurcation of Singaporean law. In political and constitutional matters, Singapore follows the so-called "four walls" doctrine, whereby Singapore laws are to be interpreted "within its own four walls," without comparison to other jurisdictions (Tey 2011); but its laws related to civil matters, in particular business and commercial operations, are "modern" and "pristine," and above all outward-looking (Rajah 2012).

Of course, any comparison between the two must be conducted with caution. China and Singapore differ greatly in size, regional diversity, and political structure. Regional variations within China are prominent and will only continue to be so. Furthermore, China's brand of populist authoritarianism means that there is likely to be more discretion and abuse that the Singaporean model would allow. What we want to point out is that, despite the changing makeup of judges, it would be wrong to assume that the Chinese judiciary has arrived at a "tipping point" where wholesale changes to the role of the courts are imminent. What is most likely to happen is a gradual development toward a mixed, eclectic model, where the courts become more specialized and professional in dealing with civil cases, particularly in economic and commercial cases, but continue to remain at once populist and controlling in criminal cases.

The Chinese party-state's view about the judicial system is well known: to develop the institutional legitimacy of the judicial system while reinforcing the nature of the system as an apparatus of state power (Traveskes 2011). In recent years, the courts have been asked to take up other functions. Rule of law is used as a means for regulating local economies, for example. Rule of law has also been offered by the central government as an ersatz reform, to defer deeper political changes. The recent policies on the judiciary indicate a paradox: courts are asked to become more professional while at the same time they have become more controllable by the central government. The central government expects more judicial accountability, not more judicial independence.

One might ask if judicial accountability without operational independence is achievable. The leaders of the Chinese party-state, like politicians in general, are pragmatic. Their immediate concerns, as always, are about the various stresses and strains that bubble up in different parts of the country, particularly in the countryside. Underneath the banner of the rule of law, they will likely continue to do what they have been doing – muddling through with a series of piecemeal, *ad hoc* and eclectic policies that demand that the Chinese judicial system be many things at once. As such, strong local variations between courts of the firm and the work-unit variants will continue to be among the most distinctive features of this purportedly simple-structured system in the world's most populous country.

Methodological Appendix

This study is based on interviews and fieldwork that the authors conducted, studying various aspects of the Chinese grassroots courts. The interviews were conducted between November 2012 and September 2015. Besides the interviews, we also had follow-up conversations with some of the judges. The bulk of the interviews were conducted in Hong Kong, when the judges were in Hong Kong to attend training courses run by City University of Hong Kong, in which the second author taught. When inviting respondents to be interviewed, we tried to include judges of different ranks, including presidents, vice presidents, division heads, and ordinary judges. However, since our focus was on the day-to-day, case-by-case routine operations of the courts, ordinary judges constituted the largest group among our interviewees.

Judges were recruited through personal connections and snowball sampling techniques. The respondents were not a random sample of frontline and senior judges. The judges interviewed were told that any quotes would be anonymous. Some of the interviews were tape-recorded, with the consent of the judges. Others were not, as some judges did not feel comfortable being taped. Notes were taken and written up as soon as possible after each interview was complete. In general, we felt that judges spoke very freely in the interviews, especially when describing their job responsibilities and what they saw to be the challenges of the courts. In an interesting way, our commitment to understand the mundane routines caught these judges off guard. They did not consider the information we sought to be sensitive or controversial. They were more cautious and guarded when discussing specific cases, especially cases that they or their colleagues had dealt with.

On average, an interview lasted for about an hour to an hour and a half. The first author was the primary interviewer. He conducted all of the interviews. The second author participated in about half of the interviews. The interviews started with the interviewer(s) outlining the study. The interviews were semi-structured. We did not follow a list of questions, but there was a list of general questions and topics that we asked about:

- Describe your court. How long have you been there?
- What kind of judicial work do you do?
- Describe your typical work day.
- What is the most challenging part of being a judge?
- What is the most satisfying aspect of being a judge?
- How would you characterize the litigants that you deal with in your work?
- How much time do you spend on mediation?
- How much time do you spend on legal research and judgment writing?
- Do you work alone? How would you describe your interactions with judges in the same division?
- Can you share a memorable case that you presided over?
- How do you view judges of different generations? Is each generation different?
- Do you see the courts as independent?
- Do you feel that you work independently?
- What are the challenges facing the courts today?
- Why did you choose to become a judge?
- Would you mind telling us your age?
- Do you think you will remain a judge a few years from now?

The list of questions was strictly for our reference. We tried to allow the interviewees to speak as much as possible on a topic that interested them. We also asked questions not included in the list, following up on the answers offered by our interviewees. The follow-up questions were asked to extract more details about their working environment and how they characterized the internal operation of their courts. Biographical questions about the interviewees were usually raised toward the end of the interview.

Despite our efforts to diversify our pool of interviewees, there was some bunching. This group of judges, though selected from different parts of the country, was not a representative sample of the incumbent Chinese judges by any means. The judges were present in Hong Kong for training and educational purposes. Apparently, there were more judges who worked in urban courts than judges who worked in the rural regions. There was also a higher number of judges from Guangdong. The proximity between Hong Kong and Guangdong could have been a factor. That said, the group represented quite a diverse group of judges. We interviewed about 50 judges in Hong Kong. The interviews together allowed us to sketch out a picture of the Chinese courts with nuanced regional and local variations.

This project is also based on the fieldwork we conducted from 2011 to 2015. As the contrast between firm and work-unit suggests, we tried to orient ourselves to the logic of comparative method. The way we present the comparison here is admittedly neater than what we thought it would be when we embarked on our research field trips. This idea of offering a variationist account of the Chinese courts grew out of the research trips we made to study specific topics about the Chinese courts, including mediation, criminal reconciliation, divorce petitions, demolition cases, court finances and social ties. We noticed that courts differ significantly. Studying their differences was to us an important way to understand the character of the Chinese court system. Our selection of court study sites was driven by our hope to compare inland and coastal courts, but also driven in part by accessibility.

The courts in which we conducted ethnographic research were mainly located in two different provinces. The first is Guangdong. We visited courts in the Pearl River Delta region. This constituted the base of our understanding of firm-type courts. The Pearl River Delta region is now the largest urban area in Asia. It is one of the most affluent regions of China. We also supplemented our understanding with discussions with judges working in cities such as Beijing and Shanghai. We made four trips to the region during the research period, each one lasting two to four weeks. The second main province for our study is Shaanxi. The second author visited courts in the rural and suburban areas of the inland province. The area was less economically developed. The facilities of the courthouses were plain. Resources were sparse. The second author made two trips to the region during the research period (and some additional trips were made earlier), each lasting for two to three weeks. This constituted the base of our understanding of work-unit courts. We supplemented this research with interviews of judges from other inland provinces. We also made occasional visits to other courts. For these short visits, which usually lasted less than a week, we did not conduct ethnographic studies of court trials.

Access to the Chinese courts is difficult for researchers. If anything, access has only become more restrictive in recent years. As our Chinese informants would like to joke, the People's Court remained closed to most people. In both Guangdong and Shaanxi, we were allowed access because of our personal connections with some of the judges there. Among these judges, the second author had known a few of them for years. Others were our former students. To our knowledge, we are the only foreign research team to have obtained this sort of access to both civil and criminal trials in China.

There were good reasons why it would have been safer if the judges had turned us down, or had revealed as little as possible. As the readers of this book can attest, we did not give a flattering portrayal of the courts we studied or the judges we interviewed. Little harm would be done if they had declined to assist us in our research. To us, it would have been a disappointing but understandable outcome. The fact that we were able to enter many grassroots courtrooms in our intellectual quest for insight was a culmination of individual acts of generosity.

Getting into the Chinese courts was not made easier by the policy of judicial transparency spearheaded by the SPC in recent years. Most trials are, by law, open to the public. In reality, it is difficult for unrelated outsiders who are not part of the litigating parties to sit in on a trial. Surely many courts are now streaming their trials live on the web. But the live streaming is *controlled* access. Courts carefully select the cases that are made available for viewing. We watched some "live" broadcasts made available on the internet (many of them were in fact pre-recorded). The trials were, by a considerable margin, more formalized, rehearsed and orderly than what we observed *in situ*. In contrast, the trials that we observed were hurried, sometimes messy, and often conducted without the presence of lawyers. Virtual access is different from corporeal access to the courts. They are two different experiences, both for the observer and for the observed. One should not believe that the availability of the former means that the latter is no big deal.

To be able to observe trials, one has first to physically enter a courthouse. Security checks have tightened considerably in recent years. When Liang (2008) did his research of Chinese courts in 2002, he wrote that the guards at the front door only *looked* intimidating – it was not difficult to walk pass the guards. Nowadays, the guards *are* intimidating, and vigilant. Often we needed to be escorted by an acquainted judge just to get inside the building. This was particularly true with the bigger courthouses in the cities. Steel gates were put up and visitors were asked to go through not just one but sometimes two security checkpoints. People who entered the court building were subject to x-ray and metal-detector screening. The guards would also take away (temporarily) any cameras and recorders that they found (but they allowed cell phones to be brought in). Visitors could only get those items back when they left the building. The enhanced security was put in place in light of violent incidents that have led to the death of a few judges in the past few years.

Once inside the courthouse, one had to know where to go. Courts were sensitive to unfamiliar faces wandering around in the building, again out of security concerns. In the lobby, one is supposed to see the latest daily case schedule conspicuously displayed. This, however, was often not the case in practice. Smaller rural courts did not bother to put out a schedule. There were fewer cases. Bigger urban courts did; but the list was often outdated, as last-minute changes were frequent.

In a couple of the Guangdong courts we visited, we let the judges know of the types of cases we wanted to study. We were then given an updated daily schedule of the cases on which we planned to focus. This gave us the most accurate information of where trials were held. We focused mainly on cases handled by Civil Division Number 1 Court – for example, divorce petitions and labor disputes. Sometimes, two trials took place at the same time. In that case, we each attended a different trial and then we briefed each other and compared notes in the evening of the same day. With criminal cases, we had a lesser degree of freedom. We were accompanied by a judge or a court staff member we knew. We were not as free to roam the courthouses we visited and to pick the criminal cases we wanted to hear. The types we observed most were cases for which the judges were keen to promote criminal reconciliation – traffic-related crimes and assaults. For the inland courts, arrangements were more informal. The second author was often allowed to accompany judges to listen to the cases they handled.

Judges in China were guarded about their courtrooms. In most cases, they were aware of our presence. Courtrooms in China were generally small and it was very rare for anyone not connected with a case to show up at trial. We were allowed to be there because the judges knew the colleague(s) we knew. They would have been less accommodating if we had walked in as strangers. Even with collegial introductions, there were visible differences in the degree of easiness that judges displayed toward us. There were occasions where we were, for example, told not to take any notes inside the courtroom. But in most cases, we were able to take notes. This was crucial for our research, as video and audio recordings were not allowed.

Oddly enough, having unfettered access was at best a mixed blessing. Unfettered access to a court would only come when the judge with whom we acquainted was the *yibashou*, i.e., court president. In one of the Guangdong courts, we gained unfettered access, but the judges treated us too respectfully. Our presence was too conspicuous because of whom we knew. We feared that as observers our presence had changed what we were observing. We did not stay in that court for long.

In all cases, we were mindful of the possibility that our observations of the judges and their trials could possibly be affected by our connections – i.e., we were treated as no ordinary outsiders. But outsiders we were. We tried to be as non-intrusive as possible. The fact that we are ethnically Chinese and know the languages helped us to "blend in" somewhat. But this superficial similarity in appearance hardly dissembled our differences from the judges we interviewed, both in the roles we took and in the perspectives we held. Both of us studied for many years in the United States. The first author works in the United States; the second in Hong Kong, a former British colony that is politically and culturally different from the Chinese mainland. The safe response was for judges to deny our access. We appreciated their consent to let us see their world.

To address the problem of the intervening effects of our presence, we did two things. We stayed for as long as we could in courts to which we were given access. After the first few days, we found that the judges we observed became more relaxed as they became accustomed to our presence. They reverted back to their routine practices and habits. We also deliberately walked into courtrooms presided over by judges to whom we were not introduced. We observed those trials as strangers. This served as a kind of "control" for us. Observations of this type offered a good way to corroborate our observations. Obviously, without a collegial introduction, our showing up at some trials became a more precarious event. In some cases, we were asked to identify who we were and then we were asked to leave. The tip offered by Liang (2008) was useful. As Liang (2008:12) suggested, one trick of avoiding being kicked out by a judge was to slip into the courtroom only after a trial had commenced. Once a trial had commenced, the judge would be busy dealing with litigants. This minimized the possibility that a judge would ask us (sitting at the back) questions.

Putonghua is the official language, and it was the language used in most trials we heard in Guangdong and Shaanxi. In the case of Guangdong, some trials were conducted in Cantonese. It happened when the litigants were more fluent in Cantonese and the judge was able to speak Cantonese. There were not many of these cases. Most younger and newer judges were from other provinces and felt more comfortable speaking in *Putonghua*. But there were older litigants who did not speak *Putonghua*. It could become a problem if the judge did not speak Cantonese. As a remedy, courts in the Pearl River Delta region would pair up a judge who did not speak Cantonese with a clerk who did. When a litigant had difficulties expressing himself in *Putonghua*, the clerk would serve as an interpreter. Both of us speak *Putonghua* and Cantonese.

Depending on what level of access we obtained, our fieldwork involved the following:

- attending civil trials, including the most common types of divorce petitions, labor disputes, personal injury cases and contractual disputes
- attending criminal trials, including traffic-related crimes, assaults, robberies and drug-related offenses
- studying courtroom interactions by observing the open sessions of both civil and criminal trials
- interviewing presiding judges to understand why they chose to do certain things in court and how they viewed the litigants' reactions
- interviewing litigants and lawyers (when available)

The cases were not randomly sampled. They were selected based on our research agenda. In-trial observations were one source of our raw data. An even more important source of data for this book was our interviews with the presiding judges we observed in courts. Between the morning and evening sessions, or sometimes after the evening session, we tried to talk with judges. Most of the judges were at least willing to have a chat with us. Some were very open. Some were more cautious and divulged few details beyond what we read about in court judgments. Our interviews with judges lasted from half an hour to an hour and a half. A handful of the interviews lasted for more two hours. Again, as in the interviews conducted in Hong Kong, we tried to allow the interviewees to speak freely and to go where they wanted to go. Some of the interviews were conducted inside court buildings, including judges' offices and meeting rooms.

Conducting interviews *in situ* was different from conducting interviews in Hong Kong. Compared to the latter set of interviews, the interviews done in our field site were more issue-specific. The focus was less on the judges and their careers. The interviews were even more open-ended. We did not use a fixed set of questions. Rather, we discussed what happened during the trial with judges and sought a better understanding of the rationale behind their decisions. We asked them about their views about the specific practices that we studied, such as mediation, criminal reconciliation and how they dealt with problem cases.

On more sensitive topics such as our examples collected on social ties, or when judges discussed the difficult part of their jobs and tensions with their superiors, we conducted interviews away from the courthouse. These interviews happened in informal settings. They took place in restaurants and sometimes during our rides with judges on their way back home. For certain topics, talking to them in an informal setting helped to open up the conversation. We did not tape the interviews. We took notes. To encourage our interviewees to speak candidly, we told them that we would not use their real names.

Together we talked to about 40 judges from our fieldwork. Our interviews with litigants and lawyers were much shorter. We saw about 150 litigants appearing in trials, with about one-third of them accompanied by a lawyer or a law firm employee. Other litigants seldom attended their trial alone. Those without a lawyer were accompanied by a relative or friend. It was difficult to tell if a person sitting next to the plaintiff/defendant was a licensed lawyer in China, as the right of audience was not exclusively confined to lawyers. In any case, the interviews we had with litigants and lawyers were in general brief. We usually talked to them before or after the trials. Some of them were reluctant to talk to us for fear that we were related to other parties of their trial.

In the course of our fieldwork, we had opportunities to observe not just the trial process proper, but how the different divisions of the courts operate, including the divisions that interact with litigants the most often: the court filing office and the pre-trial mediating office. On some occasions, we were invited to visit the offices of the judges with whom we were acquainted. This gave us the opportunity to have a first-hand look at their working environments.

The ideal types of the firm and the work-unit came up only later in the research process. But there was still interplay between theorizing and data collection. As soon as we noticed the palpable differences between the two types of courts, we engaged the judges we interviewed more on the decision-making process. And this eventually became the main theme of the book.

Another source of data was the documents produced by the courts we studied. We perused judgments of the trials we attended. We also got hold of caseload data of the courts we visited. Our analysis of the adjudication committee in Chapter 4 was based on an earlier study (He 2012) of the minutes of one of the Shaanxi courts we studied. Through a collaborative research project between a local law school and the court, the archival minutes of the adjudication committee became accessible. As a visitor of the law school, the second author was invited to advise the court staff on how to write investigative reports.

Notes

1 CHINESE COURTS AS EMBEDDED INSTITUTIONS

1. As we will show later in the book, in many rural communities, divorce is still discouraged, not so much because husband-wife disputes are disapproved of ideologically, but more because some divorces might disrupt a community.
2. Official statistics are sketchy, but some judges we talked to estimated that about 70 percent of judges are engaged in judicial work.
3. If the dispatched tribunals or mobile courts of the basic-level courts were included, the number of courts would reach more than 10,000.
4. In this book, we use the term "judiciary" in the way it is conventionally used among Anglo-American scholars to refer to the country's court system. It is, however, worth noting that in China, "judiciary" or "judicial organs" (司法机 关 *sifa jiguan*) consist(s) of courts, procuratorates, public security organs, and judicial administrative organs, an indication that the court is not treated as a separate and independent institution from police and public prosecution (see Gechlik 2005, footnote 4).
5. Even when the rates of adjudication and mediation of individual courts are reported, they do not always accurately reflect what happens on the ground (see Chapter 3).
6. There are also further organizational variations subsumed under the dichotomous distinction we here suggest. Furthermore, even within a single court, it is often the case that judges of one division (civil, criminal, administrative, etc.) operate in an institutional environment that is different from judges of others.
7. In fact, the deepening rural-urban divide dated back beyond the 1980s to state policies made during Mao Zedong's era (Brown 2012).
8. It is not our intention to create an imagery of a court filled with judges who are poor but loyal cadres of the Chinese Communist Party, poorly educated but caring of the people they serve. This Maoist imagery of a grassroots court is outdated, even when we are talking about courts situated in the most economically backward parts of China (see Balme 2010).
9. This trichotomous division is inspired by Downs (1967:61).

10. The metaphors were first applied to discuss the Chinese political system by Susan Shirk (1992:62).

11. This is not to say that the juridical field as conceived by Bourdieu is autonomous. Bourdieu notes that the juridical field enjoys a "smaller degree of autonomy." Yet the crucial feature that defines the field is its ability to translate a problem from another field (e.g., politics, economics) into a *legal* problem and resolve it by deploying the legal tools available without falling back to extralegal means. Bourdieu (1987:850) writes: "Given the determinant role it plays in social reproduction, the juridical field has a smaller degree of autonomy than other fields (…) External changes are more directly reflected in the juridical field, and internal conflicts within the field are more directly decided by external forces (…) It is as if the positions of different specialists in the organization of power within the juridical field were determined by the place occupied in the political field by the group whose interests are most closely tied to the corresponding legal realm."

12. We also argue, in line with the resource dependency literature in organizational sociology, that, given the opportunity, senior judges who administer their courts would want more autonomy. As Pfeffer (1982:193) puts it: "Managers and administrators attempt to manage their external dependencies, both to ensure the autonomy of the organization and to acquire, if possible, more autonomy and freedom from external constraint."

13. Empirical research within organizational ecology has branched out to consider factors seldom examined by economists, including institutional legitimacy (Hannah and Freeman 1987, 1988), community endorsement (Singh et al. 1986), lifestyles (McPherson 1983) and political turmoil (Carroll 1987), among others.

14. The metaphor of "inverted sieve" is used by Lampton (1992:39) to describe China's bureaucratic structure of authority. It is also applicable to decision-making structure of the Chinese court, itself a part of the mammoth bureaucracy of China's party-state.

15. From the perspective of Western liberalism, the biggest problem of the Chinese court is its lack of independence – the government and the CCP have too much say with regard to courts' verdicts and sentences (see for example, US Department of State 2014).

16. Abbott notes that "Even in statist France, one speaks of governments plural and departments plural; the Conseil d'Etat exists precisely so that the administrative state will not break out into competing factions" (2005:251). The same can be said about the plural existence of the seemingly centralized party-state of China. It is a framework rather than a neat structure.

17. Court leaders, like other senior bureaucrats, are also motivated by other goals including power, income, prestige, security, convenience, loyalty, pride in excellent work, and desire to serve the public interest (Downs 1967:2, 81–91).

18. The ideological foundation of this populist tendency can be traced back to Mao's mass-line ideology (Lubman 1999).

19. Studies by Chinese researchers indicate that local courts were deeply indebted to either the judiciary or to banks. These debts included 9.9 billion yuan for un-reimbursed travel expenses, 1.2 billion yuan for un-reimbursed medical claims and 90 billion yuan owed to the banks for courthouse renovation and construction (cited by Keith et al. 2014:114).

20. In 1978, criminal cases represented more than 30 percent of the total yearly caseloads (Liang 2008:46), a very high percentage of criminal cases by any standard.

21. The current method, adopted in 2000, is to divide the civil division into four sub-divisions. Traditional civil cases (such as personal and family relations, property disputes, torts and labor, among others) fall within the jurisdiction of Division Number 1. Civil Division Number 2 deals with domestic commercial cases, including bankruptcies, contracts, companies and securities. Civil Division Number 3 focuses on intellectual property disputes such as copyright, trademark and patent infringements. Civil Division Number 4 deals with cases with a foreign-related element, e.g., cases involving litigants from Hong Kong, Macao and Taiwan, as well as maritime disputes. See Zhu 2011.

22. It is also important to distinguish the economicalization of the law from the overall growth of the civil docket. The former concentrates in the most economically developed coastal cities of the country, while the latter is a much more generalized process.

2 THE DAILY ROUNDS OF FRONTLINE JUDGES

1. In fact, judges were reluctant to take outside visitors (such as us) to their office. They were not proud to show people their cramped office space.

2. The SPC's Fourth Five Year Reform Plan announced in 2015 aims to reduce the number of judges who are not involved in case hearings. It remains unknown whether this will lead to a substantial reduction of judicial establishment.

3. Though some judges working in the busiest courts in China hear cases every day, this is an exception to the norm.

4. According to the Article 9 of Organic Law of the People's Courts, a trial by a collegial panel made up of judges and/or people's assessors is the standard procedure.

5. Older versions of the Civil Procedure Law (Article 147) state that a collegial panel for a civil case can comprise as many as seven judges (Liang 2008:213, footnote 1; see also Luo 2000). But the current Civil Procedure Law (2012) only states that the number of members of a collegial panel shall be odd (Article 39). Liang (2008) also found that the three-member panel is the predominant norm in his study.

6. According to Article 37 of the Organic Law of the People's Courts, assessors are appointed or elected members of the community who are at least 23 years old and have full political rights. If elected, they are elected by local individuals or a people's congress; if appointed, they are appointed by the court itself.

7. According to Article 179 of the Criminal Procedure Law (2012) and Article 42 of the Civil Procedure Law (2012), the minority opinion of the collegial bench shall be entered in the records/transcripts, though the dissenting opinion is not made known to the public, including the litigating parties.

8. In 1998, the SPC published regulations to change the traditional "inquisitorial" trial model to the "adversarial" model in civil cases. In 2001, it published "Several Stipulations of the Supreme People's Court Regarding Evidence on Civil Litigations." (中国人民法院关于民事诉讼证据的若干界定 *Zuigao renmin fayuan guanyu minshi susong zhengju de ruogan guiding*).

9. See Civil Procedure Law of the People's Republic of China (2012), Articles 64, 68.

10. Article 64 of the Civil Procedure Law states that if parties or their litigation agents cannot gather evidence by themselves due to some objective reasons, or if the People's Court is of the opinion that certain evidence is necessary for the case, the People's Court shall investigate and collect evidence.

11. The SPC has recently set up a centralized online database of civil and criminal judgments from different levels of courts in China (see also Note 16). Liebman (2012:222) suggested that judges confronting new legal issues turn to the internet to learn how courts elsewhere in China, and even overseas, dealt with similar issues. He also suggested that this form of judicial networking, and the development of informal patterns of precedent, may lead to more consistent application of the law (2007:631).

12. Judge Su acknowledges that the mediation rate is a factor in promotion evaluation. She adds, "I just think a judge's mediation rate has no correlation with the quality of her job. I won't blindly pursue it."

13. Criminal cases, despite the important social control function they serve and the scrutiny they receive, now make up less than 9 percent of the total caseload of the courts combined (excluding the SPC). See www.court.gov.cn/fabuxiangqing-13879.html, last visited on June 8, 2015.

14. Both figures are made available at the SPC website, available at www.court.gov.cn/qwfb/sfsj/201105/t20110525_100996.htm and www.court.gov.cn/fabuxiangqing-13879.html, last visited on June 8, 2015.

15. This in part is because we spent more time in urban courts than in rural courts.

16. Civil and criminal judgments (sans the sensitive ones) from different levels of courts in China, including some grassroots courts, are now available online. Readers can read these judgments by visiting the SPC's database at www.court.gov.cn/zgcpwsw/

17. Civil Procedure Law (2012), Article 199.

18. Whether it is going to adjudicate is another matter; see Chapters 3 and 4.

19. Even in the United States, this is, from a historical viewpoint, a rather recent phenomenon (Friedman 2004).

20. Once a difficult case is "kicked up" the bureaucratic hierarchy, it becomes less of a concern because of the increased complexity of bureaucratic consideration.

21. See Civil Procedure Law Article 149, which states: "A People's Court shall complete the adjudication of a case to which ordinary procedure is applied within six months after the case is accepted. Where an extension of the term is necessary for special circumstances, a six-month extension may be given upon the approval of the president of the court. Any further extension shall be reported to the People's Court at a higher level for approval."

22. Article 161 of the Civil Procedure Law states: "The People's Court shall complete the adjudication of a case to which the summary procedure is applied within three months after the case is accepted."

3 COHORTS OF JUDGES

1. According to Article 2 of the Judges Law, judges are "judicial persons who exercise the judicial authority of the State according to law, and they include the presidents, vice presidents, members of judicial committees, chief judges and associate chief judges of divisions, judges and assistant judges of the Supreme People's Court, local People's Courts at various levels and special People's Courts such as military courts."

2. In fact, just the idea of a uniform itself is relatively recent for the Chinese judiciary. The old military-style uniform was only introduced in 1984 (BBC Monitoring Asia Pacific, 2000).

3. Of course, one might question the quality of some of the degrees obtained, especially for those working judges who were required by the new rules established by the SPC that sitting judges under the age of 40 would be required to obtain a degree within five years or lose their jobs (Liebman 2007:625).

4. In May 1985, the CCP Central Committee organized a national conference on education and released a policy document on education reform that highlighted legal education as a relatively weaker area requiring faster development. And, in June 1985, Deng Xiaoping stated that legal education should be developed quickly (Shen and Wang 2005:406).

5. Under the old job assignment system, which was restored in the late 1970s, central and provincial authorities drew up employment plans each year and colleges assigned their graduates to fill these slots (the so-called *fenpei* system) (Yang 2014). In 1981, when Chinese universities again began graduating classes after the Cultural Revolution, Deng Xiaoping, then Chinese *de facto* leader, continued the system of government placement of graduates, whereby university graduates were directed to take particular jobs in critical positions. Not until the end of the decade, when the number of graduates increased enough to meet the demand, did Deng introduce a two-way selection system that gave graduates some freedom to choose their own future employment (Vogel 2011:388).

6. Biddulph (2010:264–265) writes: "In 2000, the General Office of the State Council transmitted the Ministry of Education Notice on Adjusting the Management Structure of Schools under Ministries (and Units) of the State

Council … Under this scheme, some law schools, such as the China University of Politics and Law, were transferred from the Ministry of Justice to the Ministry of Education. Others, such as East China Institute of Politics and Law, Southwest Institute of Politics and Law and Northwest Institute of Politics, were transferred to the joint control of central and local governments, with local governments having primary responsibility. This reorganization completed the transformation of the previous system of 'Five Institutes, Four Departments.'"

7. More than 360,000 people took the examination, but fewer than 8 percent of them met the minimum requirement (Liang 2008:65). For a while, the examination gained a reputation as being the most difficult public examination in all of China. In recent years, the pass rate hovered around 10 percent.

8. The number of takers is likely to drop in the future. According to central government guidelines, from 2017 onward, judicial examinations will only be open to graduates who majored in law or people who have worked in law-related fields for a certain number of years (Global Times 2016).

9. In 2013, for example, a total of 436,000 people took the examination. Among them, 78,000 (about 18 percent) were college graduates of the same year (Sina News 2013).

10. According to Article 9 of the 1995 Judges Law, the youngest age for a person to be appointed a judge is 23.

11. Since the early 2000s, Chinese political-legal authorities have promoted party-led "grand mediation" (大调解 *datiaojie*) practices that involve coordinated participation from several government branches, including the judiciary, to handle potentially social destabilizing disputes, such as land seizures, corporate reorganizations of failed enterprises and collective grievances against local officials (Minzner 2011b; see also Hand 2011).

12. The number 1,000 does not seem to include judges who chose to transfer to other bureaus.

13. Some Chinese scholars criticize that university-based legal education has become too intellectualized and impractical. As one Chinese law professor suggests, legal education has been focusing too much on legal knowledge and not enough on legal skills (Yi 2012). Law professors in China are still developing an organic relationship with the growing legal sector of the country. Most of the academic law reviews in China do not target a practitioner audience. Yet, the heavy involvement of the party-state means that academic writings play a minor role in developing and interpreting the law. The insignificance of academia represents a major difference from European countries that adopt a bureaucratic model of judiciary. In France, for example, leading academics often produce *note d'arrêt*, a brief commentary explaining an otherwise-cryptic decision of the court and situating it within trends in legal development (Bell 2006:83).

14. For example, at the Eighteenth Central Committee's Third Plenum in November 2013, current Chinese leader Xi Jinping pledged to "strengthen rule of law guarantees."

4 ADMINISTRATIVE EMBEDDEDNESS: THE VERTICAL HIERARCHY OF CONTROL

1. A collegial panel is sometimes made up of judges and people's assessors (*renmin peishenyuan*). But the most common form for complex cases remains a three-judge panel. See He 2016.

2. This is of course a general framework. Individual courts vary in their practice. For example, a judge from a court in Guizhou said that if a collegial panel could not reach a unanimous decision in his court, they would report the case directly to the vice president.

3. Before the use of the judicial examination, the party-state also adopted an open selection system for judges. It was first implemented in 1999 and called for applicants from the public to apply for some positions of senior judgeships. But the number of judges recruited through this open channel (mostly lawyers, law professors and other scholars) has been minuscule (Liang 2008:66). The open channel of recruitment was recently reiterated in the decision passed by the influential 4th Plenary Session of the 18th Central Committee of the Chinese Communist Party (October 23, 2014), available at https://chinacopyrightandmedia.wordpress.com/2014/10/28/ccp-central-committee-decision-concerning-some-major-questions-in-comprehensively-moving-governing-the-country-according-to-the-law-forward/ (last visited December 19, 2014).

4. There is also no protection of a lifetime tenure: judges, even the most senior ones, can be dismissed if mistakes are made.

5. The Judges Law (Article 12) provides that "[the] presidents, vice presidents of the People's Courts shall be selected from among the best judges and *other persons who are best qualified for the post*" (emphasis added).

6. Article 9 of the Judges Law provides that for places where it is difficult to recruit academically qualified candidates to become judges, "the academic qualifications for judges may be eased for a specific period of time allowing for two-year law major graduates of colleges and universities."

7. This is despite the latest judicial reform by the SPC that seeks to assign more responsibilities and powers to frontline judges.

8. This is also reflected in the laws. Article 126 of the Chinese Constitution states that the Chinese courts have "the judicial power according to the provisions of law, and are not to be interfered by administrative agencies, social organizations, and individuals." The Judges Law of 2001 discusses independence in the following way: that people's courts should "independently exercise judicial authority according to law." The agency that independently exercises judicial authority is not an individual judge, but a court. Though Article 8 of the Judges Law states that a Chinese judge is entitled to "(1) the power and working condition for carrying out the judge's professional responsibility; (2) trial of cases according to law, free from the interference of administrative agencies, social organizations and individual persons; (3) freedom from dismissal, demotion, retirement or penalties without the cause and procedure

determined by law," its focus is still on external independence rather than internal independence.

9. We believe the judge's account is representative and accurate. We triangulated her account with those offered by other judges.

10. We translate *shenpan weiyuanhui* as "adjudication committee" rather than following the official translation, "judicial committee," in the Organic Law of the People's Court. "Adjudication committee" is the more widely used term in scholarly literature. It also renders the function of the committee more clearly, which is to decide on the outcome of important cases.

11. Through a collaborative research project between a local law school and the court, the archival minutes of the adjudication committee became accessible. As a visiting professor of the law school, one of us (Xin He) was invited as an advisor for improving the research quality of the court staff. One of the research projects of the court then was to examine the functioning of the adjudication committee, and He was thus granted access to the minutes. Since by law the minutes are not publically accessible, He was only allowed to read the minutes in a court office. While no photocopy was permitted, He was allowed to take notes. To avoid potential impact on cases that had been decided (the major concern of the court), we were required to use the materials without disclosing any case or individual identification. To understand the stories behind the minutes, He later interviewed five judges who have been involved in reporting some of the cases. Due to the sensitive nature of the topic discussed, the interviews were not recorded. Instead, He took notes of the interviews and compiled them immediately after the interviews.

12. We know of no other work whose data offer such a close look at the decision-making process in Chinese or other authoritarian judicial systems.

13. The percentage of cases reviewed by an adjudication committee varied greatly across courts in different regions and at different levels. Yang (2010) reports from a basic-level court in the city of Chongqing, for example, only 10 to 20 percent of criminal cases were reviewed by the committee. Guan (2004) reports that during 1999–2003, several basic-level courts in Shandong province only reviewed 1.26 percent of the received cases.

14. The information here comes from He Xin's interviews with judges of the court, March 1–4, 2011.

15. This is consistent with the national trend. Criminal cases make up less than 10 percent of the total caseload nationwide (Supreme People's Court 2016a).

16. In civil cases, the victim or plaintiff has a more direct stake in the decision. How much the defendant is found to be liable for determines how much money the plaintiff receives as compensation.

17. Interview with the responsible judge after the change, March 5, 2011

18. Interview with the responsible judge, March 3, 2011

19. For cases in which suggested opinions were not changed, the discussions were usually very short, and in most situations, all the members agreed with the opinions. They were less able to show the decision-making position of the president.

20. In reality, every member has his or her fixed seat, usually with the president sitting directly opposite the reporting judge. Of course, the reporting judge knows to whom he or she is reporting. In other words, the equal status of committee members exists only on the paper of the committee rules.

21. The minutes only provided the proposed decision of the collegial panel, the discussion, and the final decision. All other information came from author's interviews with the responsible judge, March 3, 2011.

22. This case's subsequent development verifies the point: the intermediate court regarded the transaction as valid. The second time that the case was discussed by the committee, all other members changed their views and supported the president.

23. We did not have access to the judgments for our study.

24. As of 2010, only 54 percent of the staff in the court obtained the qualification of judgeship, and fewer have passed the national judicial exam.

25. For the last two decades, not a single document has been issued by the committee in promoting judicial craft. (He's interview with judges of the court, March 3, 2011.)

26. It is noteworthy to point out that, in Weber's original discussion, the authority of the monocrat is meant to insulate subordinates from influences that would interfere with the work of the bureaucracy (Bendix 1977:139). But in this case, there are significant incongruities between the putative legal-technical nature of the adjudication committee and its actual practices.

27. Liu's ethnographic work (2006) also suggests that in Chinese courts, informal influence on the decision-making process based on the administrative ranking system undermines the due process of law much more severely than the formal adjudication committee does.

28. The clear directional nature of the committee's verdict seems to suggest that its changes were guided by wholesale administrative considerations rather than case-by-case legal considerations.

29. *Xu XX su Peng Yu renshen sunhai peichang jiufenan* (徐XX诉彭宇人身损害赔偿纠纷案) [Xu XX vs. Peng Yu, Personal Injury Compensation Dispute], (Nanjing Mun. Gulou Dist. People's Ct. Sept. 3, 2007). Available at http://pkulaw.cn/case/pfnl_117526495.html?keywords=%20XX%20&match=Exact; see also Chen (2007).

30. During the Cultural Revolution and other earlier political campaigns, bureaucratization was equated with bureaucratism (Harding 1981; Whyte 1989).

31. In other authoritarian states, judicial bureaucracy acquiesces to the expectations of the executive through the practice of apoliticism (Hilbink 2007). But the Chinese model is different.

32. Clearly, judiciaries in Continental Europe can be subject to the influence of actors outside the judicial system, especially from those in the executive branch and ministry of justice. But the influence asserted is channeled through the promotion process of higher-ranking judges. Judges, once appointed, do enjoy a strong degree of judicial independence. As such, political intervention in the judiciary in Europe is less direct and immediate. See Guarnieri 2001:118.

33. In these cases, the government or the land developer has already obtained the license to demolish, which gives them the legal right to ask the courts to implement the licenses for them under the law (Pils 2005; He 2014).

5 POLITICAL EMBEDDEDNESS: COURTS AS STABILITY MAINTENANCE AGENCIES

1. The latest is by Chinese President Xi Jinping, who established his network for "Comprehensively Deepening Reform" (see Saich 2015:172).
2. According to one of the directives announced in the latest judicial reform, the case filing division no longer evaluates and reviews the merits of incoming cases. Its role is limited to simply registering the complaint (see Finder 2015). The criteria used to determine whether a compliant is registerable are said to be technical – whether the complaint is compliant with the substantive aspects of the law. See Supreme People's Court 2015c. How effective the new measure is on curbing shrinking behaviors remains to be seen. Technical review can easily revert back to political review. Courts might also choose to step up grand mediation to divert cases from arriving at their doorstep.
3. Article 32 of the Marriage Law stipulates that whether the emotional relationship has broken down is the leading legal principle. It also lists non-exhaustive scenario that would warrant a divorce decision: bigamy, cohabitation, domestic violence and deserting family members, chronic bad habits such as gambling and drug addiction, and separation for two years.
4. In our fieldwork, we also observed cases when the roles of the husband and the wife reversed, i.e., the husband sought to divorce but the wife resisted, in some cases with a death threat. For details, see He (2017).
5. The analysis below is primarily based on data collected in fieldwork investigations in Nantong, Jiangsu province and Taizhou, Zhejiang province on the east coast of China during the summer of 2012. These two places were chosen on the grounds of their renown for protest-supported litigation and for being pioneers in China's legal development. Taizhou, for instance, has been known for its innovative practice in administrative justice (Beijing Times 2007). Economically, both places represent the most affluent areas in China. According to official statistics, Nantong's GNP reached around 287 billion yuan in 2009, ranking twenty-eighth among all Chinese cities and eighth among cities at the prefectural level. Its GDP per capita reached 35,040 yuan, or $5,000, in 2008, surpassing the mean in developed countries. The economy has also been industrialized during the period. In 2008, the agricultural sector accounted for less than 12 percent of its GNP. Construction, textile, petroleum-chemical, port, shipbuilding and new energy have become the pillar industries, with the construction industry alone producing more than one-third of its GNP (Baiduwenku 2011). The dynamics described here may not be the same as in economically backward areas, but it may predict what will happen when other parts of China develop.

6. There was a spike in the number of administrative cases taken up by the courts in 2015 (Supreme People's Court 2016a). A total of 241,000 first-instance administrative cases were accepted, up almost 60 percent from 2014. Time will tell if this is a one-off spike or a sustained trend.

7. The following reports are just a small part of a long list of cases reported in the Chinese-language media in recent years:

In August 2009, due to her discontent with the judges' decisions and their treatment of her in the handling of her husband's divorce petitions against her, a woman placed a coffin with statements condemning the judges on it in front of a court in Foshan. She did this before her divorce hearing commenced as a way of protesting the judges' actions (Hong Kong Commercial Daily 2009).

In June 2010, it was reported that a man who had been aggrieved by the court's earlier ruling on the division of marital property opened fire in a court in Hunan, resulting in the death of three judges and injury to another judge and two clerks. The man committed suicide at the scene by shooting himself. According to the report, none of the judges killed had handled the man's divorce case (Apple Daily 2010).

In April 2011, while the Hefei Intermediate People's Court was adjudicating a divorce appeal, the female litigant, who had opposed a divorce from her rich husband, rushed into the washroom and attempted to commit suicide by drinking pesticide (Hexun.com.tw 2011).

In September 2015, four judges in a courthouse in Hubei province were stabbed. The suspect was arrested in the basement of the Shiyan No. 1 Intermediate People's Court, where the attack took place. The suspected, a man named Hu Qinggang, stabbed the judge at her office after she informed him of her verdict. Three more judges were injured by Hu (Luo and Zhou 2015).

6 SOCIAL EMBEDDEDNESS: TIES FROM WITHIN AND FROM WITHOUT

1. We also found that judges were more amenable to discussing *guanxi* cases in casual settings. Our interviews took place in restaurants, canteens, judges' own offices and occasionally even in cars in which we rode with them during the course of our fieldwork.

2. For the division of responsibilities between a responsible judge and a presiding judge, please see Chapter 2.

7 ECONOMIC EMBEDDEDNESS: THE POLITICAL ECONOMY OF COURT FINANCES

1. Recently though, the central government has begun to reverse the trend by allocating more direct funding to courts in the economically least-developed part of the country (Wang, Yaxin 2010).

2. Growth in tort cases has also been substantial and steady, though we expect an even sharper spike in the decade of the 2010s as the new Tort Liability Law only took effect on July 1, 2010. The law covers a range of topics that have increasingly captured Chinese and international headlines, including product and medical liability, environmental pollution, motor vehicle accidents and hazardous work.

3. Of course, the Department of Education is, like the Chinese Judiciary, a weak bureaucratic actor that does not generate its own revenues but has to rely on local governments for funding. The real test is about whether the court can go after a strong bureau.

4. In fact, firm-type courts engage in this practice of active collection of cases too, but they do it with teams of dedicated staff (see Chapter 3).

5. As mentioned earlier, as part of the public security cluster of bureaus, the courts are there to monitor and relieve social unrest, to promote government's vision of society, and to coordinate various forms of "social management" (社会管理 *shehui guanli*). This role is particularly prominent for courts located in the vast rural hinterland of China.

8 CONCLUSION

1. The difference reminds us of the distinction made by Alvin Gouldner (1954) in his famous study of industrial bureaucracy. He characterizes bureaucracies as either "punishment-centered" or "representative." This dichotomy might not be the most appropriate for our purpose, but it seems to be the case that in work-unit-type courts, frontline judges consult their seniors out of fear that deviance from the rules would lead to sanctions. In firm-type courts, frontline judges consult on technical grounds and in their own interests.

2. The judges who serve on the circuit courts are seconded from the SPC on a two-year term.

Bibliography

(I) ENGLISH LANGUAGE LITERATURE

Abbott, Andrew. 2005. "Linked Ecologies: States and Universities as Environments for Professions." *Sociological Theory* 23(3):245–274.

Abe, Masaki. 1995. "The Internal Control of a Bureaucratic Judiciary: The Case of Japan." *International Journal of the Sociology of Law* 23(4):303–320.

Administrative Office of the United States Courts. 2013. *Annual Report of the Director: Judicial Business of the United States Courts*. www.uscourts.gov/Statistics/JudicialBusiness/2013.aspx

Albrow, Martin. 1970. *Bureaucracy*. New York: Praeger Press.

Alford, William, and Yuanyuan Shen. 2003. "Have You Eaten? Have You Divorced? Marriage, Divorce and the Assessment of Freedom in China." In *Ideas of Freedom in the Chinese World*, ed. William Kirby, 234–263. Stanford: Stanford University Press.

Andersen, Seth S. 2001. "Judicial Retention Evaluation Programs." *Loyola of Los Angeles Law Review* 34(4):1375–1389.

Ang, Yuen Yuen, and Nan Jia. 2014. "Perverse Complementarity: Political Connections and the Use of Courts among Private Firms in China." *The Journal of Politics* 76(2):318–332.

Arce, Dwyer. 2010. "China Judges Shot Dead in Courthouse." *Jurist*, June 2. http://jurist.org/paperchase/2010/06/china-judges-shot-dead-in-courthouse.php

Balme, Stephanie. 2010. "Local Courts in Western China: The Quest for Independence and Dignity." In *Judicial Independence in China: Lessons for Global Rule of Law Promotion*, ed. Randall Peerenboom, 154–179. New York: Cambridge University Press.

Barro, Robert J. 1997. *Determinants of Economic Growth: A Cross-Country Empirical Study*. Cambridge, MA: The MIT Press.

Barth, Frederik. 1969. "Introduction." In *Ethnic Groups and Boundaries*, ed. Frederik Barth, 9–38. London: Little, Brown.

BBC Monitoring Asia Pacific. 2000. "Chinese Judges to Abandon Military-Style Uniforms." June 30.

Beckert, Jens. 2003. "Economic Sociology and Embeddedness: How Shall We Conceptualize Economic Action?" *Journal of Economic Issues* 37(3):769–787.

Beetham, David. 1974. *Max Weber and the Theory of Modern Politics*. London: George Allen & Unwin.

——— 1996. *Bureaucracy*. 2nd edition. Minneapolis: University of Minnesota Press.

Belcher, Marc J., and Gordon White. 1979. *Micropolitics in Contemporary China: A Technical Unit during and after the Cultural Revolution*. Armonk, NY: M. E. Sharpe.

Bell, John. 2001. "Judicial Cultures and Judicial Independence." *Cambridge Yearbook of European Legal Studies* 4:47–60.
    2006. *Judiciaries Within Europe: a Comparative Review*. Cambridge: Cambridge University Press.
Bendix, Reinhard. 1949. *Higher Civil Servants in American Society*. Colorado: University of Colorado Press.
    1977. *Nation Building and Citizenship*. 2nd edition. Berkeley: University of California Press.
Bennett, James T., and Manuel H. Johnson. 1980. *The Political Economy of Federal Government Growth, 1959–1978*. College Station, TX: Texas A&M University Press.
Bian, Yanjie. 1994. "*Guanxi* and the Allocation of Jobs in Urban China." *The China Quarterly* 140:971–999.
    1997. "Bringing Strong Ties Back In." *American Sociological Review* 62(3):366–385.
Biddulph, Sarah. 2010. "Legal Education in the People's Republic of China: The Ongoing Story of Politics and Law." In *Legal Education in Asia: Globalization, Change and Contexts*, eds. Stacey Steele and Kathryn Taylor, 260–277. New York: Routledge.
Biddulph, Sarah, Sean Cooney and Ying Zhu. 2012. "Rule of Law with Chinese Characteristics: The Role of Campaigns in Lawmaking." *Law & Policy* 34(4):373–401.
Blau, Peter M. 1968. "The Hierarchy of Authority in Organizations." *American Journal of Sociology* 73(4):453–467.
Bourdieu, Pierre. 1987. "The Forces of Law: Towards a Sociology of Juridical Field." *Hastings Law Journal* 38:814–853.
    1990. *The Logic of Practice*. Stanford: Stanford University Press.
Brody, David C. 2008. "The Use of Judicial Performance Evaluation to Enhance Judicial Accountability, Judicial Independence, and Public Trust." *Denver University Law Review* 86(1):115–157.
Brown, Jeremy. 2012. *City versus Countryside in Mao's China*. New York: Cambridge University Press.
Cabestan, Jean-Pierre, Li Qinglan, Sun Ping and Yves Dolais. 2012. "The Renaissance of the Legal Professional in China." In *China, Democracy, and Law: A Historical and Contemporary Approach*, eds. Pierre-Etienne Will and Mireille Delmas-Marty, 705–739. Leiden: Brill.
Carroll, Glenn R. 1984. "Organizational Ecology." *Annual Review of Sociology* 10:71–93.
    1987. *Publish and Perish: The Organizational Ecology of Newspaper Industries*. Greenwich, CT: JAI Press.
    1990. "The Organizational Ecology of Chester Barnard." In *Organizational Theory: From Chester Barnard to the Present and Beyond*, ed. Oliver E. Williamson, 56–71. New York: Oxford University Press.
Chen, Bob. 2007. "China: Senior Sues Would-be Samaritan." *Global Voices*, September 11. http://globalvoicesonline.org/2007/09/11/china-senior-sues-would-be-samaritan
Chen, Feng, and Xin Xu. 2012. "'Active Judiciary': Judicial Dismantling of Workers' Collective Action in China." *The China Journal* 67:87–107.
Chen, Jianfu. 2015. *Chinese Law: Context and Transformation*. Boston: Martinus Nijhoff.
Chen, Te-Ping. 2016. "Slaying of Beijing Judge prompts Horror in China's Embattled Legal Community." *Wall Street Journal*, February 29. http://blogs.wsj.com/chinarealtime/2016/02/29/slaying-of-beijing-judge-prompts-horror-in-chinas-embattled-legal-community/
Chin, Josh. 2014. "China Tries to Hold on to Judges by Offering Freer Hand." *Wall Street Journal*, October 21. www.wsj.com/articles/china-tries-to-hold-on-to-judges-by-offering-freer-hand-1413822462

China Daily. 2007. "Complaint Bureau Busiest Office in Beijing." September 2. www.china daily.com.cn/china/2007–09/02/content_6142475.htm

Chung, Jae Ho. 1998. "Appendix: Study of Provincial Politics and Development in the Post-Mao Reform Era: Issues, Approaches and Sources." In *Provincial Strategies of Economic Reform in Post-Mao China: Leadership, Politics and Implementation*, eds. Peter T. Y. Cheung, Jae Ho Chung and Zhimin Lin, 429–456. New York: M. E. Sharpe.

Clarke, Donald. 1996. "Power and Politics in the Chinese Court System: The Execution of Civil Judgments." *Columbia Journal of Asian Law* 10(1):1–125.

2003. "Empirical Research into the Chinese Judicial System." In *Beyond Common Knowledge: Empirical Approaches to the Rule of Law*, eds. Erik Gilbert Jensen and Thomas C. Heller, 164–192. Stanford: Stanford University Press.

2009. "Lawsuits as Criticisms." *New York Times*, June 2. http://roomfordebate.blogs .nytimes.com/2009/06/02/chinas-new-rebels/

2015. "First Successful Case against Administrative Monopoly." *Chinese Law Professor Blog*, February 20. http://lawprofessors.typepad.com/china_law_prof_blog/2015/02/first-successful-case-against-administrative-monopoly.html

Cohen, Jerome A. 1997. "Reforming China's Civil Procedure: Judging the Courts." *American Journal of Comparative Law* 45(4):793–804.

2006. "China's Legal Reform at the Crossroads." *Far Eastern Economic Review* 169(2):23–27.

2016. "A Looming Crisis for China's Legal System." *Foreign Policy*. http://foreignpolicy.com/ 2016/02/22/a-looming-crisis-for-chinas-legal-system/

Constas, Helen. 1958. "Max Weber's Two Conceptions of Bureaucracy." *American Journal of Sociology* 63(4):400–409.

Cownie, Fiona, Anthony Bradney and Mandy Burton. 2005. *English Legal System in Context*. 3rd edition. London: LexisNexis UK.

Damaska, Mirjan R. 1986. *The Faces of Justice and State Authority: A Comparative Approach to the Legal Process*. New Haven, CT: Yale University Press.

deLisle, Jacques. 2014. "China's Legal System." In *Politics in China: An Introduction*, ed. William A. Joseph, 2nd edition, 224–53. New York: Oxford University Press.

2015. "Law and the Economy in China." In *Routledge Handbook of the Chinese Economy*, eds. Gregory C. Chow and Dwight H. Perkins, 255–279. New York: Routledge.

Depei, Han, and Stephen Kaner. 1984. "Legal Education in China." *The American Journal of Comparative Law* 32(3):543–582.

Diamant, Neil J., Stanley B. Lubman and Kevin J. O'Brien. 2005. *Engaging the Law in China: State, Society and Possibilities for Justice*. Stanford: Stanford University Press.

DiMaggio, Paul. 2001. "Introduction." In *The Twenty-First-Century Firm: Changing Economic Organization in International Perspective*, ed. Paul DiMaggio, 3–30. Princeton: Princeton University Press.

Downs, Anthony. 1967. *Inside Bureaucracy*. Boston: Little, Brown.

Dunleavy, Patrick. 1991. *Democracy, Bureaucracy and Public Choice*. New York: Harvester Wheatsheaf.

Easton, David. 1965. *A Systems Analysis of Political Life*. New York: John Wiley & Son.

Edin, Maria. 2003. "State Capacity and Local Agent Control in China: CCP Cadre Management from a Township Perspective." *The China Quarterly* 173:35–52.

Eger, Thomas, and Margot Schüller. 2007. "A Comparison of Chinese and European-Style Federalism from a Law and Economics Perspective." In *Economic Analysis of Law in China*, eds. Thomas Eger, Michael Faure and Zhang Naigen, 3–28. Cheltenham: Edward Elgar.

Erie, Matthew S. 2012. "Property Rights, Legal Consciousness and the New Media in China: The Hard Case of the Toughest Nail-House in History." *China Information* 26(1):35–59.

——— 2015. "Muslim Mandarins in Chinese Courts: Dispute Resolution, Islamic Law, and the Secular State in Northwest China." *Law & Social Inquiry* 40(4):1001–1030.

Ewick, Patricia, and Susan Silbey. 2003. "Narrating Social Structure: Stories of Resistance to Legal Authority." *American Journal of Sociology* 108(6):1328–1372.

Fei, Xiaotong. 1992. *From the Soil: The Foundation of Chinese Society.* trans. Gary Hamilton and Wang Zheng. Berkeley: University of California Press.

Feng, Yuqing. 2015. "In the Midst of Law and Politics: Legal Consciousness in Chinese Court-related Petitioning." Ph.D. Dissertation, City University of Hong Kong.

Finder, Susan. 1989. "Like Throwing an Egg against a Stone? Administrative Litigation in the People's Republic of China." *Journal of Chinese Law* 3(1):1–29.

——— 2015. "New Docketing Procedures Come to the Chinese Courts." *Supreme People's Court Monitor* (Blog) June 18. https://supremepeoplescourtmonitor.com/2015/06/18/new-docketing-procedures-come-to-the-chinese-courts/

——— 2016. "Why are Chinese Judges Resigning?" *Supreme People's Court Monitor* (Blog) August 23. https://supremepeoplescourtmonitor.com/2016/08/23/why-are-chinese-judges-resigning/

Frecklington, Cameron. 2014. "Rising Divorce Rate Adds to China's Demographic Problems." *China Outlook*, April 22. http://chinaoutlook.com/rising-divorce-rate-adds-to-chinas-demographic-problems/

Friedman, Lawrence. 1998. "Some Notes on the Civil Jury in Historical Perspective." *DePaul Law Review* 48(2):201–220.

——— 2004. "Day before Trials Vanished." *Journal of Empirical Legal Study* 1(3):689–703.

Fu, Hualing. 2003. "Putting China's Judiciary into Perspective: Is It Independent, Competent, and Fair?" In *Beyond Common Knowledge: Empirical Approaches to the Rule of Law*, eds. Erik Gilbert Jensen and Thomas C. Heller, 193–219. Stanford: Stanford University Press.

Fu, Hualing, and Richard Cullen. 2011. "From Mediatory to Adjudicatory Justice: The Limits of Civil Justice Reform in China." In *Chinese Justice: Civil Dispute Resolution in Contemporary China*, eds. Margaret Y. K. Woo and Mary E. Gallagher, 25–57. New York: Cambridge University Press.

Fu, Yulin. 2011. "Dispute Resolution and China's Grassroots Legal Services." In *Chinese Justice: Civil Dispute Resolution in Contemporary China*, eds. Margaret Y. K. Woo and Mary E. Gallagher, 314–339. New York: Cambridge University Press.

Galanter, Marc. 1974. "Why the 'Haves' Come out Ahead: Speculations on the Limits of Legal Change." *Law & Society Review* 9(1):95–160.

——— 2004. "The Vanishing Trial: an Examination of Trials and Related Matters in Federal and State Courts." *Journal of Empirical Legal Studies* 1(3):459–570.

Garland, David. 2001. *The Culture of Control.* Chicago: University of Chicago Press.

Gechlik, Mei. 2005. "Judicial Reform in China: Lessons from Shanghai." *Columbia Journal of Asian Law* 19(1):97–137.

George, Ronald M. 2005. "Challenges Facing an Independent Judiciary." *New York University Law Review* 80(5):1345–1365.

Gibson, James L. 2007. "The Legitimacy of the U.S. Supreme Court in a Polarized Polity." *Journal of Empirical Legal Studies* 4(3):507–38.

Ginsburg, Tom. 2008. "Administrative Law and the Judicial Control of Agents in Authoritarian Regimes." In *Rule by Law: The Politics of Courts in Authoritarian Regimes*, eds. Tom Ginsburg and Tamir Moustafa, 58–72. New York: Cambridge University Press.

Global Times. 2016. "Exam Changes to Make It Harder to Enter Legal Profession." September 26. www.globaltimes.cn/content/1008393.shtml

Goffee, Rob, and Gareth Jones. 1998. *The Character of a Corporation*. New York: Harper Business.

Gold, Thomas, Doug Guthrie and David Wank. 2002. "An Introduction to the Study of Guanxi." In *Social Connections in China: Institutions, Culture, and the Changing Nature of Guanxi*, eds. Thomas Gold, Doug Guthrie and David Wank, 3–20. New York: Cambridge University Press.

Gouldner, Alvin. 1954. *Patterns of Industrial Bureaucracy*. New York: Free Press.

Government of India. 2008. Judge Population Ratio by Public Information Bureau, http://pib.nic.in/newsite/erelease.aspx?relid=38105

Granovetter, Mark. 1973. "The Strength of Weak Ties," *American Journal of Sociology* 78:1360–80.

1974. *Getting a Job*. Cambridge, MA: Harvard University Press.

1985. "Economic Action and Social Structure: The Problem of Embeddedness." *American Journal of Sociology* 91(3):481–510.

1995. "Afterword." In *Getting a Job*. 2nd edition Chicago: University of Chicago Press.

Grimheden, Jonas. 2011. "Chinese Courts in Law Implementation." In *Making Law Work: Chinese Laws in Context*, eds. Mattias Burell and Marina Svensson, 103–142. Ithaca: Cornell East Asia Series.

Gu, Weixia. 2009. "Judicial Review over Arbitration in China: Assessing the Extent of the Latest Pro-Arbitration Move by the Supreme People's Court in the People's Republic of China." *Wisconsin International Law Journal* 27(2):222–269.

2015. "Courts in China: Judiciary in the Economic and Societal transitions." In *Asian Courts in Context*, eds. Jiunn-rong Yeh, and Wen-Chen Chang, 487–517. New York: Cambridge University Press.

Guarnieri, Carlo. 2001. "Judicial Independence in Latin Countries of Western Europe." In *Judicial Independence in the Age of Democracy: Critical Perspectives from around the World*, eds. Peter H. Russell and David M. O'Brien, 111–130. Charlottesville: University Press of Virginia.

Guarnieri, Carlo, and Patrizia Pederzoli. 2002. *The Power of Judges: a Comparative Study of Courts and Democracy*. New York: Oxford University Press

Guthrie, Doug. 1999. *Dragon in a Three-Piece Suit: The Emergence of Capitalism in China*. Princeton: Princeton University Press.

Haggard, Stephan, MacIntyre Andrew and Lydia Tiede. 2008. "The Rule of Law and Economic Development." *Annual Review of Political Science* 11:205–234.

Hall, Richard H. 1963. "Concept of Bureaucracy: an Empirical Assessment." *American Journal of Sociology* 69(1):32–40.

Hand, Keith J. 2011. "Resolving Constitutional Disputes in Contemporary China." *University of Pennsylvania East Asia Law Review* 7(1):51–159.

Hannan, Michael T., and John Freeman. 1977. "The Population Ecology of Organizations." *American Journal of Sociology* 82(5):929–964.

1984. *Organizational Ecology*. Cambridge, MA: Harvard University Press.

1987. "The Ecology of Organizational Founding: American Labor Unions, 1836–1985." *American Journal of Sociology* 92(4):910–943.

1988. "The Ecology of Organizational Mortality: American Labor Unions, 1836–1985." *American Journal of Sociology* 94(1):25–52.

Harding, Harry. 1981. *Organizing China*. Stanford: Stanford University Press.

Hawley, Amos, H. 1950. *Human Ecology: a Theory of Community Structure*. New York: Ronald Press.

Hazard, Geoffrey C., Jr., Martin B. McNamara and Irwin F. Sentilles. 1972. "Court Finance and Unitary Budgeting." *Yale Law Journal* 81:1286–1301.

He, Xin. 2007. "Why Did They Not Take on the Disputes? Law, Power, and Politics in the Decision-Making of Chinese Courts." *International Journal of Law in Context* 3(3):203–225.

2009a. "Routinization of Divorce Law Practice in China: Institutional Constraints' Influence on Judicial Behavior." *International Journal of Law, Policy and the Family* 23(1):83–109.

2009b. "Enforcing Commercial Judgments in the Pearl River Delta of China." *American Journal of Comparative Law* 57(2):419–457.

2009c. "Court Finance and Court Reactions to Judicial Reforms: a Tale of Two Chinese Courts." *Law & Policy* 31(4):463–486.

2009d. "Administrative Law as a Mechanism for Political Control in Contemporary China." In *Building Constitutionalism in China*, eds. Stephanie Balme and Michael Dowdle, 143–162. New York: Palgrave Macmillan.

2010. "The Judiciary Pushes Back: Law, Power, and Politics in Chinese Courts." In *Judicial Independence in China*, ed. Randall Peerenboom, 180–195. Cambridge: Cambridge University Press.

2012. "Black Hole of Responsibility: The Adjudication Committee's Role in a Chinese Court." *Law & Society Review* 46(4):681–712.

2013. "Judicial Innovation and Local Politics: Judicialization of Administrative Governance in East China." *The China Journal* 69:20–42.

2014. "Maintaining Stability by Law: Protest-Supported Housing Demolition Litigation and Social Change in China." *Law & Social Inquiry* 39(4):849–873.

2016. "Double Whammy: Lay Assessors as Lackeys in Chinese Courts." *Law & Society Review* 50(3):733–765.

2017. "'No Malicious Incidents': The Concern for Stability in China's Divorce Law Practice." *Social and Legal Studies* 26(3):1–23.

He, Xin, and Yuqing Feng. 2016. "Mismatched Discourses in the Petition Offices of Chinese Courts." *Law & Social Inquiry* 41(1):212–241.

He, Xin, and Kwai Hang Ng. 2013a. "Inquisitorial Adjudication and Institutional Constraints in China's Civil Justice." *Law & Policy* 35(4):290–317.

2013b. "Pragmatic Discourse and Gender Inequality in China." *Law & Society Review* 47 (2):279–310.

Henisz, Witold J. 2000. "The Institutional Environment for Economic Growth." *Economic & Politics* 12(1):1–31.

Hilbink, Lisa 2007. *Judges beyond Politics in Democracy and Dictatorship: Lessons from Chile*. Cambridge: Cambridge University Press.

Hirschman, Albert O. 1970. *Exit, Voice, and Loyalty*. Cambridge, MA: Harvard University Press.

Huang, Philip C. C. 2010. *Chinese Civil Justice: Past and Present*. London: Rowan and Littlefield.

Hwang, Kwang-kuo. 1987. "Face and Favor: The Chinese Power Game." *American Journal of Sociology* 92(4):944–974.

Jackall, Robert. 1988. *Moral Mazes*. New York: Oxford University Press.

Jacob, Herbert. 1996. "Courts and Politics in the United States." In *Courts, Law, and Politics in Comparative Perspective*, eds. Herbert Jacob, Erhard Blankenburg, Herbert M.

Kritzer, Doris Marie Provine and Joseph Sanders, 16–80. New Haven: Yale University Press.

Jacobs, Andrew. 2011. "Harassment and Evictions Bedevil Even China's Well-Off." *New York Times*, October 28, A4.

Jayasuriya, Kanishka. 2001. "The Exception Becomes the Norm: Law and Regimes of Exception in East Asia." *Asian Pacific Law & Policy Journal* 2(1):108–124.

Jiang, Huiling. 2010. "Judicial Reform." In *China's Journey toward the Rule of Law: Legal Reform, 1978–2008*, eds. Dingjian Cai and Chenguang Wang, 199–250. Boston: Brill.

Jones, Peter Blundell. 2013. "The Architecture and Operation of Chinese Imperial Yamen." In *Architecture and Justice: Judicial Meanings in the Public Realm*, eds. Jonathan Simon, Nicholas Temple and Renée Tobe, 131–147. Burlington: Ashgate Publishing.

Kapferer, Bruce. 1969. "Norms and the Manipulation of Relationships in a Work Context." In *Social Networks in Urban Situations*, ed. J. Clyde Mitchell, 181–244. Manchester: Manchester University Press.

Keister, Lisa A. 2002. "*Guanxi* in Business Group." In *Social Connections in China: Institutions, Culture, and the Changing Nature of Guanxi*, eds. Thomas Gold, Doug Guthrie and David Wank, 77–96. New York: Cambridge University Press.

Keith, Ronald C., Zhiqiu Lin and Shumei Hou. 2014. *China's Supreme Court*. New York: Routledge.

Kinkel, Jonathan J., and William J. Hurst. 2015. "The Judicial Cadre Evaluation System in China: From Quantification to Intra-State Legibility." *The China Quarterly* 224:933–954.

Krippner, Greta, and Anthony S. Alvarez. 2007. "Embeddedness and the Intellectual Projects of Economic Sociology." *Annual Review of Sociology* 33:219–240.

Lampton, David. 1992. "A Plum for a Peach: Bargaining, Interest, and Bureaucratic Politics in China." In *Bureaucracy, Politics, and Decision Making in Post-Mao China*, eds. Kenneth G. Lieberthal and David M. Lampton, 34–59. Berkeley: University of California Press.

Lee, Sing, and Arthur Kleinman. 2000. "Suicide as Resistance in China's Society." In *Chinese Society: Change, Conflict and Resistance*, eds. Elizabeth J. Perry and Mark Selden, 294–317. New York: Routledge.

Li, Ji. 2013. "Suing the Leviathan: an Empirical Analysis of the Changing Rate of Administrative Litigation in China." *Journal of Empirical Legal Studies* 10(4):815–846.

Li, Li. 2011. "Strategies for Judicial Restraint in Chinese Group Action Cases: a Realistic Reaction to Judicialization." doi: 10.2139/ssrn.1789564.

Li, Ling. 2010. "Corruption in China's Courts." In *Judicial Independence in China*, ed. Randall Peerenboom, 196–220. New York: Cambridge University Press.

——— 2011. "Performing Bribery in China: Guanxi-practice with a Human Face." *Journal of Contemporary China* 20(68):1–20.

——— 2012. "The 'Production' of Corruption in China's Courts: Judicial Politics and Decision Making in a One-Party State." *Law & Social Inquiry* 37(4):848–877.

Li, Yedan, Joris Kocken and Benjamin van Rooij. 2016. "Understanding China's Court Mediation Surge: Insights from a Local Court." *Law & Social Inquiry* doi: 10.1111/lsi.12234.

Li, Yuwen. 2002. "Court Reform in China: Problems, Progress and Prospects." In *Implementation of Law in the People's Republic of China*, eds. Jianfu Chen, Yuwen Li and Jan Michiel Otto, 55–84. Hague: Kluwer Law.

——— 2014. *The Judicial System and Reform in Post-Mao China: Stumbling towards Justice*. London: Routledge.

Liang, Bin. 2008. *The Changing Chinese Legal System, 1978-Present: Centralization of Power and Rationalization of the Legal System*. New York: Routledge.

Lieberthal, Kenneth. 1992. "Introduction: The 'Fragmented Authoritarianism' Model and Its limitations." In *Bureaucracy, Politics, and Decision Making in Post-Mao China*. eds. Kenneth G. Lieberthal and David M. Lampton, 1–32. Berkeley: University of California Press.

——— 2004. *Governing China: From Revolution to Reform*. 2nd edition. New York: W. W. Norton.

Liebman, Benjamin L. 2007. "China's Courts: Restricted Reform." *The China Quarterly* 191:620–638.

——— 2011. "A Populist Threat to China's Courts." In *Chinese Justice: Civil Dispute Resolution in Contemporary China*, eds. Margaret Y. K. Woo and Mary E. Gallagher, 269–313. Cambridge: Cambridge University Press.

——— 2012. "Professionals and Populists: The Paradoxes of China's Legal Reforms." In *China in and beyond the Headlines*, 3rd edition, eds. Timothy B. Weston and Lionel M. Jensen, 214–245. London: Rowman and Littlefield.

Lim, Louisa. 2010. "'Lightning Divorces' Strike China's 'Me Generation.'" *NPR*, November 17. www.npr.org/2010/11/09/131200166/china-s-me-generation-sends-divorce-rate-soaring

Liu, Nanping, and Michelle Liu. 2011. "Justice without Judges: The Case Filing Division in the People's Republic of China." *UC Davis Journal of International Law & Policy* 17:283.

Liu, Sida. 2006. "Beyond Global Convergence: Conflicts of Legitimacy in a Chinese Lower Court." *Law & Social Inquiry* 31(1):75–106.

Llewellyn, Karl. 1960. *The Common Law Tradition*. Boston: Little, Brown.

Long, Cheryl Xiaoning. 2010. "Does the Rights Hypothesis Apply to China?" *Journal of Law & Economics* 53(4):629–650.

Lü, Xiaobo. 2002. *Cadres and Corruption*. Stanford: Stanford University Press.

Lü, Xiaobo, and Elizabeth Perry. 1997. *Danwei: The Changing Chinese Workplace in Historical and Comparative Perspective*. New York: M. E. Sharpe.

Lubman, Stanley. 1999. *Bird in a Cage: Legal Reform in China after Mao*. Stanford: Stanford University Press.

Luo, Wangshu, and Zhou Lihua. 2015. "Judges Shocked by Courthouse Stabbings." *China Daily*. September 11. www.chinadaily.com.cn/china/2015–09/11/content_21842772.htm

Luo, Wei. 2000. *The Amended Criminal Procedure Law and the Criminal Court Rules of the People's Republic of China: With English Translation, Introduction, and Annotation*. Buffalo, NY: Hein.

Manion, Melanie. 1985. "The Cadre Management System Post-Mao: The Appointment, Promotion, Transfer, and Removal of Party and State Leaders," *The China Quarterly* 102:203–233.

Mann, Michael. 1986. *The Sources of Social Power*, Volume 1. Cambridge: Cambridge University Press.

Markoff, John. 1975. "Governmental Bureaucratization: General Processes and an Anomalous Case." *Comparative Studies in Society and History* 17(4):479–503.

Marsden, Peter V., and Karen E. Campbell. 1984. "Measuring Tie Strength." *Social Forces* 63(2):482–501.

Marshall, Anna-Maria. 2006. "Social Movement Strategies and the Participatory Potential of Litigation." In *Cause Lawyers and Social Movements*, eds. Stuart Scheingold and Austin Sarat, 164–181. Stanford: Stanford University Press.

McCubbins, Mathew, and Thomas Schwartz. 1984. "Congressional Oversight Overlooked: Police Patrols vs. Firm Alarms." *American Journal of Political Science* 28(1):165–179.

McPherson, Miller. 1983. "An Ecology of Affiliation." *American Sociological Review* 48(4):519–532.

Merryman, John Henry. 1985. *The Civil Law Tradition*, 2nd edition. Stanford: Stanford University Press.

Merton, Robert. 1968. "The Matthew Effect in Science." *Science* 159(3810):56–63.

Meyer, John W., and Brian Rowan. 1977. "Institutionalized Organizations: Formal Structure as Myth and Ceremony." *American Journal of Sociology* 83(2):340–363.

Michelson, Ethan, and Benjamin L. Read. 2011. "Public Attitudes toward Official Justice in Beijing and Rural China." In *Chinese Justice: Civil Dispute Resolution in Contemporary China*, eds. Margaret Y.K. Woo and Mary E. Gallagher, 169–203. New York: Cambridge University Press.

Migdal, Joel. 1994. "The State in Society: an Approach to Struggles for Domination." In *State Power and Social Forces: Domination and Transformation in the Third World*, eds. Joel S. Migdal, Atul Kohli and Vivienne Shue, 7–36. New York: Cambridge University Press.

Minzner, Carl. 2006. "Xinfang: an Alternative to Formal Chinese Legal Institutions." *Stanford Journal of International Law* 42:103–179.

2009. "Riots and Cover-ups: Counterproductive Control of Local Agents in China." *Journal of International Law* 31(1):53–123.

2011a. "Judicial Disciplinary Systems for Incorrectly Decided Cases: The Imperial Chinese Heritage Lives on." In *Chinese Justice: Civil Dispute Resolution in Contemporary China*, eds. Margaret Y. K. Woo and Mary E. Gallagher, 58–90. New York: Cambridge University Press.

2011b. "China's Turn against Law." *American Journal of Comparative Law* 59:935–984.

2013. "The Rise and Fall of Chinese Legal Education." *Fordham International Law Journal* 36(2):335–396.

Nathan, Andrew. 2003. "Authoritarian Resilience." *Journal of Democracy* 14(1):6–17.

Naughton, David. 1992. "Hierarchy and the Bargaining Economy: Government and Enterprise in the Reform Process." In *Bureaucracy, Politics, and Decision Making in Post-Mao China*, eds. Kenneth G. Lieberthal and David M. Lampton, 245–281. Berkeley: University of California Press.

Nee, Victor, and David Mozingo. 1983. *State and Society in Contemporary China*. Ithaca: Cornell University Press.

Neubauer, David W., and Stephen S. Meinhold. 2012. 6th edition. *Judicial Process: Law, Courts, and Politics in the United States*. Boston: Wadsworth Publishing.

Ng, Kwai Hang, and Xin He. 2014. "Internal Contradictions of Judicial Mediation in China." *Law & Social Inquiry* 39(2):285–312.

2017. "The Institutional and Cultural Logics of Legal Commensuration: Blood Money and Negotiated Justice in China." *American Journal of Sociology* 122(4):1104–1143.

Niskanen, William A. 1973. *Bureaucracy: Servant or Master*. London: Institute of Economic Affairs.

O'Brien, Kevin J., and Lianjiang Li. 2004. "Suing the Local State: Administrative Litigation in Rural China." *The China Journal* 51:75–96.

2006. *Rightful Resistance in Rural China*. New York: Cambridge University Press.

Oi, Jean. 1999. *Rural China Takes Off: Institutional Foundations of Economic Reform*. California: University of California Press.

Paine, Lynn. 1992. "The Education Policy Process: a Case Study of Bureaucratic Action in China." In *Bureaucracy, Politics, and Decision Making in Post-Mao China*, eds. Kenneth G. Lieberthal and David M. Lampton, 181–215. Berkeley: University of California Press.

Parish, William L., and Martin King Whyte. 1978. *Village and Family in Contemporary China*. Chicago: University of Chicago Press.

Pei, Minxin. 1997. "Citizens v. Mandarins: Administrative Litigation in China." *The China Quarterly* 152:832–862.

People's Daily. 2000. "Chinese Judges to Discard Military-Style Uniform." March 9. http://en.people.cn/english/200003/09/eng20000309N103.html

Peerendoom, Randell. 2002. *China's Long March towards Rule of Law*. Cambridge: Cambridge University Press.

———. 2009. "More Law, Less Courts: Legalized Governance, Judicialization, and Dejudicialization in China." In *Administrative Law and Governance in Asia: Comparative Perspectives*, eds. Tom Ginsburg and Albert H. Y. Chen, 175–202. New York: Routledge.

———. 2010. "Judicial Independence in China: Common Myths and Unfounded Assumptions." In *Judicial Independence in China*, ed. Randall Peerenboom, 69–94. Cambridge: Cambridge University Press.

———. 2011. "Assessing Implementation of Law in China: What Is the Standard?" In *Making Law Work: Chinese Laws in Context*, eds. Mattias Burell and Marina Svensson, 33–68. Ithaca: Cornell East Asia Series.

Perlez, Jane. 2013. "Chinese Judges Disciplined in Prostitution Scandal after Videos Circulate Online." *New York Times*, August 7. www.nytimes.com/2013/08/08/world/asia/chinese-judges-disciplined-for-cavorting-with-prostitutes.html?_r=0

Perrow, Charles. 1967. "A Framework for the Comparative Organizational Analysis." *American Sociological Review* 32(2):194–208.

Pfeffer, Jeffrey. 1982. *Organizations and Organization Theory*. Boston: Pitman.

Philips, Susan U. 1990. "The Judge as Third Party in American Trial-Court Conflict Talk." In *Building Constitutionalism in China*, ed. Allen D. Grimshaw, 197–209. Cambridge: Cambridge University Press.

Pils, Eva. 2005. "Land Disputes, Rights Assertion, and Social Unrest in China: a Case from Sichuan." *Columbia Journal of Asian Law* 19(1):235–292.

Polanyi, Karl. 1944. *The Great Transformation: The Political and Economic Origins of Our Time*. Boston: Beacon.

Pollitt, Christopher. 1986. "Democracy and Bureaucracy." In *New Forms of Democracy*, eds. David Held and Christopher Pollitt, 158–191. London: Sage.

Portes, Alejandro, and Julia Sensenbrenner. 1993. "Embeddedness and Immigration: Notes on the Social Determinants of Economic Action." *American Journal of Sociology* 98(6):1320–1350.

Potter, Pitman B. 2002. "*Guanxi* and the PRC Legal System." In *Social Connections in China: Institutions, Culture, and the Changing Nature of Guanxi*, eds. Thomas Gold, Doug Guthrie and David Wank, 179–196. New York: Cambridge University Press.

———. 2004. "Legal Reform in China: Institutions, Culture, and Selective Adaptation." *Law & Social Inquiry* 29(2):465–495.

Powell, Walter W. 1990. "Neither Market nor Hierarchy: Network Forms of Organization." In *Research in Organizational Behavior*, eds. Barry Staw and Lawrence L. Cummings, 295–336. Greenwich, CT: JAI Press.

Rajah, Jothie. 2012. *Authoritarian Rule of Law: Legislation, Discourse and Legitimacy in Singapore*. Cambridge: Cambridge University Press.

Sabel, Charles F., and Jonathan Zeitlin. 1996. *Worlds of Possibility: Flexibility and Mass Production in Western Industrialization*. Paris: Maison des Sciences de l'Homme.

Saich, Tony. 2015. *Governance and Politics of China*. 4th edition. New York: Palgrave Macmillan.

Sciulli, David. 1986. "Voluntaristic Action as a Distinct Concept: Theoretical Foundations of Societal Constitutionalism." *American Sociological Review* 51(6):743–766.

Selznick, Philip. 1949. *TVA and the Grassroots*. Berkeley: University of California Press.

Shambaugh, David. 2000. "The Chinese State in the Post-Mao Era." In *The Modern Chinese State*, ed. David Shambaugh, 161–187. New York: Cambridge University Press.

Shapiro, Martin. 1981. *Courts: a Political and Comparative Analysis*. Chicago: University of Chicago Press.

Shetreet, Shimon. 1985. "Judicial Independence: New Conceptual Dimensions and Contemporary Challenges." In *Judicial Independence: The Contemporary Debate*, eds. Shimon Shetreet and Jules Deschenes, 590–681. Dordrecht, the Netherlands: Martinus Nijhoff.

Shirk, Susan. 1992. "The Chinese Political System and the Political Strategy of Economic Reform." In *Bureaucracy, Politics, and Decision Making in Post-Mao China*, eds. Kenneth G. Lieberthal and David M. Lampton, 60–88. Berkeley: University of California Press.

　　1993. *The Political Logic of Economic Reform in China*. Berkeley: University of California Press.

Simmel, Georg. 1990. *The Philosophy of Money*. New York: Routledge.

Singh, Jitendra V., David J. Tucker and Robert J. House. 1986. "Organizational Legitimacy and the Liability of Newness." *Administrative Science Quarterly* 31(2):171–193.

Smart, Josephine, and Alan Smart. 1991. "Personal Relations and Divergent Economies: a Case Study of Hong Kong Investment in South China." *International Journal of Urban and Regional Research* 15(2):216–233.

Solomon, Peter H. 2007. "Courts and Judges in Authoritarian Regimes." *World Politics* 60(1):122–145.

Stern, Rachel E. 2013. *Environmental Litigation in China*. New York: Cambridge University Press.

Stinchcombe, Arthur L. 1959. "Bureaucratic and Craft Administration of Production." *Administrative Science Quarterly* 4(2):168–187.

Su, Yang, and Xin He. 2010. "Street as Courtroom: State Accommodation of Social Conflicts in South China." *Law & Society Review* 44(1):157–184.

Tey, Tsun Hang. 2011. *Legal Consensus: Supreme Executive, Supine Jurisprudence, Suppliant Profession of Singapore*. Hong Kong: Centre for Comparative and Public Law.

Trevaskes, Susan. 2007. *Courts and Criminal Justice in Contemporary China*. New York: Lexington Books.

　　2010. *Policing Serious Crime in China: From "Strike Hard" to "Kill Fewer"*. New York: Routledge.

　　2011. "Political Ideology, the Party, and Politicking: Justice System Reform in China." *Modern China* 37(3):315–344.

Trevaskes, Susan, Elisa Nesossi, Flora Sapio and Sarah Biddulph. 2014. "Stability and the Law." In *The Politics of Law and Stability in China*, eds. Susan Trevaskes, Elisa Nesossi, Flora Sapio and Sarah Biddulph, 1–17. Cheltenham, UK: Edward Elgar.

Udy, Stanley H. 1959. "'Bureaucracy' and 'Rationality' in Weber's Organizational Theory." *American Sociological Review* 24(6):791–795.

Upham, Frank K. 2011. "Reflections on the Rule of Law in China." *Taiwan University Law Review* 6(1):251–267.

US Department of State. 2014. "Country Reports on Human Rights Practices for 2013: China." www.state.gov/j/drl/rls/hrrpt/humanrightsreport/index.htm?year=2013&dlid=220186

Verbrugge, Lois. 1979. "Multiplexity in Adult Friendships." *Social Forces* 57(4):1286–1309.

Vogel, Ezra. 2011. *Deng Xiaoping and the Transformation of China*. Cambridge, MA: Harvard University Press.

Walder, Andrew G. 1986. *Communist Neo-Traditionalism*. Berkeley: University of California Press.

1992. "Local Bargaining Relations and Urban Industrial Finance." In *Bureaucracy, Politics, and Decision Making in Post-Mao China*, eds. Kenneth G. Lieberthal and David M. Lampton, 308–333. Berkeley: University of California Press.

Walder, Andrew G., Bobai Li and Donald J. Treiman. 2000. "Politics and Life Chances in a State Socialist Regime: Dual Career Paths into the Urban Chinese Elite, 1949–1996." *American Sociological Review* 65(2):191–209.

Wang, Chang, and Nathan H. Madson. 2013. *Inside China's Legal System*. Oxford: Chandos Publishing.

Wang, Yuhua. 2013. "Court Funding and Judicial Corruption in China." *The China Journal*. 69:43–63.

Wank, David L. 1999. *Commodifying Communism*. New York: Cambridge University Press.

Wasserstrom, Jeffrey N., and Liu Xinyong. 1995. "Student Associations and Mass Movements." In *Urban Spaces in Contemporary China: The Potential for Autonomy and Community in Post-Mao China*, ed. Deborah Davis, 362–393. New York: Cambridge University Press.

Waters, Malcolm. 1989. "Collegiality, Bureaucratization, and Professionalization: a Weberian Analysis." *American Journal of Sociology* 94(5):945–972.

Wayne, Vicki, and Ping Xiong. 2011. "The Relationship between Mediation and Judicial Proceedings in China." *Asian Journal of Comparative Law* 6(1):1–34.

Weber, Max. 1946. *From Max Weber: Essays in Sociology*, eds. H. H. Gerth and C. Wright Mills. New York: Oxford University Press.

1978. *Economy and Society*. Berkeley: University of California Press.

Whyte, Martin King. 1989. "Who Hates Bureaucracy?" In *Remaking the Economic Institutions of Socialism: China and Eastern Europe*, eds. Victor Nee and David Stark, 233–253. Stanford: Stanford University Press.

Whyte, Martin King, and William L. Parish. 1984. *Urban Life in Contemporary China*. Chicago: University of Chicago Press.

Williamson, Oliver E. 1970. *Corporate Control and Business Behavior*. New Jersey: Prentice Hall.

1981. "The Economics of Organization: The Transaction Cost Approach." *American Journal of Sociology* 87(3):548–577.

Wilson, Scott. 2015. *Tigers without Teeth*. New York: Rowman & Littlefield.

Woo, Margaret Y. K. 2003. "Shaping Citizenship: Chinese Family Law and Women." *Yale Journal of Law & Feminism* 15(1):99–134.

Woo, Margaret Y. K., and Yaxin Wang. 2005. "Civil Justice in China: an Empirical Study of Courts in Three Provinces." *American Journal of Comparative Law* 53(4):911–940.

World Bank. 2015. *East Asia's Changing Urban Landscape: Measuring a Decade of Spatial Growth*. Washington: World Bank.

Xin, Catherine R., and Jone L. Pearce 1996. "Guanxi: Connections as Substitutes for Formal Institutional Support." *Academy of Management Journal* 39(6):1641–1658.

Xinhua News Agency. 2014. "China Unveils Landmark Urbanization Plan." March 16. http://news.xinhuanet.com/english/china/2014-03/16/c_133190495.htm

Xinhua News Agency. 2016. "438,000 Sit China's National Judicial Exam." September 24. http://english.gov.cn/state_council/ministries/2016/09/24/content_281475450422690.htm

Xiong, Hao. 2014a. "Two Sides of Court Mediation in Today's Southwest Grassroots China: an Empirical Study in T Court, Yunnan Province." *Asian Journal of Law and Society* 1(2):367–394.

2014b. "The Feasibility of Court Mediation in the Grassroots Society of Southwest China: a Case Study from Yunnan." *Hong Kong Law Journal* 44(1):277–302.

Yang, Mayfair Mei-hui. 1994. *Gift, Favors, and Banquets: The Art of Social Relationship in China*. Ithaca: Cornell University Press.

Yang, Wanli. 2015. "Rural-Urban Income Gap Narrows." *China Daily*, April 22. www.china daily.com.cn/china/2015–04/22/content_20509439.htm

Yang, Yi. 2014. "Tiananmen Square Protest and College Job Placement Reform in the 1980s." *Journal of Contemporary China* 23(88):736–755.

Yeh, Wen-hsin. 1997. "The Republican Origins of the *Danwei*: The Case of Shanghai's Bank of China." In *Danwei: The Changing Chinese Workplace in Historical and Comparative Perspective*, eds. Xiaobo Lü and Elizabeth J. Perry, 60–90. New York: M. E. Sharpe.

Young, Melody W. 2013. "The Aftermath of Peng Yu: Restoring Helping Behavior in China." *Pacific Rim Law & Policy Journal*. 22(3):691–711.

Young, Susan. 1989. "Policy, Practice and the Private Sector in China." *Australia Journal of Chinese Affairs* 21:57–80.

Zhan, Jing Vivian. 2012. "Filling the Gap of Formal Institutions: The Effects of Guanxi Network on Corruption in Reform-Era China." *Crime, Law, and Social Change* 58(2):93–109.

Zhang, Qianfan. 2003. "The People's Court in Transition: The Prospects of Chinese Judicial Reform." *Journal of Contemporary China* 12(34):69–101.

Zhang, Xianchu. 2011. "Civil Justice Reform with Political Agenda." In *The Development of the Chinese Legal System*, ed. Guanghua Yu, 253–271. New York: Routledge.

Zhang, Xinbao. 2014. "Advancing Judicial System Reform." *China Today*, December 8. http://www.chinatoday.com.cn/english/report/2014–12/08/content_657401.htm

Zheng, Yongnian. 2004. *Globalization and State Transformation in China*. Cambridge: Cambridge University Press.

Zhou, Xueguang. 2010. "The Institutional Logic of Collusion among Local Governments in China." *Modern China* 36(1):47–78.

Zhu, Lizhen. 2003. "Chinese Marriage and Divorce Registration to Be Easier & More Convenient." *People's Daily Online*, August 22. http://english.peopledaily.com.cn/200308/22/eng20030822_122866.shtml

Zou, Keyuan. 2006. *China's Legal Reform: Towards the Rule of Law*. Boston: Martinus Nijhoff Publishers.

Zukin, Sharon and Paul DiMaggio. 1990. "Introduction." In *Structure of Capital: The Social Organization of the Economy*, eds. Sharon Zuckin and Paul DiMaggio, 1–36. Cambridge: Cambridge University Press.

LAWS CITED

National People's Congress. 2002. Judges Law of the People's Republic of China, effective January 1, 2002. www.lawinfochina.com/display.aspx?lib=law&id=121&CGid=

National People's Congress. 2006. Organic Law of the People's Courts, effective January 1, 2007. www.npc.gov.cn/englishnpc/Law/ 192007–12/13/content_1384078.htm

National People's Congress. 2012. Civil Procedure Law of the People's Republic of China, effective January 1, 2013. www.npc.gov.cn/englishnpc/Law/2007–12/12/content_1383880.htm

(II) CHINESE LANGUAGE LITERATURE

Anhui High Court. 2016. *Anhui sheng gaoji renmin fayuan gongzuo baogao [zhaiyao]*. (Summary of Annual Work Report 2015) *Anhui ribao* (Anhui Daily), February 27. http://epaper.anhui news.com/html/ahrb/20160227/article_3413974.shtml

Apple Daily. 2010. *Buman lihun panjue baofu niang Hunan xuean* (Revenge Due to Dissatisfaction with the Court's Divorce Decision Resulted in a Homicide Case in Hunan). June 2. http://hk.apple.nextmedia.com/international/art/20100602/14092073 (accessed 13 December 2013)

Baiduwenku. 2011. Nantong. http://wenku.baidu.com/view/796bc41cc281e53a5802ff39.html (accessed May 5, 2016)

Beijing Times. 2007. *Zhejiang Taizhou tansuo yi yidi guanxia pojie min gao guan nanti* (Taizhou in Zhejing Experiments Crossed Jurisdictions over Administrative Litigation). April 12. http://news.xinhuanet.com/local/2007-04/12/content_5964787.htm (accessed May 5, 2013)

Beijing Youth. 2013. *Canji nanzi jichang yinbao "tu zha dan"* (Disabled Man Detonated "Hand-Made Bomb" in Beijing Airport). February 2. http://bjyouth.ynet.com/3.1/1307/21/8151868.html

Cai, Yanmin. 2013. *Zhongguo minshi sifa anjian guanli jizhi touxi* (Exploring and Analyzing the Management Mechanism of Civil Judicial Cases in China). *Zhongguo faxue* (China Legal Science) 2013(1):131–143.

—— 2014. *Duanlie yu xiuzheng: woguo minshi shenpan zuzhi zhi shanbian* (Disjuncture and Revision: Changes of China's Civil Court Structure). *Zhengfa luntan* (Tribunal of Political Science and Law) 32(2):38–49.

CCP News Net. 2010. *Zhengdi chaiqian zhong bei chaiqian ren de jizhong biaoxian zhide yanjiu* (Several Phenomena of the People Affected by Land Requisition and Housing Demolition Need Attention). http://djxt.yzjsj.gov.cn/showArticle.jsp?id=9525&partyId=50 (accessed November 21, 2011)

Chen, Haiguang. 2016. *Faguan yingdang qinmian jingye* (Judges Should Work Hard and Respect Their Job). May 7. Chinacourt.org www.chinacourt.org/article/detail/2016/05/id/1852057.shtml

Chen, Weidong. 2008. *Youhua sifa zhiquan peizhi jianli gongzheng sifa zhidu* (Optimizing the Organization of Judicial Authority and Establishing a Fair Judicial system). *Fazhi ribao* (Legal Daily), December 9.

Chen, Xuefei. 2007. *Lihun anjian shenli zhong de faguan de xingbie pianxiang* (Gender Preference in Judges' Discourse during the Trial of Divorce Cases). *Zhongwai faxue (Peking University Law Journal)* 8:384–411.

China.com. 2015. *Dongguan yi zhen zhengfu lianxu liangtian dengbao ma fayuan: wanggu shishi paimai tudi* (A Township Government in Dongguan Accused Court Two Days in a Row: Auctioning Land, Ignoring Facts). December 16. http://news.china.com/domestic/945/20151216/20949603_all.html#page_2

Chongqing Municipality. 2010. *Jiceng fanying zhengdi chaiqian zhong bei chaiqian qunzhong "kua qu chuan lian" xianxiang tuchu ying yu gaodu zhongshi* (Trans-Local Association among Residents Stands Out in Housing Demolition and Deserves Special Attention). www.pacq.gov.cn/platform/news_view.asp?newsid=2070 (accessed October 26, 2010)

Ding, Wei. 2014. *Qinyao fating: jiceng sifa de shiqian luoji* (Qinyao's Court: The Logic in Elementary Legal Practice). Beijing: Sanlian Bookstore.

Du, Mong. 2007. *Zhengfu fawen jiang chuting lü naru kaohe "bi" guan chuting, fayuan qian yu jian sifa jianyi "cu" guan chuting: jiedu Jiangsu "gao guan jian guan" weihe cheng changtai* (Government Directives Pressure Officials into Taking on the Stand, More than One Thousand Judicial Suggestions Facilitate Officials to Take on the Stand: Why Can Plaintiffs Meet the Officials in Citizens vs. Mandarin Litigation in Jiangsu Province?). *Fazhi ribao* (Legal Daily). September 19. http://news.sohu.com/20070919/n252232641.shtml (accessed May 26, 2011)

Fan, Yu. 2005. *Guanyu fayuan tiaojie de shizheng yanjiu* (Empirical Analysis to Juridical Mediation). In *Falü chengxu yunzuo de shizheng fenxi* (An Empirical Analysis to Practice of Legal Procedures), ed. Wang Yaxin. Beijing: China University of Political Science and Law.

Feng, Junqi. 2010. *Zhongxian ganbu* (Cadres in Zhong County), Ph.D. dissertation, Peking University Department of Sociology, China.

Fujian High Court. 2016. *Fujian sheng gaoji renmin fayuan gongzuo baogao 2015* (Annual Work Report 2015). January 13. http://fjrb.fjsen.com/fjrb/html/2016-01/28/content_896362.htm?div=-1

Gansu High Court. 2016. *Gansu sheng gaoji renmin fayuan gongzuo baogao zhaiyao* (Summary of Annual Work Report 2015). *Gansu Daily*, February 9. http://gansu.gansudaily.com.cn/system/2016/02/09/015888538.shtml

Gao, Qichi, Weiping Zhou and Zhenye Jiang. 2009. *Xiangtu sifa: shehui bianqian zhong de yangcun renmin fating shizheng fenxi* (Rural Justice: Empirical Analysis on People's Tribunal of Yang Village in Social Change). Beijing: Law Press.

Guan, Shengying. 2004. *Shenpan weiyuan hui gongzuo jizhi tansuo ji wanshan* (Exploring and Improving the Working Mechanism of the Adjudication Committee). *Renmin sifa* (People's Judiciary) 10: 27–29.

Guangdong High Court. 2013. *Guangdong sheng gaoji renmin fayuan gongzuo baogao* (Annual Work Report 2012). January 28. www.gdcourts.gov.cn/ecdomain/framework/gdcourt/einjemnkabbmbboelkeboekheeldjmod/ibhafdicabjdbboekklboafjdjkbjamc.do?isfloat=1&disp_template=pchlilmiaebdbboeljehjhkjkkgjbjie&fileid=20141008114423625&moduleIDPage=ibhafdicabjdbboekklboafjdjkbjamc&siteIDPage=gdcourt&infoCheckd=0&keyword=&dateFrom=&dateTo=

2014. *Guangdong fayuan jianfei jingfei baozhang he guanli qingkuang de diaoyan baogao* (Research Report on Court Expenditure and Its Management). July 29. www.gdcourts.gov.cn/ecdomain/framework/gdcourt/lgedihgbabbebboelkeboekheeldjmod/jldinjpmabbgbboelkeboekheeldjmod.do?isfloat=1&disp_template=pchlilmiaebdbboeljehjhkjkkgjbjie&fileid=20140729144424785&moduleIDPage=jldinjpmabbgbboelkeboekheeldjmod&siteIDPage=gdcourt&infoChecked=0&keyword=&dateFrom=&dateTo=

Guangdong Bureau of Statistics. 2013. *Guangdong tongji nianjian 2013* (Guangdong Statistical Yearbook 2013). www.gdstats.gov.cn/tjnj/ 192013/directory/020.html

Guizhou High Court. 2016. *Guizhou sheng gaoji renmin fayuan gongzuo baogao 2015* (Annual Work Report 2015). January 28. http://gz.people.com.cn/n2/2016/0219/c194827-27765827.html

Guo, Jisheng. 2004. *Guanyu sifa jingfei baozhang tizhi gaige de ruogan wenti* (Several Issues Regarding Reforms for a System of Guaranteed Funding for the Administration of Justice). In *Zhongguode jiancha yuan fayuan gaige* (Judicial Reform Report: The Reform of Chinese Procuratorate and Court), eds. Qian Sun and Chengliang Zheng. 337–344. Beijing: Law Press.

Heilongjiang High Court. 2016. *Heilongjiang sheng gaoji renmin fayuan gongzuo baogao 2015* (Annual Work Report 2015). January 31. http://hlj.people.com.cn/n2/2016/0224/c220027-27796128.html

Henan High Court. 2014. *Henan sheng gaoji renmin fayuan gongzuo baogao 2013* (Annual Work Report 2013). January 18. www.chinacourt.org/article/detail/2014/01/id/1205214.shtml

Hexun.com.tw. 2011. *Nuzi buyuan he fuhao zhangfu lihun he nongyao yu zisha* (Woman Who Refused to Divorce Her Rich Husband Attempted Suicide by Drinking Pesticides). April 12. http://news.hexun.com.tw/192011-04-12/128657632.html (accessed December 13, 2013)

Hong Kong Commercial Daily. 2009. "Divorced Woman Who Was Dissatisfied with the Judgment Placed a Coffin Outside the Court and Insulted the Judges," 22 August. www.hkcd.com.hk/content/2009-08/22/content_2374393.htm (accessed December 13, 2013)

Hubei High Court Research Team, and Jian Zhang. 2009. *Gaige yu wanshan renmin fayuan jingfei baozhang tizhi de diaoyan baogao* (Survey Report on the Reform and Perfection of People's Court's Guaranteed Funding System). *Renmin sifa* (People's Judicature) 9:65–70.

Jiang, Lina. 2010. *Liaohe liangji fayuan minshi tiaojie anjian lüxing qingkuang de tongji fenxi* (Statistical Analysis of the Enforcement of Settled Civil Cases of Two Levels of Liaohe Courts). www.lhfy.com.cn/shownews.asp?id=347&BigClass=%C9%F3%C5%D05%D1%D0%BE%BF (accessed May 24, 2012)

Jiangsu High Court. 2016a. *Quansheng fayuan 2015 nian 1–12 yue shenpan gongzuo jiben qingkuang* (The Basic Situation about Judicial Work in 2015). www.jsfy.gov.cn/tjsj2014/sftj/2016/03/28142941597.html

Jiangxi High Court. 2016b. *Jiangxi sheng gaoji renmin fayuan gongzuo baogao 2015* (Annual Work Report 2015). http://jiangxi.jxnews.com.cn/system/2016/02/22/014695611.shtml

Li, Jie. 2008. *Tiaojielü shuoming shenme? Dui tiaojielü yu hexie zhengxiangguan mingti de fenxi* (What Does Mediation Rate Mean? An Analysis on the Assumption that Mediation Rate Reflects Harmony). *Falü shiyong* (Journal of Law Application) 10:49–54.

Liao, Yong'an, and Shenggang Li. 2005. *Woguo minshi susong feiyong zhidu zi yunxing xianzhuang* (The Current Operational Status of the System of Civil Litigation Fees in China). *Zhongwai faxue* (Peking University Law Journal) 3:304–327.

Liaowang Newsweek. 2006. *Zhongguo jiceng fayuan mianlin min gao guan anjian dafu zengzhang susong yali* (Caseload Pressures in Administrative Litigation Mounted for China's Basic-Level Courts). http://news.sina.com.cn/c/2006-04-22/12159690235.shtml

Lin, Jingbiao. 2014. *Xiyin he chuilian youxiu faguan de da wutai* (The Big Stage for Attracting and Training Outstanding Judges). *Renmin fayuan bao* (People's Court Daily). July 12. www.chinacourt.org/article/detail/2014/07/id/1337770.shtml

Liu, Jie. Directed. 2006. *Mabei shang de fating* (Courthouse on Horseback).

Liu, Zuoxiang. 2003. *Zhongguo sifa difang baohu zhuyi zhi pipan* (The Criticism about Local Protectionism in Judicial Practice in China). *Faxue yanjiu* (Chinese Journal of Law) 1:83–98.

Ministry of Civil Affairs of the People's Republic of China. 2014. *2014 nian shehui fuwu fazhan tongji gongbao* (Statistical Bulletin of Social Work Development 2014). June 10. www.mca.gov.cn/article/sj/tjgb/201506/201506008324399.shtml

Peng, Shizhong. 2011. *Nengdong sifa shiyexia minshi tiaojie gaige de jingxiang xuanze* (Paths of the Civil Mediation Reform from Judicial Activism Perspective). *Jinan xuebao [zhexue shehui kexue ban]* (Journal of Jinan University [Philosophy and Social Sciences]) 1:52–58.

Pengzhou Court Net (Pengzhou fayuanwang). 2004. *Pengzhou shi renmin fayuan shenpan weiyuan hui gongzuo guicheng* (The Working Rules of the Adjudication Committee of Pengzhou Court). www.pzfy.org/Article/swyt/spgl/200412/216.html (accessed Mar. 24, 2011)

People's Net. 2011. *Shen Deyong: Zhongguo jue buneng gao "san quan fen li" shi sifa duli* (Shen Deyong: No Room in China for Judicial Independence of the Western Style). http://192011lianghui.people.com.cn/GB/214392/14102041.html (accessed May 5, 2013)

Qiao, Shengbiao. 2004. *Fayuan guanli tizhi zhizheng jue ji gaige* (Problems and Reform of the Management of Court System). In *Zhongguo de jiancha yuan fayuan gaige* (Judicial

Reform Report: The Reform of Chinese Procuratorate and Court), eds. Qian Sun and Chengliang Zheng, 265–275. Beijing: Law Press.

Shandong High Court. 2014. *Shandong sheng gaoji renmin fayuan gongzuo baogao 2013* (Shandong High Court Annual Work Report 2013). January 19. http://sdfy.china court.org/article/detail/2014/07/id/1349563.shtml

Shanxi High Court. 2014. *Shanxi isheng gaoji renmin fayuan gongzuo baogao 2013 [zhaiyao]* (Summary of Annual Work Report 2013). *Shanxi Daily*, January 28. www.sxdaily.com.cn/ n/2014/0128/c266-5345335.html

———. 2015. *Shanxi sheng gaoji renmin fayuan gongzuo baogao 2014* (Shanxi High Court Annual Work Report 2014). January 27. www.chinacourt.org/article/detail/2015/02/ id/1546616.shtml

Shen, Guoming, and Wang Limin, eds. 2005. *20 shiji Zhongguo shehui kexue faxuejuan (Twentieth Century China Social Science: Legal Studies Volume)*. Shanghai: Shanghai People's Publisher.

Shenzhen Intermediate Court. 2011. *Shenzhen fayuan zhishi chanquan sifa baohu zhuangkuang [2006–2010 nian]* (IP Protection in Shenzhen Court [2006–2010]). www.court.gov.cn/zscq/dcyj/201101/t20110120_13220.html

Sichuan High Court. 2012. *Sichuan sheng gaoji renmin fayuan gongzuo baogao 2011*(Sichuan High Court Annual Work Report 2011). January 12. www.scspc.gov.cn/html/cwhgb_44/ 201201/2012/0320/65450.html

———. 2013. *Sichuan sheng gaoji renmin fayuan gongzuo baogao 2012* (Sichuan High Court Annual Work Report 2012). January 26. www.scspc.gov.cn/html/zls_80/gzbg_85/fygzbg/ 2013/0225/68925.html

Sina News. 2013. *Jinri 43 wan ren canjia guojia sifa kaoshi 18% wei yingjie benke sheng* (430,000 People Attend National Judicial Examination Today, 18% Are This Year's Undergraduates). September 14. http://news.sina.com.cn/c/2013–09-14/ 101728215449.shtml

Su, Li. 2000. *Songfa xiaxiang* (Bring the Law to the Countryside). Beijing: China's University of Political Science and Law Press.

Supreme People's Court. 2010. *Guanyu gaige he wanshan renmin fayuan shenpan weiyuan hui zhidu de shishi yijian* (The Implementing Opinions on Reforming and Improving the Judicial Committee System of the People's Court). Promulgated on January 11, 2010. www.lawinfochina.com/display.aspx?lib=law&id=8367&CGid=

———. 2012a. *Renmin fayuan 2011 gongzuo baogao* (Annual Work Report 2011). June 14. www.chinacourt.org/article/detail/2012/06/id/524092.shtml

———. 2012b. *Renmin fayuan zhishichanquan shenpanhan 2011* (Intellectual Property Protection by Chinese Courts 2011). www.iammagazine.com/files/People's%20Supreme%20Court %20Intellectual%20Property%20Protection%20in%20China.pdf

———. 2014. *Renmin fayuan zhishichanquan shenpanhan 2013* (Intellectual Property Protection by Chinese Courts 2013). www.court.gov.cn/zscq/bhcg/201404/t20140425_195314.html

———. 2015a. *Zuigao renmin fayuan guanyu quanmian shenhua renmin fayuan gaige yijian: Renmin fayuan disi ge wunian gaige gangyao [2014–2018]*. (Opinion of the Supreme People's Court on Deepening Reform of the People's Courts Comprehensively: Outline of the Fourth Five-Year Reform of the People's Courts [2014–2018]). February 26. www.court.gov.cn/zixun-xiangqing-13520.html

———. 2015b. *Zuigao renmin fayuan guanyu tiaozheng gaoji renmin fayuan he zhongji renmin fayuan guanxia diyi shen minshang shi anjian biaozhun de tongzhi* (The Supreme People's Court Adjusted the Jurisdiction of Higher and Intermediate Level Courts in First Instance Civil/ Commercial Cases). April 30. www.chinacourt.org/article/detail/2015/05/id/1606865.shtml

2015c. *Zuigao renmin fayuan guanyu renmin fayuan dengji li'an ruogan wenti de guiding* (SPC Provisions on Several Questions regarding Case Registration and Filing). www.chinacourt.org/law/detail/2015/04/id/148127.shtm

2015d. *Zuigao renmin fayuan gongzuo baogao* 2014 (SPC Annual Work Report 2014). March 12. www.court.gov.cn/zixun-xiangqing-13796.html

2016a. *Zuigao renmin fayuan 2016 gongzuo baogao* (SPC Annual Work Report 2015). http://lianghui.people.com.cn/192016npc/n1/2016/0313/c403052-28194909.html

2016b. *Zhongguo fayuan de sifa gaige [baipishu]* (Judicial Reform of Chinese Courts [White paper]). March 3. http://english.court.gov.cn/2016-03/03/content_23724636.htm

Tang, Humei, Feng Guo, and Jun Ji. 2011. *Quanguo fayuan jingfei baozhang tizhi gaige qingkuang* (The Survey Report on the National People's Court's Guaranteed Funding System). *Renmin sifa* (People's Judicature) 17:75–79.

Wang, Daojun, and Jun Zhong. 2010. *Xibu ji pinkun diqu faguan duanque wenti yanjiu* (Study on the Shortage of Judges in the West and Poor Areas). *Zhongong Shanxi shengzhi jiguan dangxiao xuebao* (Journal of the Party School for the Departments Directly under Shanxi Provincial Committee of the CPC) 2:30–32.

Wang, Lusheng. 2015. *Xiangma yu saima: Zhongguo churen faguan xuanren jizhi shizheng yanjiu* (Picking Horses and Racing Horses: Empirical Study on the System of New Judge Appointment in China). *Fazhi yu shehui fazhan* (Law and Social Development) 6:41–53.

Wang, Qiliang. 2012. *Falü shijie guan wenluan shidai de sifa, minyi, he zhengzhi – yi Li Changkui an wei zhongxin* (Judicature, Public Opinion, and Politics at an Age of Disordered Legal World View: A Study on the Case of Li Changkui). *Faxue jia* (The Jurist) 3:1–17.

Wang, Qinhua, and Xin Yin, eds. 2010. *Zhongguo jiceng xingzheng zhengyi jiejue jizhi de jingyan yanjiu* (An Empirical Study of Administrative Dispute Resolution in Grassroots China). Shanghai: Shanghai Sanlian Press.

Wang, Yaxin. 2010. *Sifa chengben yu sifa xiaolü: Zhongguo fayuan de caizheng baozhang yu faguan jili* (Judicial Cost and Judicial Efficiency: The Guaranteed Funding and Judges' Motivation in Chinese Court). *Faxue jia* (The Jurist) 4:132–138.

Wu, Yanping, and Genju Liu, eds. 2005. *Xingshi susong faxue cankao ziliao huibian* (A Compilation of References for Criminal Procedure Law Volume 1). Beijing, China: Peking University Press.

Wu, Yingzi. 2006. *Shenpan weiyuan hui taolun de qunti juece jiqi guizhi* (The Collective Decision-Making of the Adjudication Committee). *Nanjing daxue falü pinglun* (Nanjing University Law Review) 1:185–201.

Xu, Xin, Huang Yanhao, and Wang Xiaotang. 2015. *Zhongguo sifa gaige niandu baogao* (Annual Report on China's Judicial Reform 2014). *Zhengfa luntan* (Tribune of Political Science and Law) 33(3):125–141.

Xu, Ziliang. 2010. *Difang fayuan zai sifa gaige zhong de nengdong xing sikao* (The Dynamic Role of Local Court in Judicial Reform). *Faxue* (Legal Science) 4:153–160.

Yan, Lijie. 2013. *Qianyi jianyi chengxu minshi anjian shangsheng de yuanyin he jianyi* (The Reasons and Suggestions on the Increasing Civil Summary Procedure Cases). January 9. www.chinacourt.org/article/detail/2013/01/id/811192.shtml

Yang, Xiaoling. 2010. *Feichu yu baoliu zhijian: shenpan weiyuan hui fansi yu chonggou* (Between Abolishment or Preservation: A Reflection and Reconstruction of the Adjudication Committee). *Chongqin yi zhong fayuan wang* (Chongqing No. 1 Intermediate Court Net). www.cqyzfy.gov.cn/view.php?id=10302505201037250520104425052010512505201060250520 (accessed March 28, 2011)

Yi, Jiming. 2012. *Zhongguo faxue jiaoyu de sanci zhuanxing* (On Three Transitions of Legal Education in China). *Huanqiu falu pinglun* (Global Law Review) 3:33–48.

Ying, Xing, and Yin Xu. 2009. *Lian zhengzhixue yu xingzheng susonglu de paihuai: Huabei liangshi jiceng fayuan de duibi yanjiu* (Case Registration Politics and the Stagnation of Administrative Litigation: An Empirical Study of Two Northern China Basic Courts). *Zhengfa luntan* (Law & Politics Forum) 27(6):111–112.

Yu, Jianrong. 2005. *Zhongguo xinfang zhidu pipan* (Criticisms of the Petition System in China). *Zhongguo gaige* (China Reform) 2:26–28.

Zeng, Xianyi, Wang Jian, Yan Xiaojun, eds. 2012. *Lüxue yu faxue: Zhongguo falü jiaoyu yu falü xueshu de chuantong jiqi xiandai fazhan* (Law and Legal Studies: Tradition and Modern Developments of Chinese Legal Education and Legal Studies). Beijing: Renmin University of China Press.

Zhang, Hongtao. 2014. *Zhongguo fayuan yali zhi xiaojie: Yizhong falü zuzhi xue jiedu* (How to Dispel the Stress of China's Courts: an Interpretation from Legal History). *Faxue jia* (The Jurist) 1:19–36.

— 2015. *Sifa jingfei shengji tongguan de zhengzhi fenxi* (The Political Analysis of the Provincial Governance of Judicial Finance). *Lilun shiye* (Theoretical Horizon) 4:32–34.

Zhang, Lijun. 2010. *Fayuan jingji baozhang tizhi yanjiu* (Study on Protecting Court Budgets). July 30. www.hebeicourt.gov.cn/public/detail.php?id=1207

Zhang, Zhiquan. 2014. *Jiceng faguan liushi de yuanyin yu yingdu* (Attrition of frontline judges and Measures to Cope with it). August 16. http://www.chinacourt.org/article/detail/2014/08/id/1365926.shtml

Zhao, Qiang. 2014. *Jiang dang de quanzhong luxian guanchuan renmin fayuan gongzuo quan guocheng* (Practicing Party's Mass Line in the Works of the People's Court). July 22. www.court.gov.cn/zixun-xiangqing-6558.html

Zhejiang High Court. 2016. *Zhejiang sheng gaoji renmin fayuan gongzuo baogao 2015* (Zhejiang High Court Annual Work Report 2015). January 26. http://zjnews.zjol.com.cn/system/2016/02/02/021011445.shtml

Zhou, Yongkang. 2010. *Shenru tuijin shehui maodun huajie* (Deeply Push Forward Resolution of Social Conflict). *Qiushi* (Seeking Truth). February 16. www.qstheory.cn/zxdk/192010/201004/201002/t20100209_20841.htm

Zhu, Jingwen. 2007. *Zhongguo falü fazhan baogao* (Report on China Law Development: Database and Indicators). Beijing: Renmin University of China Press.

— 2011. *Zhongguo falü fazhan baogao* (Report on China Law Development). Beijing: Renmin University of China Press.

Zuo, Weimin. 2010. *Zhongguo faguan renyong jizhi: jiyu linian de chubu pingxi* (Judges' Appointment in China: a Conceptual Comment and Analysis). *Xiandai faxue* (Modern Law Science) 32(5):43–51.

— 2014. *Zhonguo fayuan yuanzhang juese de shizheng yanjiu* (An Empirical Study on the Role of Presidents of Courts in China). *Zhongguo faxue* (Chinese Legal Science) 1:5–25.

— 2015. *Zhongguo jiceng fayuan canzheng zhidu shizheng yanjiu* (Empirical Research on the Fiscal System of the People's Court at the Grassroots Level). *Zhongguo faxue* (Chinese Legal Science) 1:257–271.

Index

Abbott, Andrew, 19, 210
active case collection, 185, 220
adjudication, 7, 22, 209. *See also* judgment writing;
    litigation, protests and
    cities and, 194
    firm-type courts and, 13, 194, 198
    mediation avoiding, 50, 125
    political embeddedness and, 29
    post-1980 judges and, 71–72
    reporting system and, 91
    shrinking and, 125
adjudication committees, 95–114, 208, 216. *See also*
    modifications; reversals
    administrative bureaucracy and, 108
    administrative cases and, 99–100
    advisory request and, 105–106
    bureaucracy and, 95–96, 107–109
    cases reviewed by, 98–100, 216
    civil cases and, 98, 99–100, 102–104, 113
    clique culture and, 111
    collegiality and, 110
    composition of, 97–98
    consensus and, 97, 111
    corruption and, 107–108
    court presidents and, 104–105, 110–111
    criminal cases and, 98, 99–102, 105, 109, 110, 169
    discussion within, 104–105, 106, 216
    divorce and, 103
    enforcement cases and, 99–100
    fines and, 101–102
    frontline judges and, 108, 109, 111–114
    housing demolition cases and, 109
    judicial independence and, 108–109
    judicial reform and, 195–196
    local party-government coalitions and, 109, 110
    majority rule and, 105, 217
    minutes of, 96–97, 98, 216
    monocratic bureaucracy and, 109–111
    origin of, 96
    political insurance and, 103–104, 109, 112–114
    politics and, 108–109
    punishment and, 101–102
    reporting system and, 86, 106
    responsible judges and, 103, 106, 112
    risk avoidance and, 113–114
    significant cases and, 98, 102–103
    unanimity and, 110
    vertical hierarchy and, 102
administerization (*xingzhenghua*), 119–120, 194
administrative bureaucracy, 83–120
    adjudication committees as, 108
    judicial bureaucracy and, 18
administrative cases, 99–100, 139, 219. *See also*
    housing demolition cases
administrative embeddedness, 17–20, 29, 83–120,
    142, 191. *See also* vertical hierarchy
    court presidents and, 19–20
    decision-making and, 17–18
    external, 19–20
    firm-type courts and, 193
    internal, 17–19
    work-unit courts and, 28, 193
administrative hierarchy, 29. *See also* vertical
    hierarchy
    guanxi and, 24
    judicial reform and, 189
    signing off and, 114, 115
    work-unit courts and, 8
administrative income, court funding and, 171
Administrative Litigation Law, 133
administrative rank, 110, 217
adversarialism, trial hearings and, 41, 55
advisory request (*qingshi*), 94, 105–106, 217
affirmation, reporting system and, 92
anti-rightist movement, 62
apoliticism, judicial bureaucracy and, 217

CPSIA information can be obtained
at www.ICGtesting.com
Printed in the USA
LVHW050303161221
706369LV00009B/578